CHRIS DEVON

Python Development With AWS lambda

Contents

Getting Started with AWS Lambda

What is AWS Lambda?
AWS Lambda is a serverless computing service provided by Amazon Web Services (AWS) that lets developers run code without the need to manage servers or infrastructure. Introduced in 2014, Lambda was designed to make it easier for developers to build, deploy, and scale applications while eliminating much of the operational overhead associated with traditional server-based infrastructure. The essence of AWS Lambda is simplicity, scalability, and cost-efficiency, making it an attractive option for developers and businesses looking to streamline their cloud-based solutions.

At its core, AWS Lambda allows you to execute code in response to a variety of events, such as HTTP requests, changes in data within an Amazon S3 bucket, updates to a DynamoDB table, or even based on a predefined schedule. One of the most notable advantages of AWS Lambda is that it automatically scales with your workload—handling thousands or even millions of function invocations without any need for manual intervention.

The Serverless Paradigm

To fully grasp AWS Lambda's value, it is important to understand the concept of **serverless computing**. In traditional computing environments, developers have to manage servers, operating systems, patches, scaling, and other infrastructure concerns. With serverless, these responsibilities are abstracted away, allowing developers to focus purely on writing code. This approach brings several benefits, such as reduced operational complexity, faster development cycles, and often lower costs.

Lambda functions are **event-driven**, meaning they are triggered by specific events rather than running continuously. As a result, resources are consumed only when the function is actively running, which translates into a **pay-per-use** billing model—one of the most cost-efficient ways to run workloads in the cloud.

Key Characteristics of AWS Lambda

1. **Event-Driven Architecture** AWS Lambda is designed to respond to various types of events, both within and outside of the AWS ecosystem. These events can include data uploads to S3, messages in an Amazon SQS queue, changes in a DynamoDB table, or custom events triggered by other AWS services, external applications, or HTTP requests via Amazon API Gateway.

2. **Fully Managed Infrastructure** With AWS Lambda, all server management tasks—including provisioning, scaling, patching, and managing underlying compute resources—are taken care of by AWS. You no longer have to worry about configuring, scaling, or maintaining virtual machines or containers.

3. **Automatic Scaling** AWS Lambda automatically adjusts the number of function instances to handle incoming requests. Whether you have a few invocations per day or millions per minute, Lambda can scale horizontally based on the workload, ensuring your application remains responsive regardless of the traffic volume.

4. **Pay-Per-Use Billing** One of the primary cost advantages of AWS Lambda is its **pay-per-use** model. You only pay for the compute time used by your function. This billing model is based on the number of requests and the actual execution time (measured in milliseconds). There are no charges when your code is not running, which can lead to significant cost savings for applications with sporadic or variable workloads.

5. **Statelessness** Lambda functions are **stateless**, meaning they do not retain information between executions. Each invocation is independent of others, and no execution context is preserved. This encourages developers to design applications that externalize state, often using other AWS services like Amazon S3, DynamoDB, or Amazon RDS for persistence.

6. **Short-Lived Functions** AWS Lambda functions are designed to run for short periods of time, with a maximum timeout of **15 minutes** per execution. This makes Lambda ideal for tasks like data transformations, backend API processing, automation tasks, or event-driven computing. For long-running or continuous workloads, other AWS services like EC2 or Fargate may be more appropriate.

7. **Lambda Layers** Lambda Layers allow you to package libraries, custom runtimes, or other dependencies separately from your function code. This promotes code reuse, helps streamline deployments, and can simplify managing large projects where multiple functions share the same libraries or configuration.

8. **Built-in Security and IAM** AWS Lambda integrates seamlessly with AWS Identity and Access Management (IAM) for managing permissions and security. Lambda functions can be assigned specific IAM roles, ensuring that they have the necessary permissions to interact with other AWS services or resources. This fine-grained control enhances the security of your applications by adhering to the principle of least privilege.

How AWS Lambda Works

When working with AWS Lambda, the following core components come into play:

1. **Lambda Functions** A **Lambda function** is the heart of AWS Lambda. It is a block of code that is executed when an event triggers it. Functions can be written in multiple programming languages supported by

Lambda, such as Python, Node.js, Java, Go, C#, and Ruby. The function is stateless, meaning it handles each event independently without any built-in persistence of data across executions. Code is uploaded via the AWS Management Console, AWS CLI, or a Continuous Integration/Continuous Deployment (CI/CD) pipeline.

2. **Event Sources** An **event source** is any service or system that generates events that trigger a Lambda function. AWS Lambda integrates natively with numerous AWS services, such as Amazon S3 (object uploads or changes), Amazon DynamoDB (data updates), Amazon Kinesis (streaming data), Amazon SQS (queue messages), and API Gateway (HTTP requests). Lambda can also be triggered by external applications through custom events.

3. **Triggers** A **trigger** is what starts the execution of a Lambda function. AWS Lambda functions are automatically invoked in response to triggers from event sources. For example, a file uploaded to an S3 bucket can trigger a Lambda function that processes the file. Alternatively, an API Gateway HTTP request can trigger a Lambda function to serve dynamic content for a web application.

4. **Execution Environment** AWS Lambda provides a secure, isolated **execution environment** for running your function code. Each Lambda function runs in its own environment, with access to limited system resources like memory (configurable between 128 MB and 10 GB) and execution time (configurable up to 15 minutes). Lambda abstracts the underlying infrastructure so that developers don't need to worry about server configurations, operating systems, or patch management.

5. **Function Configuration** AWS Lambda requires the configuration of certain parameters when creating a function. This includes specifying the amount of memory to allocate, the timeout duration, and the permissions needed to access other AWS services. You can also define environment variables, set up VPC configurations (for accessing private resources), and configure error handling policies.

6. **AWS CloudWatch Integration** AWS Lambda automatically integrates with **AWS CloudWatch** for monitoring and logging. Each time a

function is invoked, Lambda logs details such as the duration of the execution, memory used, and any output or errors from the function. This is invaluable for troubleshooting and monitoring the performance of your serverless applications.

7. **Response Handling** After a Lambda function is executed, the result (or **response**) is returned to the event source, if applicable. For example, when invoked via an API Gateway, the result of the Lambda function is returned as an HTTP response to the client that made the request. Alternatively, if the function is triggered by an S3 file upload, the function can process the file and store the result in a separate S3 bucket or database without returning an explicit response.

Common AWS Lambda Use Cases

AWS Lambda is extremely versatile and can be used in a variety of scenarios across different industries and application types. Here are some common use cases where Lambda excels:

1. **Web Backends** Lambda is often used to build the backends for web and mobile applications. When integrated with API Gateway, Lambda can handle RESTful API requests without the need for provisioning or maintaining servers. This allows developers to create dynamic, scalable applications with minimal operational overhead.

2. **Data Processing** AWS Lambda can be used for real-time or batch data processing. For example, it can process data streams from Amazon Kinesis or Kafka, process file uploads to S3, or transform and load data into a database such as Amazon RDS or DynamoDB. Lambda's event-driven architecture makes it ideal for automating the processing of data as soon as it becomes available.

3. **Infrastructure Automation** AWS Lambda is frequently employed for automating infrastructure tasks such as creating backups, monitoring services, handling security audits, or provisioning resources. By reacting to cloud events (e.g., CloudWatch alarms or AWS Config changes),

Lambda can automatically adjust or remediate infrastructure in real-time.

4. **Microservices** Lambda plays a significant role in microservices architectures by enabling services to operate independently. Each microservice can be represented by one or more Lambda functions, ensuring the application scales seamlessly and each component can be managed, deployed, and updated independently.

5. **IoT Applications** With the growth of the Internet of Things (IoT), AWS Lambda has found utility in processing data from IoT devices. Lambda functions can be used to process and analyze real-time data streams from IoT sensors or devices, enabling low-latency responses and scalable architectures for IoT solutions.

6. **Real-Time Stream Processing** Lambda functions can process real-time data from streaming sources like Amazon Kinesis or DynamoDB Streams. For example, you can create a Lambda function that listens to a Kinesis stream, processes each incoming record, and stores the results in a database or triggers alerts based on certain criteria.

7. **Automation of DevOps Tasks** AWS Lambda is widely used in DevOps practices to automate repetitive tasks such as deployments, backups, log processing, or even monitoring and alerting systems. By reacting to infrastructure events, Lambda functions can automatically provision resources, run health checks, or clean up unused assets.

The Benefits of AWS Lambda

1. **Cost Efficiency** Lambda's pay-per-use pricing model can significantly reduce the cost of running applications. You only pay for the execution time used by your function, meaning there's no charge when your function is idle. This is especially beneficial for workloads that experience fluctuating traffic, such as seasonal web applications or sporadic data processing tasks.

2. **Scalability** AWS Lambda automatically scales with the number of incoming requests. Whether your application handles a few requests

per day or millions per second, Lambda adjusts dynamically without the need for manual intervention. This scalability is crucial for applications that require high availability and performance.

3. **Reduced Operational Overhead** By eliminating the need for server management, Lambda allows developers to focus on writing code rather than managing infrastructure. There is no need to worry about configuring servers, patching operating systems, or ensuring scalability—AWS handles it all.

4. **Fast Development Cycles** AWS Lambda is well-suited for rapid development and deployment. Since there's no need to configure infrastructure, developers can quickly iterate and deploy new features. The serverless model enables faster time-to-market and agility, which is particularly important in competitive industries.

5. **Built-in Fault Tolerance** AWS Lambda automatically manages availability and fault tolerance. If a function fails, Lambda will retry the function invocation or send the event to a dead letter queue (if configured). This built-in resilience helps ensure the reliability of your serverless applications.

AWS Lambda represents a paradigm shift in how developers build and manage applications in the cloud. With its event-driven architecture, pay-per-use pricing, and automatic scaling capabilities, Lambda enables developers to focus on writing code rather than managing infrastructure. Whether you're building APIs, automating infrastructure, or processing data in real-time, AWS Lambda offers a scalable, cost-efficient solution that simplifies cloud development. Understanding the fundamental concepts of AWS Lambda and its event-driven model is the first step towards mastering serverless architectures and unlocking the full potential of this powerful service.

Understanding Serverless Architecture

In recent years, serverless architecture has transformed the way applications are built and deployed, and AWS Lambda is a cornerstone of this revolution. To understand the value that AWS Lambda brings to serverless computing, it is important to explore the key principles and concepts that define serverless architecture and how it differs from traditional approaches.

At its most fundamental level, **serverless architecture** abstracts away the need for developers to manage servers. While servers still exist in the background, they are entirely managed by cloud providers like AWS. This architecture enables developers to write code and deploy applications without worrying about the underlying infrastructure, such as server provisioning, maintenance, scaling, and uptime.

Serverless architecture offers a new development model focused on deploying individual **functions** rather than managing entire applications or servers. In AWS Lambda, these functions are small, stateless units of logic that are invoked in response to specific events. This approach provides both flexibility and efficiency, allowing developers to break down applications into smaller, manageable units that are easier to scale, deploy, and maintain.

Key Principles of Serverless Architecture

1. **Event-Driven Computing** Serverless architecture is inherently **event-driven**, meaning functions are triggered by specific events rather than running continuously. Events can come from a wide range of sources, such as user actions (e.g., API requests), changes in data (e.g., file uploads), or scheduled tasks (e.g., cron jobs). In the AWS ecosystem, services like Amazon S3, API Gateway, DynamoDB, and SQS act as event sources that can trigger Lambda functions.
2. This event-driven nature enables developers to design applications that respond dynamically to changes in the environment, scaling effortlessly to handle varying levels of demand. By decoupling event processing from the underlying infrastructure, serverless architecture

aligns well with the principles of microservices, where each service can independently respond to events and scale as needed.

3. **No Server Management** A defining characteristic of serverless architecture is the complete abstraction of server management. In traditional cloud computing, even with virtual machines or container-based architectures, developers still need to configure and maintain servers, ensure uptime, apply patches, and monitor scaling.

4. With serverless, cloud providers like AWS take full responsibility for managing the underlying infrastructure, including server allocation, maintenance, and scaling. Developers focus exclusively on writing code. This frees up resources to focus on building features rather than worrying about operational tasks, leading to faster development cycles and reduced operational overhead.

5. **Automatic Scaling** One of the most significant advantages of serverless architecture is **automatic scaling**. Unlike traditional applications, which often require manual intervention to handle spikes in traffic, serverless applications scale automatically based on the number of events they need to process. AWS Lambda handles scaling for each function independently, meaning multiple instances of a Lambda function can run concurrently to handle high loads, and idle resources are deallocated when there are no events to process.

6. For example, if you have a Lambda function handling HTTP requests via API Gateway, and your application experiences a sudden spike in traffic, Lambda will automatically create new instances of your function to handle the incoming requests. Once the traffic decreases, Lambda will scale back, releasing the resources and ensuring that you only pay for the compute time used.

7. **Pay-Per-Use Model** Traditional server-based architectures typically involve provisioning and paying for resources regardless of whether they are fully utilized. This can result in underutilized infrastructure and increased costs. In contrast, serverless architecture follows a **pay-per-use** model, where you are charged only for the actual execution time of your code, measured in milliseconds. If a function is not invoked,

no charges are incurred.

8. AWS Lambda's pricing model is based on the number of function invocations and the amount of compute time consumed during each invocation. This makes serverless architecture highly cost-effective for workloads that experience variable traffic, such as applications with infrequent usage patterns or seasonal demand. By avoiding the need to maintain idle resources, businesses can significantly reduce operational costs.

9. **Statelessness** In serverless architecture, functions are typically **stateless**, meaning they do not retain any data or state between invocations. Every time a Lambda function is invoked, it starts with a clean execution environment, and any state that needs to be preserved must be stored externally. AWS Lambda encourages developers to externalize state by leveraging services like Amazon S3 (for object storage), DynamoDB (for data persistence), and Amazon RDS (for relational databases).

10. This stateless nature enables Lambda functions to scale easily, as there are no dependencies on prior executions or shared memory. It also simplifies the design of serverless applications, as developers do not need to worry about synchronizing state across multiple instances of a function.

11. **Ephemeral Execution** In a serverless environment, functions are designed to be short-lived and ephemeral. AWS Lambda enforces a maximum execution time of 15 minutes per invocation, meaning that each function must complete its task within that timeframe. This makes Lambda ideal for lightweight, stateless tasks such as processing API requests, transforming data, or running automation scripts.

12. While this constraint encourages developers to write efficient code, it also necessitates the use of other AWS services for handling longer-running tasks. For instance, complex workflows that require long processing times can be managed using AWS Step Functions, which coordinate multiple Lambda functions and external services to execute tasks asynchronously.

13. **Decoupling and Modularity** Serverless architecture encourages **de-**

coupling and **modularity** by breaking applications into smaller, independent units of logic, commonly referred to as **functions** or **microservices**. Each Lambda function is responsible for a specific task and can be independently developed, deployed, and scaled. This promotes a modular design where each function operates autonomously, communicating with other services or functions via well-defined interfaces, such as APIs or message queues.

14. By adopting this modular approach, developers can build more maintainable and testable applications. Each function can be updated or replaced without affecting the rest of the application, enabling faster innovation and reducing the risk of introducing errors into production.

15. **Integration with Managed Services** AWS Lambda is tightly integrated with a wide range of AWS services, making it easy to build complex applications that leverage the power of the AWS ecosystem. For example, Lambda can process events from S3 (file uploads), DynamoDB (data changes), Kinesis (streaming data), or SNS (notifications). This seamless integration allows developers to build event-driven architectures that can respond to real-time data and scale automatically based on demand.

16. Lambda also integrates with external services via API Gateway, allowing developers to expose Lambda functions as RESTful APIs for web and mobile applications. Additionally, AWS Step Functions enable the orchestration of complex workflows across multiple Lambda functions, providing a way to handle asynchronous or long-running tasks.

Serverless vs. Traditional Architectures

To better understand the benefits of serverless architecture, it's helpful to compare it with traditional, server-based architectures:

1. **Server Management** In traditional architectures, developers are responsible for provisioning, configuring, and maintaining servers, whether physical or virtual. This involves tasks like patching the operating system, configuring load balancers, scaling resources, and

ensuring security. With serverless, all of this is abstracted away by the cloud provider. Developers simply write code and deploy it, without worrying about the underlying infrastructure.

2. **Cost Efficiency** Traditional architectures often result in over-provisioning of resources, as developers must estimate the peak capacity their application may need and provision servers accordingly. This can lead to underutilized infrastructure and higher costs. In contrast, serverless architecture follows a pay-per-use model, meaning you only pay for the compute time you actually use. There's no need to provision or pay for idle resources, making serverless ideal for workloads with variable traffic patterns.

3. **Scaling** In traditional architectures, scaling often requires manual intervention or the configuration of auto-scaling mechanisms. These systems can be complex to manage and may not scale instantaneously in response to traffic spikes. Serverless architecture, on the other hand, automatically scales with demand. AWS Lambda can handle thousands of concurrent executions, scaling up or down based on the volume of incoming events without any manual intervention.

4. **Deployment and Maintenance** Deploying and maintaining traditional server-based applications often involves managing multiple layers of infrastructure, such as load balancers, web servers, databases, and caches. This can slow down development cycles and increase operational complexity. With serverless, deployment is simplified to uploading code and configuring the runtime environment. AWS Lambda takes care of provisioning infrastructure, ensuring uptime, and applying security patches, allowing developers to focus solely on writing and deploying code.

5. **State Management** Traditional server-based architectures often rely on persistent servers that maintain state across user sessions or transactions. This can introduce complexities in managing shared memory, synchronization, and data consistency. In serverless architecture, functions are stateless, meaning they do not retain data between invocations. State must be externalized to storage services like DynamoDB, S3, or

RDS. While this requires careful consideration of how to handle data persistence, it also simplifies scaling and reduces the risk of issues related to shared state.

Benefits of Serverless Architecture

1. **Faster Time to Market** Serverless architecture allows developers to rapidly prototype, develop, and deploy applications without the need for lengthy infrastructure setup and management. By focusing solely on writing code, development cycles are shortened, enabling faster time-to-market for new features and products.

2. **Reduced Operational Complexity** Since serverless architecture abstracts away the underlying infrastructure, developers no longer need to manage servers, configure scaling, or monitor uptime. This reduces operational complexity and frees up resources for innovation and feature development. AWS takes care of operational tasks like server patching, scaling, and infrastructure management, enabling developers to focus on building high-quality applications.

3. **Scalability and Elasticity** Serverless architecture offers unmatched scalability and elasticity, allowing applications to handle sudden spikes in traffic without any manual intervention. AWS Lambda automatically scales to meet demand, ensuring that applications remain highly available and performant even during peak usage. This is particularly beneficial for applications with unpredictable or seasonal traffic patterns.

4. **Cost Efficiency** The pay-per-use model of serverless architecture can result in significant cost savings, especially for applications with variable workloads. Traditional architectures often require developers to over-provision resources to handle peak traffic, resulting in wasted infrastructure costs. In contrast, serverless architecture charges only for the actual execution time of functions, making it highly cost-efficient for both small-scale and large-scale applications.

5. **Focus on Business Logic** By removing the need to manage infras-

tructure, serverless architecture enables developers to focus on writing business logic and building features that add value to users. This leads to greater agility and innovation, as teams can spend more time developing and less time on operational tasks.

6. **Environmentally Friendly** Since serverless computing scales based on actual usage, it avoids the energy waste associated with maintaining idle servers. By optimizing resource utilization, serverless architecture contributes to more sustainable computing practices and reduces the environmental impact of running applications.

Challenges of Serverless Architecture

Despite its many benefits, serverless architecture also presents certain challenges that developers must be aware of:

1. **Cold Start Latency** When a Lambda function is invoked after a period of inactivity, AWS must initialize a new execution environment, which can introduce latency known as a **cold start**. While cold starts are typically short (measured in milliseconds), they can impact performance-sensitive applications. There are strategies to mitigate cold starts, such as configuring **provisioned concurrency** or keeping functions "warm" by invoking them periodically.

2. **Timeout Limitations** AWS Lambda imposes a maximum execution time of 15 minutes per invocation. While this is sufficient for most tasks, long-running processes may require alternative solutions, such as breaking the task into smaller units or using AWS Step Functions to manage complex workflows. Developers must carefully design their functions to ensure that they complete within the allotted time frame.

3. **Vendor Lock-In** Since AWS Lambda is a proprietary service, building applications on top of Lambda may result in **vendor lock-in**. Migrating a serverless application to another cloud provider or on-premises infrastructure can be challenging, as it may require rewriting significant portions of the codebase to accommodate different APIs and services.

4. **Debugging and Monitoring** Debugging serverless applications can be more complex than traditional applications, as functions are stateless and distributed across multiple execution environments. Monitoring tools like AWS CloudWatch provide insights into function performance, but developers must adopt a distributed monitoring approach to track execution across the various services and functions in their application.

Serverless architecture, powered by AWS Lambda, represents a significant shift in how developers build and manage applications in the cloud. By abstracting away server management, enabling automatic scaling, and promoting a pay-per-use model, serverless architecture allows developers to focus on delivering value to users without being burdened by infrastructure concerns. While there are challenges to consider, the benefits of serverless architecture—such as faster development cycles, cost savings, and scalability— make it an attractive option for modern cloud-native applications. Understanding the principles of serverless architecture is essential for harnessing the full potential of AWS Lambda and building efficient, scalable, and maintainable applications in the cloud.

AWS Lambda's Core Concepts

To fully leverage the power of AWS Lambda, it's crucial to understand the core concepts that underpin the service. AWS Lambda operates within a distinct framework that abstracts much of the infrastructure traditionally associated with application development. By mastering these core concepts, developers can take advantage of Lambda's flexibility, scalability, and efficiency. These concepts form the foundation of how Lambda functions work, are triggered, and interact with other AWS services.

1. Lambda Function

At the heart of AWS Lambda is the **Lambda function** itself. A Lambda function is a discrete unit of computation that consists of code designed to perform a specific task in response to an event. Lambda functions can be written in a variety of programming languages, including Python, Node.js, Java, Go, Ruby, C#, and PowerShell. Once the function code is created, it is deployed into AWS Lambda, where it can be executed when triggered by specific events.

A Lambda function has three essential components:

- **Handler**: The entry point to your Lambda function where the event data is passed. This is the function in your code that Lambda invokes when the function is executed.
- **Event**: The data that triggers the Lambda function, such as an HTTP request, a file upload to S3, or a message in an SQS queue.
- **Context**: Metadata provided by AWS Lambda that provides information about the execution environment, including memory usage, function timeout, log stream details, and function invocation type (synchronous or asynchronous).

Lambda functions are designed to be stateless, meaning they do not retain any data or context between executions. This allows Lambda to horizontally scale by invoking multiple instances of the function in response to incoming events. Each function instance runs independently and in isolation from others.

2. Handler and Event Model

The **handler** is a key concept in Lambda as it defines the entry point for your function's logic. When Lambda is triggered, the service looks for the specified handler, which contains the code to process the event.

The signature of the handler function depends on the programming language being used. For example, in Python, a Lambda handler typically looks like this:

```python
def lambda_handler(event, context):
    # Your code here
    return {
        'statusCode': 200,
        'body': 'Hello from Lambda!'
    }
```

- The **event** parameter contains the data that triggered the function execution. This can vary widely depending on the event source. For example, if the function is triggered by an API Gateway request, the event will contain details about the HTTP request. If triggered by an S3 bucket, the event will include information about the uploaded object.
- The **context** parameter provides runtime information about the Lambda function itself. This includes function name, memory limits, log group, and request ID, as well as a function to access remaining execution time (context.get_remaining_time_in_millis()).

The handler structure ensures that Lambda functions can respond dynamically to different types of events, making them highly versatile for use in a wide range of scenarios.

3. Event Sources

AWS Lambda is an event-driven service, meaning that its functions are executed in response to events. **Event sources** are the services or systems that generate these events, which in turn trigger Lambda functions. AWS Lambda integrates with various AWS services that act as event sources. Some of the most common event sources include:

- **Amazon S3**: Trigger a Lambda function when objects are created, deleted, or modified in an S3 bucket. For example, a Lambda function can process image files uploaded to an S3 bucket, generating thumbnails or performing image recognition.
- **Amazon DynamoDB**: Trigger a Lambda function when data in a DynamoDB table is inserted, updated, or deleted. This can be used for real-time data processing and auditing.
- **Amazon SNS (Simple Notification Service)**: Trigger Lambda functions to process messages sent to an SNS topic. This is often used for messaging and notifications.
- **Amazon SQS (Simple Queue Service)**: Process messages from an SQS queue, which allows for decoupling between services by sending and receiving messages asynchronously.
- **Amazon Kinesis**: Process streaming data from a Kinesis stream, allowing for near real-time data analysis and transformation.
- **Amazon API Gateway**: Trigger Lambda functions in response to HTTP requests. This allows developers to build fully serverless APIs that are cost-effective and scalable.
- **Scheduled Events**: AWS Lambda also supports triggering functions based on scheduled events using **Amazon CloudWatch Events** or **EventBridge**. This is useful for running recurring tasks such as data cleanup or daily reporting.

Lambda's ability to integrate seamlessly with various event sources makes it a powerful tool for creating event-driven architectures. Each event source has its own format for delivering event data to the Lambda function, and understanding the structure of these events is crucial for handling them effectively.

4. Triggers and Invocations

Triggers are specific configurations that define when and how a Lambda function is invoked. For example, uploading a file to an S3 bucket can be configured as a trigger for a Lambda function. There are two main types of invocations in AWS Lambda:

- **Synchronous Invocation**: In this mode, the event source (e.g., API Gateway, an application) waits for the Lambda function to complete and return a response. The calling application or service sends the request to Lambda, and Lambda processes the function, returning the result back to the client. Synchronous invocations are commonly used in scenarios where the caller needs an immediate response, such as API requests via API Gateway.
- **Asynchronous Invocation**: In this mode, the event source sends the event to Lambda, but does not wait for a response. Lambda processes the event independently and logs the result in CloudWatch. Asynchronous invocations are often used for event sources like S3, SNS, and CloudWatch Events, where the function can execute without requiring an immediate response. This mode is useful for tasks like background processing and notifications.

5. Execution Environment

When AWS Lambda executes a function, it runs inside an **execution environment** that provides an isolated runtime for the function. This environment is managed by AWS and includes the following components:

- **Runtime**: The programming language runtime that executes your function code. AWS Lambda supports multiple runtimes, including Python, Node.js, Java, Ruby, Go, and .NET. Developers can also provide custom runtimes using Lambda Layers (discussed later).
- **Memory and CPU**: Lambda allows you to configure the memory

allocation for your function, ranging from 128 MB to 10 GB. The amount of CPU allocated to the function is directly proportional to the memory size. This means that functions with higher memory allocation also have access to more CPU power, allowing them to execute faster.

- **Ephemeral Storage**: Each Lambda function is provided with a limited amount of **ephemeral storage** (500 MB) in the /tmp directory, which can be used for storing temporary data or files during execution. This storage is only available for the duration of the function's execution and is cleared when the function completes.
- **VPC Integration**: AWS Lambda functions can be configured to run inside a **Virtual Private Cloud (VPC)**, allowing them to access resources like RDS databases or EC2 instances that are within the VPC. When a Lambda function is configured to run inside a VPC, it must also be given the appropriate network configurations such as security groups and subnet associations.
- **Environment Variables**: Lambda allows you to define **environment variables** that are accessible during the function's execution. These variables can store sensitive information such as API keys, database credentials, or configuration settings.

Each Lambda invocation occurs within an isolated environment, which means that there's no direct interaction between function instances. However, AWS does reuse execution environments between invocations when possible, which can lead to performance optimizations such as reduced cold start times. This environment reuse is an important optimization, but developers must ensure that functions remain stateless and do not rely on data from previous invocations.

6. Concurrency and Scaling

AWS Lambda is designed to automatically scale based on the number of incoming events. The concept of **concurrency** plays a significant role in how Lambda handles scaling.

- **Concurrency** refers to the number of executions of a function that can run at the same time. When an event triggers a Lambda function, Lambda creates a new instance of that function to handle the event. If multiple events occur simultaneously, Lambda automatically scales by creating multiple instances to process the events concurrently.
- **Reserved Concurrency**: AWS allows you to configure **reserved concurrency** for a Lambda function, which limits the number of concurrent executions. This ensures that the function does not consume all available resources, which is useful for applications where other services need to share resources or where traffic spikes need to be controlled.
- **Provisioned Concurrency**: AWS introduced **provisioned concurrency** to address the issue of cold start latency. By enabling provisioned concurrency, you can ensure that a pre-defined number of function instances are always initialized and ready to handle requests, thus eliminating cold starts. This is particularly beneficial for applications with high-performance requirements or unpredictable spikes in traffic.

Lambda's automatic scaling is one of its most powerful features, as it enables applications to handle traffic spikes without manual intervention or infrastructure management. This is especially useful for applications with unpredictable workloads, such as web APIs, data pipelines, or event-driven workflows.

7. AWS Lambda Limits

Although AWS Lambda abstracts much of the infrastructure complexity, it imposes certain **limits** to ensure efficient and fair usage of resources. Some key limits include:

- **Execution Timeout**: Each Lambda function has a maximum execution time of 15 minutes per invocation. If a function exceeds this limit, Lambda terminates the execution and logs an error. This constraint requires developers to design functions that complete within this time frame, often breaking complex tasks into smaller, manageable units.

- **Memory Allocation**: The amount of memory that can be allocated to a Lambda function ranges from 128 MB to 10 GB. The CPU power is proportional to the allocated memory, so increasing memory also boosts CPU performance. This flexibility allows developers to optimize their function's performance based on their specific workload.
- **Payload Size**: The maximum size of the event data (payload) passed to a Lambda function for synchronous invocations is 6 MB. For asynchronous invocations, the payload limit is 256 KB. Large payloads need to be stored in services like S3, and only a reference (such as an S3 object key) should be passed to the Lambda function.
- **Deployment Package Size**: The maximum size of the deployment package (i.e., the compressed file containing your code and dependencies) is 50 MB when uploaded directly via the AWS Management Console or 250 MB when using S3 as the source.

These limits encourage developers to optimize their code and workflows, ensuring that Lambda functions are efficient, fast, and scalable. Understanding these limits is essential for designing serverless applications that perform reliably under various conditions.

8. AWS CloudWatch Integration

CloudWatch is AWS's monitoring service that automatically collects and tracks metrics, logs, and events for your Lambda functions. Every time a Lambda function is invoked, it generates logs, performance data, and metrics that are automatically stored in **CloudWatch Logs** and **CloudWatch Metrics**. This integration is essential for monitoring and troubleshooting your Lambda functions.

- **Logs**: Lambda functions generate logs that contain details about each invocation, including the start and end time, memory usage, and any output or errors produced by the function. These logs are automatically stored in CloudWatch Logs, where they can be viewed or queried to debug and optimize the function.

- **Metrics**: CloudWatch Metrics provide real-time insights into the performance of Lambda functions. Key metrics include:
- **Invocation count**: The number of times a function is invoked.
- **Duration**: The execution time of the function.
- **Error count**: The number of failed invocations.
- **Throttles**: The number of times the function invocation was throttled due to reaching concurrency limits.
- **Memory usage**: The amount of memory used by the function during execution.

Developers can configure **CloudWatch Alarms** to trigger notifications based on specific metrics, such as error rates or memory consumption, providing automated monitoring and alerting for critical performance issues.

9. Error Handling and Retries

AWS Lambda has built-in error handling and retry mechanisms that help manage function failures and ensure that applications remain resilient.

- **Synchronous Invocations**: For synchronous invocations (e.g., API Gateway), if a function fails, the error is immediately returned to the caller. Developers can implement custom error-handling logic within their function to return appropriate HTTP status codes or retry the operation.
- **Asynchronous Invocations**: For asynchronous invocations (e.g., S3 or SNS triggers), AWS Lambda automatically retries the function twice if it encounters an error. If the function continues to fail after the retries, the event is sent to a **Dead Letter Queue (DLQ)** or **on-failure destination** if configured. DLQs allow developers to inspect failed events and determine the cause of the failure.

This built-in error handling helps ensure that transient issues are retried automatically, reducing the likelihood of data loss or incomplete processing.

AWS Lambda's core concepts are designed to simplify serverless application development by abstracting away infrastructure concerns while providing flexibility, scalability, and cost efficiency. Understanding how Lambda functions work, how they are triggered, and how they interact with other AWS services is essential for building robust, high-performance applications. With its event-driven architecture, automatic scaling, and integration with the AWS ecosystem, Lambda empowers developers to focus on writing code and solving business problems without being bogged down by operational complexities.

Setting Up Your AWS Account

Before you can begin working with AWS Lambda and other AWS services, the first step is to set up an AWS account. AWS provides a wide range of cloud services, and by creating an account, you gain access to all the tools you need for serverless development, including Lambda, API Gateway, S3, DynamoDB, and many more.

This section will walk you through the process of creating an AWS account, setting up the necessary permissions and security configurations, and preparing your environment for working with AWS Lambda. By the end of this section, you'll have everything in place to start building and deploying your Lambda functions.

1. Creating an AWS Account

If you don't already have an AWS account, you'll need to create one. Follow these steps to get started:

Visit the AWS Website:

- Go to the official AWS website at https://aws.amazon.com. You will see an option to sign up for a new account if you don't have one.

Click on "Create an AWS Account":

- On the homepage, locate the "Create an AWS Account" button. Clicking this will initiate the signup process.

Enter Your Account Information:

- You will be prompted to enter your **email address, password**, and an **AWS account name**. The account name can be your business name, personal name, or a project-specific identifier.

Provide Billing Information:

- AWS requires billing information even though many services (including AWS Lambda) have free-tier offerings. You'll need to provide a **valid credit card** or **bank account information** to complete the signup process. Don't worry—AWS will not charge you unless you exceed the limits of the free-tier services.

Choose Your Support Plan:

- AWS offers several support plans, ranging from basic (free) to enterprise-level support. For most users starting with Lambda, the **Basic Support** plan will suffice. You can always upgrade later if needed.

Verify Your Identity:

- AWS will require identity verification via **SMS** or **voice call**. Enter your phone number and follow the instructions to verify your account.

Complete Setup:

- Once you've entered all required information and verified your identity, you will receive a confirmation email. After your account is confirmed, you can log in to the AWS Management Console.

2. Navigating the AWS Management Console

The **AWS Management Console** is your central interface for accessing and managing AWS services, including Lambda. Once you've created your account and logged in, you'll be directed to the console dashboard.

Here's a brief overview of the console and how to navigate to key services:
Dashboard:

- The AWS Management Console dashboard provides an overview of recently used services and account information. You can customize this view to pin frequently used services like Lambda, S3, DynamoDB, or API Gateway.

Search Bar:

- At the top of the console, you'll find a search bar where you can quickly search for services. Type "Lambda" into the search bar and click on "AWS Lambda" to access the Lambda service.

AWS Services Menu:

- On the top-left corner of the dashboard, you'll find the "Services" menu. Clicking on this menu will open a list of all available AWS services, organized by category (e.g., Compute, Storage, Database, Machine Learning, etc.). You can navigate through this menu to access any service you need.

Region Selector:

- In the top-right corner of the console, you'll see the region selector. AWS services are distributed across multiple global regions. Choose the region closest to your target users or infrastructure to minimize latency. The selected region will affect where your Lambda functions are deployed.

3. Setting Up Billing and Cost Management

Before diving into Lambda development, it's important to understand AWS's billing system. AWS provides a **Free Tier** that allows you to experiment with many services, including Lambda, without incurring costs. However, it's a good practice to set up **billing alarms** to ensure that you don't exceed your budget.

Here's how to set up billing and monitor your AWS spending:

Access Billing and Cost Management:

- From the AWS Management Console, navigate to the "Billing and Cost Management" section. You can find this by clicking your account name in the top-right corner and selecting "Billing Dashboard."

View Free Tier Usage:

- AWS Lambda offers 1 million free requests and 400,000 GB-seconds of compute time per month under the AWS Free Tier. Monitor your usage here to ensure that you're staying within the Free Tier limits.

Set Up Billing Alarms:

- AWS offers integration with **CloudWatch** to set up billing alarms. These alarms notify you via email if your costs exceed a predefined threshold.
- Go to the **CloudWatch** service by searching for it in the console.
- Select **Alarms** from the left-hand menu, then click **Create Alarm**.

- Choose the metric: **Billing -> Total Estimated Charge**.
- Set a threshold (e.g., $10) to receive notifications if your AWS charges exceed this amount.

By configuring these alarms, you can ensure that you don't accidentally exceed your expected budget while experimenting with AWS Lambda.

4. Creating IAM Users and Roles

AWS Identity and Access Management (IAM) is a critical component of AWS security. IAM allows you to create users, groups, and roles, and assign them specific permissions. It's a best practice to avoid using the root account (the account you initially created) for day-to-day tasks. Instead, you should create IAM users and roles with appropriate permissions for working with AWS Lambda.

Here's how to set up IAM users and roles:

Access the IAM Console:

- From the AWS Management Console, search for "IAM" in the search bar and select **Identity and Access Management**.

Create an IAM User:

- Click on **Users** in the left-hand menu, then click **Add User**.
- Enter a **username** (e.g., lambda-admin) and select **Programmatic Access** if you need access via the CLI or SDK, or **AWS Management Console Access** for console access.
- Assign the necessary permissions by attaching policies like **AdministratorAccess** (for full access) or more restrictive policies like **AWSLambdaFullAccess** for Lambda-specific tasks.

Set Up User Groups (Optional):

- You can create groups to organize users with similar roles. For example, you might create a group called **Developers** and assign appropriate permissions for building and deploying Lambda functions.

Create an IAM Role for Lambda:

- AWS Lambda requires an **IAM role** to execute functions and access other AWS resources (e.g., S3, DynamoDB, or CloudWatch). This role provides the necessary permissions for Lambda to perform these actions securely.
- In the IAM console, click **Roles** from the left-hand menu, then click **Create Role**.
- Select **AWS Service** as the trusted entity and choose **Lambda** as the service that will use this role.
- Attach the necessary policies, such as **AWSLambdaBasicExecutionRole** (which allows Lambda to write logs to CloudWatch) or custom policies depending on your application's needs.
- Name the role (e.g., lambda-execution-role) and save it.

Use Roles for Fine-Grained Permissions:

- AWS best practices recommend using **least privilege** when assigning permissions. This means giving users and roles only the permissions they need to perform their tasks, rather than blanket access to all services.

5. Installing the AWS CLI and SDKs

AWS provides multiple ways to interact with its services, including the **AWS Management Console**, **Command Line Interface (CLI)**, and various **Software Development Kits (SDKs)**. While the console is user-friendly for beginners, experienced developers often prefer the CLI or SDKs for automation, scripting, and integration into CI/CD pipelines.

Here's how to install and configure the AWS CLI:

Install the AWS CLI:

- The AWS CLI allows you to manage AWS services from your terminal. It supports all AWS services, including Lambda, and can be used for tasks like deploying functions, managing permissions, and invoking Lambda functions.
- On macOS: Install via brew install awscli (Homebrew).
- On Linux: Use your distribution's package manager or download it directly from AWS.
- On Windows: Use the AWS CLI MSI installer available on the AWS website.

Configure the AWS CLI:

- After installation, configure the CLI with your AWS credentials and region:

```bash

aws configure

```

- You'll be prompted to enter your **Access Key ID**, **Secret Access Key**, **Default region name**, and **Default output format**. These credentials are generated in the IAM console.

Install AWS SDKs:

- AWS SDKs are essential for interacting with AWS services programmatically from various programming languages. If you're developing Lambda functions in Python, Node.js, Java, or other supported languages, you'll need to install the corresponding SDK to make API calls to AWS services like Lambda, S3, DynamoDB, and others.
- The **AWS SDK for Python** (also known as **Boto3**) is commonly used

for Python-based Lambda development. Here's how to install and set up Boto3:

For Python:

```bash
bash

pip install boto3
```

- For **Node.js**, install the **AWS SDK** using npm:

```bash
bash

npm install aws-sdk
```

- For **Java**, use **Maven** or **Gradle** to include the AWS SDK:

```xml
xml

<dependency>
    <groupId>com.amazonaws</groupId>
    <artifactId>aws-java-sdk</artifactId>
    <version>1.12.0</version>
</dependency>
```

AWS provides SDKs for a variety of languages, so you can choose the one that best suits your development environment. These SDKs enable seamless integration between your code and AWS services, allowing you to interact with AWS resources from within your Lambda functions.

Testing AWS CLI and SDK Integration:

- Once the AWS CLI or SDK is installed, you should test that they are configured correctly by listing available Lambda functions. This will confirm that your environment is set up properly for interacting with AWS services.

For example, using the CLI, run the following command to list Lambda functions:

```bash

aws lambda list-functions
```

If everything is set up correctly, you should see an empty list (if no functions have been created yet) or a list of existing Lambda functions in your AWS account.

6. Configuring Regions and Availability Zones

AWS Lambda is a globally distributed service, but when you create a function, it is deployed to a specific **AWS Region**. AWS regions are physical locations around the world where data centers are grouped. Each region consists of multiple **Availability Zones** (AZs) which provide redundancy and high availability.

- **Why Regions Matter**: The region you select for deploying your Lambda functions can affect latency, performance, and data residency requirements. For example, if your users are primarily in Europe, it makes sense to deploy your Lambda function in the **eu-west-1** (Ireland) region for minimal latency. Similarly, businesses with regulatory requirements may need to choose a region that complies with specific data privacy laws, such as **us-east-1** (Northern Virginia) for U.S.-based applications.
- **How to Choose a Region**: When creating a Lambda function, the AWS Console will prompt you to select a region. Some considerations for

choosing a region include:

- **Latency**: Choose the region closest to your users for faster response times.
- **Cost**: AWS pricing varies slightly by region, so you may want to compare costs across regions, especially for high-volume workloads.
- **Compliance**: Ensure that the region complies with your data residency or regulatory requirements.
- **Service Availability**: Some AWS services or features may not be available in all regions. Check that the region you choose supports all the AWS services you plan to use.

In the AWS Management Console, you can change regions using the **region selector** in the top-right corner. Be sure to select the appropriate region before creating and deploying your Lambda functions.

7. Setting Up CloudWatch for Monitoring and Logs

Once your AWS account is set up and you start deploying Lambda functions, it's important to configure monitoring and logging to track the performance of your applications and troubleshoot issues. AWS Lambda integrates seamlessly with **Amazon CloudWatch**, AWS's monitoring service that collects and tracks metrics, logs, and events for your Lambda functions.

Enabling CloudWatch Logs for Lambda:

- By default, AWS Lambda sends function logs to CloudWatch. These logs include details about function execution, errors, and the output generated by your code. Each time a Lambda function is invoked, a new log stream is created in the CloudWatch log group associated with that function.

Setting Up CloudWatch Metrics:

- AWS Lambda automatically provides key metrics that can be viewed in CloudWatch, such as:

- **Invocation count**: The number of times your function is called.
- **Duration**: The time it takes for your function to complete execution.
- **Error count**: The number of function invocations that failed.
- **Throttles**: The number of function invocations that were throttled due to concurrency limits.

You can view these metrics in the **CloudWatch Console** to monitor your function's performance and set up alerts when thresholds are breached.

Creating CloudWatch Alarms:

- You can create alarms based on CloudWatch metrics to get notified when something goes wrong, such as when the error rate exceeds a certain threshold or function duration is unusually high. To create a CloudWatch alarm:
- Navigate to the **CloudWatch Console**.
- Select **Alarms** from the left-hand menu.
- Click **Create Alarm** and select a metric (e.g., **Errors** for your Lambda function).
- Set a threshold and configure notifications to receive alerts (via email, SMS, etc.) when the threshold is exceeded.

8. Setting Up a Development Environment

To streamline the development process, it's helpful to set up a local development environment where you can write, test, and debug your Lambda functions before deploying them to AWS. This setup allows for faster iteration and more control over the development lifecycle.

Local Development Tools:

- While AWS Lambda is a cloud-based service, there are tools that allow you to develop and test Lambda functions locally. These tools simulate the Lambda environment, enabling you to run functions on your local machine.

34

- The **AWS SAM (Serverless Application Model)** CLI is a powerful tool that helps you build and test serverless applications locally. SAM supports local testing, debugging, and deployment of Lambda functions.

To install SAM CLI:

```bash

brew tap aws/tap
brew install aws-sam-cli
```

You can also use **Docker** to simulate the Lambda execution environment locally, allowing for realistic testing of functions before they are deployed.
IDE and Text Editor Configuration:

- Choose an Integrated Development Environment (IDE) that suits your language of choice. Popular options for Lambda development include **Visual Studio Code**, **PyCharm**, **Atom**, and **Sublime Text**.
- Many IDEs provide plugins or extensions for working with AWS Lambda, such as the **AWS Toolkit** for Visual Studio Code, which provides features like function deployment, local debugging, and viewing Lambda logs directly from your IDE.

9. Deploying Your First Lambda Function

With your AWS account, CLI, and SDKs all set up, you're ready to deploy your first Lambda function. AWS provides several ways to deploy functions, including through the AWS Management Console, the CLI, or using frameworks like AWS SAM or the Serverless Framework.

Here's how to deploy a simple Lambda function using the AWS Console:
Create a Lambda Function:

- In the AWS Console, search for "Lambda" and navigate to the Lambda service page.

- Click **Create Function** and choose a name for your function.
- Select a **runtime** (e.g., Python, Node.js, Java) and configure the basic execution settings.

Write Function Code:

- In the Lambda editor, write or paste your function code. For a simple "IIello World" function, you can use the following Python code:

```python
def lambda_handler(event, context):
    return {
        'statusCode': 200,
        'body': 'Hello, World!'
    }
```

Configure Permissions:

- Attach the necessary IAM role to your function. If your function needs to interact with other AWS services (e.g., S3, DynamoDB), ensure the role has the appropriate permissions.

Set Up Triggers:

- You can set up triggers such as an API Gateway, S3 event, or CloudWatch Events to invoke your Lambda function.

Deploy and Test:

- Once the function is set up, click **Deploy**. After deployment, you can test your function directly from the console by providing sample input and viewing the result.

Setting up your AWS account and configuring the necessary tools is the foundation for building serverless applications with AWS Lambda. By creating IAM users and roles, configuring billing and monitoring, and setting up a local development environment, you ensure that your Lambda development process is secure, scalable, and cost-effective. Once your environment is set up, deploying your first Lambda function is a straightforward process that will open the door to building powerful, event-driven applications in the cloud.

Why Python for AWS Lambda?

Python's Advantages in Serverless Development
Python has rapidly become one of the most popular programming languages globally, thanks to its simplicity, readability, and extensive support for various use cases, from web development to data science and machine learning. In the context of AWS Lambda, Python's popularity is even more pronounced because of its unique advantages in serverless development.

When building serverless applications, developers are often looking for a language that is easy to learn, fast to deploy, lightweight, and capable of integrating seamlessly with cloud services. Python checks all these boxes, making it an ideal choice for AWS Lambda functions.

This section will cover Python's specific advantages in serverless development, particularly within the AWS Lambda ecosystem, and why it is such a preferred language for many developers working in the cloud.

1. Simplicity and Readability

Python is widely known for its simple and clean syntax, which allows developers to write and understand code quickly. This readability is particularly valuable in serverless development, where functions are often small and isolated, and the ability to quickly comprehend and maintain code becomes essential.

- **Faster Onboarding**: Python's simplicity allows new developers to onboard quickly. Serverless architectures encourage small, independent units of logic (Lambda functions), so writing clear and concise Python code is crucial for maintaining efficiency in larger, more distributed systems.

- **Less Code, More Functionality**: Python's design philosophy emphasizes code readability and brevity. Its concise syntax enables developers to write fewer lines of code compared to other programming languages like Java or C#, resulting in faster development and easier maintenance.

For example, compare a basic "Hello, World!" Lambda function in Python versus Java:

Python:

```
def lambda_handler(event, context):
    return {
        'statusCode': 200,
        'body': 'Hello, World!'
    }
```

Java:

```
import com.amazonaws.services.lambda.runtime.Context;
import com.amazonaws.services.lambda.runtime.RequestHandler;
import java.util.Map;

public class HelloWorldHandler implements
RequestHandler<Map<String,String>, String> {
    @Override
    public String handleRequest(Map<String,String> event, Context
    context) {
        return "Hello, World!";
    }
}
```

Python's minimalism clearly stands out, making it quicker to write and deploy serverless functions.

2. Fast Deployment and Cold Start Optimization

One of the most critical factors in serverless computing is **cold start** performance—the time it takes for a cloud provider to start a function in response to an event when the function has not been invoked recently. AWS Lambda's performance during cold starts is influenced by the size of the deployment package, the function's runtime, and the initialization process.
Python excels in this area for several reasons:

- **Lightweight Deployment Packages**: Python's standard libraries are relatively lightweight compared to other languages. This results in smaller deployment packages, which means Lambda functions can be loaded faster into the execution environment. Smaller packages help reduce cold start times, improving overall application performance.
- **Quick Initialization**: Python's runtime is known for having faster initialization times compared to Java or .NET runtimes. For applications where low latency is crucial (e.g., APIs or real-time data processing), this quick start time is a key advantage.

For example, in applications with frequent cold starts, Python functions tend to initialize and execute more quickly than Java-based Lambda functions, resulting in a better user experience, especially in latency-sensitive applications.

3. Versatility and Wide Use Cases

Python's versatility is another significant advantage when working with AWS Lambda. It is widely used across a broad range of domains, making it easy to apply the same language to various serverless use cases without needing to switch to a different toolset. Here are some of the key areas where Python excels in serverless development:

- **Web and API Development**: Python, in conjunction with AWS Lambda and **Amazon API Gateway**, makes it easy to develop serverless web applications and RESTful APIs. Libraries like **Flask** or **FastAPI** can be used to create serverless APIs quickly and efficiently.

- **Data Processing and Automation**: Python's powerful libraries for data processing, such as **Pandas** and **NumPy**, are commonly used in serverless environments to handle tasks like real-time data transformations, ETL processes (extract, transform, load), or report generation. Python's ability to manipulate data effectively makes it a great choice for serverless data workflows in AWS Lambda.

- **Machine Learning and AI**: Python dominates the field of machine learning and artificial intelligence, with libraries like **TensorFlow**, **PyTorch**, and **Scikit-learn** being industry standards. AWS Lambda can be used to deploy lightweight machine learning models in Python, enabling serverless applications to provide AI-driven insights, such as real-time predictions or image classifications.

- **Automation and DevOps**: Python's role in automation and DevOps is well established. Serverless automation workflows, such as AWS Lambda functions triggered by CloudWatch Events, are commonly written in Python to handle tasks like infrastructure provisioning, monitoring, backup scheduling, or auto-remediation.

4. Extensive Libraries and Ecosystem

Python boasts an enormous ecosystem of libraries and frameworks, many of which are perfect for serverless development. AWS Lambda allows you to package these libraries alongside your Lambda function or deploy them as Lambda Layers for code reuse and better management. Some of the most widely used Python libraries in serverless applications include:

- **Boto3**: The official AWS SDK for Python, **Boto3** provides a simple and efficient way to interact with AWS services, such as S3, DynamoDB, and Lambda. With Boto3, you can easily build complex workflows and integrations within your Lambda functions.

- **Requests**: Python's **requests** library is one of the most popular libraries for making HTTP requests. It simplifies the process of calling external APIs from within Lambda functions, making Python a natural fit for integrating third-party services or handling webhooks.
- **Flask/FastAPI**: These micro-frameworks allow developers to create serverless APIs that are easily integrated with AWS Lambda via API Gateway. Python's ability to work seamlessly with API development makes it a go-to language for creating serverless backends.
- **NumPy/Pandas**: For serverless data processing, Python's **NumPy** and **Pandas** libraries are widely regarded for their efficiency in handling numerical computations and data analysis. These libraries can be used in Lambda functions to process and analyze large datasets, making Python an excellent choice for serverless data pipelines.
- **Zappa**: **Zappa** is a Python framework that simplifies the deployment of web applications to AWS Lambda. It works with Python web frameworks like Flask and Django, allowing developers to create serverless web applications and APIs with minimal configuration.

The extensive availability of these libraries means that you can build highly functional, robust applications without reinventing the wheel. Python's package ecosystem supports nearly every use case imaginable in serverless computing.

5. Integration with AWS Services

AWS Lambda does not operate in isolation—it's typically part of a larger ecosystem involving multiple AWS services. Python's **Boto3** SDK makes it incredibly easy to integrate Lambda functions with other AWS services such as:

- **Amazon S3**: Use Lambda to process file uploads to S3 (e.g., image resizing, data transformation).
- **Amazon DynamoDB**: Trigger Lambda functions when data in a Dy-

namoDB table changes, enabling real-time analytics or event-driven data processing.

- **Amazon SQS/SNS**: Build event-driven applications that respond to messages from SQS queues or SNS topics, using Python functions to process these events.
- **Amazon CloudWatch**: Automate monitoring tasks by triggering Python-based Lambda functions when CloudWatch alarms are triggered, such as automatically restarting failed services or sending notifications.

Python's integration with AWS services is seamless, making it easy to build end-to-end serverless workflows that involve multiple services.

6. Developer Community and Learning Resources

Another key advantage of Python is its vast developer community and the wealth of resources available for learning and troubleshooting. The Python community is one of the largest and most active in the world, meaning that developers working with Python in AWS Lambda are never short of tutorials, documentation, or example projects to reference.

- **Official AWS Documentation**: AWS provides extensive documentation, code samples, and SDKs specifically for Python, making it easier to build Lambda functions, manage resources, and integrate with AWS services.
- **Open-Source Projects**: Python has a thriving open-source community, with numerous tools and libraries tailored specifically for AWS Lambda and serverless development. These open-source projects often include pre-built templates, Lambda Layers, and reusable code that can be integrated into your own projects.
- **Online Communities and Forums**: From Stack Overflow to AWS-specific forums, there is a vast network of developers and AWS experts ready to help with any Python or Lambda-related questions.
- **Learning Resources**: Python's ease of learning, coupled with a large number of tutorials, courses, and books dedicated to Python in serverless

environments, makes it an excellent choice for both beginner and experienced developers. Whether you're building your first Lambda function or deploying complex serverless architectures, Python's developer community is always there to support your journey.

7. Mature Error Handling and Debugging Capabilities

Python's built-in capabilities for **error handling** and **debugging** are crucial in a serverless environment where runtime errors need to be managed effectively. With Python, developers can implement detailed exception handling using **try-except blocks**, ensuring that Lambda functions can handle failures gracefully, log errors effectively, and retry operations if necessary.

In a serverless architecture, where functions interact with external services like databases or APIs, the ability to catch, log, and resolve errors in real-time is critical. Python's mature error handling mechanisms allow for the creation of robust, fault-tolerant Lambda functions.

Here's an example of how Python handles error logging in a Lambda function:

```python
import logging
import boto3

logger = logging.getLogger()
logger.setLevel(logging.INFO)

def lambda_handler(event, context):
    try:
        # Simulating a function that may fail
        if event.get('should_fail'):
            raise ValueError('An error occurred')
        return {
            'statusCode': 200,
            'body': 'Success'
        }
```

```
except ValueError as e:
    logger.error(f'Error: {str(e)}')
    return {
        'statusCode': 500,
        'body': 'Internal Server Error'
    }
```

In this example, Python's exception handling and logging ensure that errors are captured and logged to CloudWatch Logs, making it easier to diagnose issues.

8. Cost Efficiency

Finally, Python's runtime is highly efficient in terms of resource consumption, which directly translates to cost savings when using AWS Lambda's **pay-per-use** pricing model. Since AWS Lambda charges based on the execution time and memory consumed by the function, Python's fast execution and low resource footprint can result in lower operational costs, especially for high-volume applications.

- **Efficient Memory Usage**: Python is known for its efficient memory management, which helps reduce the total runtime cost of Lambda functions, especially when handling large volumes of data or performing complex computations.
- **Optimized Performance**: Python's performance, particularly in I/O-bound applications (such as API calls or file processing), is well-suited for AWS Lambda's execution model. Its ability to handle asynchronous operations using libraries like asyncio and aiohttp further optimizes performance, reducing the overall runtime.

Python offers a multitude of advantages that make it an excellent choice for AWS Lambda and serverless development in general. Its simplicity, fast deployment times, extensive library support, and seamless integration with AWS services ensure that Python is well-suited for a wide range of serverless use cases, from web APIs to machine learning applications. With Python, developers can build scalable, efficient, and cost-effective serverless solutions quickly and confidently, leveraging the full power of AWS Lambda and the cloud.

Comparing Python with Other Lambda-Compatible Languages

AWS Lambda supports several programming languages, each with its strengths and weaknesses. When deciding which language to use for your serverless applications, factors like performance, ease of development, cold start times, runtime behavior, and integration with AWS services come into play. While Python has significant advantages in many areas, other Lambda-compatible languages, such as Node.js, Java, Go, C#, and Ruby, may offer specific benefits depending on the application requirements.

In this section, we'll compare Python to these other Lambda-supported languages to highlight the key differences and help you determine the best fit for your serverless workloads.

1. Python vs. Node.js

Node.js is one of the most popular alternatives to Python for serverless development in AWS Lambda, particularly for event-driven applications and real-time APIs. Both Python and Node.js are widely used, versatile languages that provide excellent support for AWS Lambda, but there are several important differences to consider.

Cold Start and Initialization Time

- **Python**: Python tends to have quicker initialization times compared to languages like Java and C#, but its cold start performance is somewhat slower than Node.js in specific use cases, especially when the function relies heavily on I/O operations or external HTTP calls.
- **Node.js**: Node.js generally has faster cold start times compared to Python due to its event-driven, non-blocking nature. This makes it particularly suitable for scenarios where the Lambda function is invoked frequently or requires low-latency responses.

Concurrency and Event Handling

- **Python**: Python handles concurrency using traditional multi-threading and asynchronous programming via the asyncio library. While Python's concurrency capabilities are robust, Node.js's event-driven architecture gives it an edge in high-concurrency scenarios, such as handling many API requests simultaneously.
- **Node.js**: Node.js excels in handling asynchronous, event-driven work-flows. Its non-blocking I/O model makes it a good choice for Lambda functions that involve significant external API calls, database queries, or file processing. In high-traffic, I/O-bound applications (e.g., APIs or webhooks), Node.js often provides better performance than Python.

Ease of Development

- **Python**: Python's simple, readable syntax makes it easier for developers to write, debug, and maintain code. It is often favored by data scientists and engineers who work in fields like data processing, machine learning, and automation.
- **Node.js**: Node.js, with its vast ecosystem of NPM packages, is widely used for full-stack development and is a natural fit for JavaScript developers. Its ease of use is comparable to Python, especially for developers already familiar with JavaScript.

47

Use Case Summary

- **Python**: Best for general-purpose applications, data processing, and machine learning. It's favored for simplicity and versatility.
- **Node.js**: Best for applications requiring high concurrency and asynchronous processing, such as real-time APIs or event-driven architectures.

2. Python vs. Java

Java is another Lambda-compatible language, typically used in enterprise-level applications due to its strong typing, performance, and scalability. However, when compared to Python, Java's complexities can become a disadvantage in serverless environments.

Cold Start and Performance

- **Python**: Python generally has faster cold starts compared to Java, as its runtime and packages are smaller and require less initialization overhead. This makes Python more suitable for workloads with sporadic traffic, where cold start latency can be a concern.
- **Java**: Java functions tend to suffer from longer cold start times because of the JVM (Java Virtual Machine) initialization process and the size of the deployment package. While Java offers superior performance once it's warmed up, the initial delay can be problematic for low-latency applications, particularly those that need quick responses or have unpredictable traffic patterns.

Memory and Compute Efficiency

- **Python**: Python's runtime is less memory-efficient compared to Java, especially when handling compute-intensive workloads. However, for I/O-bound tasks, Python is often more than adequate.
- **Java**: Java's strong memory management, multi-threading, and perfor-

mance optimization make it better suited for CPU-bound tasks. Java Lambda functions are typically preferred for long-running processes or high-throughput tasks that require optimization at scale.

Ease of Development

- **Python**: Python's concise and readable code allows developers to quickly write and deploy Lambda functions. It has fewer lines of boilerplate code compared to Java, which helps developers iterate faster.
- **Java**: Java's verbose syntax and strong typing system make it more complex to work with, especially for small, serverless functions where rapid development and deployment are priorities.

Use Case Summary

- **Python**: Ideal for workloads with frequent cold starts, rapid prototyping, and tasks that prioritize ease of development.
- **Java**: Best for long-running or compute-heavy tasks where performance and scalability are the top priorities.

3. Python vs. Go

Go (Golang) is a statically typed language designed for high-performance applications. Its simplicity, speed, and efficiency make it a strong contender in serverless development, especially in situations where performance is crucial.

Cold Start and Execution Performance

- **Python**: Python's interpreted nature means that its execution times may be slower compared to compiled languages like Go. Python performs well in most Lambda use cases, but for functions requiring extreme performance, it may not be as fast as Go.
- **Go**: Go is known for its fast execution and low memory usage. Go functions typically have excellent cold start times and can process more

requests per second compared to Python. This makes Go ideal for high-performance applications, such as those involving real-time data processing or heavy computation.

Concurrency

- **Python**: Python's concurrency model is solid but less performant compared to Go's concurrency mechanisms. For highly concurrent applications, Python relies on libraries like asyncio and multithreading, but these can't match Go's efficiency.
- **Go**: Go has native support for concurrency through its **goroutines**, which are lightweight threads managed by the Go runtime. This makes Go a natural choice for applications that need to handle many concurrent processes, such as streaming data processing or high-volume APIs.

Ease of Development

- **Python**: Python's developer-friendly syntax and extensive ecosystem make it easier for teams to quickly develop, test, and deploy serverless applications. Python's dynamic typing and flexibility are ideal for projects where simplicity and rapid iteration are essential.
- **Go**: Go is simpler than many other statically typed languages but requires more effort than Python due to its lower-level syntax. While Go is easy to learn, especially for developers familiar with C-like languages, it may not be as accessible as Python for beginners or for teams seeking rapid development cycles.

Use Case Summary

- **Python**: Best for projects where ease of development and flexibility are more important than raw performance. It's particularly suited for I/O-bound tasks and data processing.
- **Go**: Best for performance-sensitive applications where low-latency

execution, high concurrency, and memory efficiency are critical.

4. Python vs. C# (.NET Core)

C#, especially with the introduction of **.NET Core**, is another Lambda-compatible language. It is popular among enterprise developers and organizations with existing .NET ecosystems.

Cold Start and Initialization

- **Python**: Python's cold start performance is generally better than C# due to its smaller runtime and lightweight packages. Python Lambda functions start quickly and are ideal for workloads where rapid responses are critical.
- **C#**: .NET Core functions often have longer cold start times because of the time required to initialize the .NET runtime. This can be a disadvantage for serverless applications with sporadic traffic or latency-sensitive use cases. However, for warm invocations, C# performs comparably well to other languages.

Performance and Memory Usage

- **Python**: While Python's memory consumption is higher compared to C#, it performs efficiently for most I/O-bound and light-to-medium computational tasks. Python is generally not used for highly compute-intensive tasks due to its limitations in CPU performance.
- **C#**: .NET Core provides excellent performance for CPU-bound tasks. C# is well-suited for complex, enterprise-level serverless applications that require robust performance and efficient memory usage, particularly in environments where .NET is already in use.

Ease of Development

- **Python**: Python's simplicity and dynamic nature allow for faster development cycles. Its extensive ecosystem and built-in modules provide everything developers need to quickly build and deploy Lambda functions.

- **C#**: C# has a steeper learning curve due to its verbose syntax and statically typed structure, but it's preferred in enterprise environments where existing .NET systems are in place. For organizations with experienced .NET developers, C# may be easier to integrate into existing workflows.

Use Case Summary

- **Python**: Ideal for smaller, lightweight applications where rapid deployment and low cold start times are important.
- **C#**: Best for large, enterprise-grade applications where performance, scalability, and integration with existing .NET systems are crucial.

5. Python vs. Ruby

Ruby is a dynamic programming language that, like Python, emphasizes simplicity and productivity. It's commonly used with web frameworks such as Ruby on Rails.

Cold Start and Performance

- **Python**: Python generally has faster cold starts than Ruby, particularly because Python's runtime initialization is more optimized in Lambda environments. Python's memory usage is also lower than Ruby's, making it better suited for serverless applications where performance is a key concern.
- **Ruby**: Ruby's cold starts tend to be slower compared to Python, especially when larger deployment packages or external libraries are involved. While Ruby is highly productive for development, its performance in serverless environments can be a limitation.

Developer Productivity

- **Python**: Python and Ruby are comparable in terms of ease of development, though Python is more widely adopted in cloud computing and serverless applications. Python's extensive library ecosystem gives it a significant edge when working with AWS services, data processing, and machine learning.
- **Ruby**: Ruby's elegant syntax and productivity tools, such as Rails, make it an appealing choice for web applications. However, it lacks the broader ecosystem of cloud and serverless tools that Python offers, limiting its utility for certain AWS Lambda use cases.

Use Case Summary

- **Python**: Best for a broad range of serverless applications, especially when performance, scalability, and AWS integration are top priorities.
- **Ruby**: Best for developers and teams already working within the Ruby ecosystem, particularly for building serverless web applications with frameworks like Rails.

Python stands out among other Lambda-compatible languages due to its simplicity, rapid deployment capabilities, and extensive support for various use cases, from data processing to machine learning. While languages like Node.js, Go, and C# may offer advantages in specific scenarios (e.g., high concurrency, performance-sensitive workloads, or enterprise-level systems), Python provides a versatile and developer-friendly option that excels in a wide range of serverless use cases.

Choosing between Python and other Lambda-compatible languages depends on the specific requirements of your project. If rapid development, ease of use, and broad community support are your priorities, Python is often the best choice. For more performance-intensive or enterprise-focused applications, languages like Go, Java, or C# may be better suited. Ultimately, Python's balance of performance, readability, and flexibility makes it a top choice for AWS Lambda development.

Overview of Python SDKs and Libraries for AWS Lambda

One of Python's key advantages in serverless development, especially within the AWS Lambda ecosystem, is its extensive set of SDKs (Software Development Kits) and libraries. These tools allow developers to interact with AWS services, manage Lambda functions, and build feature-rich serverless applications more easily. Whether you are working on API integrations, data processing, or machine learning, Python's robust library ecosystem can streamline the development process, enabling you to focus on the business logic of your serverless applications.

This section provides an overview of the most important Python SDKs and libraries for AWS Lambda, including **Boto3**, **Requests**, **AWS Lambda Powertools**, **Zappa**, and various other utilities that enhance serverless workflows.

1. Boto3: The AWS SDK for Python

Boto3 is the official Python SDK for AWS, providing a simple and efficient way to interact with all AWS services, including S3, DynamoDB, Lambda, SQS, SNS, and more. It is a crucial tool for AWS Lambda developers because it enables programmatic access to AWS services directly from within Lambda functions.

Core Features of Boto3:

- **Service Clients**: Boto3 provides service clients, which are Python objects that allow you to interact with AWS services. For instance, the S3 client allows you to upload, download, and delete objects in S3 buckets.
- **Resources**: Boto3's resource model offers an abstraction that simplifies working with AWS services by providing more Pythonic and object-oriented APIs.
- **Session Management**: Boto3 handles AWS credentials and session

management, allowing developers to easily authenticate and authorize their interactions with AWS services.

Example Use Case: A simple Lambda function that uses Boto3 to upload a file to an S3 bucket:

```python
import boto3

def lambda_handler(event, context):
    s3 = boto3.client('s3')
    s3.put_object(Bucket='my-bucket', Key='file.txt', Body='Hello, World!')
    return {
        'statusCode': 200,
        'body': 'File uploaded to S3'
    }
```

Boto3 Highlights:

- **Comprehensive AWS Coverage**: Boto3 supports virtually every AWS service, making it a one-stop SDK for interacting with AWS resources.
- **Ease of Use**: With its simple interface, Boto3 abstracts much of the complexity of working directly with AWS APIs, enabling rapid development and deployment.
- **Asynchronous Programming**: Boto3 can be used with Python's asynchronous programming libraries, allowing for non-blocking calls in Lambda functions.

2. Requests: HTTP Requests in Python

When working with AWS Lambda, you may need to interact with external APIs or services, especially when building webhooks, REST APIs, or serverless automation workflows. Python's **Requests** library is one of the most popular tools for handling HTTP requests, making it easy to send GET, POST, PUT, and DELETE requests from your Lambda functions.

Core Features of Requests:

- **Simple API**: Requests abstracts the complexities of handling HTTP requests, providing a user-friendly interface for sending and receiving data from web services.
- **Timeouts and Error Handling**: Built-in support for setting timeouts and handling network-related errors, which are essential in serverless environments where failure handling is critical.

Example Use Case: A Lambda function that uses the Requests library to call an external API:

```python
import requests

def lambda_handler(event, context):
    response =
    requests.get('https://jsonplaceholder.typicode.com/posts/1')
    return {
        'statusCode': response.status_code,
        'body': response.json()
    }
```

Requests Highlights:

- **Versatility**: Whether you're making API calls, scraping web pages, or integrating third-party services, Requests simplifies HTTP interactions in Lambda functions.
- **Built-in Error Handling**: Requests provides native support for handling timeouts, retries, and exceptions, which are particularly useful in AWS Lambda's event-driven model.
- **Popularity**: Requests is widely used in the Python ecosystem, making it a well-documented, community-supported library.

3. AWS Lambda Powertools for Python

AWS Lambda Powertools is a set of utilities designed to ease the development of serverless applications using AWS Lambda. It provides powerful tools for logging, tracing, and metrics, helping developers follow best practices for observability and operational excellence in serverless applications.

Core Features of AWS Lambda Powertools:

- **Structured Logging**: Powertools provides utilities for consistent, structured logging, making it easier to trace and debug Lambda executions.
- **Tracing**: With built-in tracing, Powertools integrates with AWS X-Ray to provide deep insights into the behavior and performance of your Lambda functions.
- **Metrics**: Powertools simplifies the collection and publication of custom CloudWatch metrics, enabling you to monitor the performance and health of your serverless applications.

Example Use Case: Structured logging with AWS Lambda Powertools:

```python
from aws_lambda_powertools import Logger

logger = Logger(service="my_service")

def lambda_handler(event, context):
    logger.info("Lambda function started")
    # Your code logic here
    return {
        'statusCode': 200,
        'body': 'Success'
    }
```

AWS Lambda Powertools Highlights:

- **Improved Observability**: Powertools makes it easy to add structured logging, custom metrics, and distributed tracing to your Lambda functions, significantly improving observability.

- **Best Practices**: Built-in utilities encourage adherence to best practices for serverless application development, making your code more maintainable and scalable.
- **AWS X-Ray Integration**: The tracing features of Powertools work seamlessly with AWS X-Ray, providing a detailed view of function performance and identifying bottlenecks or failures.

4. Zappa: Serverless Framework for Python

Zappa is an open-source Python framework that allows you to build and deploy serverless applications on AWS Lambda quickly. It is particularly useful for deploying WSGI-compatible web frameworks, such as **Flask** and **Django**, as fully serverless applications.

Core Features of Zappa:

- **Automatic Deployment**: Zappa simplifies the process of packaging and deploying Python applications to AWS Lambda, including the creation of necessary API Gateway integrations.
- **API Gateway Integration**: Zappa automatically configures AWS API Gateway for you, enabling Lambda functions to be triggered by HTTP requests, making it ideal for creating serverless web APIs.
- **Django and Flask Support**: Zappa works out-of-the-box with popular Python web frameworks like Django and Flask, allowing developers to deploy fully serverless web applications without the need for complex setup.

Example Use Case: Deploying a Flask application to AWS Lambda using Zappa:

```
pip install zappa
zappa init
```

```
zappa deploy
```

Flask Example:

```
from flask import Flask

app = Flask(__name__)

@app.route('/')
def hello_world():
    return 'Hello, World!'
```

Zappa Highlights:

- **Serverless Web Applications**: Zappa makes it easy to convert traditional Python web applications into fully serverless architectures, leveraging the scalability of AWS Lambda and API Gateway.
- **Effortless Deployment**: The simplicity of deploying Python applications with Zappa reduces the operational overhead, allowing developers to focus on building features instead of managing infrastructure.
- **Python Web Framework Support**: Zappa is ideal for teams that want to deploy web applications or APIs written in Python frameworks like Flask or Django, offering a fast path to serverless architectures.

5. Pandas and NumPy: Data Processing Libraries

For Lambda functions that perform data processing tasks, Python's **Pandas** and **NumPy** libraries are invaluable. These libraries are highly optimized for numerical and data manipulation tasks and are frequently used in serverless workflows that handle real-time data processing, ETL pipelines, or machine learning preprocessing.

Core Features of Pandas:

- **Data Manipulation**: Pandas provides powerful tools for data wrangling, including filtering, sorting, grouping, and merging large datasets.

- **DataFrames**: The Pandas DataFrame is a highly efficient structure for working with tabular data, making it easy to manipulate CSV files, database results, or JSON data within a Lambda function.

Core Features of NumPy:

- **Numerical Computation**: NumPy provides efficient multi-dimensional arrays and functions for numerical computation, enabling Lambda functions to handle matrix operations, statistical analysis, and complex mathematical calculations.

Example Use Case: A Lambda function that processes a CSV file using Pandas:

```python
import pandas as pd
import boto3

def lambda_handler(event, context):
    s3 = boto3.client('s3')
    response = s3.get_object(Bucket='my-bucket', Key='data.csv')
    df = pd.read_csv(response['Body'])

    # Perform data manipulation with Pandas
    result = df.groupby('category').sum()

    return {
        'statusCode': 200,
        'body': result.to_json()
    }
```

Pandas and NumPy Highlights:

- **Efficient Data Processing**: Both Pandas and NumPy are highly optimized for processing large datasets in memory, making them excellent tools for Lambda functions that need to handle complex data transformations or calculations.

- **Versatility**: These libraries support a wide range of data types and formats, including CSV, JSON, Excel, and SQL databases, allowing seamless integration into serverless data pipelines.
- **Machine Learning and AI**: For serverless machine learning workflows, Pandas and NumPy are essential for preprocessing data before feeding it into machine learning models.

6. SciPy and Scikit-learn: Machine Learning and Scientific Computing

For more advanced serverless applications involving machine learning, scientific computing, or algorithmic processing, Python's **SciPy** and **Scikit-learn** libraries provide a comprehensive set of tools. These libraries allow you to integrate machine learning models and perform complex calculations within your Lambda functions.

Core Features of SciPy:

- **Scientific Computing**: SciPy provides modules for optimization, integration, interpolation, eigenvalue problems, and more, making it essential for complex mathematical and scientific applications.

Core Features of Scikit-learn:

- **Machine Learning Models**: Scikit-learn includes tools for machine learning, including classification, regression, clustering, and dimensionality reduction. Models can be trained offline and deployed into AWS Lambda for real-time inference.

Example Use Case: A Lambda function that uses a pre-trained Scikit-learn model to classify input data:

```python
import joblib
import numpy as np

# Load a pre-trained model (stored in S3)
def lambda_handler(event, context):
    model = joblib.load('/tmp/model.pkl')
    data = np.array(event['input'])

    # Predict using the loaded model
    prediction = model.predict(data)

    return {
        'statusCode': 200,
        'body': {'prediction': prediction.tolist()}
    }
```

SciPy and Scikit-learn Highlights:

- **Serverless AI/ML**: These libraries make it easy to bring machine learning and scientific computing capabilities to serverless architectures, allowing Lambda functions to perform real-time analysis and predictions.
- **Efficient Computation**: SciPy and Scikit-learn are highly optimized for numerical computation, making them well-suited for serverless tasks that require fast, efficient processing of large datasets.

Python's extensive library and SDK ecosystem make it one of the most versatile and powerful languages for AWS Lambda development. From **Boto3** for seamless AWS integration to **Pandas** and **NumPy** for efficient data processing, these libraries enable developers to build scalable, feature-rich serverless applications. Whether you are working on data-driven workflows, API integrations, or machine learning applications, Python's SDKs and libraries provide the tools necessary to maximize the potential of AWS Lambda.

AWS Lambda Function Basics

Creating **Your First Lambda Function**
AWS Lambda allows developers to build applications that automatically scale based on incoming events, eliminating the need to manage underlying infrastructure. In this chapter, we'll guide you through the process of creating your first Lambda function. We will cover how to configure it, how to trigger it manually or through an event, and explain key elements you'll need to understand for successful Lambda development.

Whether you are creating an API, processing files from an S3 bucket, or implementing a backend service, AWS Lambda makes it easy to deploy and manage your application logic. We'll focus on using **Python** for this guide, but the steps apply to other supported languages as well.

1. Prerequisites

Before creating a Lambda function, ensure you have the following:

- **AWS Account**: If you don't have one, you can sign up at https://aws.am azon.com.
- **IAM Role with Lambda Permissions**: Your function will need permissions to execute. You can create a new role or use an existing one with basic Lambda execution permissions.
- **Familiarity with Python**: Although this guide uses Python for the function code, no advanced knowledge is required.

2. Setting Up Your Lambda Function: Step-by-Step

Step 1: Log in to the AWS Management Console

1. Visit https://aws.amazon.com and log in with your credentials.
2. From the dashboard, use the **search bar** at the top and type "Lambda." Select **AWS Lambda** from the search results.

Step 2: Create a New Lambda Function

1. In the Lambda Console, click **Create function**.
2. You will be prompted to choose how to create the function. Choose **Author from scratch** to build a new function manually.

Configuration Options:

- **Function Name**: Enter a name for your function (e.g., HelloWorldFunction).
- **Runtime**: Select **Python 3.9** (or any other supported version).
- **Permissions**: Under **Execution role**, choose **Create a new role with basic Lambda permissions**. This role allows your function to write logs to Amazon CloudWatch.

Click **Create function**. AWS will create your Lambda function and redirect you to the function's configuration page.

Step 3: Writing Your Lambda Function Code

On the function's configuration page, scroll down to the **Code** section. Here, AWS provides an inline code editor where you can write or edit your function code.

Let's write a simple "Hello World" function in Python:

```
def lambda_handler(event, context):
    return {
        'statusCode': 200,
        'body': 'Hello, World from AWS Lambda!'
    }
```

- **lambda_handler**: This is the entry point for your Lambda function. AWS Lambda invokes this function when it runs your code.
- **event**: This parameter contains the event data that triggered the function. It could be an API Gateway request, an S3 event, or a custom event.
- **context**: This parameter provides metadata about the function's execution environment, such as function name, memory limits, and execution time.

Step 4: Deploy and Test the Lambda Function

After writing your code, click **Deploy** in the upper-right corner of the editor. This action saves your changes and deploys the function.

Now, you can test the function directly from the console:

1. At the top of the page, click **Test**.
2. In the **Configure test event** dialog box, select **Create new test event**.
3. For simplicity, use the default **Hello World** event template, and name the event TestEvent.
4. Click **Create** and then click **Test** to execute the function.

After a few seconds, you'll see the output of the function execution. The result should look like this:

```
{
  "statusCode": 200,
  "body": "Hello, World from AWS Lambda!"
}
```

Congratulations! You have successfully created, deployed, and tested your first Lambda function.

3. Key Concepts in Lambda Function Creation

Now that you've created a basic Lambda function, it's important to understand some core concepts that will help you as you build more complex applications.

Lambda Handler

The **Lambda handler** is the entry point of the Lambda function. It is the function AWS Lambda invokes when your Lambda function is triggered.

In our example, the function lambda_handler is the handler:

```
def lambda_handler(event, context):
```

- **event**: This parameter contains the data passed by the trigger event. For example, if the function is triggered by an API Gateway, this will contain the HTTP request data.
- **context**: This parameter includes runtime information, such as function name, request ID, remaining execution time, and memory allocation.

Return Value

The return value from the Lambda handler function is used to construct the HTTP response if the function is invoked via services like API Gateway. In the example, the response contains a statusCode and a body:

```
return {
    'statusCode': 200,
    'body': 'Hello, World from AWS Lambda!'
}
```

- **statusCode**: This represents the HTTP status code, such as 200 (OK) or

400 (Bad Request).

- **body**: This is the content of the response, which can be a simple string, a JSON object, or more complex data.

4. Configuring Lambda Function Settings

Once your function is created, AWS Lambda provides various configuration options that you can modify to control its behavior and optimize performance.

Memory and Timeout Settings

- **Memory Allocation**: Lambda allocates CPU power proportional to the memory setting of the function. You can set memory anywhere from 128 MB to 10 GB.
- **Timeout**: Lambda functions have a maximum timeout limit of 15 minutes. The default is set to 3 seconds, but you can adjust this based on your function's needs.

To adjust these settings:

1. Scroll to the **General Configuration** section of the function page.
2. Click **Edit** next to the Memory or Timeout settings.

Environment Variables

You can pass configuration data to your Lambda function using **Environment Variables**, which helps avoid hardcoding values such as API keys or database connection strings.

To set environment variables:

1. Go to the **Configuration** tab.
2. Under **Environment variables**, click **Edit** and add key-value pairs.

For example:

```
DB_HOST = "database.example.com"
API_KEY = "1234567890abcdef"
```

You can access these variables in your code like this:

```
import os

db_host = os.getenv('DB_HOST')
api_key = os.getenv('API_KEY')
```

IAM Role and Permissions

Lambda functions execute with an **IAM role** that defines what AWS resources the function can access. For example, if your function needs to interact with S3, DynamoDB, or RDS, the role must have the appropriate permissions.

1. In the **Configuration** tab, under **Permissions**, you can view or edit the function's execution role.
2. Add policies to the role as needed, such as granting access to an S3 bucket or a DynamoDB table.

VPC Configuration

If your Lambda function needs to access resources inside a **Virtual Private Cloud (VPC)** (e.g., RDS databases), you'll need to configure VPC settings.

1. Go to the **Configuration** tab, and click **VPC**.
2. Choose the VPC, subnets, and security groups that the function will use to interact with resources.

Be aware that placing your Lambda function inside a VPC may increase cold start times, as Lambda has to create network interfaces.

5. Testing and Monitoring Your Lambda Function

AWS Lambda integrates with several tools for testing and monitoring your functions in real-time.

CloudWatch Logs

Whenever a Lambda function runs, it generates logs. These logs are stored in **Amazon CloudWatch**, which you can access from the Lambda Console:

1. Under **Monitoring**, click on **View logs in CloudWatch**.
2. This takes you to the CloudWatch Logs page, where you can view logs for each invocation of your Lambda function.

CloudWatch logs are particularly useful for debugging and performance optimization. You can use logging statements in your Lambda function like this:

```
import logging

logger = logging.getLogger()
logger.setLevel(logging.INFO)

def lambda_handler(event, context):
    logger.info('Lambda function invoked')
    return {
        'statusCode': 200,
        'body': 'Hello, World!'
    }
```

CloudWatch Metrics

AWS Lambda automatically tracks several key metrics, including:

- **Invocations**: The number of times your function has been triggered.
- **Duration**: The execution time of your function.
- **Errors**: The number of invocations that resulted in an error.
- **Throttles**: The number of times your function was throttled due to

hitting concurrency limits.

You can view these metrics in the **Monitoring** tab of your Lambda function.
Setting Up Alarms
To monitor your function's performance and get alerts when something goes wrong, you can set up CloudWatch **Alarms**.

1. Go to **Amazon CloudWatch** and create a new alarm.
2. Set up an alarm to monitor a specific metric, such as invocation errors or function duration.
3. Configure notifications (via email or SMS) for when the threshold is exceeded.

6. Adding Event Triggers to Your Lambda Function

Lambda functions can be triggered automatically by events from other AWS services. Some common event sources include:

- **Amazon S3**: Trigger a function when an object is created, updated, or deleted in a bucket.
- **Amazon DynamoDB**: Trigger a function when items in a DynamoDB table are modified.
- **Amazon API Gateway**: Use API Gateway to invoke your Lambda function in response to HTTP requests.
- **Amazon SQS**: Process messages in an SQS queue by triggering Lambda functions.

To add a trigger:

1. In the **Designer** section of the Lambda console, click **Add trigger**.
2. Choose the service that will trigger your function (e.g., S3, DynamoDB, or API Gateway).
3. Configure the settings for the trigger, such as selecting the S3 bucket or

API Gateway resource.

4. Click **Add** to save the trigger.

Creating your first Lambda function is the starting point of serverless development on AWS. By understanding the fundamental concepts like handlers, event data, permissions, and memory settings, you can build robust and scalable applications. AWS Lambda's seamless integration with other AWS services enables developers to implement event-driven architectures without the need to manage infrastructure. As you continue to explore Lambda, you will learn how to build more complex applications, use triggers, and leverage AWS's monitoring tools for performance optimization and troubleshooting.

Exploring the AWS Lambda Console

The AWS Lambda Console is the central interface for managing Lambda functions, providing developers with all the tools needed to configure, test, and monitor their serverless applications. In this section, we'll explore the Lambda Console in detail, covering the main components, how to interact with functions, and the tools available for managing triggers, configurations, and logs. Understanding the Lambda Console is essential for developing, deploying, and maintaining efficient serverless functions on AWS.

1. Lambda Console Overview

Once logged into the **AWS Management Console**, the Lambda Console can be accessed by searching for **Lambda** in the top search bar and selecting it from the list of services. The Lambda Console opens to a dashboard that provides an overview of your Lambda functions.

Main Dashboard Features:

- **Function List**: Displays all the Lambda functions created within your current AWS region. Each entry shows the function name, last modified date, and configuration details.
- **Create Function**: The **Create function** button is located at the top-right corner, allowing you to start building new Lambda functions from scratch or based on predefined templates.
- **Search Bar**: You can search for specific Lambda functions by name using the search bar, which is especially useful when managing many functions.

2. Function Configuration Page

Once you select a Lambda function, you'll be taken to the **Function Configuration** page, where you can manage and adjust all aspects of that function. This page is divided into several key sections that provide access to the function's code, settings, triggers, logs, and performance metrics.

Designer: Visual Overview

The **Designer** section provides a visual representation of the function's architecture. It shows how the Lambda function interacts with other AWS services and event sources. This section is useful for understanding the relationships between your Lambda function and the AWS services it integrates with.

Designer Components:

- **Function Overview**: The Lambda function's basic information, such as its name, runtime, and role, is displayed here.
- **Triggers**: This shows the services or events that trigger the Lambda function, such as Amazon S3, DynamoDB, or API Gateway. You can add or remove triggers directly from this section.
- **Destination**: Displays the destination of the function's output. It could be another AWS service, such as Amazon SQS, SNS, or even another Lambda function.

To add a trigger:

1. Click **Add trigger** under the **Designer** section.
2. Choose the service that will invoke the Lambda function (e.g., S3, DynamoDB, or API Gateway).
3. Configure the settings for the trigger, such as bucket name or API resource, and save.

Code Source: Writing and Managing Code

The **Code Source** section allows you to write, upload, and manage the code for your Lambda function.

Inline Code Editor:

Lambda provides an inline code editor where you can write and modify your function code directly in the console. This editor supports several programming languages (Python, Node.js, Java, Go, and more) and is ideal for quick edits or simple functions.

1. To edit the code, you can type directly into the inline editor.
2. After making changes, click **Deploy** to save and apply the new version of your Lambda function.

Upload ZIP or Image:

For more complex Lambda functions that include external libraries or dependencies, you can upload your code as a ZIP file or a **container image** (via Amazon Elastic Container Registry). This is particularly useful when managing large-scale applications or when working with development environments outside of the Lambda Console.

1. Under the **Code Source** section, click **Upload from** and select **ZIP file** or **container image**.
2. Upload the relevant file and click **Deploy**.

Test and Debug Lambda Functions

AWS Lambda provides built-in tools for testing and debugging your functions, enabling you to simulate event triggers, view logs, and analyze function output.

Testing Your Lambda Function:

Lambda allows you to create test events that simulate different scenarios or inputs that would trigger your function. These test events help ensure your function is behaving as expected before deploying it in production.

1. At the top of the Lambda function configuration page, click **Test**.
2. If this is your first time testing the function, create a **Test Event**:

- Choose a test event template (e.g., **S3 Put** or **API Gateway**).
- Modify the event data as needed to match the real-world inputs your function will process.

1. Click **Create** and then **Test** to execute the function using the test event.

After running the test, you'll see the execution result, including the output, logs, and any errors that occurred during the invocation.

Monitoring and Logging

AWS Lambda automatically integrates with **Amazon CloudWatch** for monitoring, logging, and metrics collection. From the Lambda Console, you can quickly access logs and view key performance metrics.

CloudWatch Logs:

Every time a Lambda function is invoked, logs are generated that contain information about the function's execution, including any log statements added to the code, errors, and performance details.

To view logs:

1. Under the **Monitoring** tab, click **View logs in CloudWatch**.
2. This will redirect you to the **CloudWatch Logs** console, where you can see detailed logs for each invocation.

Logging is crucial for debugging and monitoring. You can add logging to your Lambda function using Python's logging module:

```
import logging

logger = logging.getLogger()
logger.setLevel(logging.INFO)

def lambda_handler(event, context):
    logger.info('Lambda function invoked')
    return {
        'statusCode': 200,
        'body': 'Hello, World!'
    }
```

CloudWatch Metrics:

AWS Lambda tracks several key performance metrics by default, including:

- **Invocations**: The number of times your function is invoked.
- **Duration**: The time taken for each execution of your function.
- **Error Count**: The number of failed invocations.
- **Throttles**: The number of invocations that were throttled due to reaching concurrency limits.

You can view these metrics in the **Monitoring** tab of the Lambda Console. These metrics are invaluable for performance tuning and troubleshooting.

Creating CloudWatch Alarms:

You can set up alarms to monitor your Lambda function's behavior, such as when it exceeds a certain error rate or execution time.

1. Navigate to **Amazon CloudWatch**.
2. Select **Alarms** from the left-hand menu and click **Create Alarm**.
3. Choose a metric (e.g., error count or duration) and set a threshold. Configure notifications to alert you when the threshold is exceeded.

Configuration: Fine-Tuning Function Settings

The **Configuration** tab is where you can adjust critical settings for your

Lambda function. These include memory allocation, timeout settings, environment variables, and execution roles.

Memory and Timeout:

- **Memory Allocation**: Lambda functions are allocated memory, ranging from 128 MB to 10 GB. The amount of CPU power available to the function is proportional to the memory size, so more memory means faster execution for CPU-bound tasks.
- **Timeout**: Lambda functions can run for up to 15 minutes. You can adjust the timeout setting to match the expected execution time of your function.

To adjust memory and timeout:

1. Under the **Configuration** tab, click **General configuration**.
2. Click **Edit** and adjust the **Memory (MB)** and **Timeout** settings as needed.

Environment Variables:

You can set **environment variables** that your Lambda function can access during runtime. This allows you to pass configuration data, such as database connection strings or API keys, without hardcoding them into the code.

To add environment variables:

1. In the **Configuration** tab, click **Environment variables**.
2. Click **Edit** to add or update key-value pairs.

Example:

```
DB_HOST = "database.example.com"
API_KEY = "1234567890abcdef"
```

In your code, access the environment variables using:

```
import os

db_host = os.getenv('DB_HOST')
api_key = os.getenv('API_KEY')
```

VPC Configuration:

If your Lambda function needs to access resources inside a **Virtual Private Cloud (VPC)**, such as an Amazon RDS database, you'll need to configure VPC access.

1. Go to the **VPC** section of the **Configuration** tab.
2. Click **Edit** to select the appropriate VPC, subnets, and security groups that the function will use.

Keep in mind that running Lambda inside a VPC can introduce additional latency (cold start times), as Lambda needs to establish network interfaces within the VPC.

Execution Role (IAM Permissions):

The Lambda function's **execution role** determines what AWS resources the function is allowed to access. If your function needs to interact with other services like S3, DynamoDB, or RDS, you need to ensure that the role has the appropriate permissions.

1. In the **Permissions** section of the **Configuration** tab, you can view the IAM role attached to your Lambda function.
2. You can attach additional policies to the role by navigating to the **IAM Console** and editing the role's permissions.

For example, if your Lambda function needs to access an S3 bucket, the role should have the AmazonS3ReadOnlyAccess or AmazonS3FullAccess policy attached.

3. Versioning and Aliases

Lambda provides the ability to create **versions** and **aliases** for your functions, which is crucial for managing deployments in production environments.

Versions:

Each time you make changes to your function, you can publish a new version. This version becomes immutable and can be referenced by different environments (e.g., dev, staging, prod).

To create a version:

1. In the **Code Source** section, click **Actions** and select **Publish new version**.
2. Name the version (e.g., v1.0) and click **Publish**.

Aliases:

Aliases allow you to map different versions to a name, such as prod or dev. This allows you to switch between function versions without changing the code or trigger configurations.

To create an alias:

1. Under the **Aliases** section, click **Create alias**.
2. Enter the alias name (e.g., prod) and select the version it should point to.

Aliases are particularly useful for blue-green deployments or rolling out new features to a subset of users.

The AWS Lambda Console is a powerful and flexible tool for managing all aspects of your serverless applications. From writing and deploying code to testing and monitoring performance, the console provides all the necessary tools to build, maintain, and optimize Lambda functions. Understanding how to use each section of the console—from triggers and permissions to

CloudWatch logs and metrics—will help you get the most out of AWS Lambda and enable you to build robust, scalable applications with ease.

Managing Permissions and Roles with IAM

Permissions and roles are critical components of AWS Lambda's security model. AWS Lambda relies on **AWS Identity and Access Management (IAM)** to manage permissions that control what a Lambda function can access and which services are allowed to invoke the function. Correctly managing permissions ensures that your Lambda functions can interact with necessary resources without granting excessive privileges, thus adhering to the **principle of least privilege**.

This section will guide you through the key concepts of IAM in relation to AWS Lambda, how to create and attach roles to your Lambda function, and best practices for managing permissions securely.

1. Understanding IAM Roles and Policies for Lambda

IAM roles and policies determine what actions a Lambda function can perform and what AWS services can invoke it. Lambda functions require an **execution role** to access other AWS resources (such as reading from an S3 bucket or writing logs to CloudWatch).

Key Concepts:

- **IAM Role**: An IAM role is an entity that defines a set of permissions for making AWS service requests. Lambda functions assume this role when they execute.
- **IAM Policy**: A policy is a document that specifies the permissions associated with an IAM role. Policies can grant or deny specific AWS actions on services, such as s3:GetObject or dynamodb:PutItem.
- **Execution Role**: The role that the Lambda function assumes to access other AWS services.
- **Resource-based Policy**: Some AWS services (such as S3 and API

Gateway) support resource-based policies that grant permissions directly to AWS Lambda to interact with those resources.

2. Creating an IAM Role for AWS Lambda

When creating a Lambda function, you need to assign an IAM role that defines the permissions the function will have. This role allows the Lambda function to interact with other AWS services (such as S3, DynamoDB, CloudWatch, etc.).

Step-by-Step Guide: Creating an IAM Role for Lambda
  Log in to the AWS Management Console.
  Navigate to **IAM** by searching for it in the services search bar.
  Create a New Role:

- In the IAM dashboard, select **Roles** from the left-hand menu and click **Create role**.
- Choose **AWS Service** as the trusted entity, and then select **Lambda** from the list of services. This tells AWS that this role will be assumed by a Lambda function.

Attach Permissions Policies:

- After selecting the Lambda service, the next step is attaching permissions policies.
- For example, if your Lambda function needs to log information to CloudWatch Logs, attach the policy **AWSLambdaBasicExecutionRole**. This policy allows the function to write logs to CloudWatch.
- To give the Lambda function access to other services like S3 or DynamoDB, you can attach additional managed policies (e.g., **AmazonS3ReadOnlyAccess**, **AmazonDynamoDBFullAccess**).

Name and Create the Role:

- Give the role a meaningful name (e.g., LambdaExecutionRole) and click **Create role**.

Assign the Role to a Lambda Function:
Once the IAM role is created, you need to assign it to your Lambda function.

1. Go to the **AWS Lambda Console** and select the function you want to configure.
2. Under the **Configuration** tab, navigate to the **Permissions** section.
3. Click on the role name, which will take you to the IAM role configuration. You can attach the newly created role or change the existing role here.

By following these steps, you ensure that your Lambda function has the necessary permissions to interact with other AWS services securely.

3. Fine-Tuning Permissions with Custom Policies

For more granular control, you can create custom IAM policies that define specific permissions for your Lambda function. This allows you to restrict access to specific actions or resources.
Creating a Custom IAM Policy:
Navigate to IAM:

- Go to the **IAM Console** and click on **Policies** from the left-hand menu. Click **Create policy**.

Choose the Service:

- Select the service the policy will apply to (e.g., **S3**, **DynamoDB**, or **CloudWatch**).
- For example, if you want the Lambda function to read from a specific S3 bucket, choose the **S3** service.

Set Actions:

- Choose the actions the policy will allow. For example, you can grant the action s3:GetObject to allow the function to read objects from an S3 bucket.

Set Resources:

- Specify the resource the policy applies to. For example, provide the ARN (Amazon Resource Name) of the S3 bucket the function should access:

```
"Resource": "arn:aws:s3:::my-bucket/*"
```

1. **Review and Create**:

- Name the policy (e.g., LambdaS3ReadPolicy) and review the details before creating the policy.

1. **Attach the Custom Policy to the IAM Role**:

- After creating the policy, navigate to the **Roles** section, find the IAM role assigned to your Lambda function, and attach the custom policy to it.

By creating custom policies, you can control exactly which actions your Lambda function can perform and which resources it can access, reducing the risk of over-privileging your Lambda functions.

4. Using Resource-Based Policies

Some AWS services, such as S3, API Gateway, and SNS, support **resource-based policies** that grant permissions directly to AWS Lambda functions. Resource-based policies complement IAM roles by allowing you to control which AWS services can invoke the Lambda function.

Example: S3 Bucket Resource Policy

If you want an S3 bucket to trigger your Lambda function when a new object is uploaded, you can create a resource-based policy on the S3 bucket that allows it to invoke your Lambda function.

Navigate to the S3 Console:

- Go to the **S3 Console** and select the bucket that will trigger the Lambda function.

Add a Bucket Policy:

- Under the **Permissions** tab, find the **Bucket Policy** section and add the following JSON policy, replacing the LambdaFunctionARN with the actual ARN of your Lambda function:

```
{
  "Version": "2012-10-17",
  "Statement": [
    {
      "Effect": "Allow",
      "Principal": {
        "Service": "lambda.amazonaws.com"
      },
      "Action": "lambda:InvokeFunction",
      "Resource":
      "arn:aws:lambda:us-east-1:123456789012:function:MyLambdaFunction"
    }
  ]
```

```
}
```

This policy allows the S3 bucket to invoke the Lambda function whenever a new object is uploaded.

5. Best Practices for Managing IAM Roles and Permissions

To ensure your Lambda functions remain secure and scalable, follow these best practices when managing IAM roles and permissions:

Principle of Least Privilege:

- Only grant the permissions that are absolutely necessary for the function to perform its tasks. Avoid using broad policies like AdministratorAccess unless it's essential.

Use Managed Policies:

- AWS provides **managed policies** for common use cases, such as **AWSLambdaBasicExecutionRole** or **AWSLambdaVPCAccessE xecutionRole**. These policies are maintained by AWS and are a good starting point for securing your Lambda functions.

Review Permissions Regularly:

- Periodically review the permissions attached to your Lambda function's role to ensure that no excessive permissions are granted. AWS provides **IAM Access Analyzer** to help you detect overly permissive policies.

Separate Development and Production Roles:

- Create different IAM roles for development and production environments. This way, development Lambda functions are restricted from accessing sensitive production resources.

Monitor Permissions with CloudTrail:

- Use **AWS CloudTrail** to monitor and log all actions performed by your Lambda functions. This allows you to audit access and detect any unauthorized attempts to access AWS resources.

Rotate Credentials and Keys:

- If your Lambda function uses environment variables to store sensitive information (such as database credentials), make sure to rotate these credentials regularly. Consider using **AWS Secrets Manager** or **AWS Systems Manager Parameter Store** to securely manage these secrets.

6. IAM Policies for Cross-Account Lambda Access

In scenarios where you need to invoke Lambda functions across AWS accounts (e.g., triggering a Lambda function in Account A from resources in Account B), you can configure cross-account permissions using IAM policies and resource-based policies.

Steps for Cross-Account Lambda Access:
In Account A (Where Lambda Resides):

- Attach a **resource-based policy** to the Lambda function that allows the trusted AWS account (Account B) to invoke the function.

Example policy attached to the Lambda function in Account A:

```
{
  "Version": "2012-10-17",
  "Statement": [
    {
      "Effect": "Allow",
      "Principal": {
```

```
      "AWS": "arn:aws:iam::123456789012:root"
    },
    "Action": "lambda:InvokeFunction",
    "Resource":
    "arn:aws:lambda:us-east-1:987654321098:function:MyLambdaFunction"
  }
 ]
}
```

In Account B:

• Create an IAM policy that allows resources in Account B (e.g., an S3 bucket) to invoke the Lambda function in Account A.

By setting up cross-account access securely, you can extend your Lambda functions to work across different AWS accounts in multi-account environments.

Managing permissions and roles with IAM is essential for the secure and efficient operation of Lambda functions in AWS. By creating the appropriate IAM roles, attaching custom policies, and following security best practices, you can control access to AWS resources while ensuring that your Lambda functions remain secure. IAM's flexibility allows you to fine-tune permissions, ensuring that your functions have just the right level of access to do their job and nothing more.

Deploying Your First Python Lambda Function

After writing and testing your Python code in the AWS Lambda Console, the next step is to deploy it so it can handle real-world events or API requests. AWS Lambda offers several methods for deploying your function, including via the Lambda Console, AWS CLI, or Infrastructure as Code (IaC) tools like

AWS CloudFormation and AWS SAM (Serverless Application Model). In this section, we will cover the different ways you can deploy your Lambda function, focusing on Python code deployment.

1. Deploying via the AWS Lambda Console

The simplest way to deploy your first Python Lambda function is by using the AWS Lambda Console. This method is ideal for small-scale functions, quick changes, or testing.

Step-by-Step Guide: Deploying via the Lambda Console
Navigate to the AWS Lambda Console:

- Open the AWS Lambda Console and select the function you want to deploy or create a new one (if you haven't already done so).

Write or Upload Your Python Code:

- In the **Code** section of the Lambda function page, you can directly write or modify your Python code in the inline code editor.
- Alternatively, you can upload a ZIP file containing your code and dependencies if your function uses external libraries.

Deploy the Code:

- Once you've written or uploaded your Python code, click the **Deploy** button located at the top-right corner of the Lambda function editor.
- The deployment process takes just a few seconds, and AWS Lambda immediately makes the function available for invocation.

Testing the Deployment:

- After deploying, you can test the function directly from the console using the **Test** button.

- Set up a **Test Event** (e.g., a sample API Gateway request or a DynamoDB stream event) and execute the function to verify that it runs as expected.

Deploying Lambda Functions with Dependencies

If your Lambda function relies on external libraries, such as requests or boto3, you can package these dependencies along with your function in a ZIP file.

Here's how to do it:

Create a project directory on your local machine and write your Lambda function code inside it:

```
mkdir my-lambda-function
cd my-lambda-function
```

Install any required dependencies in the same directory using pip:

```
pip install requests -t .
```

Zip the entire contents of the directory:

```
zip -r function.zip .
```

Go back to the AWS Lambda Console and choose **Upload from > .zip file**, then upload the function.zip file you created. Once uploaded, click **Deploy**.

2. Deploying via AWS CLI

The AWS Command Line Interface (CLI) provides a powerful and flexible way to deploy Lambda functions. This method is useful when automating deployments, integrating with CI/CD pipelines, or managing Lambda functions programmatically.

Step-by-Step Guide: Deploying via AWS CLI

Install AWS CLI: Ensure the AWS CLI is installed on your machine. If you haven't installed it, follow the installation instructions here.

Set Up Your AWS CLI Credentials: Configure your AWS credentials by running:

```
aws configure
```

You'll be prompted to enter your AWS Access Key ID, Secret Access Key, region, and output format.

Package Your Lambda Function: If your Lambda function has dependencies, follow the steps to create a ZIP file, as described earlier. Ensure the function code and dependencies are in the same directory and then zip them into a package.

Deploy Your Lambda Function: Use the aws lambda command to create or update your Lambda function. Here's how to create a new Lambda function using the CLI:

```
aws lambda create-function \
    --function-name MyPythonFunction \
    --runtime python3.9 \
    --role
    arn:aws:iam::123456789012:role/service-role/MyLambdaRole \
    --handler lambda_function.lambda_handler \
    --zip-file fileb://function.zip \
    --timeout 60 \
    --memory-size 128
```

Parameters:

- —function-name: The name of your Lambda function.
- —runtime: The runtime environment, in this case, python3.9.
- —role: The ARN of the IAM role that Lambda will assume to execute the function.
- —handler: Specifies the handler function. In this example, lambda_function.lambda_handler means the handler function is lambda_handler

inside lambda_function.py.

- —zip-file: The path to the ZIP file that contains your Lambda function and its dependencies.
- —timeout: The maximum execution time in seconds for the function.
- —memory-size: The amount of memory allocated to the function.

Update the Function: If the function already exists and you want to update it, use the update-function-code command:

```
aws lambda update-function-code \
    --function-name MyPythonFunction \
    --zip-file fileb://function.zip
```

1. **Test Your Function**: After deploying your function, you can test it using the AWS CLI. Create a test event and invoke the function:

```
aws lambda invoke \
    --function-name MyPythonFunction \
    --payload '{"key": "value"}' \
    output.json
```

The function's response will be saved to output.json.

3. Deploying via AWS SAM (Serverless Application Model)

The **AWS Serverless Application Model (SAM)** is an open-source framework that simplifies the creation, testing, and deployment of serverless applications on AWS. SAM extends AWS CloudFormation to provide a simplified way of defining serverless resources, such as Lambda functions, API Gateway, and DynamoDB tables.

Step-by-Step Guide: Deploying via AWS SAM

1. **Install AWS SAM CLI**: Install the AWS SAM CLI on your machine. You can follow the installation instructions here.
2. **Define Your Lambda Function in a SAM Template**: Create a **template.yaml** file that defines your Lambda function and any other serverless resources. For example:

```yaml
AWSTemplateFormatVersion: '2010-09-09'
Transform: AWS::Serverless-2016-10-31
Resources:
  MyPythonFunction:
    Type: AWS::Serverless::Function
    Properties:
      Handler: lambda_function.lambda_handler
      Runtime: python3.9
      CodeUri: ./src
      MemorySize: 128
      Timeout: 60
      Policies:
        - AWSLambdaBasicExecutionRole
```

Package and Deploy Your Function: Run the following commands to package and deploy your Lambda function with SAM:

```
sam package \
    --template-file template.yaml \
    --output-template-file packaged.yaml \
    --s3-bucket my-sam-deployments
```

The sam package command uploads your function code to an S3 bucket and generates a deployment package.

Next, deploy the application:

```
sam deploy \
    --template-file packaged.yaml \
    --stack-name my-lambda-stack \
    --capabilities CAPABILITY_IAM
```

1. **Monitor and Manage**: After deployment, you can monitor and manage your Lambda functions from the AWS Management Console or using the SAM CLI.

4. Deploying with AWS CloudFormation

AWS CloudFormation is an Infrastructure as Code (IaC) service that allows you to define and provision AWS infrastructure through code. You can use CloudFormation to automate the deployment of Lambda functions, ensuring consistency and repeatability across environments.

Step-by-Step Guide: Deploying via CloudFormation
Create a CloudFormation Template: Define your Lambda function in a **CloudFormation template**. This template can include other AWS resources as well, such as S3 buckets, API Gateway, and IAM roles.
Example CloudFormation template:

```
Resources:
  MyLambdaFunction:
    Type: AWS::Lambda::Function
    Properties:
      Handler: lambda_function.lambda_handler
      Runtime: python3.9
      Role: arn:aws:iam::123456789012:role/MyLambdaRole
      Code:
        S3Bucket: my-code-bucket
        S3Key: function.zip
      MemorySize: 128
      Timeout: 60
```

1. **Upload Your Lambda Function Code to S3**: Before running the CloudFormation stack, upload your Lambda function code (ZIP file) to the specified S3 bucket.
2. **Deploy the CloudFormation Stack**: Use the AWS CLI to deploy the

CloudFormation stack:

```
aws cloudformation create-stack \
    --stack-name my-lambda-stack \
    --template-body file://template.yaml \
    --capabilities CAPABILITY_IAM
```

1. **Update the Stack**: To update the function after making changes to the code or configuration, update the CloudFormation stack:

```
aws cloudformation update-stack \
    --stack-name my-lambda-stack \
    --template-body file://template.yaml \
    --capabilities CAPABILITY_IAM
```

Using CloudFormation, you can define, deploy, and manage Lambda functions along with their associated resources as part of a single infrastructure deployment.

5. Best Practices for Lambda Deployment

1. Use Versioning:

Whenever you deploy a new version of your Lambda function, publish it as a new version. This enables you to roll back to previous versions if necessary and provides a clear deployment history.

2. Use Aliases:

Lambda **aliases** allow you to point an alias (e.g., prod or dev) to a specific version of your function. This makes it easier to manage deployments and safely roll out updates to different environments.

3. Package Dependencies Efficiently:

For Python Lambda functions with external libraries, package only the necessary dependencies to keep your deployment package lightweight and reduce cold start times.

4. Automate with CI/CD Pipelines:

For production-level applications, integrate Lambda deployments into a **CI/CD pipeline** using services like **AWS CodePipeline, Jenkins**, or **GitHub Actions**. This automates testing, building, and deploying Lambda functions.

5. Monitor Deployment Metrics:

After deployment, monitor your Lambda function's performance using **Amazon CloudWatch**. Keep an eye on key metrics like invocation count, error rates, and execution duration to ensure that your function performs as expected.

Deploying your first Python Lambda function is a straightforward process, whether you choose to use the AWS Management Console, AWS CLI, or an Infrastructure as Code tool like SAM or CloudFormation. By following best practices—such as using versioning, packaging dependencies efficiently, and automating deployments—you can ensure that your Lambda functions are scalable, maintainable, and easy to manage. Understanding the different deployment methods allows you to choose the one that best fits your development workflow and project requirements.

Building and Deploying Lambda Functions Using Python

AWS Lambda Handlers and Events
  At the heart of AWS Lambda's serverless architecture lies the **Lambda handler**—the function's entry point that AWS invokes when your function is triggered by an event. Understanding Lambda handlers and the types of events that can trigger them is crucial for designing and developing efficient serverless applications. In this section, we will dive deep into the concept of Lambda handlers, explore how they process events, and examine the different types of events that Lambda functions handle.

1. Understanding the Lambda Handler

The **Lambda handler** is the function in your code that AWS Lambda calls when your function is executed. Every Lambda function needs a handler, which receives input from the event that triggers it and returns a response.

Lambda Handler Syntax

The handler function follows a specific signature depending on the programming language. Since we are focusing on Python, the Python Lambda handler signature is:

```
def lambda_handler(event, context):
    # Your code logic here
```

```
return response
```

- **event**: This parameter contains the event data that triggered the function. The format of this data depends on the event source, such as an API Gateway request, an S3 bucket event, or a DynamoDB stream record.
- **context**: This parameter provides runtime information about the function, including invocation details, resource limits, and AWS request ID.

Example Lambda Handler

Here's a simple example of a Python Lambda handler that processes an HTTP request event from Amazon API Gateway and returns a response:

```
def lambda_handler(event, context):
    return {
        'statusCode': 200,
        'body': 'Hello, World from AWS Lambda!'
    }
```

In this example:

- The function receives an event that contains the HTTP request data (which can include parameters, headers, and body).
- The function returns a JSON response with an HTTP status code of 200 and a message body.

2. The event Parameter

The event parameter contains the input data that the Lambda function receives when triggered. This data varies based on the event source (e.g., API Gateway, S3, SNS, DynamoDB). Understanding the structure of the event parameter is crucial for building Lambda functions that respond to a wide variety of triggers.

Common Event Sources and Event Formats

1. Amazon API Gateway Event

When AWS Lambda is triggered by an **API Gateway** request, the event parameter contains details about the incoming HTTP request, including the method (GET, POST, etc.), headers, query parameters, and body. The Lambda function can then process the request and return an HTTP response.

Example Event (API Gateway):

```json
{
    "resource": "/hello",
    "path": "/hello",
    "httpMethod": "GET",
    "headers": {
        "Accept": "application/json"
    },
    "queryStringParameters": {
        "name": "John"
    },
    "body": null,
    "isBase64Encoded": false
}
```

Example Lambda Handler:

```python
def lambda_handler(event, context):
    name = event['queryStringParameters']['name']
    return {
        'statusCode': 200,
        'body': f'Hello, {name}!'
    }
```

2. Amazon S3 Event

When an object is created, modified, or deleted in an S3 bucket, it can trigger a Lambda function. The event parameter will include details about the S3 event, such as the bucket name, object key, and event type.

Example Event (S3):

```
{
    "Records": [
        {
            "eventVersion": "2.1",
            "eventSource": "aws:s3",
            "awsRegion": "us-west-2",
            "eventTime": "2022-01-01T12:00:00.000Z",
            "eventName": "ObjectCreated:Put",
            "s3": {
                "bucket": {
                    "name": "my-s3-bucket"
                },
                "object": {
                    "key": "example.txt"
                }
            }
        }
    ]
}
```

Example Lambda Handler:

```
def lambda_handler(event, context):
    bucket_name = event['Records'][0]['s3']['bucket']['name']
    object_key = event['Records'][0]['s3']['object']['key']
    print(f'New object created in {bucket_name}: {object_key}')
    return {
        'statusCode': 200,
        'body': 'S3 event processed successfully.'
    }
```

In this case, the function processes the S3 event by extracting the bucket name and object key from the event and performing the necessary actions (e.g., processing the file).

3. DynamoDB Stream Event

When an item in a DynamoDB table is added, modified, or deleted, a **DynamoDB stream** can trigger a Lambda function. The event parameter will contain details about the DynamoDB record that changed.

Example Event (DynamoDB Stream):

```
{
    "Records": [
        {
            "eventID": "1",
            "eventName": "INSERT",
            "dynamodb": {
                "Keys": {
                    "id": {"S": "123"}
                },
                "NewImage": {
                    "id": {"S": "123"},
                    "name": {"S": "John Doe"}
                }
            }
        }
    ]
}
```

Example Lambda Handler:

```
def lambda_handler(event, context):
    for record in event['Records']:
        if record['eventName'] == 'INSERT':
            new_data = record['dynamodb']['NewImage']
            print(f'New item added: {new_data["name"]["S"]}')
    return {
        'statusCode': 200,
        'body': 'DynamoDB stream event processed.'
    }
```

This function handles DynamoDB stream events, checks if the event was an INSERT operation, and processes the new data added to the DynamoDB table.

4. Amazon SNS Event

AWS Lambda can be triggered by an **Amazon SNS** (Simple Notification Service) topic when a message is published. The event parameter will contain the SNS message details, including the subject and message body.

Example Event (SNS):

```
{
    "Records": [
        {
            "EventSource": "aws:sns",
            "Sns": {
                "Message": "Hello, this is a test message!",
                "Subject": "Test Subject"
            }
        }
    ]
}
```

Example Lambda Handler:

```
def lambda_handler(event, context):
    sns_message = event['Records'][0]['Sns']['Message']
    sns_subject = event['Records'][0]['Sns']['Subject']
    print(f'Received SNS message: {sns_message} with subject:
    {sns_subject}')
    return {
        'statusCode': 200,
        'body': 'SNS message processed.'
    }
```

In this example, the Lambda function reads the SNS message and subject and prints them.

Custom Events

In addition to predefined events from AWS services, you can trigger Lambda functions with **custom events**. For example, you might invoke a Lambda function from another service (such as a mobile app or a microservice), passing a custom JSON payload as the event.

Example Custom Event:

```
{
    "userId": "abc123",
    "action": "purchase",
    "amount": 150
}
```

Example Lambda Handler:

```
def lambda_handler(event, context):
    user_id = event['userId']
    action = event['action']
    amount = event['amount']
    print(f'User {user_id} performed {action} action with amount:
    {amount}')
    return {
        'statusCode': 200,
        'body': f'{action} action processed for user {user_id}.'
    }
```

Custom events are versatile and can be triggered from a variety of applications, such as microservices or third-party integrations.

3. The context Parameter

The context parameter provides runtime information about the Lambda function and its execution environment. While the event parameter contains the data that triggered the function, context provides useful metadata, such as the function name, execution time remaining, and AWS request ID.

Key Attributes of the context Object:

- **function_name**: The name of the Lambda function.
- **memory_limit_in_mb**: The amount of memory allocated to the function.
- **aws_request_id**: A unique identifier for the request. This can be useful

for tracing and debugging specific invocations.

- **log_group_name**: The name of the CloudWatch Logs group where the function's logs are stored.
- **log_stream_name**: The name of the CloudWatch Logs stream where the function's logs are recorded.
- **get_remaining_time_in_millis()**: A method that returns the number of milliseconds remaining before the function times out.

Example Usage of the context Parameter:

```python
def lambda_handler(event, context):
    print(f'Function Name: {context.function_name}')
    print(f'Memory Limit: {context.memory_limit_in_mb} MB')
    print(f'AWS Request ID: {context.aws_request_id}')
    print(f'Time Remaining (ms):
    {context.get_remaining_time_in_millis()}')
    return {
        'statusCode': 200,
        'body': 'Context data logged successfully.'
    }
```

In this example, the Lambda function logs key details about its execution environment, including the function name, memory allocation, and time remaining before timeout. This information can be useful for debugging or performance monitoring.

4. Error Handling in Lambda Functions

When working with Lambda functions, error handling is crucial to ensure that your function can gracefully handle unexpected situations. AWS Lambda provides mechanisms for handling errors, retrying invocations, and capturing logs.

1. Try-Except Block (Error Handling)

You can use Python's try-except blocks to catch and handle exceptions within your Lambda function.

Example:

```
import logging

def lambda_handler(event, context):
    try:
        result = 10 / 0  # This will raise a ZeroDivisionError
    except ZeroDivisionError as e:
        logging.error(f'Error occurred: {str(e)}')
        return {
            'statusCode': 500,
            'body': 'Internal Server Error'
        }
    return {
        'statusCode': 200,
        'body': 'Success'
    }
```

In this example, a ZeroDivisionError is caught by the except block, and an appropriate error message is logged and returned.

2. AWS Lambda Retries and Dead Letter Queues (DLQ)

If a Lambda function fails due to an error, AWS Lambda may automatically retry the function, depending on the event source. For asynchronous invocations (e.g., triggered by S3, SNS, or CloudWatch Events), Lambda automatically retries the function twice if it fails. To handle persistent failures, you can configure a **Dead Letter Queue (DLQ)** where failed events are sent for further investigation.

To enable DLQs:

1. Go to your Lambda function in the AWS Management Console.
2. Under the **Asynchronous invocation** section, configure the **Dead Letter Queue** with an Amazon SQS queue or an SNS topic.

This ensures that failed invocations are not lost and can be reprocessed or investigated later.

5. Best Practices for Lambda Handlers and Events

To ensure the performance, security, and maintainability of your Lambda functions, follow these best practices:

- **Validate Event Input**: Always validate incoming event data to ensure it meets expected formats and types. This prevents invalid data from causing runtime errors.
- **Use Environment Variables**: Instead of hardcoding configuration values (such as API keys or database connections), use environment variables to pass configuration into your Lambda function securely.
- **Log and Monitor**: Use logging (print() or logging module) and Cloud-Watch Logs to monitor your Lambda function's behavior. This helps with debugging and understanding performance issues.
- **Timeouts and Memory**: Ensure that your function has appropriate memory allocation and timeout settings. Use the context.get_remaining _time_in_millis() method to check for timeouts dynamically within the function.
- **Error Handling**: Implement robust error handling using try-except blocks and configure retries or Dead Letter Queues (DLQ) for asynchronous invocations.

AWS Lambda handlers and events are the foundation of serverless application development. The handler serves as the entry point for the function, while events drive the invocation of Lambda from various AWS services or custom sources. Understanding the structure of events and the context provided by AWS Lambda enables developers to create powerful, scalable, and responsive applications that can handle diverse workloads. By following best practices for error handling, logging, and configuration, you can ensure that your Lambda functions are resilient and easy to manage.

Writing and Testing Your Python Code for AWS Lambda

Writing and testing Python code for AWS Lambda functions is a crucial part of developing serverless applications. AWS Lambda functions need to be optimized for performance and correctness while handling diverse events and workloads. In this section, we will cover best practices for writing Python code, how to structure your Lambda functions, and how to efficiently test your functions locally and in the AWS environment.

1. Structuring Python Code for AWS Lambda

To build efficient and maintainable Lambda functions, it's important to adopt a clear structure for your Python code. This includes organizing your code into reusable modules, handling configuration, and managing dependencies effectively.

Basic Structure of a Python Lambda Function

At the core of every Lambda function is the lambda_handler function, which AWS invokes when the function is triggered. Here's a basic example of a Python Lambda function:

```python
import json

def lambda_handler(event, context):
    # Process the incoming event
    body = {
        'message': 'Hello, World from AWS Lambda!',
        'input': event
    }

    return {
        'statusCode': 200,
        'body': json.dumps(body)
    }
```

Best Practices for Structuring Your Code:

- **Separation of Concerns**: Keep the core logic separate from the Lambda handler. This makes the code easier to test and maintain. For example, the lambda_handler should only handle input and output while delegating business logic to separate functions or classes.
- **Configuration**: Use environment variables to configure sensitive data like API keys, database credentials, or external service URLs. You can access environment variables in Python using the os module:

```
import os
db_url = os.getenv('DB_URL')
```

- **Dependencies**: Include external libraries (such as requests or boto3) in your Lambda function by packaging them with your code or deploying them via AWS Lambda Layers (discussed later in this chapter).

2. Handling Dependencies

AWS Lambda lets you import third-party Python libraries via **Lambda Layers** or by packaging the libraries within a ZIP file along with your function code.

Method 1: Packaging Dependencies Locally

If your Lambda function uses external libraries, such as requests for HTTP calls or pandas for data processing, you can package them alongside your function code.

Steps for Packaging Dependencies:
Create a Project Directory:

- Start by creating a directory for your Lambda function and its dependencies.

```
mkdir my-lambda-function
cd my-lambda-function
```

Install Dependencies Locally:

- Use pip to install your dependencies into the project directory. This ensures that all the required libraries are packaged with the function.

```
pip install requests -t .
```

Add Your Python Code:

- Create a Python file for your Lambda function, such as lambda_function.py.

```python
# lambda_function.py
import requests

def lambda_handler(event, context):
    response = requests.get('https://api.example.com/data')
    return {
        'statusCode': 200,
        'body': response.text
    }
```

Package the Code and Dependencies:

- Zip the contents of the directory (your code and dependencies) into a deployment package.

```
zip -r function.zip .
```

1. **Upload to AWS Lambda**:

- In the AWS Lambda Console, upload the ZIP file under the **Code** section and click **Deploy**.

Method 2: Using AWS Lambda Layers
Lambda Layers allow you to package libraries, custom runtimes, and other function dependencies separately from the main Lambda function code. This improves modularity, reduces the size of your function deployment package, and promotes reuse across multiple Lambda functions.

Steps for Creating a Lambda Layer:
  Create a Directory for the Layer:

- The directory structure for a Python Lambda Layer must include the python folder:

```
mkdir -p my-layer/python
```

Install Dependencies in the Layer:

- Use pip to install the required libraries into the python subdirectory.

```
pip install requests -t my-layer/python
```

Package the Layer:

- Zip the contents of the my-layer directory:

```
cd my-layer
zip -r my-layer.zip .
```

Create the Layer in AWS Lambda:

- Go to the **AWS Lambda Console**, select **Layers**, and create a new layer.
- Upload the ZIP file you created and specify the compatible runtime (Python 3.8, 3.9, etc.).

Use the Layer in Your Lambda Function:

- In the Lambda function configuration, go to the **Layers** section and add the newly created layer. The function can now import any libraries included in the layer.

3. Logging and Monitoring in AWS Lambda

Logging is essential for tracking your function's execution and diagnosing issues. AWS Lambda integrates with **Amazon CloudWatch** to automatically log all function invocations and output. You can use the print() function or Python's built-in logging module to write logs to CloudWatch.

Example of Logging in Lambda:

```
import logging

logger = logging.getLogger()
logger.setLevel(logging.INFO)

def lambda_handler(event, context):
    logger.info("Function invoked")

    try:
        result = 10 / 0  # Simulate an error
    except ZeroDivisionError as e:
```

```
        logger.error(f"Error occurred: {str(e)}")
        return {
            'statusCode': 500,
            'body': 'Internal Server Error'
        }

    return {
        'statusCode': 200,
        'body': 'Success'
    }
```

- **Log Levels**: You can control the verbosity of logs using log levels such as INFO, DEBUG, WARNING, and ERROR. These logs are automatically sent to CloudWatch and can be viewed from the **Logs** section of the AWS Lambda Console.

4. Testing Lambda Functions

Testing your Lambda function is critical to ensure it behaves as expected. You can test Lambda functions locally or directly within the AWS environment.

Testing in the AWS Lambda Console

You can manually test Lambda functions in the AWS Lambda Console by creating **test events**.

Steps to Test in the AWS Console:

1. Navigate to the **Lambda Console** and select your function.
2. Click the **Test** button at the top of the function configuration page.
3. In the **Configure test event** dialog, select a test event template or create a custom event in JSON format based on the event source (e.g., API Gateway, S3, or DynamoDB).
4. Save the test event and click **Test** again to execute the function.
5. The console will display the execution result and logs, helping you validate the function's behavior.

Testing Locally Using AWS SAM CLI

The **AWS Serverless Application Model (SAM) CLI** allows you to test Lambda functions locally on your machine, emulating the AWS environment.

Steps for Testing Locally with AWS SAM:

Install AWS SAM CLI:

- Install the SAM CLI by following the installation guide here.

Set Up Your Lambda Function with SAM:

- Create a SAM template (template.yaml) that defines your Lambda function:

```
AWSTemplateFormatVersion: '2010-09-09'
Transform: AWS::Serverless-2016-10-31
Resources:
  MyLambdaFunction:
    Type: AWS::Serverless::Function
    Properties:
      Handler: lambda_function.lambda_handler
      Runtime: python3.9
      CodeUri: .
      MemorySize: 128
      Timeout: 60
```

Run SAM Locally:

- Use the SAM CLI to build and test your Lambda function locally:

```
sam local invoke MyLambdaFunction --event event.json
```

The event.json file contains a sample event that simulates a real AWS event (e.g., an API Gateway request or an S3 event).

111

Debugging:

- You can debug your Lambda function locally using tools like **VSCode** or **PyCharm** by integrating them with the SAM CLI. This allows you to set breakpoints and step through your function code.

5. Handling Errors and Exceptions

Robust error handling is essential for Lambda functions to ensure they fail gracefully and provide meaningful feedback. AWS Lambda automatically retries certain failed invocations, but it's best to handle common errors within your code.

Common Error Handling Patterns:

- **Try-Except Blocks**: Catch and handle errors using try-except blocks. Log the errors for debugging and return appropriate responses.
- **Example**:

```
def lambda_handler(event, context):
    try:
        # Simulate an error
        result = 10 / 0
    except ZeroDivisionError as e:
        return {
            'statusCode': 500,
            'body': f'Error: {str(e)}'
        }

    return {
        'statusCode': 200,
        'body': 'Success'
    }
```

- **Retries and Dead Letter Queues (DLQ)**: For asynchronous events (e.g.,

S3, SNS), AWS Lambda automatically retries failed invocations twice. To handle persistent failures, configure a **Dead Letter Queue (DLQ)** to capture failed events for further analysis or reprocessing.

- To set up a DLQ:
- Go to the **Asynchronous invocation** section of the Lambda function configuration.
- Choose an **SQS** queue or **SNS** topic as the DLQ.
- Any events that fail after the retries will be sent to the DLQ for investigation.

6. Best Practices for Writing and Testing Python Code in Lambda

1. Optimize Cold Start Performance

Minimize the code executed during function initialization to reduce the **cold start** latency. This can be achieved by loading dependencies lazily and minimizing the size of deployment packages.

2. Leverage Environment Variables

Use environment variables to store configuration data like database credentials, API keys, and external URLs. This avoids hardcoding sensitive data in the code.

3. Modularize Code for Reusability

Break down your Lambda function logic into smaller, reusable components or helper functions. This improves testability and maintainability.

4. Use AWS X-Ray for Tracing

For complex functions, enable **AWS X-Ray** to trace requests and identify bottlenecks in your Lambda execution. AWS X-Ray integrates with Lambda and provides detailed insights into how the function interacts with other services.

5. Test Locally and in AWS

While local testing using tools like SAM is valuable, it's essential to test Lambda functions in the actual AWS environment as well. This ensures your function works correctly with real AWS services and configurations.

Writing and testing Python code for AWS Lambda requires a balance of good coding practices, robust error handling, and thoughtful testing. By following these guidelines, you can create efficient, scalable Lambda functions that respond to events reliably. Whether you're working on simple APIs or complex workflows, AWS Lambda's integration with services like CloudWatch, S3, DynamoDB, and SAM CLI provides all the tools needed to build and maintain production-ready serverless applications.

Deploying AWS Lambda Functions via AWS Console, CLI, and SAM

Once you've written and tested your AWS Lambda function, the next step is deploying it to the cloud where it can be triggered by events and handle real-time workloads. AWS offers several methods for deploying Lambda functions, each suited to different workflows and preferences. Whether you're using the **AWS Management Console, AWS Command Line Interface (CLI),** or **AWS Serverless Application Model (SAM),** each deployment method provides flexibility for managing your Lambda functions in production.

1. Deploying via the AWS Management Console

The AWS Management Console is the simplest way to deploy Lambda functions. It is particularly useful for developers who prefer a visual interface and are deploying small-scale functions without the need for automation.

Steps to Deploy via AWS Console
1.1 Create a Lambda Function
Navigate to the AWS Lambda Console:

- Go to the AWS Management Console and log in.
- Use the search bar to find **AWS Lambda** and open the Lambda Console.

Create a New Function:

- Click **Create Function**.
- Select **Author from scratch** and provide a function name (e.g., MyPythonFunction).
- Choose **Python** as the runtime (e.g., Python 3.9).
- Under **Permissions**, either select an existing role with the required permissions or let Lambda create a new role for basic execution.
- Click **Create Function** to initialize the function.

1.2 Upload and Configure the Code
Write or Upload Your Code:

- In the **Code** section, either write your Lambda function code directly in the inline editor or upload a deployment package (ZIP file) if your function has dependencies.
- If uploading a ZIP file, ensure it contains both the code and any necessary dependencies (as mentioned in the previous section on packaging dependencies).

Configure Function Settings:

- **Memory Allocation**: Adjust the amount of memory your function needs (between 128 MB and 10 GB).
- **Timeout**: Set the function timeout based on your expected execution time (maximum of 15 minutes).
- **Environment Variables**: Add key-value pairs for any environment variables your function requires (e.g., API keys, database URLs).

1.3 Deploy the Function

1. Once you've written or uploaded the function code, click the **Deploy** button at the top-right of the code editor to save and deploy the function.
2. After deployment, you can manually test the function by using the **Test** button to simulate an event, or you can set up real event triggers such as

API Gateway or S3.

2. Deploying via AWS CLI

The AWS Command Line Interface (CLI) provides a flexible and powerful way to automate the deployment of Lambda functions. This method is particularly useful for continuous integration (CI) and continuous deployment (CD) pipelines, where repeatable and consistent deployment processes are required.

Steps to Deploy via AWS CLI

2.1 Prepare Your Lambda Function

Create a Deployment Package:

- Package your Lambda function code and dependencies into a ZIP file (as described earlier).
- For example:

```
zip -r function.zip .
```

2.2 Create or Update the Lambda Function Using CLI

Create a New Lambda Function:

- If you are deploying the function for the first time, use the create-function command:

```
aws lambda create-function \
    --function-name MyPythonFunction \
    --runtime python3.9 \
    --role arn:aws:iam::123456789012:role/MyLambdaRole \
    --handler lambda_function.lambda_handler \
    --zip-file fileb://function.zip \
```

```
--timeout 60 \
--memory-size 128
```

In this command:

- **—function-name**: The name of the Lambda function.
- **—runtime**: The runtime environment (e.g., Python 3.9).
- **—role**: The IAM role ARN that grants permissions to the Lambda function.
- **—handler**: The entry point of your function (e.g., lambda_function.lambda_handler).
- **—zip-file**: The path to the ZIP file containing your code and dependencies.
- **—timeout**: The maximum execution time in seconds.
- **—memory-size**: The amount of memory allocated to the function.

1. **Update an Existing Lambda Function**:

- If you've already created the Lambda function and are updating the code, use the update-function-code command:

```
aws lambda update-function-code \
    --function-name MyPythonFunction \
    --zip-file fileb://function.zip
```

This command uploads the updated deployment package to the existing Lambda function.

2.3 Test the Lambda Function via CLI

After deploying the function, you can invoke it from the CLI for testing purposes:

```
aws lambda invoke \
    --function-name MyPythonFunction \
    --payload '{"key1": "value1"}' \
    output.json
```

This command will invoke the Lambda function and store the output in the output.json file. You can review this file to validate the response.

3. Deploying via AWS SAM (Serverless Application Model)

The AWS Serverless Application Model (SAM) is an open-source framework that simplifies the creation, testing, and deployment of serverless applications, including Lambda functions, API Gateway, DynamoDB tables, and more. SAM is a powerful tool for defining infrastructure as code and managing complex serverless applications.

Steps to Deploy via AWS SAM
3.1 Install AWS SAM CLI
To use SAM, you must first install the SAM CLI on your local machine. Follow the installation guide here for your operating system.

3.2 Define a SAM Template
The **SAM template** is a YAML file that defines your serverless resources, including Lambda functions, APIs, and other AWS services. Here's an example template for a Python Lambda function:

```
AWSTemplateFormatVersion: '2010-09-09'
Transform: AWS::Serverless-2016-10-31
Resources:
  MyLambdaFunction:
    Type: AWS::Serverless::Function
    Properties:
      Handler: lambda_function.lambda_handler
      Runtime: python3.9
      CodeUri: ./src
```

```
MemorySize: 128
Timeout: 60
Policies:
  - AWSLambdaBasicExecutionRole
```

In this example:

- **Handler**: Specifies the function entry point.
- **Runtime**: Sets the runtime environment (Python 3.9).
- **CodeUri**: Points to the directory containing the function code.
- **Policies**: Grants basic execution permissions (e.g., logging to Cloud-Watch).

3.3 Package the Application

Use the SAM CLI to package your Lambda function. This command packages the application and uploads it to an S3 bucket.

```
sam package \
    --template-file template.yaml \
    --output-template-file packaged.yaml \
    --s3-bucket my-s3-bucket
```

- **—template-file**: The path to your SAM template.
- **—output-template-file**: The output file where the packaged template is stored.
- **—s3-bucket**: The name of the S3 bucket where your deployment package will be stored.

3.4 Deploy the Application

After packaging, deploy the Lambda function using the SAM CLI:

```
sam deploy \
    --template-file packaged.yaml \
    --stack-name my-lambda-stack \
    --capabilities CAPABILITY_IAM
```

In this command:

- **—stack-name**: The name of the CloudFormation stack where the Lambda function and related resources are deployed.
- **—capabilities**: Specifies the necessary permissions for deploying IAM resources.

3.5 Test Locally Using SAM

One of the advantages of SAM is that you can test Lambda functions locally before deploying them to AWS. The SAM CLI emulates the Lambda execution environment on your local machine.

```
sam local invoke MyLambdaFunction --event event.json
```

In this example:

- **MyLambdaFunction**: The name of your Lambda function as defined in the SAM template.
- **—event**: A JSON file containing the event data that will trigger the Lambda function.

4. Deploying Lambda with AWS CloudFormation

CloudFormation allows you to manage and deploy AWS infrastructure as code. For complex applications involving multiple AWS services, you can use CloudFormation to deploy Lambda functions along with their associated resources (e.g., API Gateway, DynamoDB).

Steps to Deploy via CloudFormation

4.1 Create a CloudFormation Template

A CloudFormation template defines the resources that you want to provision in AWS. Here's an example for deploying a Lambda function:

```
Resources:
  MyLambdaFunction:
    Type: AWS::Lambda::Function
    Properties:
      Handler: lambda_function.lambda_handler
      Runtime: python3.9
      Role: arn:aws:iam::123456789012:role/MyLambdaRole
      Code:
        S3Bucket: my-s3-bucket
        S3Key: function.zip
      MemorySize: 128
      Timeout: 60
```

4.2 Deploy the CloudFormation Stack

To deploy your Lambda function via CloudFormation, use the following AWS CLI command:

```
aws cloudformation create-stack \
    --stack-name my-lambda-stack \
    --template-body file://template.yaml \
    --capabilities CAPABILITY_IAM
```

This command creates a CloudFormation stack and provisions the resources defined in the template.

5. Best Practices for Lambda Deployment

1. Use Versioning

Each time you deploy a new version of your Lambda function, publish it as a new version. This ensures that you can roll back to a previous version if necessary and allows for better tracking of changes.

121

2. Implement Aliases

Use Lambda **aliases** to manage different environments (e.g., dev, staging, prod). You can point an alias to a specific version of your Lambda function, making it easier to manage deployment cycles and roll out updates.

3. Automate Deployment with CI/CD Pipelines

Integrate Lambda deployments into your **CI/CD** pipeline using tools like **AWS CodePipeline, Jenkins**, or **GitHub Actions**. Automating deployments ensures consistency and speeds up the process of pushing new code to production.

4. Monitor Deployment Metrics

After deployment, use **Amazon CloudWatch** to monitor key metrics like invocation counts, error rates, and latency. This helps you ensure that your function is performing as expected.

Deploying AWS Lambda functions is a crucial step in building serverless applications. Whether you prefer the visual AWS Management Console, the automation capabilities of AWS CLI, or the infrastructure-as-code approach with AWS SAM or CloudFormation, AWS provides a range of tools to help you manage Lambda deployments. By following best practices, such as using versioning, aliases, and automating with CI/CD pipelines, you can ensure a smooth and efficient deployment process, regardless of the scale of your application.

Working with AWS SDK (Boto3) in Lambda

The **AWS SDK for Python (Boto3)** is the primary tool that enables Python developers to interact with AWS services programmatically. When building AWS Lambda functions, Boto3 allows you to interact with various AWS services such as S3, DynamoDB, SNS, SQS, and more. Integrating Boto3 into your Lambda functions empowers you to build rich, serverless applications that automate workflows, manage cloud infrastructure, and perform complex operations on AWS services.

In this section, we'll explore how to use Boto3 within Lambda functions, common use cases, and best practices for efficiently integrating AWS services.

1. Introduction to Boto3

Boto3 is the official Python SDK for AWS. It allows developers to interact with AWS APIs to perform actions such as reading and writing to S3 buckets, querying DynamoDB tables, publishing messages to SNS topics, sending emails via SES, and more.

Installing and Importing Boto3

AWS Lambda functions come pre-installed with the Boto3 library, so you don't need to manually include it in your deployment package unless you're using specific AWS services that require custom configurations or versions.

To use Boto3 in your Lambda function, simply import it as follows:

```
import boto3
```

You can then create clients or resources to interact with specific AWS services, such as S3, DynamoDB, SNS, and more.

2. Creating AWS Clients and Resources in Boto3

Boto3 offers two main abstractions for interacting with AWS services: **clients** and **resources**.

- **Clients**: Low-level APIs that map directly to AWS service operations.
- **Resources**: High-level object-oriented abstractions that provide more intuitive ways to work with AWS services (available for some services like S3, DynamoDB).

Creating a Client

A **client** allows you to call AWS service operations. For example, to interact with S3 or DynamoDB:

```
s3_client = boto3.client('s3')
dynamodb_client = boto3.client('dynamodb')
```

Creating a Resource

A **resource** provides object-oriented methods for working with AWS services and is generally easier to use for common operations.

```
s3_resource = boto3.resource('s3')
dynamodb_resource = boto3.resource('dynamodb')
```

3. Common Use Cases for Boto3 in Lambda Functions

AWS Lambda functions often need to interact with multiple AWS services to perform tasks such as file storage, database operations, and messaging. Below are some common use cases for Boto3 in Lambda functions.

Use Case 1: Reading and Writing Files to Amazon S3

S3 is one of the most commonly used services with Lambda, enabling serverless applications to store and retrieve objects (files).

Example: Writing a File to an S3 Bucket

```
import boto3
import json

s3_client = boto3.client('s3')

def lambda_handler(event, context):
    data = {'message': 'Hello, S3!'}
    file_content = json.dumps(data)
```

```
# Write file to S3
s3_client.put_object(
    Bucket='my-bucket-name',
    Key='hello.json',
    Body=file_content
)

return {
    'statusCode': 200,
    'body': 'File successfully uploaded to S3'
}
```

In this example:

- **put_object()**: Uploads the hello.json file to the specified S3 bucket (my-bucket-name).

Example: Reading a File from S3

```
import boto3

s3_client = boto3.client('s3')

def lambda_handler(event, context):
    # Read a file from S3
    response = s3_client.get_object(Bucket='my-bucket-name',
    Key='hello.json')
    file_content = response['Body'].read().decode('utf-8')

    return {
        'statusCode': 200,
        'body': file_content
    }
```

In this example:

- **get_object()**: Retrieves the file from S3, and we then read and decode the file content.

Use Case 2: Managing Data in DynamoDB

DynamoDB is a fully managed NoSQL database, and it's often used with Lambda for serverless applications. Boto3 makes it easy to query, insert, and delete items in DynamoDB.

Example: Inserting an Item into DynamoDB

```python
import boto3

dynamodb = boto3.resource('dynamodb')
table = dynamodb.Table('my-table-name')

def lambda_handler(event, context):
    item = {
        'id': '123',
        'name': 'John Doe',
        'email': 'john.doe@example.com'
    }

    # Insert item into DynamoDB table
    table.put_item(Item=item)

    return {
        'statusCode': 200,
        'body': 'Item successfully added to DynamoDB'
    }
```

In this example:

- **put_item()**: Inserts a new item (JSON object) into the DynamoDB table (my-table-name).

Example: Querying Data from DynamoDB

```python
import boto3

dynamodb = boto3.resource('dynamodb')
table = dynamodb.Table('my-table-name')
```

```python
def lambda_handler(event, context):
    # Query an item by its key (id)
    response = table.get_item(Key={'id': '123'})

    if 'Item' in response:
        return {
            'statusCode': 200,
            'body': response['Item']
        }
    else:
        return {
            'statusCode': 404,
            'body': 'Item not found'
        }
```

In this example:

- **get_item()**: Retrieves an item from DynamoDB using its primary key (id).

Use Case 3: Sending Notifications with Amazon SNS

AWS Lambda can send notifications to users or services via **Amazon SNS** (Simple Notification Service). You can use SNS to publish messages, send text messages (SMS), or trigger other systems based on events.

Example: Sending a Notification via SNS

```python
import boto3

sns_client = boto3.client('sns')

def lambda_handler(event, context):
    message = "Hello, this is a test notification!"

    sns_client.publish(
        TopicArn='arn:aws:sns:us-west-2:123456789012:MyTopic',
        Message=message,
```

```
        Subject='Test Notification'
    )

    return {
        'statusCode': 200,
        'body': 'Message successfully sent to SNS'
    }
```

In this example:

- **publish()**: Publishes a message to an SNS topic (MyTopic). The message can be sent to multiple subscribers, including email addresses and other Lambda functions.

Use Case 4: Managing Message Queues with Amazon SQS

Amazon SQS (Simple Queue Service) is a message queue that enables you to decouple the components of a cloud application. Lambda can both send and receive messages to/from SQS queues.

Example: Sending a Message to an SQS Queue

```
import boto3

sqs_client = boto3.client('sqs')

def lambda_handler(event, context):
    queue_url =
    'https://sqs.us-west-2.amazonaws.com/123456789012/my-queue'

    sqs_client.send_message(
        QueueUrl=queue_url,
        MessageBody='Hello from Lambda!',
        DelaySeconds=10
    )

    return {
        'statusCode': 200,
```

```
    'body': 'Message successfully sent to SQS'
}
```

In this example:

- **send_message()**: Sends a message to the SQS queue. You can also specify a delay (e.g., 10 seconds) before the message becomes available for processing.

Example: Reading a Message from an SQS Queue

```python
import boto3

sqs_client = boto3.client('sqs')

def lambda_handler(event, context):
    queue_url =
    'https://sqs.us-west-2.amazonaws.com/123456789012/my-queue'

    # Receive a message from the queue
    response = sqs_client.receive_message(
        QueueUrl=queue_url,
        MaxNumberOfMessages=1,
        WaitTimeSeconds=5
    )

    if 'Messages' in response:
        message = response['Messages'][0]
        receipt_handle = message['ReceiptHandle']

        # Process the message (e.g., print its contents)
        print(f"Received message: {message['Body']}")

        # Delete the message after processing
        sqs_client.delete_message(
            QueueUrl=queue_url,
            ReceiptHandle=receipt_handle
```

```
        )

        return {
            'statusCode': 200,
            'body': 'Message processed and deleted successfully'
        }

    return {
        'statusCode': 204,
        'body': 'No messages in the queue'
    }
```

In this example:

- **receive_message()**: Retrieves a message from the SQS queue.
- **delete_message()**: Deletes the message from the queue after it has been successfully processed.

4. Best Practices for Using Boto3 in Lambda Functions

1. Minimize Latency with Efficient Resource Management

Avoid creating new clients or resources multiple times within a Lambda function execution. Instead, define them outside the handler function to reuse them across invocations. This helps reduce latency caused by initializing the Boto3 client.

Example:

```
import boto3

s3_client = boto3.client('s3')

def lambda_handler(event, context):
    # Reuse the client created outside the handler
    response = s3_client.list_buckets()
    return {
        'statusCode': 200,
```

```
        'body': response['Buckets']
    }
```

2. Use Environment Variables for Configuration

To avoid hardcoding configuration settings (like bucket names or table names) into your code, use environment variables. This makes the function easier to maintain and secure.

```python
import os

bucket_name = os.getenv('S3_BUCKET_NAME')
```

3. Handle Errors and Exceptions Gracefully

When using Boto3, it's important to handle errors, especially for network failures or permission issues. Use try-except blocks to catch exceptions and log error messages.

```python
import boto3
import logging

s3_client = boto3.client('s3')
logger = logging.getLogger()
logger.setLevel(logging.INFO)

def lambda_handler(event, context):
    try:
        response = s3_client.list_buckets()
        return {
            'statusCode': 200,
            'body': response['Buckets']
        }
    except Exception as e:
        logger.error(f"Error occurred: {str(e)}")
        return {
            'statusCode': 500,
            'body': 'Internal Server Error'
```

}

4. Monitor and Optimize Usage

Use **Amazon CloudWatch** to monitor the execution of your Lambda functions and analyze any performance bottlenecks. By tracking metrics like invocation duration and error rates, you can optimize your function's performance and reduce costs.

Boto3 is an essential tool for Python developers working with AWS Lambda. By leveraging the power of Boto3, you can easily interact with various AWS services such as S3, DynamoDB, SNS, and SQS to build powerful, serverless applications. Whether you're managing files, sending notifications, querying databases, or interacting with message queues, Boto3 makes it simple to integrate AWS services into your Lambda functions. Following best practices such as reusing clients, handling errors gracefully, and monitoring performance will help you build robust and efficient serverless applications.

Common Use Cases for AWS Lambda in Python

Automating Cloud Tasks with AWS Lambda
    AWS Lambda has become an essential tool for automating cloud tasks, allowing developers and operations teams to automate processes without managing servers. By combining AWS Lambda with other AWS services, you can streamline workflows, optimize resource management, and execute repetitive or event-driven tasks efficiently. In this section, we'll explore how you can use AWS Lambda to automate common cloud tasks in Python, focusing on real-world scenarios and best practices.

1. Introduction to Cloud Task Automation with AWS Lambda

AWS Lambda allows you to run code in response to events from various AWS services or on a schedule. This serverless computing model is perfect for automating cloud tasks because it eliminates the need to provision and manage infrastructure, allowing the focus to remain on the task logic itself. Python, with its simplicity and versatility, is ideal for automating tasks such as data processing, file management, database maintenance, notifications, and scaling cloud resources.

Automation with Lambda enables:

- **Event-Driven Automation**: Trigger Lambda functions in response to events (e.g., S3 uploads, database changes, or SNS messages).

- **Scheduled Tasks**: Automate recurring tasks with time-based triggers using **Amazon CloudWatch Events**.
- **On-Demand Execution**: Execute tasks automatically when an API call or event occurs.

2. Common Cloud Automation Use Cases

AWS Lambda is widely used for automating several cloud-related tasks. Below, we explore some common use cases where Lambda can help automate workflows and cloud processes.

1. Scheduled Data Backups

Automating data backups is a common requirement for ensuring business continuity and data protection. Using AWS Lambda and Amazon CloudWatch Events, you can automate regular backups of data from S3, DynamoDB, or RDS (Relational Database Service) to ensure they are securely stored.

Example: Backing Up S3 Objects to Glacier

In this example, we use Lambda to automatically move objects from an S3 bucket to Amazon S3 Glacier for archival purposes, which helps reduce storage costs.

Step 1: Define a CloudWatch Event Rule

You can schedule Lambda to run at regular intervals (e.g., once a day) using **CloudWatch Events**:

- Go to the **CloudWatch Console**, select **Rules**, and create a new rule.
- Choose **Event Source** as **Schedule** (using **cron** or **rate expressions**) to define when the function should run (e.g., daily at midnight).

Step 2: Lambda Code for Moving Objects to Glacier

Here's how you can automate the archival of S3 objects using Python and Boto3:

```python
import boto3
import os

s3 = boto3.client('s3')

def lambda_handler(event, context):
    source_bucket = os.getenv('SOURCE_BUCKET')
    destination_bucket = os.getenv('DESTINATION_BUCKET')

    # List objects in the source bucket
    response = s3.list_objects_v2(Bucket=source_bucket)

    if 'Contents' in response:
        for obj in response['Contents']:
            key = obj['Key']
            # Copy object to Glacier
  storage class in the destination bucket
            s3.copy_object(
                Bucket=destination_bucket,
                CopySource={'Bucket': source_bucket, 'Key': key},
                Key=key,
                StorageClass='GLACIER'
            )
            print(f"Archived {key} to Glacier in
            {destination_bucket}")

    return {
        'statusCode': 200,
        'body': 'Backup and archive complete.'
    }
```

Explanation:

- **CloudWatch Events** triggers this function on a schedule.
- The Lambda function lists objects in the source_bucket and moves them to the destination_bucket in Glacier storage class using the copy_object() method.

2. Auto-Scaling and Resource Optimization

135

Cloud infrastructure resources (like EC2 instances, RDS databases, and S3 storage) need to be optimized based on demand to minimize costs and ensure efficient usage. AWS Lambda can automate the scaling of cloud resources based on specific conditions or thresholds.

Example: Automatically Starting and Stopping EC2 Instances

EC2 instances often need to be started and stopped based on business hours to reduce costs. You can use Lambda to automate this process by starting instances in the morning and stopping them at the end of the day using **CloudWatch Events**.

Lambda Code to Start EC2 Instances:

```python
import boto3

ec2 = boto3.client('ec2')

def lambda_handler(event, context):
    # Define the instance IDs to be started
    instance_ids = ['i-0123456789abcdef0', 'i-0abcdef1234567890']

    # Start EC2 instances
    response = ec2.start_instances
(InstanceIds=instance_ids)

    print(f"Started instances: {instance_ids}")

    return {
        'statusCode': 200,
        'body': f"EC2 instances {instance_ids}
started successfully."
    }
```

Lambda Code to Stop EC2 Instances:

```python
import boto3
```

```
ec2 = boto3.client('ec2')

def lambda_handler(event, context):
    # Define the instance IDs to be stopped
    instance_ids = ['i-0123456789abcdef0',
'i-0abcdef1234567890']

    # Stop EC2 instances
    response = ec2.stop_instances
(InstanceIds=instance_ids)

    print(f"Stopped instances: {instance_ids}")

    return {
        'statusCode': 200,
        'body': f"EC2 instances
{instance_ids} stopped successfully."
    }
```

Explanation:

- Use **CloudWatch Event Rules** to schedule two separate Lambda functions: one to start EC2 instances in the morning and another to stop them at the end of the workday.
- This automation reduces EC2 costs by running the instances only when needed.

3. Automating Cloud Resource Cleanup

Unused resources like orphaned EC2 volumes, unattached Elastic IPs, or stale S3 objects can accumulate over time, leading to increased costs. Lambda can automatically detect and clean up such resources based on specific criteria.

Example: Cleaning Up Unused EBS Volumes

AWS Lambda can automate the identification and deletion of unused Elastic Block Store (EBS) volumes to prevent unnecessary costs.

137

Lambda Code to Delete Unused EBS Volumes:

```
import boto3

ec2 = boto3.client('ec2')

def lambda_handler(event, context):
    # Get all EBS volumes that are available
(i.e., not attached to any instance)
    volumes = ec2.describe_volumes
(Filters=[{'Name': 'status', 'Values': ['available']}])

    for volume in volumes['Volumes']:
        volume_id = volume['VolumeId']
        # Delete the unused volume
        ec2.delete_volume(VolumeId=volume_id)
        print(f"Deleted unused EBS volume: {volume_id}")

    return {
        'statusCode': 200,
        'body': 'Unused EBS volumes cleaned up successfully.'
    }
```

Explanation:

- The function lists all EBS volumes that are in the available state (i.e., not attached to any EC2 instance).
- It then deletes these volumes to free up resources and reduce costs.

4. Automating Security and Compliance Monitoring

Automating security and compliance tasks ensures that your cloud environment remains secure without manual intervention. AWS Lambda, combined with services like **AWS Config, CloudWatch**, and **CloudTrail**, allows you to automate security checks and enforcement.

Example: Automatically Enforcing S3 Bucket Encryption

You can use Lambda to ensure that all S3 buckets have default encryption enabled, and if any bucket is found to be non-compliant, Lambda can automatically enable encryption.

Lambda Code to Enforce S3 Bucket Encryption:

```python
import boto3

s3_client = boto3.client('s3')

def lambda_handler(event, context):
    # List all S3 buckets
    buckets = s3_client.list_buckets()

    for bucket in buckets['Buckets']:
        bucket_name = bucket['Name']

        # Check if default encryption is enabled
        try:
            response =
            s3_client.get_bucket_encryption(Bucket=bucket_name)
            print(f"Bucket {bucket_name}
is already encrypted.")
        except s3_client.exceptions.ClientError as e:
            # If encryption is not enabled,
set default encryption to AES256
            if 'ServerSideEncryption
ConfigurationNotFoundError' in str(e):
                s3_client.put_bucket_encryption(
                    Bucket=bucket_name,
                    ServerSideEncryptionConfiguration={
                        'Rules': [{
'ApplyServerSideEncryptionByDefault': {
'SSEAlgorithm': 'AES256'
                        }
                    }]
                }
                )
print(f"Enabled encryption on bucket: {bucket_name}")
            else:
                raise e

    return {
```

```
        'statusCode': 200,
    'body': 'S3 bucket encryption enforcement complete.'
        }
```

Explanation:

- This function scans all S3 buckets in the account and checks if encryption is enabled.
- If encryption is not enabled, it configures the bucket to use **AES256** encryption automatically.

5. Automating Notifications and Alerts

AWS Lambda can automate notifications based on certain cloud events or conditions. Combined with services like **SNS**, **SES**, and **CloudWatch**, you can send automated notifications when something significant happens in your environment.

Example: Sending Alerts for EC2 CPU Usage

If an EC2 instance's CPU usage exceeds a threshold, Lambda can be triggered by **CloudWatch Alarms** to send a notification to the operations team.

Step 1: Set Up CloudWatch Alarm

- Create a CloudWatch Alarm that monitors the **CPUUtilization** metric for your EC2 instance.
- Set the alarm to trigger when CPU utilization exceeds 80% over a certain period.

Step 2: Lambda Code to Send Notification

```
import boto3
import json
import os
```

```python
sns_client = boto3.client('sns')

def lambda_handler(event, context):
    # Extract alarm details from the CloudWatch event
    alarm_name = event['detail']['alarmName']
    state = event['detail']['state']['value']
    reason = event['detail']['state']['reason']

    # Compose message
    message = {
        'AlarmName': alarm_name,
        'State': state,
        'Reason': reason
    }

    # Send SNS notification
    sns_client.publish(
        TopicArn=os.getenv('SNS_TOPIC_ARN'),
        Message=json.dumps(message),
        Subject=f"CloudWatch Alarm Triggered: {alarm_name}"
    )

    return {
        'statusCode': 200,
        'body': 'Notification sent successfully.'
    }
```

Explanation:

- The Lambda function is triggered by a CloudWatch Alarm when the CPU utilization of an EC2 instance exceeds the threshold.
- The function sends a notification to an SNS topic, which can notify subscribers (such as email addresses or Lambda functions).

3. Best Practices for Automating Cloud Tasks with AWS Lambda

1. Use Environment Variables

Environment variables allow you to manage configuration settings (like bucket names, table names, and thresholds) dynamically without hardcoding them in your Lambda function. This makes the automation task reusable across different environments (dev, prod, etc.).

2. Monitor Function Performance

Use **CloudWatch Metrics** to monitor your Lambda function's performance, such as invocation count, error rate, and execution duration. Automating cloud tasks can be sensitive to performance and timing, so it's important to keep track of your function's behavior.

3. Implement Error Handling and Retries

Always include error handling in your Lambda functions using try-except blocks to catch and log exceptions. If your tasks are time-sensitive or critical, configure **Dead Letter Queues (DLQ)** to handle failed invocations.

4. Optimize Resource Usage

Ensure that you're using the appropriate memory and timeout settings for your Lambda functions to avoid over-provisioning. For large-scale automation tasks, distribute workloads across multiple Lambda functions to avoid hitting timeout or memory limits.

AWS Lambda is a powerful tool for automating cloud tasks across your AWS environment. Whether you're managing infrastructure resources, securing your environment, or performing scheduled backups, Lambda can simplify and scale these processes without the need for manual intervention. By following best practices and leveraging Boto3 and AWS services, you can automate repetitive cloud tasks, optimize resource usage, and maintain a robust cloud infrastructure efficiently.

Real-Time Data Processing with AWS Lambda

AWS Lambda is highly effective for building **real-time data processing** pipelines. Lambda's ability to respond immediately to events from services like **Amazon Kinesis, Amazon S3, Amazon DynamoDB Streams**, and **Amazon SNS** enables it to process and transform data as soon as it is ingested. In this section, we'll explore how AWS Lambda can be used to build real-time data processing applications in Python, with a focus on common use cases, architecture patterns, and best practices.

1. Introduction to Real-Time Data Processing

Real-time data processing involves analyzing and acting on data as soon as it arrives, typically with minimal delay. This is critical for applications that need instant insights, such as fraud detection, monitoring, IoT data analysis, and log processing.

AWS Lambda, combined with event-driven services like **Amazon Kinesis, DynamoDB Streams**, and **S3**, allows developers to process streams of data in real-time. By scaling automatically based on the volume of incoming data and integrating seamlessly with other AWS services, Lambda makes it easy to build scalable, real-time data pipelines.

2. Common Real-Time Data Processing Use Cases

Real-time data processing using AWS Lambda can be applied across various scenarios. Below are some common use cases:

1. Real-Time Log Processing

Logs generated by applications, servers, or security systems need to be processed in real time to extract valuable insights, detect anomalies, or trigger alerts. By ingesting logs into **Amazon Kinesis Data Streams** or **Amazon CloudWatch Logs**, you can use Lambda to process these logs immediately.

Example: Processing CloudWatch Logs for Error Detection

In this use case, a Lambda function automatically processes log data from

Amazon CloudWatch Logs, detects error patterns, and sends notifications when errors are detected.

Step 1: Configure CloudWatch Log Subscription

Create a CloudWatch Log subscription to stream log data to a Lambda function.

Step 2: Lambda Code to Process Logs

```python
import json
import boto3
import re

sns_client = boto3.client('sns')

def lambda_handler(event, context):
    # Decode CloudWatch Logs data
    logs_data = json.loads(event['awslogs']['data'])

    # Iterate through log events
    for log_event in logs_data['logEvents']:
        message = log_event['message']

        # Look for error patterns using regex
        if re.search(r"ERROR", message):
            # Send notification to SNS if an error is found
            sns_client.publish(
                TopicArn='arn:aws:sns:us-west-2:123456789012:ErrorAlerts',
                Message=message,
                Subject='Error Detected in Logs'
            )

    return {
        'statusCode': 200,
        'body': 'Logs processed successfully.'
    }
```

Explanation:

- The Lambda function decodes the log data and processes each log event.

- It uses a regular expression (re.search()) to identify errors.
- If an error is detected, the function publishes an alert to an SNS topic, which can notify system administrators or trigger automated workflows.

2. Streaming Data Ingestion and Transformation

AWS Lambda works seamlessly with **Amazon Kinesis Data Streams** to process and transform large volumes of streaming data in real time. This is useful in applications such as telemetry processing, analytics, or monitoring sensor data from IoT devices.

Example: Processing Data from Kinesis Streams

In this use case, Lambda is triggered by a Kinesis Data Stream to process real-time data and store transformed results in **Amazon DynamoDB** for further analysis.

Step 1: Set Up Kinesis Stream

Set up an **Amazon Kinesis Data Stream** to ingest real-time data, such as telemetry from IoT devices or clickstream data from a web application.

Step 2: Lambda Code to Process and Store Data in DynamoDB

```python
import boto3
import json

dynamodb = boto3.resource('dynamodb')
table = dynamodb.Table('ProcessedDataTable')

def lambda_handler(event, context):
    for record in event['Records']:
        # Decode the Kinesis data
        data = json.loads(record['kinesis']['data'])

        # Perform data transformation (e.g., normalization)
        transformed_data = {
            'deviceId': data['deviceId'],
            'temperature': (data['temperature']
 - 32) * 5.0 / 9.0,
```

145

```
# Convert Fahrenheit to Celsius
        'timestamp': data['timestamp']
    }

    # Store the transformed data in DynamoDB
    table.put_item(Item=transformed_data)

return {
    'statusCode': 200,
    'body': 'Data processed and stored successfully.'
}
```

Explanation:

- The function processes incoming records from Kinesis, decodes the data, and transforms it (e.g., converting temperature data from Fahrenheit to Celsius).
- The transformed data is then stored in a DynamoDB table for further analysis or dashboarding.

3. Real-Time Image Processing

AWS Lambda can also be used for real-time image processing by automatically responding to **Amazon S3 events**. For example, you can trigger a Lambda function when an image is uploaded to an S3 bucket to perform operations like resizing, filtering, or running machine learning models on the image.

Example: Resizing Images Automatically

In this example, Lambda automatically resizes images uploaded to an S3 bucket and stores the resized versions in another S3 bucket.

Step 1: Set Up an S3 Bucket Trigger

Create an S3 bucket and configure it to trigger a Lambda function when a new object (image) is uploaded.

Step 2: Lambda Code to Resize Images

```python
import boto3
from PIL import Image
import io

s3_client = boto3.client('s3')

def lambda_handler(event, context):
    bucket_name = event['Records'][0]['s3']['bucket']['name']
    object_key = event['Records'][0]['s3']['object']['key']

    # Download the image from S3
    image_obj = s3_client.get_object(Bucket=bucket_name,
    Key=object_key)
    image_data = image_obj['Body'].read()

    # Open the image using Pillow
    image = Image.open(io.BytesIO(image_data))

    # Resize the image
    resized_image = image.resize((800, 600))

    # Save the resized image back to another S3 bucket
    buffer = io.BytesIO()
    resized_image.save(buffer, 'JPEG')
    buffer.seek(0)

    s3_client.put_object(
        Bucket='resized-images-bucket',
        Key=f"resized-{object_key}",
        Body=buffer,
        ContentType='image/jpeg'
    )

    return {
        'statusCode': 200,
        'body': 'Image resized and uploaded successfully.'
    }
```

Explanation:

- The Lambda function is triggered by an image upload to S3.
- The function resizes the image using the **Pillow** library and stores the resized image in another S3 bucket.
- This process is useful for applications that need to optimize image sizes for web delivery or perform real-time image transformations.

4. Real-Time Notification Systems

Real-time notifications can be triggered when specific conditions are met in the data, such as anomalies, high-frequency events, or predefined thresholds. Using services like **Amazon SNS** or **Amazon SQS** with Lambda, you can build a robust notification system.

Example: Real-Time IoT Sensor Alerts

Lambda can be used to process IoT sensor data in real time and trigger alerts when certain conditions are met, such as temperature thresholds being exceeded.

Step 1: Process IoT Data Stream

IoT sensor data is streamed to **Amazon Kinesis Data Streams** or **AWS IoT Core**.

Step 2: Lambda Code to Process Data and Trigger Alerts

```
import boto3
import json

sns_client = boto3.client('sns')

def lambda_handler(event, context):
    for record in event['Records']:
        # Decode IoT data
        sensor_data = json.loads(record['kinesis']['data'])

        # Check if temperature exceeds the threshold
        if sensor_data['temperature'] > 100:
            message = f"Alert:
Temperature exceeded 100 degrees! Current temperature:
{sensor_data['temperature']}"
```

```
            # Send alert via SNS
            sns_client.publish(
                TopicArn='arn:
aws:sns:
us-west-2:
123456789012:
TemperatureAlerts',
                Message=message,
                Subject='High Temperature Alert'
            )

    return {
        'statusCode': 200,
        'body': 'Alerts processed successfully.'
    }
```

Explanation:

- The function processes IoT sensor data in real time.
- If the temperature exceeds a threshold, an alert is sent via SNS to notify the relevant parties.
- This setup can be expanded to process other types of sensor data or to trigger actions based on different criteria.

3. Real-Time Data Processing Architecture

When designing a real-time data processing pipeline using AWS Lambda, it's essential to understand how various AWS services fit together. Below is a common architecture pattern for real-time data processing:

Data Ingestion:

- Use **Amazon Kinesis Data Streams**, **AWS IoT Core**, or **Amazon S3** to ingest real-time data.
- Kinesis can handle high-throughput streams, such as log data or click-stream data, while S3 is ideal for file-based data like images or videos.

Lambda for Processing:

- Lambda functions are triggered in real time by the event sources (Kinesis, S3, or IoT Core).
- Lambda processes, transforms, or filters the incoming data.

Data Storage:

- Store processed data in **Amazon DynamoDB**, **Amazon RDS**, or **Amazon S3** depending on the use case. DynamoDB is ideal for structured data, while S3 is perfect for file-based storage.

Notifications or Alerts:

- Use **Amazon SNS** or **Amazon SQS** to notify users or trigger further actions based on data analysis results.

Monitoring and Logging:

- Use **Amazon CloudWatch** to monitor Lambda function performance and capture logs for auditing and troubleshooting purposes.

4. Best Practices for Real-Time Data Processing

1.Minimize Latency

To minimize processing delays, avoid complex logic within the Lambda function. Keep the code lightweight and offload heavy processing to more suitable services like **AWS Batch**, **Amazon EMR**, or **Athena**.

2. Monitor and Scale

Leverage **CloudWatch Metrics** to monitor the execution of your Lambda functions, including the number of invocations, errors, and execution duration. Use these metrics to tune the scaling and performance of your real-time pipeline.

3. Efficient Error Handling

In real-time pipelines, errors or delays in processing can disrupt the entire workflow. Implement proper error handling using retries and **Dead Letter Queues (DLQ)** to ensure that failed records are not lost and can be reprocessed later.

4. Use Environment Variables

Configure environment variables for bucket names, thresholds, or DynamoDB table names. This makes it easier to manage your Lambda function across different environments (development, staging, and production).

Real-time data processing with AWS Lambda allows organizations to build scalable, event-driven applications that can handle large volumes of data instantly. Whether you're processing logs, transforming streaming data, handling real-time image processing, or building notification systems, AWS Lambda's ability to integrate seamlessly with other AWS services makes it an ideal solution for real-time workloads. By following best practices and designing efficient architectures, you can harness the full potential of AWS Lambda for your real-time data processing needs.

Scheduling Functions with CloudWatch Events

AWS Lambda, in combination with **Amazon CloudWatch Events** (also known as **Amazon EventBridge**), provides a powerful and flexible solution for scheduling tasks without needing to provision servers or worry about infrastructure management. With CloudWatch Events, you can trigger Lambda functions on a regular schedule (e.g., every minute, hourly, daily) or based on specific events that occur within your AWS environment.

In this section, we'll explore how to use CloudWatch Events to schedule

Lambda functions in Python, covering the most common use cases and best practices for building efficient and reliable scheduled tasks.

1. What is Amazon CloudWatch Events?

Amazon CloudWatch Events (or **Amazon EventBridge**) is an AWS service that allows you to respond to changes in your AWS resources by routing event data to other AWS services. One of its key features is the ability to create **scheduled rules** to invoke AWS Lambda functions at predefined intervals, similar to how **cron jobs** work in Unix-like systems.

Scheduled CloudWatch Events can be configured to:

- Run Lambda functions at specific time intervals (e.g., every 5 minutes).
- Execute tasks on a daily, weekly, or monthly basis (e.g., backups or reports).
- Automate infrastructure changes (e.g., start/stop EC2 instances).

2. Common Use Cases for Scheduling Lambda Functions

Scheduling Lambda functions is commonly used for automating repetitive tasks, such as:

- **Data backups**: Regularly backing up data from databases (e.g., DynamoDB) or S3 to an archive (e.g., Glacier).
- **Resource management**: Automatically starting or stopping EC2 instances based on business hours.
- **Data cleanup**: Removing unused or stale resources, such as cleaning up old S3 objects or deleting unused EBS volumes.
- **Report generation**: Generating and sending reports on a daily or weekly basis.

3. Creating Scheduled Events with CloudWatch

There are two primary ways to create scheduled rules in CloudWatch Events:

- **Rate Expressions**: Used for simple schedules, such as running a Lambda function every X minutes or hours.
- **Cron Expressions**: For more complex scheduling, such as running a Lambda function at specific times or days of the week.

1. Using Rate Expressions

A **rate expression** is used to create simple recurring schedules. For example:

- Run every 5 minutes: rate(5 minutes)
- Run every hour: rate(1 hour)
- Run once every day: rate(1 day)

Example: Running a Lambda Function Every 5 Minutes

You can create a scheduled rule using the AWS Management Console:

1. Navigate to **CloudWatch > Rules**.
2. Click **Create rule**.
3. Under **Event Source**, select **Event Schedule**.
4. Choose **Rate** and set it to run every 5 minutes.
5. Under **Targets**, choose **Lambda Function** and select the Lambda function you want to trigger.

Alternatively, you can create this rule using the **AWS CLI**:

```
aws events put-rule \
    --schedule-expression "rate(5 minutes)" \
    --name "RunLambdaEvery5Minutes"
```

Then, add a Lambda function as the target of the rule:

```
aws events put-targets \
    --rule "RunLambdaEvery5Minutes" \
    --targets
"Id"="1","Arn"="
arn:aws:lambda:
us-west
-2:123456789012
:function:MyFunction"
```

2. Using Cron Expressions

For more granular control, use **cron expressions**. Cron expressions allow you to define specific times or dates for running your Lambda function, such as running a task every Monday at 8:00 AM or on the first day of every month.

Cron expressions follow this format:

```
cron(Minutes Hours Day-of-month Month Day-of-week Year)
```

Example Cron Expressions:

- Every day at midnight: cron(0 0 * * ? *)
- Every Friday at 6:00 PM: cron(0 18 ? * FRI *)
- On the first day of every month at 12:00 PM: cron(0 12 1 * ? *)

Explanation of the Fields:

- **Minutes**: (0–59)
- **Hours**: (0–23)
- **Day-of-month**: (1–31)
- **Month**: (1–12 or JAN–DEC)
- **Day-of-week**: (1–7 or SUN–SAT)
- **Year**: Optional (e.g., 2024, 2025)

Example: Running a Lambda Function Every Day at 8:00 AM

```
aws events put-rule \
    --schedule-expression
"cron(0 8 * * ? *)" \
    --name "RunLambdaEveryDayAt8AM"
```

Once again, you need to add your Lambda function as the target of this rule:

```
aws events put-targets \
    --rule
"RunLambdaEveryDayAt8AM" \
    --targets "Id"="1",
"Arn"="arn:aws:
lambda:us-west-2:
123456789012:
function:MyFunction"
```

4. Lambda Code for Scheduled Tasks

Scheduled Lambda functions can perform various tasks like generating reports, cleaning up resources, or backing up data. Below are a few examples.

Example 1: Running a Daily Backup Task

In this example, a scheduled Lambda function runs every day at midnight to back up a DynamoDB table to an S3 bucket.

Step 1: Create a Scheduled Rule

```
aws events put-rule \
    --schedule-expression "cron(0 0 * * ? *)" \
    --name "DailyDynamoDBBackup"
```

Step 2: Lambda Code for Backing Up DynamoDB Data

```python
import boto3
import json
import datetime
import os

dynamodb = boto3.resource('dynamodb')
s3 = boto3.client('s3')

table = dynamodb.Table('MyDynamoDBTable')

def lambda_handler(event, context):
    # Fetch data from DynamoDB
    response = table.scan()
    items = response['Items']

    # Prepare file name with current date
    backup_file = f"dynamodb_backup_{datetime.
datetime.now().strftime('%Y-%m-%d')}.json"

    # Save backup to S3
    s3.put_object(
        Bucket=os.getenv('S3_BACKUP_BUCKET'),
        Key=backup_file,
        Body=json.dumps(items)
    )

    return {
        'statusCode': 200,
        'body': f"Backup saved as {backup_file}"
    }
```

Explanation:

- This function scans the DynamoDB table and saves the data to an S3 bucket.
- The function is triggered every day at midnight by a CloudWatch Event rule.

Example 2: Scheduled EC2 Instance Management

In this example, Lambda is used to automatically stop EC2 instances outside business hours to save costs.

Step 1: Create a Cron-Based Schedule

```
aws events put-rule \
    --schedule-expression
"cron(0 20 ? * MON-FRI *)" \
    --name "StopEC2InstancesAt8PMWeekdays"
```

This cron expression will run at 8:00 PM on weekdays (Monday to Friday).

Step 2: Lambda Code to Stop EC2 Instances

```
import boto3

ec2 = boto3.client('ec2')

def lambda_handler(event, context):
```

instance_ids = ['i-0123456789abcdef0',

```
'i-0abcdef1234567890']

    # Stop EC2 instances
    response = ec2.stop_instances
(InstanceIds=instance_ids)

    print(f"Stopping instances: {instance_ids}")

    return {
        'statusCode': 200,
        'body': 'EC2 instances stopped successfully.'
    }
```

Explanation:

- The Lambda function is triggered by a cron-based CloudWatch Event rule at 8:00 PM on weekdays.

• It stops the specified EC2 instances to save costs outside business hours.

5. Monitoring and Logging Scheduled Lambda Functions

CloudWatch Logs

Every Lambda invocation, including scheduled tasks, automatically generates logs in **Amazon CloudWatch Logs**. This allows you to monitor the execution of scheduled functions and debug issues when needed. Each log entry includes details such as:

• Start and end time of the function.
• Logs generated by the function (using print() or Python's logging module).
• Any errors or exceptions encountered during execution.

To access the logs:

1. Navigate to **CloudWatch > Logs** in the AWS Management Console.
2. Select the log group for your Lambda function (/aws/lambda/function-name).
3. Review the log streams corresponding to each invocation of your scheduled task.

CloudWatch Metrics

CloudWatch also tracks key metrics for Lambda functions, including:

• **Invocations**: The number of times the function is invoked.
• **Duration**: The time the function takes to execute.
• **Errors**: The number of errors encountered during execution.
• **Throttles**: The number of times the function was throttled due to exceeding concurrency limits.

These metrics help you monitor your scheduled Lambda functions and ensure they're running as expected. You can also create CloudWatch Alarms to notify you if a function starts failing or takes too long to execute.

6. Best Practices for Scheduling Lambda Functions

1. Use Dead Letter Queues (DLQ) for Error Handling

If your Lambda function fails, you can configure a **Dead Letter Queue (DLQ)** to capture failed events. This ensures that failed invocations are not lost and can be reprocessed or reviewed later.

2. Monitor for Missed Invocations

For critical scheduled tasks, set up **CloudWatch Alarms** to alert you if your Lambda function doesn't execute as expected. This could be due to throttling, permission issues, or errors in the function.

3. Optimize Function Timeout and Memory

Set the appropriate timeout and memory allocation for your scheduled Lambda function. For longer-running tasks, ensure that the timeout is sufficient, and adjust memory based on the function's resource usage to optimize performance and reduce costs.

4. Use Environment Variables

Instead of hardcoding values like bucket names or instance IDs, use **environment variables** to store configuration settings. This makes your Lambda function more maintainable and adaptable to different environments.

Scheduling AWS Lambda functions with **CloudWatch Events** enables you to automate and manage recurring tasks without the need for servers or manual intervention. Whether you're performing daily backups, managing EC2 instances, or running routine maintenance jobs, Lambda and CloudWatch Events offer a scalable and reliable solution. By following best practices such as error handling, monitoring, and resource optimization, you can ensure that your scheduled tasks run smoothly and efficiently across your AWS infrastructure.

Building Event-Driven Architectures with AWS Lambda

Event-driven architectures (EDA) are designed to respond to events in real time, enabling highly responsive, scalable, and decoupled systems. AWS Lambda plays a central role in building event-driven architectures on AWS, thanks to its ability to trigger functions automatically in response to a wide range of events from various AWS services. In this section, we'll dive into how you can use AWS Lambda to build event-driven architectures in Python, along with common patterns, use cases, and best practices.

1. What is an Event-Driven Architecture?

An **event-driven architecture** is a design pattern in which system components react to events generated by other components or external sources. Rather than following a predefined sequence of steps (as in traditional request-response architectures), event-driven systems respond dynamically to the occurrence of events such as user actions, data changes, or system events.

Event-driven architectures typically consist of the following key components:

- **Producers**: Components or systems that generate events (e.g., user actions, database updates, sensor data).
- **Events**: Data or messages that represent a change in state or trigger actions (e.g., S3 file uploads, DynamoDB stream updates, SNS messages).
- **Consumers**: Components or systems that react to events (e.g., AWS Lambda functions, Amazon SQS queues).
- **Event Routers**: Services that deliver events to consumers (e.g., Amazon EventBridge, S3, Kinesis).

2. Why AWS Lambda for Event-Driven Architectures?

AWS Lambda is well-suited for event-driven architectures because:

- **Serverless**: No need to manage or provision servers—Lambda automatically scales based on event load.
- **Event Sources**: Lambda integrates natively with multiple AWS services (such as S3, DynamoDB, SNS, SQS, and Kinesis), making it easy to build event-driven systems.
- **Automatic Scaling**: Lambda automatically scales up and down based on the volume of events, handling both high and low throughput workloads efficiently.
- **Cost-Effective**: You pay only for the time your Lambda function runs, making event-driven architectures cost-efficient for infrequent events or bursty workloads.

3. Common Event-Driven Use Cases

Event-driven architectures powered by AWS Lambda are used across a wide variety of applications. Some common use cases include:

1. Real-Time Data Processing

AWS Lambda can be triggered by data streams (e.g., **Amazon Kinesis** or **DynamoDB Streams**) to process data in real time. This is useful in use cases such as log analysis, clickstream analysis, and IoT telemetry.

Example: Processing Real-Time Stream Data with Kinesis

In this example, Lambda processes clickstream data from a Kinesis Data Stream, normalizes it, and stores the results in an S3 bucket.

```
import boto3
import json

s3 = boto3.client('s3')
```

```python
def lambda_handler(event, context):
    for record in event['Records']:
        # Decode the base64-encoded Kinesis data
        payload = json.loads(record['kinesis']['data'])

        # Normalize data (e.g., convert timestamp to UTC)
        payload['timestamp'] = payload['timestamp'] + " UTC"

        # Save the normalized data to S3
        s3.put_object(
            Bucket='processed-clickstream-data',
            Key=f"{payload['session_id']}.json",
            Body=json.dumps(payload)
        )

    return {
        'statusCode': 200,
        'body': 'Data processed and saved to S3.'
    }
```

- **Event Source**: The Kinesis stream pushes clickstream data into the Lambda function.
- **Event Processing**: Lambda normalizes and processes the data.
- **Data Storage**: The processed data is saved in an S3 bucket.

2. Asynchronous Task Execution

Lambda can be triggered asynchronously by services like **Amazon S3, Amazon SNS**, and **Amazon SQS**, enabling you to execute tasks such as image processing, email notifications, and background data processing.

Example: Image Processing with S3

In this use case, Lambda automatically triggers when an image is uploaded to S3, processes the image (e.g., resizing), and stores the transformed image in a separate S3 bucket.

```python
import boto3
from PIL import Image
import io

s3 = boto3.client('s3')

def lambda_handler(event, context):
    # Get the S3 bucket and key details
    source_bucket = event['Records']
[0]['s3']['bucket']['name']
    object_key = event['Records']
[0]['s3']['object']['key']

    # Download the image from the S3 bucket
    image_obj = s3.get_object
(Bucket=source_bucket, Key=object_key)
    image_data = image_obj['Body'].read()

    # Open the image using Pillow
    image = Image.open(io.BytesIO(image_data))

    # Resize the image
    resized_image = image.resize((800, 600))

    # Save the resized image back to S3
    buffer = io.BytesIO()
    resized_image.save(buffer, 'JPEG')
    buffer.seek(0)

    s3.put_object(
        Bucket='resized-images-bucket',
        Key=f"resized-{object_key}",
        Body=buffer,
        ContentType='image/jpeg'
    )

    return {
        'statusCode': 200,
        'body': 'Image processed and saved successfully.'
    }
```

- **Event Source**: The Lambda function is triggered by an **S3 PutObject event**.
- **Event Processing**: The image is resized using the **Pillow** library.
- **Data Storage**: The resized image is saved to a different S3 bucket.

3. Event-Driven Notifications

Lambda can be integrated with services like **Amazon SNS** or **Amazon SES** to send notifications or alerts when specific events occur. This is commonly used for monitoring, alerting, or notifying users when certain thresholds or conditions are met.

Example: Sending Notifications Based on DynamoDB Changes

In this example, a Lambda function is triggered when an item is added to a DynamoDB table. The function processes the event and sends a notification to the relevant users via SNS.

```python
import boto3
import json

sns = boto3.client('sns')

def lambda_handler(event, context):
    for record in event['Records']:
        if record['eventName'] == 'INSERT':
            new_item = record['dynamodb']['NewImage']
            message = f"New item added:
  {new_item['id']['S']}"

            # Send an SNS notification
            sns.publish(
                TopicArn='arn:aws:sns:
us-west-2:
123456789012:
NewItemNotifications',
                Message=message,
                Subject='New DynamoDB Item Added'
            )
```

```
return {
    'statusCode': 200,
    'body': 'Notification sent successfully.'
}
```

- **Event Source**: The Lambda function is triggered by a **DynamoDB Stream**.
- **Event Processing**: The function processes the new item and sends a notification via SNS.
- **Outcome**: Users are notified whenever a new item is added to the DynamoDB table.

4. Event Sources for Lambda in Event-Driven Architectures

AWS Lambda can be triggered by a variety of event sources, each of which can be used to build different types of event-driven workflows. Here are the key AWS services that can serve as event sources for Lambda:

1. Amazon S3

S3 events (such as PutObject or DeleteObject) can trigger Lambda functions. This is commonly used for automating file processing tasks, such as generating thumbnails for uploaded images, converting document formats, or performing security scans.

- **Event Examples**: File uploads, object deletions, object metadata updates.

2. Amazon DynamoDB Streams

When items in a DynamoDB table are added, updated, or deleted, these changes are captured in **DynamoDB Streams**, which can trigger a Lambda function to process the change. This is commonly used for building real-time analytics, audit logs, or maintaining materialized views.

- **Event Examples**: Insertions, updates, deletions of items in a DynamoDB table.

3. Amazon SNS (Simple Notification Service)

SNS can trigger Lambda functions when a message is published to an SNS topic. This is often used for sending notifications, triggering background processes, or distributing tasks across multiple Lambda functions.

- **Event Examples**: Published SNS messages.

4. Amazon SQS (Simple Queue Service)

Lambda can poll messages from **Amazon SQS** queues, allowing you to decouple event producers from event consumers and handle tasks asynchronously. This is useful for building queue-based, event-driven workflows.

- **Event Examples**: Queued messages in SQS.

5. Amazon Kinesis

Kinesis Data Streams and **Kinesis Firehose** allow Lambda to process large streams of real-time data. Kinesis is typically used for event-driven architectures that require real-time processing, such as telemetry, log analysis, or sensor data processing.

- **Event Examples**: Streaming data from IoT devices, application logs, clickstreams.

6. Amazon CloudWatch Events / EventBridge

CloudWatch Events (also known as **EventBridge**) can be used to trigger Lambda functions based on system events (e.g., EC2 instance state changes) or custom events. This is useful for automating operational tasks, such as monitoring infrastructure health or automating resource scaling.

- **Event Examples**: EC2 state changes, RDS failover events, custom application events.

5. Event-Driven Architecture Patterns

There are several common patterns for designing event-driven architectures using AWS Lambda. Some of the most widely used patterns include:

1. Simple Event Processing

This pattern involves a direct flow from event producers to event consumers. For example, when an event occurs (e.g., a file is uploaded to S3), a Lambda function is triggered to process the event and take immediate action (e.g., resize an image, send a notification, or update a database).

2. Event-Stream Processing

This pattern involves continuously processing streams of data using Lambda functions triggered by Kinesis or DynamoDB Streams. The stream data can be analyzed, filtered, transformed, or enriched in real-time, with results stored in a database or data lake for future analysis.

3. Event-Driven Microservices

Event-driven architectures are commonly used in microservices, where services communicate by emitting and consuming events. For example, a user registration service might emit a "UserRegistered" event that triggers other services, such as a welcome email service or a CRM update service.

4. Fan-Out Architecture with SNS

This pattern involves broadcasting a single event to multiple consumers. For example, when a new order is placed, a message can be published to an SNS topic. Multiple Lambda functions, each responsible for a different task (e.g., updating inventory, sending a confirmation email, generating an invoice), can subscribe to the topic.

6. Best Practices for Building Event-Driven Architectures with AWS Lambda

1. Decouple Event Sources and Consumers

Use services like **Amazon SNS**, **Amazon SQS**, or **EventBridge** to decouple event producers from consumers. This allows you to scale each component independently and handle failures or retries more effectively.

2. Use Dead Letter Queues (DLQ)

In an event-driven architecture, errors in processing can disrupt the system. Use **Dead Letter Queues (DLQs)** to capture failed Lambda invocations, ensuring that no events are lost and allowing you to troubleshoot and reprocess the failed events later.

3. Monitor and Trace Events

Use **AWS X-Ray** to trace the flow of events through your architecture. This helps you understand the interactions between different components, measure performance, and troubleshoot bottlenecks.

4. Ensure Idempotency

Ensure that your Lambda functions are **idempotent**, meaning they can handle the same event multiple times without side effects. This is important for scenarios where events may be retried due to failures or network issues.

5. Use Event Filtering

For services like **SNS** and **EventBridge**, use event filters to route only relevant events to specific Lambda functions. This reduces unnecessary processing and improves the efficiency of your architecture.

Building event-driven architectures with AWS Lambda allows you to create scalable, decoupled, and highly responsive systems that react to events in real time. By leveraging event sources like S3, DynamoDB Streams, Kinesis, SNS, and SQS, you can build flexible architectures that are both cost-effective and resilient. Following best practices such as decoupling components, using DLQs, and ensuring idempotency will help you create reliable event-driven systems capable of handling large-scale workloads with ease.

Working with External Libraries and Dependencies

Packaging Python Dependencies for AWS Lambda
When building AWS Lambda functions in Python, you often need to include external libraries and dependencies that are not part of the standard Lambda runtime environment. AWS Lambda provides flexibility in incorporating these dependencies, but it's essential to package them properly to ensure that your Lambda functions work as expected in the serverless environment.

In this section, we'll cover how to package Python dependencies for AWS Lambda, including local packaging, using AWS Lambda Layers, and best practices for managing and optimizing Lambda deployments with dependencies.

1. Understanding Python Dependencies in AWS Lambda

By default, AWS Lambda provides a Python runtime (e.g., Python 3.8, 3.9) with built-in libraries such as boto3 for interacting with AWS services. However, many serverless applications require additional third-party libraries (such as requests, numpy, or pandas) to perform specific tasks, such as HTTP requests, data processing, or machine learning.

To ensure these external libraries are available in your Lambda function, you need to package them along with your code. There are two primary ways to package Python dependencies:

- **Locally package dependencies**: Manually package your code and its dependencies in a ZIP file and upload it to AWS Lambda.
- **Use AWS Lambda Layers**: Package and reuse dependencies across multiple Lambda functions using Lambda Layers.

2. Method 1: Packaging Dependencies Locally

The most straightforward way to package Python dependencies is to bundle them with your function code in a deployment package (ZIP file). This method is ideal when:

- Your Lambda function uses a small number of external dependencies.
- You are not reusing the same dependencies across multiple Lambda functions.

Steps to Package Dependencies Locally
Step 1: Create a Project Directory

First, create a directory on your local machine where you will store your Lambda function code and its dependencies.

```
mkdir my_lambda_function
cd my_lambda_function
```

Inside this directory, create your Lambda function file. For example, create a file called lambda_function.py.

```
# lambda_function.py
import requests

def lambda_handler(event, context):
    response = requests.get("https://api.example.com/data")
    return {
        'statusCode': 200,
```

```
        'body': response.text
    }
```

In this example, we're using the requests library to make an HTTP request. Since requests is not included in the Lambda runtime by default, we need to package it along with our code.

Step 2: Install Dependencies Locally

Use **pip** to install the external dependencies in the current directory. The -t option tells pip to install the libraries into the specified target directory (the current directory in this case).

```
pip install requests -t .
```

After running this command, your project directory should contain:

- lambda_function.py
- A folder called requests (along with any other dependencies).

Step 3: Create a Deployment Package

Now, package your Lambda function code and the installed dependencies into a ZIP file. This ZIP file will be your deployment package that you'll upload to AWS Lambda.

```
zip -r function.zip .
```

This command recursively zips all files and directories in the current directory into a file called function.zip. The package will contain your Lambda function code and all the external dependencies required to run it.

Step 4: Upload the Deployment Package to AWS Lambda

1. Navigate to the **AWS Lambda Console**.
2. Select **Create Function** or choose an existing function.
3. Under the **Function code** section, choose **Upload from > .zip file**.

4. Upload the function.zip file.
5. Click **Deploy**.

Your Lambda function is now deployed with all the necessary dependencies included.

Pros and Cons of Local Packaging
Pros:

- Simple and quick for small, self-contained projects.
- Works well for one-off functions with specific dependency requirements.

Cons:

- Inefficient if you need to reuse the same dependencies across multiple functions (each function will require its own ZIP file).
- Deployment packages can become large, especially if the dependencies are heavy (e.g., pandas, numpy).

3. Method 2: Using AWS Lambda Layers

AWS Lambda Layers provide a more modular way to package and share external dependencies across multiple Lambda functions. A **Lambda Layer** is essentially a separate ZIP file that contains libraries, custom runtimes, or other assets that your Lambda functions can use.

Lambda Layers are particularly useful when:

- Multiple Lambda functions require the same dependencies.
- You want to avoid redeploying the same dependencies with each function update.
- You need to reduce the size of your deployment package by offloading large dependencies to a layer.

Steps to Create a Lambda Layer

Step 1: Create a Project Directory for the Layer

Create a new directory for your Lambda Layer. Inside this directory, create a subdirectory called python, which is the required structure for Lambda Layers that use Python dependencies.

```
mkdir my_layer
cd my_layer
mkdir python
```

Step 2: Install Dependencies into the Layer

Use **pip** to install your external dependencies into the python subdirectory of your Lambda Layer.

```
pip install requests -t python/
```

This installs the requests library and its dependencies into the python directory. Your directory structure should now look like this:

```
my_layer/  └──────
  python/  └──────
     requests/  └──────
     <other dependency folders>
```

Step 3: Create the Lambda Layer ZIP File

Next, zip the contents of the my_layer directory. The ZIP file will serve as the deployment package for the Lambda Layer.

```
cd my_layer
zip -r my_layer.zip .
```

Step 4: Create the Layer in AWS Lambda

1. Navigate to the **AWS Lambda Console**.

2. On the left-hand side, click **Layers**.
3. Click **Create Layer**.
4. Enter a name for your layer (e.g., requests-layer).
5. Upload the my_layer.zip file.
6. Specify the compatible runtimes (e.g., Python 3.9).
7. Click **Create**.

Step 5: Attach the Layer to a Lambda Function

1. Go to your Lambda function in the **Lambda Console**.
2. In the **Layers** section, click **Add a layer**.
3. Select **Custom layers** and choose the layer you created (requests-layer).
4. Click **Add**.

Your Lambda function can now access all the dependencies included in the layer without needing to package them in the function's deployment package.

Step 6: Modify Your Lambda Function Code

You can now remove the dependencies from your Lambda function's deployment package since they are provided by the layer. In this example, the requests library will be available to the function via the layer:

```
import requests

def lambda_handler(event, context):
    response = requests.get("https://api.example.com/data")
    return {
        'statusCode': 200,
        'body': response.text
    }
```

Pros and Cons of Using Lambda Layers
  Pros:

• Allows you to reuse dependencies across multiple Lambda functions,

175

reducing redundancy.

- Helps keep Lambda function deployment packages smaller.
- Makes updating dependencies easier—simply update the layer rather than each function.

Cons:

- Lambda layers have a size limit of 250 MB (unzipped), which may be limiting for very large dependencies.
- If you update a layer, you must re-deploy all Lambda functions that depend on the updated layer.

4. Using Serverless Frameworks for Dependency Packaging

Frameworks like the **Serverless Framework** and **AWS SAM (Serverless Application Model)** can simplify the process of packaging and deploying Lambda functions with dependencies. These frameworks automatically handle dependency packaging and deployment, making it easier to manage serverless applications at scale.

Serverless Framework Example

The **Serverless Framework** automates the packaging and deployment process for Lambda functions. You define your function, its dependencies, and layers in a configuration file (serverless.yml), and the framework takes care of the rest.

Install the Serverless Framework:

```
npm install -g serverless
```

Initialize a new Serverless project:

```
serverless create --template aws-python --path my-service
cd my-service
```

Define your Lambda function and dependencies in the serverless.yml file:

```
service: my-service

provider:
  name: aws
  runtime: python3.9

functions:
  hello:
    handler: handler.lambda_handler

plugins:
  - serverless-python-requirements

custom:
  pythonRequirements:
    dockerizePip: true
```

Install your dependencies locally:

```
pip install requests -t .
```

Deploy the function with dependencies:

```
serverless deploy
```

This automatically packages your Python dependencies and uploads them to AWS Lambda.

5. Best Practices for Packaging Python Dependencies

1. Keep Deployment Packages Small

To reduce cold start times and improve function performance, it's best to keep your Lambda deployment package as small as possible. Use Lambda Layers or selectively package only the required dependencies to avoid bundling unnecessary libraries.

2. Use Lambda Layers for Reusability

If multiple Lambda functions require the same dependencies (e.g., requests, numpy), create a Lambda Layer to share those dependencies across functions. This reduces duplication and makes your serverless application easier to maintain.

3. Monitor Function Performance

Packaging large dependencies or layers can affect the performance of your Lambda function, particularly for cold starts. Use **Amazon CloudWatch** to monitor metrics like invocation duration and memory usage, and optimize the packaging of your code and dependencies accordingly.

4. Remove Unused Dependencies

Periodically review and clean up your Lambda function's dependencies to remove any libraries that are no longer used. This helps reduce the size of your deployment package and keeps your function efficient.

Packaging Python dependencies for AWS Lambda is an essential task when building serverless applications that rely on external libraries. Whether you package dependencies locally or use Lambda Layers, understanding the right method for your use case is critical for maintaining efficient, scalable Lambda functions. By following best practices such as keeping deployment packages small, using layers for reusable dependencies, and monitoring performance, you can ensure your serverless applications remain performant and cost-effective.

Using Lambda Layers for Reusable Code in AWS Lambda

AWS Lambda Layers provide a powerful mechanism for sharing and reusing code, libraries, and other dependencies across multiple Lambda functions without having to package them with each deployment. By separating common functionality and dependencies into layers, you can reduce duplication, simplify maintenance, and improve the performance of your Lambda applications.

In this section, we will explore how to effectively use Lambda Layers for reusable code, focusing on key concepts, best practices, and practical use cases for streamlining Lambda function development in Python.

1. What are AWS Lambda Layers?

AWS Lambda Layers are a feature that allows you to package and manage external dependencies, libraries, and reusable code separately from your Lambda function code. You can think of a Lambda Layer as an additional ZIP archive that contains supporting files such as Python libraries, utility functions, or shared configurations. Once created, Lambda Layers can be attached to any Lambda function, making the contents of the layer available to the function at runtime.

Each Lambda function can include up to **five layers**, which allows you to break down dependencies or code into modular components. Layers make it easier to:

- **Reuse common code** across multiple functions without duplicating it.
- **Reduce the size** of your Lambda deployment package, minimizing the impact on cold start times.
- **Easily update shared code** without redeploying individual Lambda functions.
- **Share code** across different projects or teams in your organization.

2. Common Use Cases for Lambda Layers

Lambda Layers are particularly useful for packaging and sharing:

- **Third-party libraries**: Dependencies such as requests, numpy, pandas, or machine learning frameworks.
- **Utility functions**: Common helper functions or utilities (e.g., logging, error handling, or custom authentication) that are used across multiple functions.
- **Configuration files**: Environment-specific configurations that are required by several Lambda functions (e.g., API keys, database connection strings).
- **Custom runtimes**: For Lambda functions that require a runtime not natively supported by AWS, such as a specific version of Python or a different programming language.

3. Steps for Creating and Using Lambda Layers

Let's walk through the process of creating a Lambda Layer in Python, adding reusable code or libraries to the layer, and then attaching the layer to Lambda functions.

Step 1: Creating a Lambda Layer with Reusable Code

Suppose you have a set of utility functions (e.g., logging and error handling) that you want to use in multiple Lambda functions. You can package these functions into a Lambda Layer.

Step 1.1: Prepare the Code for the Layer

First, create a directory for your Lambda Layer, which will hold the reusable Python code. Inside the directory, create a subdirectory named python, which is required for Lambda Layers.

```
mkdir my-layer
cd my-layer
mkdir python
```

Now, inside the python directory, create a Python module for your reusable utilities. For example, create a file called utils.py with some utility functions:

```
# python/utils.py

import logging

def setup_logger(log_level=logging.INFO):
    logger = logging.getLogger()
    logger.setLevel(log_level)
    return logger

def error_handler(func):
    def wrapper(*args, **kwargs):
        try:
            return func(*args, **kwargs)
        except Exception as e:
            logger = logging.getLogger()
            logger.error(f"An error occurred: {str(e)}")
            raise
    return wrapper
```

In this example, the setup_logger function configures logging for your Lambda function, while the error_handler decorator provides centralized error handling.

Step 1.2: Create a ZIP File for the Layer

To package the reusable code as a Lambda Layer, you need to ZIP the contents of the python directory. The ZIP file must follow this specific directory structure for Python layers:

```
cd my-layer
zip -r my-layer.zip .
```

This command creates a my-layer.zip file containing the python directory and the utils.py file within it.

Step 2: Create the Lambda Layer in AWS

Now that you've packaged the reusable code, you need to create the Lambda Layer in the AWS Management Console.

1. Navigate to the **AWS Lambda Console**.
2. In the left-hand menu, click **Layers**.
3. Click the **Create layer** button.
4. Enter a name for your layer (e.g., my-utils-layer).
5. Under **Upload a .zip file**, upload the my-layer.zip file.
6. Under **Compatible runtimes**, select the appropriate Python versions (e.g., Python 3.9).
7. Click **Create**.

Your Lambda Layer is now available and can be attached to any Lambda function.

Step 3: Attach the Layer to a Lambda Function

To use the Lambda Layer in one of your Lambda functions, follow these steps:

1. Go to your Lambda function in the **Lambda Console**.
2. In the **Layers** section, click **Add a layer**.
3. Select **Custom layers**, and choose the my-utils-layer you just created.
4. Click **Add**.

Your Lambda function now has access to the reusable code in the my-utils-layer.

Step 4: Modify the Lambda Function to Use the Layer

Once the layer is attached, you can import and use the utilities from the utils.py module in your Lambda function. For example:

```
from utils import setup_logger, error_handler

logger = setup_logger()

@error_handler
def lambda_handler(event, context):
    logger.info("Lambda function started")

    # Simulate processing
    result = 10 / 0  # This will trigger an error and be handled
    by the error handler

    return {
        'statusCode': 200,
        'body': 'Processing complete'
    }
```

In this Lambda function:

- The setup_logger function from the layer is used to configure logging.
- The error_handler decorator from the layer is applied to the lambda_handler function to handle any runtime errors.

4. Best Practices for Using Lambda Layers

To get the most out of Lambda Layers, follow these best practices:

1. Keep Layers Small and Focused

Layers should contain only the code or dependencies needed by multiple Lambda functions. Avoid bundling unrelated libraries or code into a single layer, as this can lead to unnecessary bloat and complexity. Instead, create multiple layers for different purposes (e.g., one layer for logging utilities, another for database access libraries).

2. Monitor the Layer Size

AWS Lambda Layers have a size limit of **250 MB (unzipped)**. Ensure that your layers stay well within this limit by packaging only the necessary code or libraries. For large dependencies like pandas or numpy, consider creating separate layers or using pre-built optimized layers provided by the community.

3. Version Your Layers

Each time you update a Lambda Layer, AWS creates a new version of the layer. This versioning allows you to deploy updates without breaking existing Lambda functions that rely on earlier versions of the layer.

- When creating a new layer version, test it thoroughly before attaching it to production functions.
- Attach specific layer versions to Lambda functions rather than using the latest version, so you can control when updates are applied.

4. Share Layers Across Teams and Accounts

If you work in an organization with multiple teams, consider sharing Lambda Layers across AWS accounts. You can do this by setting appropriate permissions for the layer, allowing other accounts to use it.

- Set permissions when creating the layer to share it across AWS accounts or with your organization.
- Ensure proper documentation for any shared layers so that other teams understand how to use them effectively.

5. Optimize Cold Starts with Layers

When using Lambda Layers, particularly with large dependencies, be mindful of cold start times. A cold start occurs when a Lambda function is invoked for the first time or after a period of inactivity, and Lambda needs to initialize the runtime environment. Large layers can increase cold start times, especially if they contain heavyweight libraries.

To mitigate cold starts:

- **Use only essential libraries** in your layers.
- **Keep layer sizes minimal** by stripping unnecessary files (e.g., documentation, tests).
- Consider **layer pre-warming strategies**, such as invoking your Lambda function periodically to keep the runtime environment active.

5. Updating and Managing Lambda Layers

When you need to update a Lambda Layer (e.g., to patch a security vulnerability or upgrade a library version), follow these steps:

Step 1: Update the Layer Code

Modify the code or dependencies in your python directory as needed. For example, you may update the utils.py file or install a new version of a dependency.

```
pip install requests==2.26.0 -t python/
```

Step 2: Create a New Layer Version

After updating the code, repackage the layer and create a new ZIP file:

```
zip -r my-layer-v2.zip .
```

Then, create a new version of the layer in the AWS Lambda Console:

1. Go to the **Layers** section of the Lambda Console.
2. Select your existing layer (my-utils-layer).
3. Click **Create version**.
4. Upload the updated ZIP file (my-layer-v2.zip).
5. Click **Create** to finalize the new version.

Step 3: Update Lambda Functions to Use the New Layer Version

You can now update your Lambda functions to use the new version of the layer:

1. Go to the Lambda function that uses the layer.
2. In the **Layers** section, click **Edit**.
3. Select the new version of the layer (e.g., Version 2).
4. Click **Save** to apply the changes.

This ensures that your Lambda functions are using the latest code or dependencies from the updated layer.

6. Real-World Use Cases for Lambda Layers

Here are some real-world examples of how Lambda Layers can be used in production applications:

1. Centralized Logging

Create a Lambda Layer that provides a centralized logging utility. This layer can be reused across multiple Lambda functions to ensure consistent logging formats and log levels, making it easier to monitor and troubleshoot distributed serverless applications.

2. Shared Database Access Code

If several Lambda functions interact with the same database (e.g., RDS or DynamoDB), you can create a Lambda Layer containing shared database connection code and query utilities. This approach reduces duplication and ensures that changes to the database logic are centralized in one place.

3. Machine Learning Inference Layer

For applications that perform machine learning inference, you can create a Lambda Layer containing pre-trained models and the necessary libraries (e.g., TensorFlow, PyTorch). This allows you to update models independently from the Lambda function code and use the same models across multiple functions.

4. Shared Authentication Logic

If your Lambda functions require authentication (e.g., validating JWT tokens), you can package the authentication logic into a Lambda Layer. This ensures that authentication checks are consistent across all functions and can be updated centrally.

AWS Lambda Layers provide an efficient and scalable way to reuse code, manage dependencies, and improve maintainability across multiple Lambda functions. By following best practices, such as versioning layers, minimizing layer size, and keeping code modular, you can create flexible serverless applications that are easier to manage and update. Whether you're sharing utility functions, external libraries, or custom runtimes, Lambda Layers are a powerful tool for enhancing the development and deployment of serverless applications.

Managing Dependencies with Docker for AWS Lambda

Using Docker to manage dependencies in AWS Lambda provides greater flexibility and control over the environment in which your Lambda function runs. While AWS Lambda's traditional runtime allows you to package code and dependencies into deployment packages or Lambda Layers, Docker allows you to create custom images that can include specific operating system configurations, language runtimes, and dependencies that are not easily achievable with Lambda's built-in environment.

In this section, we will explore how to use Docker for managing dependencies in AWS Lambda, the benefits of this approach, and how to build, deploy, and optimize Lambda functions with Docker images.

1. Why Use Docker for AWS Lambda?

AWS Lambda now supports **container images** as an alternative deployment method, allowing you to package and deploy your Lambda functions as Docker containers. Using Docker gives you the following benefits:

- **Custom Runtime and OS Packages**: You can include custom operating system packages, specific language versions, or other runtime dependencies that are not supported natively in AWS Lambda.

- **Better Dependency Management**: For complex applications with many dependencies, using Docker simplifies dependency management by allowing you to control the environment in which your Lambda runs.
- **Reuse of Existing Docker Infrastructure**: If you already use Docker in your development process, you can leverage your existing Docker files and images to deploy Lambda functions.

By using Docker, you package everything your Lambda function needs, including:

- The Python runtime and any specific version required.
- Operating system libraries or packages (e.g., if you need to use native binaries).
- Python dependencies and external libraries (e.g., requests, pandas, or machine learning libraries).

2. When to Use Docker for AWS Lambda

While the traditional Lambda runtime with deployment packages and layers is sufficient for many use cases, Docker is particularly beneficial when:

- **You need custom dependencies**: Your Lambda function requires system-level dependencies that are not included in the default AWS Lambda runtime (e.g., custom binaries or non-standard libraries).
- **You require full control of the runtime**: You want complete control over the Python version or configuration beyond the default AWS Lambda options.
- **You're managing complex dependencies**: Your function uses multiple dependencies that may cause package conflicts or require specific installation steps.
- **You want to standardize development environments**: Docker allows you to create consistent environments across development, testing, and production by packaging your Lambda function as a container image.

3. Building a Custom Docker Image for AWS Lambda

To deploy a Python Lambda function using Docker, you'll first need to build a Docker image that contains your Lambda function code and any dependencies required. AWS Lambda provides a base image that you can use as a starting point for building custom images.

Step 1: Set Up a Dockerfile

The **Dockerfile** defines the environment in which your Lambda function will run. You can start by using one of AWS's official **Lambda base images** for Python. Here's how to set up a simple Dockerfile for a Lambda function using Python 3.9:

```
# Use the official AWS Lambda Python 3.9 base image
FROM public.ecr.aws/lambda/python:3.9

# Copy the function code and any dependencies to the container
image
COPY app/ ${LAMBDA_TASK_ROOT}

# Install any dependencies defined in the requirements.txt file
RUN pip install -r ${LAMBDA_TASK_ROOT}/requirements.txt

# Specify the handler for AWS Lambda (app.lambda_handler)
CMD ["app.lambda_handler"]
```

Let's break this down:

- **Base Image**: We start with AWS's official **Lambda Python 3.9 base image** (public.ecr.aws/lambda/python:3.9). This base image includes the Lambda runtime API for Python, allowing your container to work with AWS Lambda.
- **COPY Command**: The COPY command copies your Lambda function code from the app/ directory on your local machine into the container's working directory (${LAMBDA_TASK_ROOT}).

189

- **RUN Command**: The RUN pip install command installs the Python dependencies listed in the requirements.txt file. This ensures that all required libraries are available inside the container.
- **CMD Command**: The CMD instruction specifies the Lambda handler (app.lambda_handler) to be invoked when the function is triggered. The handler function should be defined in the app.py file.

Step 2: Create Your Lambda Function Code

Next, create the **app.py** file that contains your Lambda function and the **requirements.txt** file that lists your Python dependencies.

app.py:

```python
import requests

def lambda_handler(event, context):
    response = requests.get("https://api.example.com/data")
    return {
        'statusCode': 200,
        'body': response.text
    }
```

requirements.txt:

```
requests
```

In this example:

- The lambda_handler function uses the requests library to fetch data from an external API.
- The requirements.txt file specifies that the requests library needs to be installed in the container.

Step 3: Build the Docker Image

Now that you have the Dockerfile, app.py, and requirements.txt in place, you can build the Docker image.

1. Navigate to the directory containing the Dockerfile.
2. Build the Docker image by running the following command:

```
docker build -t my-lambda-function .
```

This command will create a Docker image tagged as my-lambda-function, based on the instructions in the Dockerfile.

Step 4: Test the Docker Image Locally

Before deploying the Docker image to AWS Lambda, you can test it locally using Docker. AWS provides a Lambda runtime interface emulator (RIE) that can simulate Lambda invocations locally.

To run the Lambda function locally, use the following command:

```
docker run -p 9000:8080 my-lambda-function
```

This command starts a local instance of the Lambda container. You can then invoke the function by sending a request to http://localhost:9000/2015-03-31/functions/function/invocations:

```
curl -XPOST
"http://localhost:9000/2015-03-31/functions/function/invocations"
-d '{}'
```

This will invoke the Lambda function, and the response will be printed to the terminal.

Step 5: Push the Docker Image to Amazon ECR

To deploy your Docker image to AWS Lambda, you need to store it in **Amazon Elastic Container Registry (ECR)**, which is a fully managed container registry provided by AWS.

Log in to ECR using the AWS CLI:

191

```
aws ecr get-login-password --region <your-region> | docker login
--username AWS --password-stdin
<aws-account-id>.dkr.ecr.<your-region>.amazonaws.com
```

Create a new ECR repository:

```
aws ecr create-repository --repository-name my-lambda-function
```

Tag the Docker image with the repository URL:

```
docker tag my-lambda-function:latest
<aws-account-id>.dkr.
ecr.<your-region>.
amazonaws.com/my-lambda
-function:latest
```

Push the Docker image to the ECR repository:

```
docker push <aws-account-id>.
dkr.ecr.<your-region>.
amazonaws.com/my-
lambda-function:latest
```

The Docker image is now stored in ECR and ready to be deployed as a Lambda function.

Step 6: Deploy the Docker Image to AWS Lambda

Once the Docker image is in ECR, you can create a new Lambda function that uses this image:

1. Navigate to the **AWS Lambda Console**.
2. Click **Create Function**.
3. Select **Container image** as the function's package type.
4. Choose the image from **Amazon ECR**.
5. Configure the function's settings (e.g., memory, timeout, etc.), and click

Create.

Your Lambda function is now deployed using the Docker container image.

4. Best Practices for Using Docker with AWS Lambda

1. Keep Docker Images Small

Minimize the size of your Docker image by including only the necessary dependencies and using lightweight base images. Large images increase deployment times and cold start latency.

- Use **multistage builds** in your Dockerfile to separate the build environment from the runtime environment.
- Exclude unnecessary files and directories (e.g., .git, documentation) from the image by using .dockerignore.

2. Leverage Base Images from AWS

Use the official AWS Lambda base images for Python to ensure compatibility with Lambda's execution environment. These base images are optimized for Lambda's event-driven model and include the Lambda runtime API.

- Base images are available for multiple runtimes (e.g., Python, Node.js, Java) and can be customized further to fit your needs.

3. Test Locally Before Deployment

Testing your Lambda function locally using Docker's runtime interface emulator (RIE) helps you identify and fix issues early, before deploying the function to AWS. This is especially useful for functions with complex dependencies or custom configurations.

- Make sure to test Lambda functions with real-world events and configurations that mirror your production environment.

4. Automate Builds and Deployments with CI/CD

Integrate Docker builds and Lambda deployments into your **CI/CD pipeline** to automate testing, image builds, and deployments. AWS Code-Pipeline, CodeBuild, or third-party tools like Jenkins or GitHub Actions can be used to manage continuous deployment workflows.

5. Monitor Lambda Performance

Even when using Docker, monitor your Lambda function's performance metrics (e.g., cold start time, memory usage) using **Amazon CloudWatch**. Analyze logs to identify any bottlenecks caused by large images or inefficient configurations, and optimize accordingly.

5. Managing Versioning and Updates with Docker

Managing versions of Lambda functions deployed as Docker containers is straightforward because Docker images are inherently versioned via tags. To update a function:

- Build a new version of your Docker image.
- Tag it with a new version number (e.g., my-lambda-function:v2).
- Push the new image to ECR.
- Update the Lambda function to use the new image.

This versioning system ensures that you can roll back to a previous version easily if something goes wrong with the new deployment.

Using Docker to manage dependencies for AWS Lambda gives you more control over the runtime environment, allowing you to handle complex dependencies, use custom binaries, or manage libraries that are not natively supported by Lambda's built-in environment. By following best practices, such as keeping images small, testing locally, and leveraging CI/CD pipelines, you can ensure efficient, scalable, and flexible serverless applications with Lambda. Docker's ability to encapsulate dependencies and configurations within a containerized environment makes it an invaluable tool for advanced serverless architecture and development.

Project 1: Serverless REST API with AWS Lambda

Integrating AWS Lambda with API Gateway
Building a serverless REST API with AWS Lambda and **Amazon API Gateway** is a common use case in modern serverless architectures. API Gateway serves as the front door for your API, handling HTTP requests and routing them to your Lambda functions. This setup allows you to build scalable, secure, and cost-effective APIs without having to manage the underlying infrastructure.

In this section, we'll cover how to integrate AWS Lambda with API Gateway, including setting up the API Gateway, configuring routes and methods, securing the API, and testing the integration. By the end, you will have a fully functional serverless API that can handle client requests and execute business logic in Lambda.

1. What is Amazon API Gateway?

Amazon API Gateway is a fully managed service that allows you to create, publish, maintain, monitor, and secure REST, HTTP, and WebSocket APIs. It acts as a gateway between your API clients and your backend services (such as AWS Lambda, EC2, or external services).

Key features of API Gateway include:

- **Scalability**: Automatically handles scaling based on traffic demand.

- **Security**: Supports authorization mechanisms like API keys, IAM roles, and AWS Cognito.
- **Monitoring**: Provides detailed logs and metrics via CloudWatch.
- **Integration**: Seamlessly integrates with AWS Lambda, enabling you to trigger Lambda functions in response to HTTP requests.

In a typical architecture, API Gateway receives incoming HTTP requests, maps those requests to the corresponding AWS Lambda function, and routes the response back to the client.

2. Steps for Integrating AWS Lambda with API Gateway

The following steps will guide you through setting up API Gateway to route HTTP requests to AWS Lambda functions, building a serverless REST API that processes client requests.

Step 1: Create a Lambda Function

Before configuring API Gateway, you need a Lambda function that will serve as the backend for your API. This function will contain the business logic and respond to API requests.

Example Lambda Function Code (API to manage a list of items):

```
import json

def lambda_handler(event, context):
    # Extract the HTTP method and the request body (if any)
    method = event['httpMethod']
    body = json.loads(event['body']) if event['body'] else None

    # Define some example data (in a real app, you would interact
    with a database)
    items = [
        {'id': 1, 'name': 'Item 1'},
        {'id': 2, 'name': 'Item 2'}
    ]
```

```
if method == 'GET':
    # Return the list of items
    return {
        'statusCode': 200,
        'body': json.dumps(items)
    }
elif method == 'POST' and body:
    # Add a new item (mock logic for this example)
    new_item = {'id': len(items) + 1, 'name': body['name']}
    items.append(new_item)
    return {
        'statusCode': 201,
        'body': json.dumps(new_item)
    }
else:
    return {
        'statusCode': 405,
        'body': json.dumps({'message': 'Method not allowed'})
    }
```

In this function:

- We handle both **GET** and **POST** HTTP methods.
- For **GET** requests, we return a list of items (in a real application, this data could come from a database like DynamoDB).
- For **POST** requests, we add a new item based on the incoming request body.

Deploy the Lambda Function:

1. Navigate to the **AWS Lambda Console**.
2. Click **Create function**.
3. Choose **Author from scratch** and provide a name (e.g., ItemManagem entFunction).
4. Select **Python 3.9** as the runtime and click **Create**.
5. Paste the function code into the code editor.

6. Click **Deploy**.

Step 2: Create an API in API Gateway

Now that we have a Lambda function, the next step is to create an API in **Amazon API Gateway** that will route HTTP requests to this function.

Navigate to the API Gateway Console:

- Go to the **Amazon API Gateway Console**.
- Click **Create API**.

Choose the API Type:

- Select **HTTP API** (simpler and lower-latency than REST API for most use cases).
- Click **Build**.

Configure API Settings:

- Provide a name for the API (e.g., ItemManagementAPI).
- For **API endpoint**, leave it as default (Regional).
- Click **Next**.

Set Up Routes:

- Define routes (HTTP methods and paths) that map to your Lambda function.

Example: Add routes for **GET** and **POST** methods on the /items path.

- Click **Add integration** to integrate the routes with your Lambda function.
- Choose **Lambda Function** as the integration type.
- Enter the name of your Lambda function (e.g., ItemManagementFunctio

n).

Deploy the API:

- Review your routes and integrations, then click **Next**.
- Click **Create** to deploy the API.

API Gateway will generate an **invoke URL** for the API. You can use this URL to make HTTP requests to your API.

Step 3: Test the API Gateway and Lambda Integration

Once the API is deployed, you can test the API using tools like **Postman** or **cURL**.

- **GET Request** to retrieve items:

```
curl -X GET
https://<api-id>.execute-api.<region>.amazonaws.com/items
```

- **POST Request** to add a new item:

```
curl -X POST
https://<api-id>.execute-api.<region>.amazonaws.com/items \
-H "Content-Type: application/json" \
-d '{"name": "New Item"}'
```

You should see responses from your Lambda function for both the GET and POST requests. API Gateway acts as the front-end, handling HTTP requests and invoking the Lambda function to process them.

Step 4: Enable CORS (Cross-Origin Resource Sharing)

If your API will be accessed by browsers from different origins (domains), you need to enable **CORS** to allow cross-origin requests. CORS is a security feature enforced by browsers.

To enable CORS for your API Gateway routes:

1. In the API Gateway Console, go to your API.
2. Select a route (e.g., /items).
3. Click on **Configure CORS**.
4. Enable CORS for the required HTTP methods (e.g., GET, POST).
5. Click **Save**.

Step 5: Securing Your API with Authorization

API Gateway provides several ways to secure your API, including **API keys**, **IAM roles**, and **Cognito User Pools** for authentication and authorization. Here's a brief overview of the most common methods:

- **IAM Roles**: Use **IAM permissions** to restrict access to the API. This is suitable for internal or server-to-server APIs.
- **Cognito User Pools**: Integrate with **Amazon Cognito** to authenticate and authorize users using standard OAuth 2.0 tokens.
- **API Keys**: Require clients to include an API key with their requests. API keys are useful for controlling access to public APIs.

Example: Securing the API with Cognito User Pools

1. In the API Gateway Console, select your API.
2. In the **Authorization** section, choose **Cognito User Pool**.
3. Select an existing **Cognito User Pool** or create a new one for user authentication.
4. Apply the authorization settings to the necessary routes (e.g., /items).

Once enabled, only authenticated users can access the API endpoints, ensuring that your API is secure.

3. Handling Errors and Responses

When building a serverless REST API, it's essential to handle errors and return meaningful HTTP responses. API Gateway allows you to configure both integration responses (from the Lambda function) and gateway responses (from API Gateway itself).

- **Lambda Integration Responses**: Your Lambda function should return appropriate HTTP status codes based on the request outcome. For example:
- 200 OK for successful operations.
- 201 Created for resource creation.
- 400 Bad Request for invalid input.
- 404 Not Found if a resource does not exist.

Example of a Response Object in Lambda:

```
return {
    'statusCode': 200,
    'body': json.dumps({'message': 'Item retrieved successfully'})
}
```

- **API Gateway Gateway Responses**: API Gateway itself can also generate responses, such as for missing API keys, unauthorized access, or throttling.

To customize these responses:

1. In the API Gateway Console, go to **Gateway Responses**.
2. Select the response you want to customize (e.g., Unauthorized or Throttled).
3. Edit the response message to provide a more user-friendly error message.

4. Monitoring and Logging with CloudWatch

Monitoring your API and Lambda functions is crucial for understanding their performance and identifying issues. AWS provides several tools, such as **Amazon CloudWatch** and **X-Ray**, to monitor and trace requests in real-time.

Enable CloudWatch Logs for API Gateway

To enable logging for your API Gateway:

1. In the API Gateway Console, go to your API.
2. Navigate to **Stages** and select the deployed stage (e.g., prod).
3. In the **Logs/Tracing** section, enable **CloudWatch Logs**.
4. Optionally, enable **AWS X-Ray** for distributed tracing.

This will log all incoming requests, responses, and errors in **CloudWatch Logs**, allowing you to analyze API usage and troubleshoot issues.

Monitor Lambda Function Metrics

In the **AWS Lambda Console**, you can view detailed metrics for your Lambda functions, such as:

- **Invocations**: The number of times your function was triggered.
- **Duration**: How long each invocation took.
- **Errors**: The number of failed invocations.
- **Throttles**: The number of requests throttled due to concurrency limits.

You can also set up **CloudWatch Alarms** to be notified when certain thresholds are reached (e.g., a high error rate).

5. Scaling and Optimizing the API

One of the main benefits of using AWS Lambda and API Gateway is automatic scalability. Both services scale automatically based on the volume of incoming traffic, allowing your API to handle sudden spikes without manual intervention.

However, to optimize performance and minimize costs, consider the following:

- **Optimize Lambda Function Memory and Timeout**: Adjust the memory allocation and timeout settings of your Lambda function to match your API's workload. Over-provisioning memory can increase costs, while under-provisioning can slow down execution.
- **Enable Caching in API Gateway**: API Gateway allows you to enable caching for specific routes. By caching responses, you can reduce the number of times your Lambda function is invoked, improving performance and reducing costs.

To enable caching:

1. In the API Gateway Console, go to your API.
2. Navigate to **Stages**, select the stage, and go to **Cache Settings**.
3. Enable **Caching** for routes that return frequently requested data.

Integrating AWS Lambda with API Gateway is a powerful way to build a serverless REST API that is scalable, secure, and cost-effective. By using API Gateway to route HTTP requests to Lambda functions, you can build a wide range of APIs, from simple CRUD services to complex microservice architectures. Additionally, API Gateway provides features like security, monitoring, and caching, making it an essential tool for building production-grade serverless applications.

By following best practices for error handling, security, and performance monitoring, you can ensure that your serverless API is robust, scalable, and reliable for your users or clients.

Handling HTTP Requests with Python in AWS Lambda

When integrating AWS Lambda with Amazon API Gateway to build a serverless REST API, it's crucial to handle incoming HTTP requests correctly in Python. API Gateway sends incoming HTTP requests to Lambda functions as structured events, and your Lambda function needs to parse the request, process the data, and return appropriate HTTP responses.

In this section, we'll cover how to handle HTTP requests in Python for AWS Lambda, including reading the HTTP method, extracting request parameters and body content, and responding with proper status codes and payloads.

1. Understanding the API Gateway Request Event Format

When API Gateway triggers an AWS Lambda function, it sends an **event** to the Lambda function in JSON format. This event contains details about the incoming HTTP request, such as the HTTP method, request headers, path parameters, query string parameters, and the request body.

Here's an example of what the event object from API Gateway looks like:

```json
{
  "resource": "/items",
  "path": "/items",
  "httpMethod": "POST",
  "headers": {
    "Content-Type": "application/json"
  },
  "queryStringParameters": {
    "category": "electronics"
  },
  "pathParameters": {
    "id": "123"
  },
  "body": "{\"name\": \"New Item\"}",
  "isBase64Encoded": false
}
```

Key components of this event object:

- **httpMethod**: The HTTP method (e.g., GET, POST, PUT, DELETE) of the request.
- **path**: The requested resource path (e.g., /items).
- **headers**: Any headers sent with the HTTP request (e.g., Content-Type, Authorization).
- **queryStringParameters**: Query parameters included in the URL (e.g., ?category=electronics).
- **pathParameters**: Path parameters (e.g., /items/123 where 123 is the path parameter).
- **body**: The body of the request, typically used in POST and PUT methods. It is often a JSON string that must be parsed.

2. Handling HTTP Methods

The first step in handling HTTP requests is identifying the **HTTP method** being used. Your Lambda function should behave differently depending on whether the request is a GET, POST, PUT, or DELETE request.

Here's how to extract the HTTP method from the event object:

```python
def lambda_handler(event, context):
    method = event['httpMethod']

    if method == 'GET':
        return handle_get(event)
    elif method == 'POST':
        return handle_post(event)
    elif method == 'PUT':
        return handle_put(event)
    elif method == 'DELETE':
        return handle_delete(event)
    else:
        return {
            'statusCode': 405,
```

```
        'body': json.dumps({'message': 'Method Not Allowed'})
    }
```

In this example:

- The httpMethod from the event object is used to determine the HTTP method.
- Each HTTP method is handled by a different function (handle_get, handle_post, etc.).
- If the request method is not supported, we return a 405 Method Not Allowed response.

3. Extracting Request Parameters and Body

API Gateway allows clients to pass data in several ways:

- **Path parameters**: Typically used for resource identifiers (e.g., /items/{id}).
- **Query string parameters**: Used for filtering or modifying the behavior of requests (e.g., ?category=electronics).
- **Request body**: Used for sending data with POST, PUT, or PATCH requests.

Path Parameters

Path parameters are extracted from the **pathParameters** section of the event object. For example, if your API route is /items/{id}, the id value is a path parameter.

Here's how to extract path parameters:

```
def handle_get(event):
    item_id = event['pathParameters'].get('id')  # Extracting the
    'id' from the path
    return {
```

```
        'statusCode': 200,
        'body': json.dumps({'message': f'Retrieved item with ID
        {item_id}'})
    }
```

Query String Parameters

Query string parameters are passed in the URL and can be extracted from the **queryStringParameters** field of the event.

Here's an example:

```
def handle_get(event):
    # Extract query parameters (e.g., ?category=electronics)
    category = event['queryStringParameters'].get('category',
    'all')  # Default to 'all' if not provided
    return {
        'statusCode': 200,
        'body': json.dumps({'message': f'Retrieved items in
        category: {category}'})
    }
```

Request Body

For POST, PUT, or PATCH requests, the request body contains data, typically in JSON format. To handle the request body, you need to:

1. Check if the body exists.
2. Parse the body (from a string into a Python dictionary).

Here's how to handle the request body in Python:

```
import json

def handle_post(event):
    # Check if the body exists and decode it
    body = event.get('body')
    if body:
```

```
        body_data = json.loads(body)  # Parse the JSON string
        item_name = body_data.get('name')
        return {
            'statusCode': 201,
            'body': json.dumps({'message': f'Created item:
            {item_name}'})
        }
    else:
        return {
            'statusCode': 400,
            'body': json.dumps({'message': 'Invalid request body'})
        }
```

4. Constructing HTTP Responses

After processing the request, your Lambda function needs to return a response in a format that API Gateway understands. The response should contain:

- **statusCode**: The HTTP status code (e.g., 200 OK, 404 Not Found, 500 Internal Server Error).
- **body**: The response body, typically as a JSON string.
- **headers** (optional): Any custom headers you want to include (e.g., Content-Type, Access-Control-Allow-Origin).

Here's an example of a typical HTTP response:

```
def lambda_handler(event, context):
    response = {
        'statusCode': 200,  # HTTP OK
        'body': json.dumps({'message': 'Request processed
        successfully'}),
        'headers': {
            'Content-Type': 'application/json',
```

```
                'Access-Control-Allow-Origin': '*'
            }
        }
    return response
```

In this response:

- The statusCode indicates the outcome of the request (e.g., 200 for success).
- The body contains a JSON-encoded message that will be returned to the client.
- The headers field includes common headers, such as Content-Type and CORS headers.

Returning Error Responses

In addition to successful responses, it's important to return meaningful error messages when something goes wrong. Common HTTP status codes include:

- 400 Bad Request: The client sent an invalid request.
- 404 Not Found: The requested resource does not exist.
- 500 Internal Server Error: A server-side error occurred.

Here's how to return an error response:

```
def lambda_handler(event, context):
    try:
        # Simulate some processing
        if not event['body']:
            raise ValueError('Missing request body')

        return {
            'statusCode': 200,
            'body': json.dumps({'message': 'Success'}),
            'headers': {
```

```
                    'Content-Type': 'application/json'
                }
            }
    except ValueError as e:
        return {
            'statusCode': 400,  # Bad Request
            'body': json.dumps({'message': str(e)}),
            'headers': {
                'Content-Type': 'application/json'
            }
        }
    except Exception as e:
        return {
            'statusCode': 500,  # Internal Server Error
            'body': json.dumps({'message': 'An error occurred',
            'details': str(e)}),
            'headers': {
                'Content-Type': 'application/json'
            }
        }
```

This ensures that clients receive clear feedback if there are issues with their request or if an unexpected error occurs on the server side.

5. Handling CORS in Responses

If your API will be accessed by a browser (especially from a different domain), you must ensure that **Cross-Origin Resource Sharing (CORS)** is enabled. Without CORS, browsers will block cross-origin requests, preventing access to your API.

To handle CORS, you need to include the Access-Control-Allow-Origin header in your Lambda function's response. You can enable CORS for specific methods or globally in API Gateway.

Example of adding CORS headers in a response:

```
def lambda_handler(event, context):
    return {
        'statusCode': 200,
        'body': json.dumps({'message': 'Request successful'}),
        'headers': {
            'Content-Type': 'application/json',
            'Access-Control-Allow-Origin': '*'  # Allow all origins
        }
    }
```

In this example:

- The Access-Control-Allow-Origin header allows any origin (*) to access the API. You can restrict this to specific origins if needed.

6. Validating Input and Query Parameters

When handling HTTP requests, it's crucial to validate the incoming data to prevent issues such as malformed requests, missing parameters, or invalid data types. For example, if your API expects an integer id in the path or a name field in the request body, you should validate these inputs before proceeding.

Here's how to validate inputs in Python:

```
def handle_post(event):
    # Parse the request body
    body = json.loads(event['body']) if event['body'] else {}

    # Validate the 'name' field
    if 'name' not in body:
        return {
            'statusCode': 400,
            'body': json.dumps({'message': 'Missing required
            field: name'})
        }
```

```
# Proceed with processing if the validation passes
item_name = body['name']
return {
    'statusCode': 201,
    'body': json.dumps({'message': f'Created item:
    {item_name}'})
}
```

In this example, if the name field is missing from the request body, the Lambda function responds with a 400 Bad Request error.

Handling HTTP requests in AWS Lambda using Python requires you to correctly interpret the event object sent by API Gateway, process the HTTP method, extract and validate parameters, and return structured responses. By following these best practices and using the built-in mechanisms for handling HTTP requests, you can build robust serverless APIs that handle a wide range of client interactions efficiently and securely.

With Lambda's flexibility and API Gateway's seamless integration, you can build highly scalable APIs that serve different business logic requirements while maintaining minimal infrastructure overhead.

Securing Your API with IAM Roles and Authorizers

When building a serverless API with AWS Lambda and API Gateway, securing the API is critical to ensure that only authorized clients can access your resources. AWS provides multiple ways to secure API Gateway endpoints, with **IAM roles** and **Lambda authorizers** being two powerful options.

In this section, we'll explore how to secure your API by using **IAM roles** and **Lambda authorizers**. We will discuss when and how to use these methods, along with practical examples and best practices for securing your serverless REST API.

213

1. IAM Roles for API Gateway

AWS Identity and Access Management (IAM) roles allow you to control access to API Gateway and AWS Lambda at a fine-grained level. By assigning IAM roles to users, groups, or AWS services, you can define what actions they are allowed to perform on specific AWS resources.

Using **IAM permissions** is an ideal solution for server-to-server communication, where the API clients are other AWS services, EC2 instances, or Lambda functions. When an AWS resource (e.g., EC2 instance) makes a request to API Gateway, you can use IAM roles to restrict which API endpoints can be accessed.

Step 1: Create an IAM Role for API Gateway Access

To secure an API with IAM, first, you need to create a role or attach permissions to an existing role to grant access to the API Gateway.

Go to the IAM Console:

- Navigate to the **IAM Console** and click **Roles**.

Create a New Role:

- Click **Create role**.
- Select **AWS service** as the trusted entity, and choose **Lambda** or any other AWS service that needs to access the API.

1. **Attach Policies**:

- Select or create an IAM policy that allows invoking the API Gateway.
- An example of a policy that allows invoking an API Gateway:

```
{
  "Version": "2012-10-17",
```

```
"Statement": [
  {
    "Effect": "Allow",
    "Action": "execute-api:Invoke",
    "Resource":
    "arn:aws:execute-api:<region>:<account-id>:<api-id>/*"
  }
]
}
```

Replace <region>, <account-id>, and <api-id> with your API Gateway's details.

Assign the Role to Your AWS Service:

- Assign this IAM role to the AWS service (e.g., Lambda, EC2) that will be invoking the API. The service can now use this role to securely access the API Gateway.

Step 2: Require IAM Authentication for API Requests

To enforce IAM authentication for your API Gateway endpoints, you need to configure the **Authorization** setting in API Gateway.

Navigate to API Gateway:

- Open the **API Gateway Console** and select your API.

Enable IAM Authorization for Methods:

- For each method (e.g., GET, POST), select **Method Request**.
- Under **Authorization**, choose **AWS_IAM**.

Deploy the API:

- After configuring the authorization settings, deploy the API to apply the changes.

Now, any requests made to the API must be signed with IAM credentials. This is done using **AWS Signature Version 4**, which securely signs each request with IAM credentials (e.g., access keys).

Step 3: Making IAM-Signed Requests

To call the secured API, clients must sign their requests using IAM credentials. Here's how to sign requests using the **AWS SDK** or **AWS CLI**.

Example with AWS SDK (Python - Boto3)

```python
import boto3
import requests
from botocore.auth import SigV4Auth
from botocore.awsrequest import AWSRequest
from botocore.credentials import get_credentials
from botocore.session import get_session

# Create a signed request using IAM credentials
def sign_request(url, region, service):
    credentials = get_credentials()
    session = get_session()

    request = AWSRequest(method='GET', url=url)
    SigV4Auth(credentials, service, region).add_auth(request)

    response = requests.get(url, headers=request.headers)
    return response

url = 
'https://<api-id>.execute-api.<region>.amazonaws.com/prod/items'
response = sign_request(url, '<region>', 'execute-api')
print(response.text)
```

This example signs the request using AWS Signature Version 4, allowing access to the API secured with IAM roles.

2. Securing API Gateway with Lambda Authorizers

In addition to IAM roles, API Gateway provides **Lambda Authorizers** (formerly known as custom authorizers), which give you more flexibility for securing APIs, especially when dealing with token-based authentication such as OAuth, JWT, or custom tokens.

A **Lambda authorizer** is a custom Lambda function that API Gateway calls to authenticate or authorize requests. The Lambda function evaluates the request and determines whether to allow or deny access based on custom logic, such as verifying a JWT or querying a database for permissions.

Lambda authorizers are useful in scenarios where:

- You're using **JWT tokens** (e.g., from Amazon Cognito or an external identity provider).
- You need to implement **custom authentication logic**.
- You want to validate **API keys, OAuth tokens**, or other tokens dynamically.

Step 1: Create the Lambda Authorizer Function

A Lambda authorizer function examines the request (e.g., headers, tokens) and returns an IAM policy that grants or denies access to the API endpoint.

Here's an example of a Lambda authorizer function that validates a JWT token:

```
import json
import jwt  # Install the PyJWT library

def lambda_handler(event, context):
    token = event['authorizationToken']
    method_arn = event['methodArn']

    try:
        # Decode the JWT token (use your secret or public key for
        validation)
```

217

```
        decoded = jwt.decode(token, 'your-secret-key',
        algorithms=['HS256'])

        # If token is valid, return an IAM policy that allows
        access
        return generate_policy('user', 'Allow', method_arn)
    except jwt.ExpiredSignatureError:
        return generate_policy('user', 'Deny', method_arn)
    except jwt.InvalidTokenError:
        return generate_policy('user', 'Deny', method_arn)


def generate_policy(principal_id, effect, resource):
    # Generate an IAM policy for the authorizer
    auth_response = {
        'principalId': principal_id,
        'policyDocument': {
            'Version': '2012-10-17',
            'Statement': [
                {
                    'Action': 'execute-api:Invoke',
                    'Effect': effect,
                    'Resource': resource
                }
            ]
        }
    }
    return auth_response
```

This function decodes and validates a JWT token. If the token is valid, it generates an IAM policy that allows access to the API. If the token is invalid, it denies access.

Step 2: Configure the Authorizer in API Gateway
Create a Lambda Authorizer:

- In the **API Gateway Console**, select your API.
- Go to the **Authorizers** section and click **Create New Authorizer**.
- Enter a name for the authorizer (e.g., JWTAuthorizer).
- Select **Lambda** as the authorizer type, and choose the Lambda function

218

you created (JWTAuthorizerFunction).

- Set the **Token Source** to Authorization (this specifies which header contains the token).

Apply the Authorizer to API Methods:

- For each method (e.g., GET, POST) that requires authorization, select **Method Request**.
- Under **Authorization**, choose your custom Lambda authorizer (JWTAuthorizer).

Deploy the API:

- Deploy the API to apply the changes.

Now, the Lambda authorizer will be invoked before API Gateway routes requests to the Lambda backend. If the authorizer allows the request (e.g., valid JWT), the API will proceed. If it denies the request (e.g., invalid token), API Gateway will return a 403 Forbidden response.

Step 3: Testing the Secured API

To test the secured API, you can use **cURL** or **Postman** to make an HTTP request with a valid JWT token:

```
curl -X GET
https://<api-id>.execute-api.<region>.amazonaws.com/prod/items \
-H "Authorization: <JWT_TOKEN>"
```

If the JWT is valid, the API Gateway will forward the request to your backend Lambda function. If the token is invalid or missing, API Gateway will return a 403 Forbidden response.

3. Best Practices for Securing Your API

1. Use IAM for Server-to-Server Authentication

For internal services or AWS resources communicating with your API, using **IAM roles** and **AWS Signature Version 4** is the most secure and scalable method. This approach ensures that API requests are signed and authenticated with AWS credentials.

2. Use Lambda Authorizers for Custom Authentication

When dealing with **token-based authentication** (such as OAuth or JWT), Lambda Authorizers provide flexibility to enforce custom authorization logic. They are ideal for public APIs that use third-party authentication providers or need custom security policies.

3. Implement API Throttling and Rate Limiting

To prevent abuse or overuse of your API, implement throttling and rate-limiting policies using **API Gateway Stages**. You can configure the maximum number of requests allowed per second and set burst limits to protect your API from excessive traffic.

4. Use HTTPS and API Gateway Custom Domain Names

Ensure all traffic to your API is encrypted by enforcing **HTTPS** for all endpoints. You can also configure **Custom Domain Names** in API Gateway to provide a branded, secure API endpoint for your users.

5. Monitor API Access and Errors

Use **CloudWatch Logs** and **AWS X-Ray** to monitor API access, identify errors, and track unauthorized attempts. This helps you detect potential security breaches and troubleshoot issues in real-time.

Securing your API with **IAM roles** and **Lambda authorizers** is essential for building robust, scalable, and secure serverless applications on AWS. IAM roles provide strong authentication and authorization for AWS resources, while Lambda authorizers offer flexibility in handling custom authentication logic. By following best practices for securing API Gateway, you can ensure that your serverless API remains protected against unauthorized access and abuse while providing a seamless experience for authorized clients.

Best Practices for Designing Scalable APIs with AWS Lambda and API Gateway

Designing scalable APIs is crucial for handling varying levels of demand and ensuring that your applications remain responsive and cost-effective. With AWS Lambda and API Gateway, you can create serverless APIs that automatically scale based on incoming traffic without needing to manage the underlying infrastructure. However, achieving optimal scalability requires implementing several key best practices.

In this section, we'll explore best practices for designing scalable APIs using AWS Lambda and API Gateway. These practices include optimizing Lambda performance, managing API Gateway configurations, handling asynchronous operations, and improving overall reliability.

1. Optimize Lambda Function Performance

The performance of your Lambda functions directly affects the responsiveness and scalability of your API. Here are some key strategies to optimize Lambda function performance:

1.1. Right-Size Memory and Timeout Settings

AWS Lambda allows you to configure the memory allocation for each function, ranging from 128 MB to 10 GB. The amount of memory allocated also influences CPU power. To optimize performance:

- **Start with a baseline** memory allocation and monitor execution times.
- Gradually **increase memory** to identify the optimal point where additional memory doesn't yield significant performance improvements.
- **Set appropriate timeout values** to avoid unnecessary billing for long-running functions.

1.2. Minimize Cold Starts

Cold starts occur when a Lambda function is invoked after being idle for a period. This involves initializing the runtime environment, which can cause a delay in execution. To minimize cold starts:

- **Keep deployment packages small** by excluding unnecessary files or using Lambda Layers for common dependencies.
- **Use Provisioned Concurrency** for critical functions that require predictable latency. This keeps a certain number of Lambda instances warm and ready to handle traffic.

1.3. Efficiently Handle Dependencies

Loading large dependencies or performing heavy initialization during each invocation can impact performance. Use these strategies:

- **Use Lambda Layers** to package shared dependencies separately from function code.
- **Lazy-load dependencies** within the handler function to delay initialization until required.

2. Design Efficient API Gateway Configurations

API Gateway serves as the entry point for your serverless API, and its configuration plays a significant role in ensuring scalability. Here are some best practices for configuring API Gateway:

2.1. Use REST API vs. HTTP API Appropriately

REST APIs and **HTTP APIs** are two main types of APIs supported by API Gateway. Choose the one that best fits your requirements:

- **Use HTTP API** for most scenarios due to its lower latency and cost, especially for simple use cases like invoking Lambda functions.
- **Use REST API** when you need advanced features such as request transformations, custom authorizers, or API Gateway's integrated response

capabilities.

2.2. Implement Caching for Frequently Accessed Data

API Gateway supports caching, allowing you to store responses for specific routes and reduce the load on Lambda functions. Implement caching for:

- **Frequently accessed resources** (e.g., product lists, user profiles).
- Routes that serve **read-heavy** traffic.

To enable caching:

1. In the **API Gateway Console**, go to **Stages** and select a stage.
2. Under **Cache Settings**, enable **Caching** and configure the cache size and TTL (Time-to-Live).

2.3. Leverage Throttling and Rate Limiting

API Gateway allows you to define throttling limits to protect your API from excessive requests. Throttling helps maintain stability by limiting the number of requests a client can make within a certain period.

- Set **Burst Limit** to handle sudden spikes and a **Rate Limit** to control sustained traffic.
- Define different throttling policies for different stages (e.g., dev, prod) to match their specific traffic patterns.

3. Handle Asynchronous Workloads with Lambda

Not all requests to your API need to be processed synchronously. Offloading non-critical tasks to asynchronous workflows can significantly improve scalability and responsiveness.

3.1. Use SQS or SNS for Asynchronous Processing

For long-running or resource-intensive tasks, consider:

- **Amazon SQS** (Simple Queue Service): Ideal for queuing tasks that need to be processed in order.
- **Amazon SNS** (Simple Notification Service): Useful for distributing tasks to multiple subscribers or notifying other systems of events.

Example: A user submits an order through the API. API Gateway triggers a Lambda function that places the order in an SQS queue. A separate Lambda function then processes the orders asynchronously from the queue.

3.2. Use Event-Driven Patterns with Lambda and EventBridge

For event-driven architectures, use **Amazon EventBridge** to connect various services and route events to Lambda functions. This enables you to decouple services and build scalable, event-driven workflows.

- **Define custom event buses** to capture and route events across multiple applications.
- Configure Lambda functions to automatically react to specific events (e.g., data processing when new data is uploaded to S3).

4. Ensure API Security and Access Control

Scalable APIs should also be secure, with well-defined access controls and monitoring. Here are some security best practices:

4.1. Use Appropriate Authorization Mechanisms

Choose the right authorization mechanism based on the nature of your API:

- **IAM Roles**: Ideal for server-to-server communication within AWS.
- **Lambda Authorizers**: Useful for implementing custom authentication or validating tokens.
- **Cognito User Pools**: Best for user authentication with OAuth 2.0 support.

4.2. Implement TLS/SSL Encryption

To protect data in transit, enforce HTTPS on all API endpoints. API Gateway automatically provisions SSL certificates for the default domain names, but you can also use **Custom Domain Names** with your SSL certificates for better branding and security.

4.3. Monitor and Audit API Access with CloudTrail and CloudWatch

Enable **AWS CloudTrail** to log all API Gateway and Lambda activity for auditing purposes. Additionally, use **CloudWatch Alarms** to detect unusual patterns of activity or unauthorized access attempts.

5. Design for Reliability and Redundancy

Building scalable APIs also involves ensuring reliability and redundancy to handle unexpected failures or disruptions.

5.1. Use Lambda's Built-in Retry and Error Handling

AWS Lambda automatically retries failed invocations, but you can fine-tune these settings:

- Configure **Maximum Retry Attempts** and **Dead Letter Queues (DLQs)** for failed invocations to ensure no data is lost.
- Implement proper exception handling within Lambda functions to return meaningful errors.

5.2. Implement Circuit Breaker Patterns

If your API interacts with external services (e.g., third-party APIs), use the **circuit breaker pattern** to prevent your application from repeatedly trying to connect to an unresponsive service. This can reduce the load on your API and improve its overall stability.

5.3. Distribute Workloads Across Multiple Regions

For APIs serving a global audience, consider deploying your Lambda functions and API Gateway endpoints across multiple AWS regions. This approach:

- Reduces latency for international users.
- Provides failover options in case of regional disruptions.

6. Use Monitoring and Analytics for Proactive Scalability

Continuously monitor the performance and usage of your API to identify and address scaling issues proactively.

6.1. Set Up CloudWatch Alarms and Dashboards

Use **Amazon CloudWatch** to monitor key metrics such as Lambda invocation counts, duration, and error rates. Create **dashboards** to visualize the health of your API and set up **alarms** to notify you of any unusual patterns or issues.

6.2. Enable X-Ray for Distributed Tracing

AWS X-Ray helps trace requests as they move through your API and backend Lambda functions. Use X-Ray to:

- Identify bottlenecks or latency issues in your API workflow.
- Analyze end-to-end request traces to optimize processing times.

7. Plan for Scalability in Data Storage

When building scalable APIs, it's essential to choose data storage options that can scale with demand:

- **Amazon DynamoDB**: A fully managed NoSQL database that automatically scales based on traffic. Ideal for handling high-velocity, low-latency data needs.
- **Amazon RDS**: For applications that require relational databases. Use **read replicas** and **Multi-AZ deployments** for scalability and reliability.
- **Amazon S3**: For storing and serving large volumes of static content or files.

By following these best practices, you can design scalable, secure, and reliable serverless APIs using AWS Lambda and API Gateway. Optimizing Lambda function performance, configuring API Gateway efficiently, handling asynchronous tasks, and ensuring robust security and monitoring are key elements in building APIs that can automatically scale to meet changing demand while maintaining responsiveness and availability.

With AWS's serverless architecture and these strategies, your APIs will be equipped to handle real-world traffic patterns and unexpected load spikes, delivering a consistent experience to users.

Project 2: Real-Time Data Processing Pipeline

Processing S3 File Uploads with Lambda Triggers
One of the most common serverless architectures involves using **Amazon S3** as a storage solution and **AWS Lambda** to process files or data in real time. By combining S3 with Lambda, you can create a scalable, event-driven data processing pipeline that automatically triggers data transformation, analytics, or notifications when new files are uploaded to an S3 bucket.

In this section, we will explore how to set up **S3 and Lambda triggers** to process file uploads automatically. We will cover key concepts, step-by-step implementation, and best practices for building a robust and scalable real-time data processing pipeline.

1. Overview of S3 and Lambda Integration

Amazon S3 (Simple Storage Service) is a scalable object storage service used to store and retrieve data files. When combined with **AWS Lambda**, you can automatically trigger a Lambda function whenever an object is created, updated, or deleted in an S3 bucket.

Typical use cases for processing S3 file uploads with Lambda triggers include:

- **Image processing** (e.g., resizing, generating thumbnails, adding watermarks).

- **Data transformation** (e.g., parsing CSV files and storing data in a database).
- **Content indexing** (e.g., extracting metadata and indexing documents).
- **Notifications** (e.g., sending alerts or email notifications when a file is uploaded).

2. Key Components of the Solution

The solution involves the following key AWS services:

- **Amazon S3**: Acts as the storage layer for uploaded files.
- **AWS Lambda**: Processes the files or data in real time based on S3 event notifications.
- **Amazon CloudWatch**: Provides monitoring and logging for the Lambda function's execution.

3. Step-by-Step Implementation

We'll create a real-time data processing pipeline where an S3 bucket receives files, triggering a Lambda function to process them automatically. In this example, we will set up a pipeline to process uploaded CSV files and store the transformed data in a DynamoDB table.

Step 1: Create an S3 Bucket
Go to the Amazon S3 Console:

- Open the **Amazon S3 Console** and click **Create Bucket**.

Configure the Bucket Settings:

- Provide a unique name for your bucket (e.g., data-processing-pipeline-bucket).
- Choose an appropriate AWS region for your bucket.

- Leave other settings as default and click **Create**.

Configure Bucket Permissions:

- Ensure that the bucket policy or ACL allows Lambda access to read from the bucket. For demonstration purposes, we'll focus on enabling permissions later through an IAM role.

Step 2: Create a Lambda Function to Process Files

Next, create a Lambda function that will process CSV files uploaded to the S3 bucket. The Lambda function should read and parse the CSV data and store it in a DynamoDB table (or any other processing task based on your use case).

Go to the AWS Lambda Console:

- Open the **AWS Lambda Console** and click **Create Function**.
- Choose **Author from scratch**.

Configure the Lambda Function:

- Name the function (e.g., ProcessS3FileUpload).
- Select **Python 3.9** as the runtime.
- Choose or create an **IAM role** with permission to access S3 and DynamoDB.

Add the Function Code:

Here's an example Lambda function code that processes uploaded CSV files:

```
import boto3
import csv
import json
```

```python
# Initialize the S3 client
s3 = boto3.client('s3')
dynamodb = boto3.resource('dynamodb')
table = dynamodb.Table('ProcessedData')


def lambda_handler(event, context):
    # Get the bucket and object key from the event
    bucket_name = event['Records'][0]['s3']['bucket']['name']
    object_key = event['Records'][0]['s3']['object']['key']

    # Retrieve the CSV file from S3
    csv_file = s3.get_object(Bucket=bucket_name, Key=object_key)
    csv_content =
    csv_file['Body'].read().decode('utf-8').splitlines()

    # Process the CSV data
    csv_reader = csv.DictReader(csv_content)
    for row in csv_reader:
        # Transform the data as needed and store it in DynamoDB
        item = {
            'id': row['ID'],
            'name': row['Name'],
            'email': row['Email']
        }
        table.put_item(Item=item)

    return {
        'statusCode': 200,
        'body': json.dumps({'message': 'File processed
        successfully'})
    }
```

In this code:

- The function retrieves the file details from the S3 event.
- It reads the CSV file content from S3, parses it, and processes each row.
- The processed data is stored in a DynamoDB table called ProcessedData.

Deploy the Lambda Function:

231

• Click **Deploy** to save and deploy the function.

Step 3: Create an S3 Trigger for the Lambda Function

To automatically trigger the Lambda function whenever a file is uploaded to the S3 bucket:

Go to the S3 Bucket Settings:

• Open the **Amazon S3 Console** and select your bucket (data-processing-pipeline-bucket).

Configure Bucket Notifications:

• Go to the **Properties** tab of the bucket.
• Under **Event notifications**, click **Create event notification**.

Set Up an S3 Event Trigger:

• Provide a name for the event notification (e.g., ProcessFileUpload).
• Choose **All object create events** as the event type (or specify the event types relevant to your use case).
• Under **Destination**, select **Lambda function**.
• Choose the Lambda function you created (ProcessS3FileUpload).

Save the Event Notification:

• Save the configuration to activate the event trigger.

Now, every time a file is uploaded to the S3 bucket, it will trigger the Lambda function to process the file.

Step 4: Test the Real-Time Data Processing Pipeline

To test the pipeline, upload a sample CSV file to the S3 bucket:

Prepare a Sample CSV File: Create a CSV file with the following format:

```
ID,Name,Email
1,John Doe,johndoe@example.com
2,Jane Smith,janesmith@example.com
```

Upload the CSV File to S3:

- Go to the **S3 Console** and select your bucket.
- Click **Upload** and upload the sample CSV file.

Monitor the Lambda Function:

- Open the **AWS Lambda Console** and view the **Monitoring** tab for your function.
- Check the CloudWatch Logs to see the output of the function. The logs should confirm that the file was processed successfully.

Verify the Processed Data in DynamoDB:

- Go to the **DynamoDB Console** and select the ProcessedData table.
- Verify that the items from the CSV file have been added to the table.

4. Best Practices for Processing S3 File Uploads

4.1. Use Dead Letter Queues (DLQs) for Error Handling

To handle failed Lambda executions gracefully, enable a **Dead Letter Queue (DLQ)**. This allows you to capture failed events and investigate issues without losing data.

- Create an SQS queue and configure it as a **DLQ** in the Lambda function settings.
- Monitor the DLQ for failed events and reprocess them as needed.

4.2. Optimize Function Execution Time

233

To optimize function execution and minimize costs:

- **Keep the function lightweight** by offloading heavy processing tasks to external services like EMR or Athena.
- **Process files in batches** if dealing with large volumes of data, reducing the execution time of individual invocations.

4.3. Implement Fine-Grained S3 Permissions

Apply **least privilege** principles when assigning IAM roles to Lambda functions. Grant your Lambda function access to only the specific S3 bucket and prefix it needs to process files.

Example policy:

```
{
  "Version": "2012-10-17",
  "Statement": [
    {
      "Effect": "Allow",
      "Action": ["s3:GetObject"],
      "Resource": "arn:aws:s3:::data-processing-pipeline-bucket/*"
    },
    {
      "Effect": "Allow",
      "Action": ["dynamodb:PutItem"],
      "Resource":
      "arn:aws:dynamodb:region:account-id:table/ProcessedData"
    }
  ]
}
```

4.4. Monitor and Scale with CloudWatch Metrics

Use **CloudWatch Metrics** to monitor key metrics such as:

- **Number of S3 events triggered.**
- **Lambda invocation duration** and **error rates**.
- **DynamoDB read and write throughput**.

Set up **CloudWatch Alarms** to be alerted when thresholds are breached, allowing you to take proactive measures to scale or debug.

4.5. Leverage S3 Object Versioning for Data Integrity

Enable **versioning** on your S3 bucket to protect against accidental overwrites or deletions. This helps maintain data integrity by allowing you to restore previous versions of files.

5. Advanced Use Cases and Extensions

Beyond the basic setup, there are several advanced use cases and features that you can implement to enhance your real-time data processing pipeline:

5.1. Real-Time Image Processing

For applications that process images (e.g., resizing, watermarking), you can extend the Lambda function to use the **Pillow** library or other image processing libraries. Store processed images in a separate S3 bucket or distribute them using **Amazon CloudFront**.

5.2. Content Indexing with Elasticsearch

If you need to index documents or media files for full-text search, set up an **Amazon Elasticsearch Service (Amazon OpenSearch)** cluster. Configure your Lambda function to extract metadata from uploaded files and index it into the Elasticsearch cluster.

5.3. Serverless Data Analytics

For more extensive data processing or analytics tasks:

- Integrate Lambda with **Amazon Kinesis** to process streaming data.
- Use **AWS Glue** or **Amazon Athena** for batch data processing and querying large datasets stored in S3.

Processing S3 file uploads with Lambda triggers allows you to create a highly scalable and cost-effective data processing pipeline. By leveraging the power of AWS Lambda and Amazon S3, you can automatically handle tasks such as data transformation, image processing, or content indexing without managing servers or complex infrastructure.

By following best practices for permissions, error handling, monitoring, and scaling, you can build reliable and secure pipelines capable of handling large volumes of real-time data. This architecture forms the backbone of many modern applications, from content delivery networks to big data analytics platforms, making it an essential skill for building serverless solutions on AWS.

Storing Processed Data in DynamoDB

In a real-time data processing pipeline, storing processed data efficiently is crucial to ensure data availability, fast retrieval, and scalability. **Amazon DynamoDB** is an ideal solution for serverless applications due to its fully managed nature, low latency, and seamless integration with AWS services like **Lambda** and **API Gateway**. In this section, we'll discuss how to store processed data from S3 uploads into DynamoDB using AWS Lambda.

1. Overview of Amazon DynamoDB

Amazon DynamoDB is a NoSQL database service that offers high availability, scalability, and low-latency performance. DynamoDB is well-suited for applications requiring real-time data processing and high read/write throughput.

Key features that make DynamoDB a good fit for this use case:

- **Automatic scaling** to handle varying read and write demands.
- **Fine-grained access control** with IAM permissions.
- **Low-latency data access** for real-time applications.
- **Seamless integration** with AWS services like Lambda, S3, and API Gateway.

2. Setting Up a DynamoDB Table

Before implementing the Lambda function to store processed data, create a DynamoDB table to hold the processed results.

Step 1: Create a DynamoDB Table
Open the DynamoDB Console:

- Go to the **Amazon DynamoDB Console** and click **Create Table**.

Define the Table Name and Primary Key:

- **Table Name**: Provide a meaningful name for your table (e.g., Processed-Data).
- **Partition Key**: Define a unique identifier for each item in the table. For example, use id as the partition key with a data type of **String**.

Configure Table Settings:

- Choose **On-Demand Capacity** for automatic scaling based on traffic, or configure **Provisioned Capacity** if you prefer to set read and write capacity units manually.
- Enable **Encryption** for data at rest to ensure security.

Create the Table:

- Click **Create** to create the DynamoDB table.

Step 2: Define IAM Permissions for DynamoDB Access
For the Lambda function to write data to DynamoDB, you need to create or update an IAM role with the necessary permissions.
Go to the IAM Console:

- Open the **IAM Console** and select **Roles**.

Attach a Policy to the Lambda Execution Role:

- Find the IAM role assigned to your Lambda function (e.g., lambda_exec ution_role).
- Attach a policy that allows writing to the DynamoDB table. Here's an example policy:

```
{
  "Version": "2012-10-17",
  "Statement": [
    {
      "Effect": "Allow",
      "Action": [
        "dynamodb:PutItem",
        "dynamodb:UpdateItem"
      ],
      "Resource":
      "arn:aws:dynamodb:<region>:<account-id>:table/ProcessedData"
    }
  ]
}
```

Replace <region> and <account-id> with your AWS region and account ID.

3. Integrating Lambda with DynamoDB

Now that the DynamoDB table is set up and permissions are configured, update your Lambda function to store processed data in the DynamoDB table. We'll extend the example Lambda function from the previous section to save each processed row into DynamoDB.

Step 1: Update the Lambda Function Code

The updated Lambda function will read the uploaded CSV file from S3, process each row, and store the data in DynamoDB.

Here's the updated code:

PROJECT 2: REAL-TIME DATA PROCESSING PIPELINE

```python
import boto3
import csv
import json

# Initialize the S3 client and DynamoDB resource
s3 = boto3.client('s3')
dynamodb = boto3.resource('dynamodb')
table = dynamodb.Table('ProcessedData')

def lambda_handler(event, context):
    # Get the bucket and object key from the event
    bucket_name = event['Records'][0]['s3']['bucket']['name']
    object_key = event['Records'][0]['s3']['object']['key']

    try:
        # Retrieve the CSV file from S3
        csv_file = s3.get_object(Bucket=bucket_name,
        Key=object_key)
        csv_content =
        csv_file['Body'].read().decode('utf-8').splitlines()

        # Process the CSV data
        csv_reader = csv.DictReader(csv_content)
        for row in csv_reader:
            # Transform the data as needed and store it in DynamoDB
            item = {
                'id': row['ID'],  # Use a unique identifier for
                each row
                'name': row['Name'],
                'email': row['Email'],
                'timestamp': csv_file['LastModified'].isoformat()
                # Add metadata if needed
            }
            # Store the item in DynamoDB
            table.put_item(Item=item)

        return {
            'statusCode': 200,
            'body': json.dumps({'message': 'File processed and
            data stored in DynamoDB successfully'})
```

```
        }
    except Exception as e:
        return {
            'statusCode': 500,
            'body': json.dumps({'error': str(e)})
        }
```

Code Explanation:

- **Read the CSV File**: The Lambda function reads the uploaded CSV file from the S3 bucket.
- **Parse and Process the Data**: It uses Python's csv.DictReader to parse the file and read each row as a dictionary.
- **Store the Data in DynamoDB**: The function creates an item for each row and stores it in the ProcessedData table using DynamoDB's put_item method.
- **Handle Errors Gracefully**: If an error occurs during processing, the function returns an error message with a 500 status code.

Step 2: Deploy the Lambda Function

1. **Open the AWS Lambda Console**.
2. Select your Lambda function (ProcessS3FileUpload).
3. Paste the updated code into the code editor.
4. Click **Deploy** to save and deploy the changes.

4. Test the Data Processing Pipeline

To verify that the Lambda function is storing data in DynamoDB correctly:

1. **Upload a New CSV File to S3**:

- Go to the **Amazon S3 Console** and select your bucket.
- Upload a new CSV file with the following content:

```
ID,Name,Email
1,John Doe,johndoe@example.com
2,Jane Smith,janesmith@example.com
```

1. **Monitor the Lambda Function Execution**:

- Go to the **AWS Lambda Console** and view the **Monitoring** tab for your Lambda function.
- Check the CloudWatch Logs to ensure that the function executed successfully.

1. **Check the DynamoDB Table**:

- Go to the **Amazon DynamoDB Console** and open the ProcessedData table.
- Verify that the items from the CSV file have been added to the table.

5. Best Practices for Storing Data in DynamoDB

5.1. Design the Table Schema for Efficient Queries
When designing a DynamoDB table schema, consider the following:

- **Choose a suitable partition key**: Ensure that the partition key is unique to avoid overwriting data. In this case, we used the id field.
- **Add additional attributes**: Include additional fields in each item as needed for filtering or searching.

5.2. Use Batch Writes for High-Volume Data
If you need to process and store large amounts of data, use DynamoDB's **BatchWriteItem** API to insert multiple items at once. This reduces the number of API calls and improves efficiency.

Example of using BatchWriteItem:

```python
with table.batch_writer() as batch:
    for row in csv_reader:
        item = {
            'id': row['ID'],
            'name': row['Name'],
            'email': row['Email']
        }
        batch.put_item(Item=item)
```

5.3. Monitor DynamoDB Performance and Scaling

DynamoDB provides **CloudWatch metrics** for monitoring table through-put, latency, and errors. Set up **CloudWatch Alarms** to be notified of issues like:

- **Throttled requests** due to exceeding provisioned capacity.
- **Increased read/write latency** indicating a performance bottleneck.

6. Implementing Fine-Grained Access Control

To enforce security, use **IAM policies** to limit DynamoDB access based on user roles or specific actions. For example, create a policy that allows only write access to the ProcessedData table for the Lambda function role:

```json
{
  "Version": "2012-10-17",
  "Statement": [
    {
      "Effect": "Allow",
      "Action": "dynamodb:PutItem",
      "Resource":
      "arn:aws:dynamodb:<region>:<account-id>:table/ProcessedData"
    }
  ]
}
```

7. Extending the Solution for Advanced Use Cases

7.1. Real-Time Analytics with DynamoDB Streams

To enable real-time analytics, enable **DynamoDB Streams** on your table. This allows you to capture every data modification and trigger Lambda functions in response to these changes. You can use this feature to:

- **Sync data with other databases** (e.g., Elasticsearch for full-text search).
- **Trigger notifications** or run analytics on newly added data.

7.2. Implement Data Versioning

For applications that need to track changes or maintain a history of modifications, implement data versioning in DynamoDB. Store a **version number** with each item and update it with every modification.

Storing processed data in DynamoDB provides a highly scalable, low-latency solution for real-time data processing pipelines. By integrating S3 with Lambda and DynamoDB, you can create a seamless, serverless architecture that processes data automatically in response to file uploads, with DynamoDB serving as the durable and scalable storage backend.

By following best practices for table design, data storage, and monitoring, you can build a robust and secure real-time data processing pipeline capable of handling high volumes of data with low latency. This architecture is well-suited for applications in e-commerce, analytics, IoT, and beyond, making it an essential pattern for building modern serverless solutions on AWS.

Real-Time Data Analytics with AWS Lambda and Kinesis

For applications that require real-time data analytics and streaming, integrating **AWS Lambda** with **Amazon Kinesis** provides a powerful, serverless solution. **Amazon Kinesis** enables you to ingest large streams of data in real-time and process it with Lambda functions, allowing for scalable, low-latency data analysis.

In this section, we'll explore how to set up a real-time data analytics pipeline using **Amazon Kinesis Data Streams** and **AWS Lambda**. We will cover key concepts, step-by-step implementation, and best practices for building a reliable real-time analytics solution.

1. Overview of Amazon Kinesis Data Streams

Amazon Kinesis Data Streams is a managed service that allows you to capture, process, and analyze real-time streaming data. Kinesis Data Streams can handle a variety of data sources, such as application logs, website clickstreams, IoT data, and more.

Key features of Kinesis Data Streams include:

- **Real-time data ingestion and processing**: Capture and process data in real-time, with low-latency response times.
- **Scalability**: Scale automatically to handle high-velocity data streams.
- **Durability**: Stores data records in shards for a specified retention period (default is 24 hours, extendable up to 7 days).

2. Key Components of the Real-Time Analytics Pipeline

The pipeline consists of the following components:

- **Amazon Kinesis Data Streams**: Ingests real-time data.
- **AWS Lambda**: Processes each incoming data record in real time.
- **Amazon DynamoDB, S3, or another storage solution**: Stores pro-

cessed results.
- **Amazon CloudWatch**: Monitors and logs Lambda execution metrics.

3. Step-by-Step Implementation

We'll create a real-time analytics pipeline where Kinesis Data Streams receive streaming data, and a Lambda function processes each data record. For this example, we will simulate website clickstream data and analyze it using a Lambda function.

Step 1: Create a Kinesis Data Stream
Go to the Amazon Kinesis Console:

- Open the **Amazon Kinesis Console** and select **Data Streams**.

Create a New Data Stream:

- Click **Create Data Stream** and provide a name (e.g., ClickstreamDataSt ream).
- Set the number of **shards** based on the expected data volume (for testing, start with 1 shard).

Configure the Data Stream:

- Leave the default settings for other options and click **Create Data Stream**.

Each **shard** can handle up to 1 MB of data per second for writes and 2 MB per second for reads, along with up to 1,000 records per second.

Step 2: Create a Lambda Function to Process Data Records
The Lambda function will read records from the Kinesis stream, analyze them, and store the results in a DynamoDB table.
Go to the AWS Lambda Console:

- Open the **AWS Lambda Console** and click **Create Function**.
- Choose **Author from scratch**.

Configure the Lambda Function:

- Name the function (e.g., ProcessClickstreamData).
- Select **Python 3.9** as the runtime.
- Choose or create an **IAM role** with permission to read from Kinesis and write to DynamoDB.

Add the Function Code:

Here's an example Lambda function code that processes clickstream data from Kinesis:

```python
import json
import boto3

# Initialize the DynamoDB resource
dynamodb = boto3.resource('dynamodb')
table = dynamodb.Table('ClickstreamAnalytics')

def lambda_handler(event, context):
    # Process each record from the Kinesis event
    for record in event['Records']:
        # Kinesis data is base64-encoded, so decode it
        payload = record['kinesis']['data']
        decoded_data = json.loads(base64.b64decode(payload))

        # Extract fields from the decoded data
        user_id = decoded_data.get('user_id')
        page = decoded_data.get('page')
        timestamp = decoded_data.get('timestamp')

        # Perform analytics processing (e.g., counting page views)
        result = {
            'user_id': user_id,
            'page': page,
```

```
        'timestamp': timestamp,
        'page_views': 1  # Increment page view count for this
        example
    }

    # Store the result in DynamoDB
    table.put_item(Item=result)

return {
    'statusCode': 200,
    'body': json.dumps({'message': 'Records processed
    successfully'})
}
```

Code Explanation:

- **Read Kinesis Records**: The Lambda function reads records from the Kinesis event.
- **Decode and Parse Data**: The function decodes the base64-encoded payload and parses the JSON data.
- **Process Analytics**: For this example, we increment the page view count based on the extracted fields.
- **Store Results in DynamoDB**: The processed data is stored in the ClickstreamAnalytics table in DynamoDB.

Step 3: Create a DynamoDB Table for Storing Analytics
Go to the Amazon DynamoDB Console:

- Open the **Amazon DynamoDB Console** and click **Create Table**.

Define the Table Name and Primary Key:

- **Table Name**: Provide a meaningful name (e.g., ClickstreamAnalytics).
- **Partition Key**: Use a unique identifier, such as user_id with a **String** data type.

247

Create the Table:

- Click **Create** to create the DynamoDB table.

Step 4: Set Up Kinesis as a Trigger for Lambda
Go to the AWS Lambda Console:

- Open the **AWS Lambda Console** and select your Lambda function (ProcessClickstreamData).

Add a Trigger for the Lambda Function:

- Under the **Designer** section, click **Add Trigger**.
- Select **Kinesis** as the trigger type.
- Choose the Kinesis Data Stream you created (ClickstreamDataStream).
- Set **Batch size** to an appropriate number (default is 100 records).

Configure the Trigger:

- Enable **Stream starting position** (choose TRIM_HORIZON to read from the beginning for testing).
- Click **Add** to add the trigger.

4. Simulate Streaming Data into Kinesis

To test the pipeline, you can use the **AWS CLI** or a Python script to put records into the Kinesis stream.

Python Script to Simulate Clickstream Data
Here's a Python script to simulate clickstream data and send it to Kinesis:

```
import boto3
import json
```

```python
import time
import random

# Initialize the Kinesis client
kinesis = boto3.client('kinesis')

def generate_clickstream_data():
    pages = ['home', 'about', 'contact', 'products', 'cart']
    while True:
        data = {
            'user_id': f"user-{random.randint(1, 100)}",
            'page': random.choice(pages),
            'timestamp': int(time.time())
        }
        # Send the data to the Kinesis stream
        kinesis.put_record(
            StreamName='ClickstreamDataStream',
            Data=json.dumps(data),
            PartitionKey='partition-key'
        )
        time.sleep(1)  # Send a record every second

if __name__ == '__main__':
    generate_clickstream_data()
```

5. Monitor and Analyze the Real-Time Pipeline

5.1. Check Lambda Logs in CloudWatch

- Go to the **AWS CloudWatch Console** and select **Logs**.
- Open the log group for your Lambda function and verify that the function is processing records correctly.

5.2. Check Data in DynamoDB

- Go to the **Amazon DynamoDB Console** and select the ClickstreamAn-

alytics table.
- Verify that the table contains entries corresponding to the simulated clickstream data.

6. Best Practices for Real-Time Data Processing with Lambda and Kinesis

6.1. Optimize Lambda Concurrency and Scaling

- Configure the **Lambda concurrency limit** to match your data processing requirements. Use **reserved concurrency** if you want to allocate a specific number of concurrent executions to this function.

6.2. Use Enhanced Fan-Out for High-Throughput Streams

If your Kinesis Data Stream has high throughput, consider enabling **enhanced fan-out** to provide dedicated throughput for each Lambda function consumer. This reduces the impact of competing consumers on data processing latency.

6.3. Handle Lambda Retries and Error Scenarios

Kinesis triggers automatically retry processing Lambda functions up to the configured number of attempts. To handle errors gracefully:

- **Log failed records** in **CloudWatch** for manual inspection.
- Use **DynamoDB Streams** to store failed records in a **dead letter queue** (DLQ) for reprocessing.

6.4. Monitor Kinesis Stream Metrics with CloudWatch

Use **CloudWatch metrics** to monitor the performance of your Kinesis Data Stream, including:

- **Incoming records**: The number of records being ingested per second.
- **Iterator age**: The age of the last processed record, indicating any lag in processing.

7. Advanced Use Cases and Extensions

7.1. Real-Time Data Enrichment with AWS Lambda

Extend the Lambda function to enrich incoming data records by:

- **Querying external databases** for additional metadata.
- **Calling external APIs** to add contextual information to each record.

7.2. Stream Aggregation with AWS Kinesis Data Analytics

For more advanced real-time analytics, integrate Kinesis Data Streams with **Kinesis Data Analytics** to run SQL queries on streaming data. This allows you to perform aggregations, filtering, and anomaly detection in real time.

7.3. Visualizing Real-Time Data with Amazon QuickSight

To visualize processed data, integrate DynamoDB with **Amazon QuickSight** or export data to **Amazon S3** and use **Athena** for ad-hoc querying.

Integrating AWS Lambda with Amazon Kinesis Data Streams enables you to build scalable, real-time data analytics pipelines that can handle high-velocity streaming data. By leveraging Kinesis's scalability and Lambda's serverless architecture, you can process and analyze data with minimal latency and without managing infrastructure.

By following best practices for Lambda scaling, error handling, and Kinesis monitoring, you can build reliable and efficient real-time analytics solutions capable of handling diverse workloads such as clickstream analysis, IoT data ingestion, and real-time user behavior tracking. This architecture is a foundational building block for modern serverless applications requiring real-time insights and analytics.

Monitoring Pipeline Performance

Building a real-time data processing pipeline using **AWS Lambda** and **Amazon Kinesis** provides a robust, scalable architecture, but maintaining it effectively requires comprehensive monitoring and performance analysis. By actively monitoring the pipeline, you can identify bottlenecks, troubleshoot issues, and ensure that your pipeline meets the expected throughput and latency requirements.

In this section, we will explore various strategies and AWS tools to monitor the performance of your real-time data pipeline. These include setting up **CloudWatch metrics and alarms**, **tracing with AWS X-Ray**, and implementing **custom logging and analytics**.

1. Monitoring Lambda Metrics with Amazon CloudWatch

Amazon CloudWatch is a monitoring and management service that collects and visualizes operational data from AWS services. CloudWatch provides detailed metrics for AWS Lambda functions, allowing you to track the health and performance of your real-time pipeline.

Key Lambda Metrics to Monitor

The following are key CloudWatch metrics for monitoring AWS Lambda functions:

- **Invocations**: The number of times your Lambda function is triggered. This indicates the volume of incoming events from Kinesis.
- **Duration**: The execution time of each Lambda invocation. Monitoring this metric helps ensure that the function is running efficiently and within the configured timeout.
- **Errors**: The number of errors thrown during Lambda execution. High error counts indicate potential issues in the data processing logic.
- **Throttles**: The number of times Lambda invocations were throttled due to reaching the concurrency limit. Throttling can lead to processing delays and should be addressed by increasing concurrency limits if

necessary.

- **Iterator Age**: In the context of Kinesis, this metric measures the age of the last record processed by Lambda from the Kinesis stream. A high iterator age indicates a lag in processing.

Setting Up CloudWatch Alarms for Key Metrics

To proactively manage pipeline performance, set up CloudWatch alarms to notify you when critical metrics breach predefined thresholds. For example:

- **Create an alarm** for **Duration** to alert you if the Lambda execution time exceeds an expected threshold.
- **Set up an alarm** for **Iterator Age** to monitor delays in processing Kinesis data records.

Steps to Create CloudWatch Alarms
Go to the CloudWatch Console:

- Open the **Amazon CloudWatch Console** and click **Alarms**.

Create a New Alarm:

- Click **Create Alarm** and select a **Lambda function metric** (e.g., Duration, Errors, Iterator Age).

Define Thresholds:

- Set up the alarm condition by specifying a threshold value (e.g., alert if Duration exceeds 1 second, or if Errors exceed 0 for a specific period).

Configure Notifications:

- Set up notifications via **SNS** (Simple Notification Service) to receive email or SMS alerts when an alarm is triggered.

253

2. Tracing Data Flows with AWS X-Ray

AWS X-Ray helps trace requests as they flow through your pipeline, providing end-to-end visibility of data processing. X-Ray collects detailed information about each request, including latency, error rates, and execution details for each Lambda function.

Benefits of Using X-Ray for Tracing

- **Identify Latency Issues**: Analyze segments of your data flow to detect bottlenecks in Lambda functions, Kinesis streams, or downstream services.
- **Track Request Paths**: Visualize the entire request path, from data ingestion in Kinesis to processing and storage in DynamoDB or other services.
- **Debug Errors and Exceptions**: View detailed error traces to pinpoint the root causes of failures in the pipeline.

Enabling X-Ray in AWS Lambda

To enable X-Ray tracing for a Lambda function:

Go to the AWS Lambda Console:

- Select your Lambda function and navigate to the **Configuration** tab.

Enable X-Ray Tracing:

- Under **Monitoring and Operations Tools**, enable **Active Tracing** with AWS X-Ray.

Deploy the Changes:

- Save and deploy the updated configuration.

3. Monitoring Kinesis Stream Metrics

In addition to monitoring Lambda metrics, you should also keep track of metrics related to **Kinesis Data Streams**. This helps ensure that the stream is handling the incoming data load efficiently and without performance degradation.

Key Kinesis Metrics to Monitor

- **IncomingRecords**: The number of records successfully put into the Kinesis stream. Monitor this metric to understand data ingestion rates.
- **ReadProvisionedThroughputExceeded**: Indicates the number of times your data stream exceeds the read throughput limits. If you see this metric spike, consider increasing the read capacity or enabling enhanced fan-out for consumers.
- **WriteProvisionedThroughputExceeded**: Indicates the number of times the stream exceeds its write capacity. If this happens frequently, increase the write capacity or add more shards.

Setting Up CloudWatch Alarms for Kinesis Metrics

Similar to Lambda, you can create CloudWatch alarms for Kinesis metrics to get notified when issues arise. For example:

- **Create an alarm** for WriteProvisionedThroughputExceeded to alert you if the stream exceeds its write capacity.
- **Set up an alarm** for IncomingRecords to notify you of unusual drops or spikes in data volume.

4. Custom Logging with Amazon CloudWatch Logs

While CloudWatch automatically logs basic metrics for Lambda, it's essential to implement custom logging for more granular insights into data processing.

Implementing Custom Logging in Lambda Functions

Use the **boto3** library's logger to record custom events, errors, and processing details within your Lambda function. Here's an example of adding custom logging to a Lambda function:

```python
import json
import logging
import boto3

# Set up logging
logger = logging.getLogger()
logger.setLevel(logging.INFO)

# Initialize the DynamoDB resource
dynamodb = boto3.resource('dynamodb')
table = dynamodb.Table('ClickstreamAnalytics')

def lambda_handler(event, context):
    for record in event['Records']:
        try:
            # Decode and process the record
            payload = record['kinesis']['data']
            decoded_data = json.loads(base64.b64decode(payload))

            # Extract fields
            user_id = decoded_data.get('user_id')
            page = decoded_data.get('page')
            timestamp = decoded_data.get('timestamp')

            # Log processing information
            logger.info(f"Processing record for user_id:
{user_id}, page: {page}")

            # Store the result in DynamoDB
            table.put_item(Item={
                'user_id': user_id,
                'page': page,
                'timestamp': timestamp,
                'page_views': 1
            })

        except Exception as e:
```

```
        # Log the error
        logger.error(f"Error processing record: {e}")

    return {
        'statusCode': 200,
        'body': json.dumps({'message': 'Records processed
        successfully'})
    }
```

In this example:

- **INFO logs** record successful processing events, allowing you to track the pipeline's operational details.
- **ERROR logs** capture exceptions, enabling quick troubleshooting of issues.

Analyzing CloudWatch Logs

Use **CloudWatch Logs Insights** to search and filter logs, analyze trends, and extract insights from log data. For example:

- Search for **ERROR** messages to find Lambda function failures.
- Query logs to identify specific patterns, such as processing delays or anomalies.

5. Performance Optimization Strategies

5.1. Optimize Lambda Execution Duration

- **Right-Size Lambda Memory and Timeout**: Allocate sufficient memory and set an appropriate timeout to ensure efficient processing without incurring unnecessary costs.
- **Avoid Unnecessary Initialization**: Only load external libraries and dependencies when needed to reduce cold start durations.

5.2. Enhance Throughput with Kinesis Shards and Enhanced Fan-Out

If your data volume grows, consider scaling up by increasing the number of Kinesis shards. You can also enable **enhanced fan-out** for consumers to provide dedicated throughput for each Lambda function or application reading from the stream.

5.3. Handle Data Processing Failures Gracefully

To minimize data loss in case of Lambda function errors:

- Implement a **Dead Letter Queue (DLQ)** using Amazon SQS to capture failed records.
- Use **AWS Step Functions** to build fault-tolerant workflows for retrying failed processing tasks.

6. Using CloudWatch Dashboards for Real-Time Visibility

CloudWatch Dashboards provide a unified view of all your pipeline metrics and alarms, helping you track performance in real time. You can create custom dashboards with widgets for Lambda, Kinesis, and DynamoDB metrics.

Steps to Create a CloudWatch Dashboard
Open the CloudWatch Console:

- Go to the **CloudWatch Console** and click **Dashboards**.

Create a New Dashboard:

- Click **Create Dashboard** and provide a name for the dashboard.

Add Widgets for Key Metrics:

- Add widgets for Lambda and Kinesis metrics, such as **Duration**, **Errors**, **Throttles**, **IncomingRecords**, and **Iterator Age**.
- Customize each widget to show relevant data for specific time periods.

Save the Dashboard:

- Save the dashboard and configure it to refresh automatically for near real-time monitoring.

Monitoring the performance of your real-time data processing pipeline is crucial for maintaining its efficiency, reliability, and scalability. By leveraging AWS services like **CloudWatch**, **X-Ray**, and **Kinesis metrics**, you can gain deep visibility into the operational health of your pipeline, proactively address performance issues, and ensure that your application meets its SLA requirements.

Comprehensive monitoring and alerting allow you to respond quickly to failures or latency spikes, enabling a resilient, real-time analytics solution that scales seamlessly with your data demands. Implementing these best practices and monitoring tools positions your pipeline for long-term success in handling diverse workloads.

Project 3: Automating Infrastructure with Python

C reating CloudFormation Templates with Lambda
Infrastructure as Code (IaC) is a critical practice in modern cloud architecture, allowing you to define, deploy, and manage infrastructure resources using code. **AWS CloudFormation** is a service that enables IaC by providing a simple way to model and set up Amazon Web Services resources. In combination with **AWS Lambda**, you can automate the creation and deployment of CloudFormation templates dynamically, enabling scalable and efficient infrastructure management.

In this section, we'll explore how to create CloudFormation templates using Python with AWS Lambda. We'll cover the concepts, implementation steps, best practices, and use cases, focusing on dynamically creating and deploying infrastructure based on business logic or events.

1. Overview of AWS CloudFormation and Lambda Integration

AWS CloudFormation allows you to model and manage AWS resources using JSON or YAML templates. These templates define the resources and their configurations, which are automatically provisioned and managed by CloudFormation.

AWS Lambda can be used to dynamically generate CloudFormation templates and trigger infrastructure provisioning based on events or business logic. This approach is useful in scenarios like:

- **Automated environment setup** for new applications or deployments.
- **Dynamic resource scaling** based on user requests or demand.
- **Configurable multi-account deployments** where each account may require slightly different configurations.

2. Key Components of the Solution

The following components will be used in the project:

- **AWS Lambda**: Executes Python code to generate CloudFormation templates and create or update stacks.
- **AWS CloudFormation**: Defines and provisions the required infrastructure resources based on templates generated by Lambda.
- **Amazon S3** (optional): Stores generated templates for later use or auditing.

3. Step-by-Step Implementation

We'll create a Lambda function that generates a CloudFormation template to provision a **simple web application infrastructure**, which includes an **EC2 instance** and an **S3 bucket**. The Lambda function will automatically create or update the CloudFormation stack with the generated template.

Step 1: Create an IAM Role with Necessary Permissions

Before creating the Lambda function, set up an IAM role that grants the function permissions to work with CloudFormation.

Go to the IAM Console:

- Open the **AWS IAM Console** and click **Roles**.

Create a New Role for Lambda:

- Click **Create Role** and choose **AWS Lambda** as the trusted entity.

261

- Attach the following policies:
- **AWSLambdaBasicExecutionRole** (for basic Lambda execution).
- **AWSCloudFormationFullAccess** (to allow Lambda to create and manage CloudFormation stacks).

Create the Role:

- Name the role (e.g., LambdaCloudFormationRole) and create it.

Step 2: Create a Lambda Function
   Go to the AWS Lambda Console:

- Open the **AWS Lambda Console** and click **Create Function**.

Configure the Lambda Function:

- Name the function (e.g., GenerateCloudFormationTemplate).
- Choose **Python 3.9** as the runtime.
- Select the **IAM role** you created (LambdaCloudFormationRole).

Add the Function Code:

The following Python code dynamically generates a CloudFormation template and creates a stack using the **boto3** library:

```
import boto3
import json

# Initialize the CloudFormation client
cloudformation = boto3.client('cloudformation')

def generate_template():
    # Define a simple CloudFormation template
for an EC2 instance and an S3 bucket
    template = {
```

```
        "AWSTemplateFormatVersion": "2010-09-09",
        "Description": "CloudFormation
template to provision an EC2 instance and an S3 bucket",
        "Resources": {
            "WebServerInstance": {
                "Type": "AWS::EC2::Instance",
                "Properties": {
                    "ImageId":
"ami-0c55b159cbfafe1f0",  # Example Amazon Linux 2 AMI
                    "InstanceType": "t2.micro",
                    "KeyName": "my-key-pair",
 # Replace with your key pair
                    "SecurityGroups": ["default"]
                }
            },
            "MyS3Bucket": {
                "Type": "AWS::S3::Bucket",
                "Properties": {
                    "BucketName":
"my-unique-bucket-name-123456"
 # Replace with a unique name
                }
            }
        }
    }
    return json.dumps(template)


def lambda_handler(event, context):
    # Generate the CloudFormation template
    template_body = generate_template()

    try:
        # Create or update the CloudFormation stack
        response = cloudformation.create_stack(
            StackName='MyWebAppStack',
            TemplateBody=template_body,
            Capabilities=['CAPABILITY_IAM']
        )
        return {
            'statusCode': 200,
```

```
                'body': json.dumps({
                    'message': 'CloudFormation stack
creation initiated',
                    'stackId': response['StackId']
                })
        }
    except cloudformation.exceptions.AlreadyExistsException:
        # If the stack already exists, update it
        response = cloudformation.update_stack(
            StackName='MyWebAppStack',
            TemplateBody=template_body,
            Capabilities=['CAPABILITY_IAM']
        )
        return {
            'statusCode': 200,
            'body': json.dumps({
                'message': 'CloudFormation stack
update initiated',
                'stackId': response['StackId']
            })
        }
    except Exception as e:
        return {
            'statusCode': 500,
            'body': json.dumps({
                'message': str(e)
            })
        }
```

Code Explanation:

- **generate_template()**: This function defines a CloudFormation template in JSON format. The template includes an EC2 instance and an S3 bucket as examples.
- **lambda_handler()**: This function serves as the Lambda entry point. It generates the CloudFormation template and uses the **boto3** library to create or update the stack.
- **Error Handling**: The function handles errors, such as an existing stack,

by attempting to update the stack instead.

Step 3: Deploy the Lambda Function

1. **Paste the Code** into the Lambda function's editor.
2. **Click Deploy** to save and deploy the function.

4. Testing the CloudFormation Automation

To test the automation, trigger the Lambda function manually or set up an **event source** (such as an API Gateway or an S3 upload) to trigger it automatically.

Manually Trigger the Lambda Function:

- Go to the **AWS Lambda Console**.
- Select your function (GenerateCloudFormationTemplate) and click **Test**.
- Use an empty event JSON ({}) to trigger the function.

Monitor Stack Creation in CloudFormation:

- Open the **AWS CloudFormation Console** and check the status of your stack (MyWebAppStack).
- You should see a new stack being created or updated based on the generated template.

5. Storing Templates in S3 (Optional)

To make the solution more flexible, you can store the generated templates in **Amazon S3** and refer to them in CloudFormation stacks. This approach is useful for managing multiple versions of templates or auditing purposes.

Steps to Store and Retrieve Templates from S3:

Upload the Generated Template to S3:

- Modify the Lambda function to upload the generated template to an S3 bucket using **boto3**.

```python
import boto3
import json

# Initialize the CloudFormation and S3 clients
cloudformation = boto3.client('cloudformation')
s3 = boto3.client('s3')

def generate_template():
    template = {
        "AWSTemplateFormatVersion": "2010-09-09",
        "Description": "CloudFormation
template to provision an EC2 instance and an S3 bucket",
        "Resources": {
            "WebServerInstance": {
                "Type": "AWS::EC2::Instance",
                "Properties": {
                    "ImageId": "ami-0c55b159cbfafe1f0",
                    "InstanceType": "t2.micro",
                    "KeyName": "my-key-pair",
                    "SecurityGroups": ["default"]
                }
            },
            "MyS3Bucket": {
                "Type": "AWS::S3::Bucket",
                "Properties": {
                    "BucketName": "my-unique-bucket-name-123456"
                }
            }
        }
    }
    return json.dumps(template)

def lambda_handler(event, context):
    # Generate the CloudFormation template
    template_body = generate_template()
```

```python
    # Upload the template to S3
    s3_bucket = 'my-cloudformation-templates-bucket'
    template_key = 'my-web-app-template.json'
    s3.put_object(Bucket=s3_bucket, Key=template_key,
    Body=template_body)

    try:
        # Create or update the CloudFormation stack using the S3
        template URL
        response = cloudformation.create_stack(
            StackName='MyWebAppStack',
            TemplateURL=f'
https://{s3_bucket}.s3.
amazonaws.com/{template_key}',
            Capabilities=['CAPABILITY_IAM']
        )
        return {
            'statusCode': 200,
            'body': json.dumps({
                'message':
'CloudFormation stack creation initiated',
                'stackId': response['StackId']
            })
        }
    except cloudformation.exceptions.AlreadyExistsException:
        response = cloudformation.update_stack(
            StackName='MyWebAppStack',
            TemplateURL=f
'https://{s3_bucket}.s3.
amazonaws.com/{template_key}',
            Capabilities=['CAPABILITY_IAM']
        )
        return {
            'statusCode': 200,
            'body': json.dumps({
                'message': 'CloudFormation stack update initiated',
                'stackId': response['StackId']
            })
        }
```

```
except Exception as e:
    return {
        'statusCode': 500,
        'body': json.dumps({
            'message': str(e)
        })
    }
```

6. Best Practices for Automating Infrastructure with Lambda

6.1. Parameterize CloudFormation Templates

To make the templates reusable, use **CloudFormation Parameters**. This allows you to pass different values when creating or updating stacks, making the templates more flexible and configurable.

Example of adding parameters to the template:

```
"Parameters": {
    "InstanceType": {
        "Description": "EC2 instance type",
        "Type": "String",
        "Default": "t2.micro"
    }
}
```

6.2. Implement Stack Policies for Controlled Updates

Use **stack policies** to control which resources can be updated during a stack update. This helps prevent accidental modifications to critical resources.

6.3. Monitor Stack Creation and Changes with CloudWatch

Configure CloudWatch Alarms to notify you of stack failures or unexpected changes. Additionally, use CloudTrail to audit all CloudFormation operations for better

Automating infrastructure using AWS Lambda and CloudFormation enables a fully serverless and scalable approach to managing AWS resources.

By dynamically generating and deploying CloudFormation templates with Python, you can create flexible infrastructure automation solutions that adapt to changing business needs and scale effortlessly.

Following best practices for parameterization, version control, and monitoring ensures that your automated infrastructure remains reliable, secure, and efficient. This architecture empowers organizations to embrace Infrastructure as Code principles, reducing manual efforts and improving deployment consistency.

Automated Resource Monitoring with Lambda and CloudWatch

Efficient monitoring of your AWS infrastructure is crucial for maintaining application performance, reliability, and security. While **Amazon CloudWatch** provides extensive monitoring capabilities, combining it with **AWS Lambda** allows you to automate monitoring tasks and respond proactively to events or anomalies in your infrastructure.

In this section, we'll explore how to set up **automated resource monitoring** using Lambda and CloudWatch. We will cover key concepts, implementation steps, and best practices for creating an automated monitoring and alerting solution that can dynamically track infrastructure resources and automatically respond to changes or issues.

1. Overview of CloudWatch and Lambda Integration

Amazon CloudWatch is a monitoring and observability service that collects and visualizes metrics, logs, and events from AWS services. CloudWatch can automatically track metrics such as CPU usage, memory utilization, disk I/O, network traffic, and much more. When combined with **AWS Lambda**, you can extend CloudWatch's capabilities to dynamically create alarms, trigger automated responses, and conduct more complex monitoring tasks.

2. Key Components of the Automated Monitoring Solution

- **Amazon CloudWatch Metrics and Alarms**: Tracks and monitors key metrics for AWS services.
- **Amazon CloudWatch Events (or EventBridge)**: Generates events based on changes or thresholds, which can be used to trigger Lambda functions.
- **AWS Lambda**: Executes custom monitoring logic, automatically adjusts alarms, or performs corrective actions based on events or metric thresholds.

3. Step-by-Step Implementation

We will create a solution where CloudWatch monitors the CPU utilization of an **EC2 instance** and triggers a Lambda function if CPU usage exceeds a certain threshold. The Lambda function will then automatically scale up the instance size or notify administrators.

Step 1: Create CloudWatch Alarms for Key Metrics

First, create CloudWatch alarms to monitor your EC2 instance's CPU utilization.

Go to the Amazon CloudWatch Console:

- Open the **Amazon CloudWatch Console** and click **Alarms**.

Create a New Alarm:

- Click **Create Alarm** and choose a **metric**.
- Select **EC2 metrics** and find the **CPUUtilization** metric for your target EC2 instance.
- Click **Select metric**.

Configure the Alarm Conditions:

- Set a threshold (e.g., trigger the alarm if CPU utilization exceeds 70% for 5 consecutive minutes).
- Define the alarm state as **ALARM** when the threshold is breached.

Configure Actions:

- Under **Actions**, choose **Send to an SNS Topic** to notify administrators, and add an action to **trigger a Lambda function** for automated responses.

Create the Alarm:

- Name the alarm (e.g., HighCPUUtilization) and click **Create alarm**.

Step 2: Create a Lambda Function to Respond to Alarms

Next, create a Lambda function that will be triggered when the CloudWatch alarm is in the ALARM state. The function can scale up the instance or send notifications.

Go to the AWS Lambda Console:

- Open the **AWS Lambda Console** and click **Create Function**.
- Choose **Author from scratch**.

Configure the Lambda Function:

- Name the function (e.g., ScaleEC2Instance).
- Select **Python 3.9** as the runtime.
- Choose an **IAM role** with permissions to describe and modify EC2 instances.

Add the Function Code:

Here's an example Lambda function code to scale up the instance type:

```python
import boto3
import json

# Initialize the EC2 client
ec2 = boto3.client('ec2')

def lambda_handler(event, context):
    # Extract the instance ID from the CloudWatch alarm event
    instance_id = 'i-1234567890abcdef0'  # Replace with your EC2
    instance ID

    try:
        # Stop the EC2 instance before modifying it
        ec2.stop_instances(InstanceIds=[instance_id])
        print(f'Stopping instance {instance_id}...')
        waiter = ec2.get_waiter('instance_stopped')
        waiter.wait(InstanceIds=[instance_id])
        print(f'Instance {instance_id} stopped.')

        # Modify the instance type (e.g., scale up to t3.medium)
        ec2.modify_instance_attribute(
            InstanceId=instance_id,
            InstanceType={'Value': 't3.medium'}
        )
        print(f'Instance {instance_id} type changed to t3.medium.')

        # Restart the EC2 instance
        ec2.start_instances(InstanceIds=[instance_id])
        print(f'Starting instance {instance_id}...')
        return {
            'statusCode': 200,
            'body': json.dumps
({'message': f'Successfully scaled
 instance {instance_id}'})
        }
    except Exception as e:
        print(f'Error scaling instance: {str(e)}')
        return {
            'statusCode': 500,
            'body': json.dumps({'message': str(e)})
```

```
    }
```

Code Explanation:

- The function stops the EC2 instance, modifies its instance type, and restarts it. This simulates scaling up based on the high CPU usage detected by CloudWatch.
- The instance ID and desired instance type can be made dynamic by extracting them from the event payload or using environment variables.

Step 3: Add a CloudWatch Event Rule to Trigger the Lambda Function

To automate the response to alarms, set up a CloudWatch Events rule that triggers the Lambda function.

Go to the CloudWatch Console:

- Open the **Amazon CloudWatch Console** and navigate to **Rules** under **Events**.

Create a New Rule:

- Click **Create Rule** and choose **Event Source** as **CloudWatch Alarms**.
- Select the **HighCPUUtilization** alarm as the source event.

Configure the Rule's Target:

- Under **Targets**, select **Lambda Function**.
- Choose the Lambda function you created (ScaleEC2Instance).

Save the Rule:

- Name the rule (e.g., RespondToHighCPU) and create it.

4. Best Practices for Automated Resource Monitoring

4.1. Implement Granular Alarms for Critical Resources

Set up alarms for a variety of critical metrics, including:

- **Memory usage**: Using custom CloudWatch metrics for applications that require memory-intensive operations.
- **Disk I/O and Network Traffic**: For workloads heavily reliant on storage or networking.
- **Application-specific metrics**: Such as request latency, database query times, or active user sessions.

4.2. Use AWS Systems Manager for Additional Automation

For complex remediation actions, integrate **AWS Systems Manager** to execute automated runbooks or scripts across multiple resources. This is useful for tasks like updating multiple EC2 instances, rotating keys, or deploying patches.

4.3. Leverage Lambda for Custom Metrics Collection

Extend your Lambda function to collect and publish **custom CloudWatch metrics** that provide deeper insights into application behavior. This is especially useful for monitoring non-standard metrics such as queue lengths, job processing times, or resource utilization beyond what's natively supported.

4.4. Optimize Lambda Execution Time and Costs

While using Lambda for monitoring automation, minimize unnecessary executions by:

- **Setting conditional logic** within Lambda functions to skip redundant operations.
- **Using Amazon EventBridge** (enhanced version of CloudWatch Events) for more flexible event filtering and routing.

5. Advanced Use Cases and Extensions

5.1. Automated Security Incident Responses

Extend the monitoring solution to include **security monitoring** by creating CloudWatch alarms for suspicious events detected by **AWS GuardDuty** or **AWS Config** rules. Trigger Lambda functions to:

- **Isolate compromised instances**.
- **Rotate access keys** or **revoke credentials** for suspected accounts.

5.2. Cross-Region or Multi-Account Monitoring

For organizations with a multi-account or multi-region setup, use **AWS Organizations** and **CloudWatch cross-account functionality** to consolidate monitoring and automate responses across accounts. You can trigger centralized Lambda functions to perform account-wide actions, such as scaling resources, updating configurations, or synchronizing states.

6. Monitoring and Auditing with CloudTrail and CloudWatch Dashboards

To audit and visualize automated responses and infrastructure events:

- **Enable AWS CloudTrail**: CloudTrail records all API calls made by CloudWatch, Lambda, and other AWS services. This is essential for auditing and security compliance.
- **Create CloudWatch Dashboards**: Set up dashboards with key metrics and alarm statuses to provide a comprehensive view of infrastructure health and automated responses.

By combining CloudWatch with AWS Lambda, you can automate the monitoring and response to changes or issues within your AWS environment. This approach allows you to maintain a proactive stance towards infrastructure management, reduce manual intervention, and ensure that critical resources are always running optimally.

Following best practices such as setting granular alarms, leveraging custom metrics, and implementing security responses ensures that your automated monitoring solution is both comprehensive and resilient. This architecture empowers organizations to build dynamic, self-healing infrastructure capable of handling the most demanding workloads and rapidly responding to operational events.

Event-Driven Infrastructure Remediation

In a modern cloud environment, **event-driven infrastructure remediation** is a critical approach to maintaining the health and resilience of your systems. By combining **AWS CloudWatch**, **AWS Lambda**, and **Amazon EventBridge**, you can automatically detect and remediate infrastructure issues based on pre-defined events or triggers. This approach not only reduces the mean time to recovery (MTTR) but also enhances the reliability and security of your infrastructure.

In this section, we'll explore how to implement event-driven infrastructure remediation using AWS services. We will cover key concepts, step-by-step implementation, and best practices for creating an automated remediation solution that responds to events such as resource failures, security breaches, or performance bottlenecks.

1. Overview of Event-Driven Architecture

Event-driven architecture involves generating and responding to events in real-time. In AWS, **Amazon EventBridge** (previously known as CloudWatch Events) acts as the event bus, capturing various events from AWS services such as **CloudWatch Alarms**, **AWS Config**, **GuardDuty**, or even custom events. Based on these events, you can trigger **AWS Lambda** functions, **Step Functions**, or other AWS services to automatically respond to incidents or anomalies.

Key Benefits of Event-Driven Remediation:

- **Proactive Incident Response**: Automatically detects and mitigates issues before they impact users.
- **Reduced Manual Effort**: Minimizes human intervention by automating common troubleshooting and recovery tasks.
- **Improved Security Posture**: Enables real-time security responses based on threat detection and policy violations.

2. Key Components of the Event-Driven Remediation Solution

The event-driven remediation architecture includes the following components:

- **Amazon EventBridge**: Acts as the central event bus, capturing and routing events from AWS services or custom sources.
- **AWS CloudWatch Alarms**: Monitors key metrics and generates alarms based on pre-defined thresholds.
- **AWS Lambda**: Executes remediation logic based on triggered events.
- **AWS Systems Manager** (optional): Executes more complex remediation tasks or scripts using Run Command or Automation Documents.

3. Step-by-Step Implementation

We will create a solution where an EC2 instance with high CPU utilization triggers an event via EventBridge. A Lambda function will be invoked to respond by either restarting the instance or scaling its capacity.

Step 1: Define the Event Rule in Amazon EventBridge
   Go to the EventBridge Console:

   • Open the **Amazon EventBridge Console** and click **Rules**.

Create a New Rule:

   • Click **Create Rule** and name it (e.g., HighCPUUtilizationRemediation).
   • Choose **Event Source** as **CloudWatch Alarms**.

Define the Event Pattern:

   • Choose **Event Source** and select **AWS CloudWatch Alarms**.
   • Specify an event pattern to match the ALARM state of a specific CloudWatch Alarm, such as HighCPUUtilization.

```
{
  "source": ["aws.cloudwatch"],
  "detail-type": ["CloudWatch Alarm State Change"],
  "detail": {
    "state": {
      "value": ["ALARM"]
    },
    "alarmName": ["HighCPUUtilization"]
  }
}
```

Add the Lambda Function as a Target:

- Under **Targets**, select **Lambda Function**.
- Choose the Lambda function that will perform the remediation action (e.g., RemediateHighCPU).

Create the Rule:

- Save the rule to automatically trigger the Lambda function based on the specified alarm state.

Step 2: Create the Lambda Function to Remediate High CPU Utilization
Go to the AWS Lambda Console:

- Open the **AWS Lambda Console** and click **Create Function**.

Configure the Lambda Function:

- Name the function (e.g., RemediateHighCPU).
- Choose **Python 3.9** as the runtime.
- Select an **IAM role** with permissions to describe and modify EC2 instances.

Add the Function Code:

Here's an example Lambda function that responds to high CPU utilization by restarting the affected EC2 instance:

```
import boto3
import json

# Initialize the EC2 client
ec2 = boto3.client('ec2')

def lambda_handler(event, context):
    # Extract the instance ID from the event
(assume single instance remediation)
```

```
    instance_id = 'i-1234567890abcdef0'
 # Replace with your actual instance ID

    try:
        # Check the current state of the instance
        instance_state = ec2.describe
_instance_status(InstanceIds=
[instance_id])['InstanceStatuses']
[0]['InstanceState']['Name']
        if instance_state == 'running':
            # Stop the instance for remediation
            ec2.stop_instances
(InstanceIds=[instance_id])
            print(f'Stopping instance
{instance_id} due to high CPU utilization...')
            waiter = ec2.get_waiter('instance_stopped')
            waiter.wait(InstanceIds=[instance_id])

            # Start the instance after a brief delay
            ec2.start_instances(InstanceIds=[instance_id])
            print(f'Restarting instance {instance_id}...')

        return {
            'statusCode': 200,
            'body': json.dumps({'message':
 f'Instance {instance_id} remediated successfully'})
        }
    except Exception as e:
        print(f'Error remediating instance: {str(e)}')
        return {
            'statusCode': 500,
            'body': json.dumps({'message': str(e)})
        }
```

Code Explanation:

- The function checks the current state of the EC2 instance. If it is running, the function stops and restarts the instance as a remediation action. This is a simple example and can be extended to include scaling, snapshot creation, or notifications.

Step 3: Test the Remediation Solution
Simulate a High CPU Event:

- Manually increase the CPU load on the EC2 instance (e.g., by running a stress test).

Trigger the CloudWatch Alarm:

- Monitor the CloudWatch alarm and verify that it transitions to the ALARM state.

Verify the Lambda Function Execution:

- Check the Lambda function's **CloudWatch Logs** to confirm that it executed successfully in response to the alarm.

4. Advanced Event-Driven Remediation Use Cases

4.1. Security Remediation with AWS GuardDuty
You can extend event-driven remediation to automatically respond to security incidents. For example:

- Use **AWS GuardDuty** to detect suspicious activity such as port scans or brute-force attacks.
- Create EventBridge rules to trigger Lambda functions that automatically **isolate compromised instances**, **revoke credentials**, or **block malicious IPs** using **AWS WAF**.

4.2. Configuration Compliance with AWS Config
Use **AWS Config** rules to enforce infrastructure compliance. When a rule is violated (e.g., an unencrypted S3 bucket), an EventBridge rule can

trigger a Lambda function to **automatically apply encryption** or notify the compliance team.

5. Best Practices for Event-Driven Remediation

5.1. Use IAM Policies for Granular Access Control

Ensure that Lambda functions only have the minimum required permissions to perform remediation actions. Apply **least privilege principles** to reduce the risk of accidental or malicious changes.

5.2. Implement Conditional Logic in Lambda Functions

Add conditional checks within Lambda functions to verify the severity and context of an event before performing remediation. This prevents overreaction to minor issues or false positives.

5.3. Automate Notifications and Escalation

In addition to automated remediation, set up **notification and escalation mechanisms** using **Amazon SNS**. This ensures that administrators are aware of critical incidents and can manually intervene if necessary.

6. Extending Remediation with AWS Systems Manager

For more complex tasks, integrate **AWS Systems Manager** to run scripts, apply patches, or execute runbooks across multiple resources. For example, you can:

- Use **Systems Manager Run Command** to update software packages or restart services on compromised instances.
- Create **Systems Manager Automation Documents** for predefined workflows, such as disaster recovery or server reboots.

Event-driven infrastructure remediation is a powerful approach to maintaining a reliable and secure cloud environment. By leveraging **EventBridge**, **Lambda**, and other AWS services, you can automate responses to common incidents, enforce compliance, and proactively mitigate performance issues.

Following best practices such as implementing granular IAM policies, adding conditional logic, and automating notifications ensures that your remediation solution is both effective and controlled. This architecture empowers organizations to build resilient cloud environments capable of responding dynamically to operational events and security incidents.

Cost Optimization and Cleanup Automation

Managing cloud infrastructure effectively involves not only provisioning resources but also optimizing costs and cleaning up unused or underutilized assets. **Cost Optimization** and **Cleanup Automation** help organizations maintain efficient cloud operations by identifying and eliminating wasteful spending, ensuring that resources are only paid for when needed, and automating routine cleanup tasks.

In this section, we'll explore strategies and implementation steps to achieve cost optimization and automated cleanup using AWS services such as **AWS Lambda, Amazon CloudWatch, AWS Cost Explorer**, and **AWS Config**.

1. Overview of Cost Optimization and Cleanup Automation

Cost optimization involves continuously monitoring, analyzing, and adjusting resources to achieve the desired performance at the lowest possible cost. Automation plays a crucial role in this process by eliminating manual interventions, reducing human errors, and ensuring continuous improvement in cloud cost management.

Typical cost optimization and cleanup tasks include:

- **Identifying and terminating unused or underutilized EC2 instances.**
- **Rightsizing instances based on utilization patterns.**
- **Cleaning up unattached EBS volumes.**
- **Deleting outdated snapshots or old backups.**
- **Removing unused Elastic IPs or load balancers.**

2. Key Components of the Solution

To automate cost optimization and cleanup tasks, you will use a combination of the following AWS services:

- **AWS Lambda**: Executes cleanup logic based on utilization metrics or schedule.
- **AWS CloudWatch Metrics and Alarms**: Monitors key utilization metrics and triggers actions when thresholds are crossed.
- **AWS Cost Explorer**: Provides insights into cost and usage trends.
- **AWS Config**: Monitors and assesses AWS resource configurations for compliance and cost-efficiency.

3. Step-by-Step Implementation

We'll create a solution that automatically identifies and terminates **underutilized EC2 instances** and cleans up **unattached EBS volumes** using AWS Lambda and CloudWatch. We will also leverage AWS Cost Explorer to generate insights for further cost optimization.

Step 1: Identify and Tag Underutilized EC2 Instances
Create CloudWatch Alarms for Underutilized EC2 Instances:

- In the **Amazon CloudWatch Console**, create a new alarm for the **CPUUtilization** metric of your EC2 instances.
- Set the threshold to a low value (e.g., below 5%) for a significant period (e.g., 7 days) to detect consistently underutilized instances.

Example Alarm Configuration:

- **Metric**: CPUUtilization
- **Threshold**: Less than 5%
- **Evaluation Period**: 168 hours (7 days)
- **Action**: **Trigger a Lambda function** to mark or terminate the instance.

Tag Underutilized Instances:

- Before terminating instances automatically, tag them for easier identification or manual review. Use AWS Lambda to add a tag (e.g., Underutilized) to the instances that breach the CloudWatch alarm threshold.

Example Lambda function code for tagging:

```python
import boto3

ec2 = boto3.client('ec2')

def lambda_handler(event, context):
    instance_id = event['detail']['instance-id']
    ec2.create_tags(
        Resources=[instance_id],
        Tags=[{'Key': 'Underutilized', 'Value': 'true'}]
    )
    print(f"Tagged instance
{instance_id} as underutilized.")
```

Schedule a Periodic Review and Termination of Tagged Instances:

- Create a Lambda function that periodically checks for instances tagged as Underutilized and terminates them if no action has been taken manually. Schedule this Lambda function using a **CloudWatch Event rule**.

Example Lambda function for termination:

285

```
import boto3

ec2 = boto3.client('ec2')

def lambda_handler(event, context):
    # Describe instances with the 'Underutilized' tag
    response = ec2.describe_instances(
        Filters=[
            {'Name': 'tag:Underutilized',
'Values': ['true']}
        ]
    )
    instances_to_terminate = [
        instance['InstanceId']
        for reservation in response['Reservations']
        for instance in reservation['Instances']
        if instance['State']['Name'] == 'running'
    ]

    if instances_to_terminate:
        ec2.terminate_instances
(InstanceIds=instances_to_terminate)
        print(f"Terminated instances:
{instances_to_terminate}")
    else:
        print("No underutilized instances found to terminate.")
```

Step 2: Clean Up Unattached EBS Volumes

Unattached **EBS volumes** can incur costs without being in use. To automate cleanup, you can use AWS Lambda to periodically identify and delete unattached volumes.

1. **Create a Lambda Function to Delete Unattached EBS Volumes**:

```
import boto3

ec2 = boto3.client('ec2')

def lambda_handler(event, context):
    # Describe unattached EBS volumes
    response = ec2.describe_volumes(
        Filters=[
            {'Name': 'status', 'Values': ['available']}
        ]
    )
    unattached_volumes = [
        volume['VolumeId']
        for volume in response['Volumes']
    ]

    for volume_id in unattached_volumes:
        try:
            ec2.delete_volume(VolumeId=volume_id)
            print(f"Deleted unattached volume:
{volume_id}")
        except Exception as e:
            print(f"Failed to delete volume
{volume_id}: {str(e)}")
```

Schedule the Lambda Function:

- Use **CloudWatch Events** to schedule this Lambda function to run periodically (e.g., every day or week).

Step 3: Automate Cost Analysis with AWS Cost Explorer

To gain deeper insights into cost trends, use **AWS Cost Explorer** to identify spending patterns and areas for optimization. Create a Lambda function that periodically retrieves cost data and generates reports.

Create an IAM Role for Cost Explorer Access:

- Grant the Lambda function permissions to access AWS Cost Explorer by

287

attaching the **CostExplorerReadOnlyAccess** policy to its IAM role.

Create a Lambda Function to Retrieve Cost Data:

```
import boto3
from datetime import datetime, timedelta

cost_explorer = boto3.client('ce')

def lambda_handler(event, context):
    # Set the time range for the cost report
    end_date = datetime.today().strftime('%Y-%m-%d')
    start_date = (datetime.today() -
    timedelta(days=30)).strftime('%Y-%m-%d')

    # Get cost data for the last 30 days
    response = cost_explorer.get_cost_and_usage(
        TimePeriod={
            'Start': start_date,
            'End': end_date
        },
        Granularity='DAILY',
        Metrics=['UnblendedCost']
    )

    # Print or store the cost report
    print("Cost report for the last 30 days:")
    for result in response['ResultsByTime']:
        print(f"Date: {result[
'TimePeriod']['Start']}, Cost:
${result['Total']['UnblendedCost']['Amount']}")
```

1. **Schedule the Lambda Function**:

- Use **CloudWatch Events** to schedule this Lambda function to run monthly or weekly. Store the generated cost data in an **S3 bucket** for reporting or analysis.

4. Advanced Cleanup and Optimization Use Cases

4.1. Cleanup Old Snapshots

To further reduce costs, automate the cleanup of old EBS snapshots. Create a Lambda function that checks the age of snapshots and deletes those older than a certain threshold (e.g., 90 days).

4.2. Remove Unused Elastic IPs and Load Balancers

Identify and release unused Elastic IPs or decommission old load balancers that are not in use. This can be automated using Lambda functions that periodically scan for unused resources and perform cleanup actions.

5. Best Practices for Cost Optimization and Cleanup Automation

5.1. Use Tags for Resource Tracking

Apply consistent tagging to resources for better cost allocation and tracking. For example, use tags like Project, Environment, or Owner to associate costs with specific teams or projects.

5.2. Implement a Governance and Approval Process

For critical resources, implement an approval workflow using **AWS Step Functions** or **AWS Systems Manager** to ensure that cleanup actions are reviewed before being executed.

5.3. Regularly Review and Optimize Reserved Instances and Savings Plans

Use **AWS Cost Explorer** to identify opportunities for savings through **Reserved Instances** or **Savings Plans**. Automate periodic checks to identify unused reservations or misaligned resources.

6. Monitoring and Reporting Cost Optimization Results

- **Create CloudWatch Dashboards** to visualize cost savings, underutilized instances, and cleaned-up resources over time.
- **Store cleanup and cost reports in S3** for long-term analysis and trend identification.

- **Automate notifications using SNS** to inform stakeholders of cost optimization and cleanup activities.

Cost optimization and cleanup automation are essential for efficient cloud operations. By leveraging AWS Lambda, CloudWatch, Cost Explorer, and other services, you can automate the identification and cleanup of underutilized resources, eliminate unnecessary costs, and maintain a lean cloud environment.

Implementing best practices such as using tags, reviewing savings plans, and automating governance ensures that your optimization and cleanup efforts remain controlled and effective. This proactive approach empowers organizations to maximize the value of their cloud investments while minimizing wasteful spending.

Performance Optimization for AWS Lambda

Optimizing Lambda Cold Starts
AWS Lambda offers an efficient way to run code without provisioning or managing servers, but one of the common challenges associated with Lambda functions is **cold starts**. A **cold start** refers to the latency introduced when a Lambda function is invoked for the first time or after a period of inactivity. This latency occurs because AWS needs to create a new execution environment for the function, load the code, and initialize dependencies before executing the request.

Cold starts can be especially noticeable in time-sensitive applications or those that require consistent low-latency responses, such as APIs, user-facing applications, and real-time processing tasks. In this section, we'll explore the causes of cold starts, strategies to mitigate them, and best practices to optimize Lambda function performance.

1. Understanding Cold Starts in AWS Lambda

When a Lambda function is invoked, AWS attempts to use an **existing execution environment** if one is available. If no existing environment is available or if the function hasn't been invoked recently, AWS must create a new execution environment. This process involves:

- **Creating a new container** to run the function.

- **Allocating the required memory and CPU resources**.
- **Initializing the runtime** (such as Python, Node.js, Java, etc.).
- **Loading the function's code and dependencies**.
- **Running any initialization code** (e.g., importing libraries, setting up database connections).

A cold start only occurs when a new execution environment is required. Once the environment is created, subsequent invocations (known as **warm starts**) reuse the existing environment, resulting in lower latency.

Factors Affecting Cold Start Latency:

- **Runtime Choice**: Languages like Java and .NET typically have longer cold starts due to runtime initialization, while Node.js and Python have shorter cold starts.
- **Function Size and Dependencies**: Larger deployment packages with heavy dependencies lead to longer cold start times.
- **VPC Configuration**: Lambda functions running inside a VPC (Virtual Private Cloud) take longer to initialize due to the time required to attach to the VPC and network interfaces.

2. Strategies to Mitigate Cold Starts

2.1. Use Provisioned Concurrency

Provisioned Concurrency is a feature that keeps your Lambda function environments warm and ready to respond instantly. When you enable Provisioned Concurrency for a Lambda function, AWS pre-creates execution environments based on the specified concurrency value, ensuring that your function always has a certain number of environments running.

How to Set Up Provisioned Concurrency:
  Go to the AWS Lambda Console:

- Open the **AWS Lambda Console** and choose your function.

Enable Provisioned Concurrency:

- Under **Concurrency settings**, click **Add provisioned concurrency**.
- Specify the amount of concurrency you need (e.g., 10) based on expected traffic patterns.

Monitor Costs:

- Be aware that enabling Provisioned Concurrency incurs additional costs, as you are paying to keep the environments warm even when they are not actively processing requests.

2.2. Optimize Function Code and Dependencies

The size of your Lambda deployment package and the number of dependencies you include can have a significant impact on cold start latency. To optimize code and reduce the package size:

- **Use Smaller Libraries**: Prefer lightweight libraries over larger ones whenever possible. For example, if you only need to make HTTP requests, consider using **urllib3** instead of installing the entire **requests** library.
- **Minimize Initialization Code**: Only include initialization logic that is necessary. For example, avoid making unnecessary database connections or loading large datasets during initialization.

Example of Optimized Initialization:

```
# Avoid unnecessary initialization outside the handler
import boto3

def lambda_handler(event, context):
    # Initialize S3 client only when needed
    s3 = boto3.client('s3')
    response = s3.list_buckets()
    return response
```

2.3. Use Lambda Layers for Reusable Code

If your Lambda functions share common libraries or dependencies, you can use **Lambda Layers** to package these shared components separately. This approach reduces the size of individual deployment packages and minimizes the time needed to load dependencies during cold starts.

Steps to Use Lambda Layers:
Create a Lambda Layer:

- Package the required dependencies (e.g., a ZIP file with Python libraries) and upload them as a Lambda Layer.

Attach the Layer to Your Lambda Function:

- In the Lambda Console, navigate to **Layers** under your function and add the required layers.

2.4. Optimize VPC Configuration

If your Lambda function requires access to resources within a VPC, such as an RDS database, it's essential to optimize VPC settings to reduce cold start times. Cold start latency can increase when Lambda functions are configured to connect to a VPC due to the time required to create **Elastic Network Interfaces (ENIs)**.

Best Practices for VPC Optimization:

- **Minimize Subnets and Security Groups**: Reduce the number of subnets and security groups associated with the Lambda function to lower ENI creation times.
- **Use AWS PrivateLink**: Consider using **AWS PrivateLink** to access services like S3, DynamoDB, or others privately without the need to connect your Lambda function to a VPC.

2.5. Optimize Runtime and Execution Memory Allocation

Selecting the right runtime and memory allocation can have a significant impact on cold start performance. Some runtimes, such as **Python** and **Node.js**, are known to have shorter cold start times compared to **Java** and **.NET** due to lighter-weight initialization requirements.

Adjust Memory Settings:

- Allocating more memory to a Lambda function not only increases CPU capacity but can also reduce cold start times. You can experiment with different memory settings using the **AWS Lambda Power Tuning tool** to find the optimal memory-to-performance ratio.

2.6. Keep Execution Environments Warm with Scheduled Invocations

If you are unable to use Provisioned Concurrency or need to keep costs low, you can use a **CloudWatch Event Rule** to invoke your Lambda function at regular intervals to keep the execution environments warm. This approach, known as **"warming up"**, reduces the likelihood of a cold start for infrequent or sporadic invocations.

How to Set Up a Scheduled Rule:

1. **Go to the CloudWatch Console** and create a **new rule**.
2. **Choose Schedule Expression** and set the frequency (e.g., every 5 minutes).
3. **Select Your Lambda Function** as the target of the rule.

2.7. Adopt Asynchronous Invocation Patterns

For workloads that are not latency-sensitive, consider using **asynchronous invocation** patterns. Asynchronous invocations in Lambda automatically queue incoming requests and process them as soon as an execution environment becomes available. This approach is ideal for background processing tasks or batch workloads.

3. Measuring and Monitoring Cold Starts

3.1. Use CloudWatch Metrics

AWS Lambda automatically publishes several key metrics to **Amazon CloudWatch**, including **Duration, Invocation Count, Error Count**, and **Init Duration**. The **Init Duration** metric specifically measures the time taken for a cold start, allowing you to monitor cold start occurrences.

- **Track Init Duration**: Set up CloudWatch alarms to alert you if the **Init Duration** metric exceeds an acceptable threshold for your application.

3.2. Leverage AWS X-Ray for Tracing

AWS X-Ray provides detailed tracing and insights into your Lambda function's execution path. By enabling X-Ray for your Lambda functions, you can:

- Identify where cold starts occur.
- Measure the impact of cold starts on overall response times.
- Analyze initialization delays in specific segments of your function's execution.

4. Best Practices for Reducing Cold Starts

- **Deploy functions using lighter runtimes** like **Python** or **Node.js** if your application does not have specific requirements for other runtimes.
- **Keep deployment packages small** by only including the essential dependencies needed for the function.
- **Use Provisioned Concurrency** for high-traffic functions or critical functions where latency is a key concern.
- **Optimize VPC configurations** and avoid unnecessary VPC attachments whenever possible.
- **Monitor cold start latency** using CloudWatch metrics and proactively take measures when cold start times impact application performance.

Optimizing cold starts in AWS Lambda is essential for achieving low-latency performance in serverless applications. By implementing strategies like using Provisioned Concurrency, optimizing code and dependencies, reducing VPC attachment latency, and monitoring key metrics, you can significantly reduce cold start times and enhance the responsiveness of your Lambda functions.

Following these best practices will enable you to build scalable and efficient serverless architectures that meet user expectations for real-time performance, even in the face of fluctuating workloads. By proactively addressing cold starts, you can leverage the full potential of AWS Lambda to power your applications reliably and cost-effectively.

Tuning Memory and Timeout Settings for Efficiency

Memory and timeout settings in AWS Lambda are crucial factors influencing both the performance and cost-efficiency of your functions. AWS Lambda allows you to configure memory in 1MB increments (from 128MB to 10GB) and set timeouts ranging from 1 second to 15 minutes. These settings not only determine the resources allocated to your Lambda functions but also impact their execution time, concurrency limits, and pricing.

In this section, we will explore how to effectively tune **memory and timeout settings** to achieve the optimal balance between performance and cost.

1. Understanding the Relationship Between Memory and Performance

The memory setting in Lambda not only determines the amount of memory available to the function but also allocates proportional CPU and network resources. Increasing the memory allocation results in higher CPU power, which can lead to a significant reduction in execution time for CPU-bound functions.

For instance:

- **Higher memory allocation** results in more CPU and faster execution, reducing the overall duration of the function. This can be especially beneficial for compute-heavy functions like image processing, data transformations, or machine learning inference.
- **Lower memory allocation** saves cost but may lead to higher execution time and potential timeouts, particularly for CPU-intensive tasks.

2. Strategies for Memory and Timeout Optimization

2.1. Analyze Function Execution Time with Different Memory Settings

AWS Lambda allows you to experiment with different memory configurations to find the optimal balance between performance and cost. When tuning memory settings, keep the following considerations in mind:

- **Identify the Bottlenecks**: Determine if your Lambda function is **CPU-bound** (tasks like data processing or encryption) or **memory-bound** (handling large in-memory datasets). CPU-bound functions benefit more from additional memory due to proportional CPU allocation.
- **Measure Execution Time**: Increasing memory allocation can often lead to significant reductions in execution time. However, higher memory also means higher costs per millisecond of execution, so there's a trade-off to consider.

Example: Python Function Execution Time and Cost Analysis

If you have a Python Lambda function that processes large JSON files, you may want to compare its performance with different memory settings.

```python
import json

def lambda_handler(event, context):
    # Simulate JSON processing
    data = json.loads(event['body'])
    result = {key: len(value) for key, value in data.items()}

    return {
        'statusCode': 200,
        'body': json.dumps(result)
    }
```

For the above function, you can deploy it with memory settings ranging from 128MB to 1024MB and use **AWS CloudWatch** to monitor the duration and cost for each setting.

2.2. Use the AWS Lambda Power Tuning Tool

AWS Lambda Power Tuning is an open-source tool provided by AWS that helps you find the optimal memory and timeout configuration for your functions. It runs your Lambda function with different memory settings and generates a visualization of the performance and cost trade-offs.

Steps to Use the Power Tuning Tool:

Deploy the AWS Lambda Power Tuning State Machine:

- The tool is available as a pre-built **AWS Step Functions** state machine. You can find deployment instructions on the AWS GitHub repository for Lambda Power Tuning.

Run the State Machine:

- Specify the Lambda function ARN, payload (if any), and the memory range you want to test (e.g., from 128MB to 1024MB).

Analyze the Results:

- The tool generates a report showing the execution duration and estimated cost for each memory configuration. Choose the memory setting that provides the best balance between performance and cost for your specific use case.

2.3. Set Appropriate Timeout Values

The **timeout setting** determines the maximum execution duration allowed for a Lambda function. If your function exceeds this duration, AWS automatically terminates it and returns a Task timed out error. When tuning the timeout value:

- **Base the Timeout on Average and Peak Execution Times**: Analyze the average execution time of your Lambda function using CloudWatch logs or X-Ray traces. Set the timeout slightly above the longest expected duration, allowing a buffer for unpredictable latency spikes.
- **Monitor and Adjust**: Regularly monitor execution times, especially if your function's workload or dependencies change over time. For example, if a downstream API starts responding more slowly, your Lambda function may require a longer timeout.

3. Measuring and Monitoring Execution Metrics

3.1. Leverage CloudWatch Metrics

CloudWatch provides several key metrics that help you understand how your Lambda function is performing with different memory and timeout settings. The key metrics to monitor include:

- **Duration**: The execution time of the function, measured in milliseconds.
- **Throttles**: The number of times Lambda throttles invocations due to concurrency limits.
- **Errors**: The number of failed function invocations.

- **Timeouts**: Instances where the function exceeded its specified timeout.

3.2. Analyze Logs to Fine-Tune Performance

Review **CloudWatch Logs** for details on each invocation, including:

- **Execution start and end times**.
- **Initialization latency** for cold starts.
- **Error messages or stack traces** for functions that fail due to timeouts or memory exhaustion.

By analyzing these logs, you can identify specific areas where memory or timeout settings need adjustment.

4. Balancing Performance and Cost

4.1. Evaluate the Cost Implications of Higher Memory Allocation

While increasing memory allocation typically improves performance, it also raises the cost per execution. AWS charges for Lambda based on both **execution duration** and **memory size**, so it's essential to evaluate the cost impact of increasing memory.

For example:

- If increasing memory from 256MB to 512MB reduces execution time from 5 seconds to 3 seconds, the cost increase may be justified. However, if the execution time only drops slightly, a lower memory setting may be more cost-effective.

4.2. Monitor Timeout-Related Errors

Timeout errors can lead to increased costs, especially if your function is re-invoked automatically or retried. When tuning timeouts:

- **Avoid Excessively High Timeouts**: Setting an unnecessarily high timeout can increase costs if your function runs into unexpected delays.

- **Use Exponential Backoff for Retries**: If your Lambda function is part of a larger workflow or event chain, implement exponential backoff and retry logic to avoid unnecessary re-invocations.

5. Best Practices for Tuning Memory and Timeout Settings

- **Use the Lambda Power Tuning Tool**: Leverage the Power Tuning tool to find the optimal memory configuration for your function.
- **Start with a Balanced Configuration**: Start with a moderate memory allocation (e.g., 512MB) and observe the initial execution times before fine-tuning.
- **Measure Performance with Realistic Data**: Use real-world event payloads and conditions to test the function's performance, ensuring that your optimizations are effective in production scenarios.
- **Set Timeouts Slightly Above Expected Duration**: Allow enough buffer to handle occasional latency spikes without terminating the function prematurely.

Tuning memory and timeout settings for AWS Lambda is a crucial step in optimizing function performance and cost-efficiency. By understanding the relationship between memory, CPU, and execution time, you can make informed decisions on the appropriate configurations for your functions.

Using tools like the AWS Lambda Power Tuning tool, monitoring key metrics with CloudWatch, and balancing performance with cost considerations enables you to create highly efficient Lambda functions that meet your application's requirements. Following these best practices will help you achieve the optimal trade-off between performance, cost, and reliability in your serverless applications.

Reducing Lambda Execution Time with Python Best Practices

AWS Lambda is designed to offer highly scalable, event-driven computing without the need for server management. However, efficient Lambda execution hinges not only on memory and timeout configurations but also on following best coding practices. When using **Python**, there are several techniques and optimizations you can apply to minimize execution time, reduce costs, and enhance overall function performance.

In this section, we'll explore Python-specific best practices for reducing AWS Lambda execution time and ensuring high-performing, reliable serverless applications.

1. Optimize Python Code for Speed

1.1. Minimize Package Imports

One of the easiest ways to improve Lambda execution speed is by **reducing unnecessary package imports**. Python allows importing modules and libraries at the global level, but this can increase the initialization time if you import too many packages. Instead, consider importing libraries only when needed, within specific functions.

Example: Importing Only When Needed

```python
# Importing at the top level increases cold start latency
import boto3
import pandas as pd  # Only import heavy libraries when absolutely
necessary

def lambda_handler(event, context):
    # Use lightweight modules by default
    import json

    # Only use boto3 when required
    s3 = boto3.client('s3')
    response = s3.list_buckets()
    return response
```

Best Practices:

- **Avoid importing large libraries** (like Pandas or Numpy) unless necessary. Use lighter alternatives if possible.
- If you're using multiple functions within a Lambda file, organize your imports and only load dependencies in the respective functions.

1.2. Reduce Execution Time with List Comprehensions and Generators

Using Python's built-in features such as **list comprehensions** and **generator expressions** can lead to significant improvements in execution speed. These features allow you to perform tasks in fewer lines of code and more efficiently.

Example: Using List Comprehension

```
# Using list comprehension for faster data processing
numbers = [1, 2, 3, 4, 5]
squared_numbers = [x**2 for x in numbers]  # List comprehension is
faster than traditional loops
```

Generators are particularly useful when dealing with large datasets, as they yield items lazily and consume less memory.

Example: Using Generators

```
# Yield data items one at a time instead of creating a large list
in memory
def process_large_data(data):
    for item in data:
        yield item * 2
```

2. Optimize Data Handling and Processing

2.1. Avoid Inefficient Data Conversions

Data conversions in Python can be time-consuming and memory-intensive. To minimize execution time:

- **Limit type conversions** unless they are necessary. For instance, avoid repeatedly converting a list to a set in every iteration of a loop.
- **Use efficient data structures** like sets and dictionaries for lookups instead of lists.

Example: Optimize Data Lookups

```
# Use a set for fast lookups
valid_items = {'apple', 'banana', 'orange'}

def is_valid(item):
    return item in valid_items  # Faster lookup compared to lists
```

2.2. Streamline File I/O Operations

Reading and writing files in Lambda should be done judiciously, as these operations can slow down execution. Where possible:

- **Read data in chunks** instead of loading entire files into memory.
- **Use built-in Python modules like csv** for processing large CSV files efficiently.

Example: Reading Large Files in Chunks

```
import csv

def process_large_file(file_path):
    with open(file_path, 'r') as file:
        reader = csv.reader(file)
        for row in reader:
            # Process each row without loading entire file into
            memory
            process_row(row)
```

3. Optimize Network Calls

3.1. Reduce Number of Network Requests

Making network calls, such as querying AWS services or third-party APIs, can increase Lambda execution time. Minimize the number of requests by:

- **Batching API requests** whenever possible.
- **Caching frequently used data** in memory or temporary storage.

Example: Batching S3 Get Requests

```python
import boto3

s3 = boto3.client('s3')

def get_files(bucket_name, keys):
    # Use batch processing to minimize the number of API calls
    return s3.get_objects(Bucket=bucket_name, Keys=keys)
```

3.2. Optimize Third-Party API Calls with Connection Pooling

If your Lambda function interacts with external services, such as databases or REST APIs, use **connection pooling** to minimize connection overhead.

Example: Using requests with Connection Pooling

```python
import requests

session = requests.Session()  # Create a persistent connection pool

def fetch_data(url):
    response = session.get(url)  # Reuse the same connection
    session
    return response.json()
```

4. Efficiently Manage AWS SDK Interactions

4.1. Reuse AWS SDK Clients

When working with AWS services like **S3**, **DynamoDB**, or **Lambda**, it's essential to reuse SDK clients instead of creating them every time the function is invoked. Reusing clients at the global level avoids repeated initialization, which can save execution time.

Example: Reusing a Boto3 Client

```python
import boto3

# Initialize Boto3 clients globally to reduce cold start latency
s3_client = boto3.client('s3')
dynamodb_client = boto3.client('dynamodb')

def lambda_handler(event, context):
    # Reuse clients for AWS interactions
    s3_response = s3_client.list_buckets()
    return s3_response
```

4.2. Leverage Asynchronous SDK Calls

In use cases where multiple AWS service calls need to be made concurrently, using **asynchronous execution** can improve overall performance. For example, you can use **Python's asyncio module** to perform asynchronous calls with **Boto3**.

5. Optimize Data Serialization and Deserialization

5.1. Use Efficient Data Formats

Serializing and deserializing data is often necessary for AWS Lambda functions. To reduce execution time:

- Use more efficient data formats such as **JSON** instead of **XML**.
- Avoid unnecessary conversions between strings, bytes, and other data types.

307

Example: Using JSON for Efficient Serialization

```
import json

def lambda_handler(event, context):
    # Use JSON for fast serialization and deserialization
    data = json.loads(event['body'])
    return json.dumps({'result': data})
```

6. Monitor and Profile Lambda Performance

6.1. Use AWS X-Ray for Detailed Tracing

Enable **AWS X-Ray** for your Lambda function to gain insights into execution paths and latency breakdowns. X-Ray allows you to:

- **Identify bottlenecks** in function initialization or external service calls.
- **Measure latency** for each segment of your function's execution.

6.2. Profile Your Code with Python Profiling Tools

Use Python's built-in profiling tools like **cProfile** to identify which parts of your code are consuming the most time. This helps you focus optimization efforts where they will have the most impact.

Example: Profiling Code with cProfile

```
import cProfile

def my_function():
    # Function logic here
    pass

cProfile.run('my_function()')
```

Reducing Lambda execution time with Python best practices can lead to substantial improvements in both performance and cost-efficiency. By optimizing your code, minimizing unnecessary operations, reusing AWS clients, and managing data effectively, you can achieve significant gains in execution speed.

Implementing these best practices ensures that your AWS Lambda functions run efficiently, providing a seamless experience for users while keeping costs under control. With continuous monitoring and profiling, you can stay proactive in refining your code and adapting to changing workloads.

Analyzing Performance Using AWS X-Ray

AWS X-Ray is a powerful service that enables developers to gain deep insights into their distributed applications, including **AWS Lambda** functions. It provides detailed tracing of application requests as they flow through different services, which helps in identifying performance bottlenecks, visualizing service dependencies, and debugging latency issues.

In this section, we'll explore how to leverage **AWS X-Ray** to analyze the performance of AWS Lambda functions and other integrated services. We'll cover the core concepts of X-Ray, step-by-step implementation, and best practices for effectively utilizing X-Ray to monitor and optimize serverless applications.

1. Overview of AWS X-Ray

AWS X-Ray provides tracing capabilities that allow developers to monitor the requests made to their applications. X-Ray traces the path of requests and records latency data for each segment of the request flow. It enables you to visualize the interaction between Lambda functions, APIs, databases, and other AWS services, and identify areas of improvement.

Key Features of AWS X-Ray:

- **Trace Generation**: Automatically generates traces for Lambda invocations, API Gateway calls, and other integrated services.
- **Latency Analysis**: Breaks down response times into individual segments, allowing you to pinpoint delays in specific operations.
- **Error Detection**: Identifies errors, exceptions, and throttling events.
- **Service Map**: Provides a visual representation of service interactions, helping you understand dependencies and architecture complexity.

2. Enabling AWS X-Ray for Lambda Functions

Step 1: Enable X-Ray Tracing in Lambda Console
Go to the AWS Lambda Console:

- Open the **AWS Lambda Console** and select your Lambda function.

Enable Active Tracing:

- Under **Configuration**, select **Monitoring and operations tools**.
- In the **X-Ray** section, select **Active tracing** to enable X-Ray tracing for your Lambda function.
- Save the changes.

Attach the Required IAM Role:

- Ensure that your Lambda function has an IAM role with the AWSXRayDa emonWriteAccess policy. This policy allows Lambda to send trace data to X-Ray.

Step 2: Configure X-Ray in Your Application Code (Optional)
While enabling X-Ray at the console level is sufficient, you can further configure X-Ray in your Python code using the **AWS X-Ray SDK**. This is

useful if you want to add custom annotations or subsegments to the trace data.

Example of Integrating X-Ray SDK in Python Code:

```python
from aws_xray_sdk.core import xray_recorder
from aws_xray_sdk.core import patch_all
import boto3

# Patch all supported libraries (like boto3, requests, etc.)
patch_all()

def lambda_handler(event, context):
    # Start a custom subsegment to trace this specific block of
    code
    with xray_recorder.in_subsegment('custom-segment'):
        s3 = boto3.client('s3')
        response = s3.list_buckets()

    return response
```

Key Points:

- **Patch Libraries**: Use the patch_all() method to automatically trace calls to supported libraries like **Boto3** and **Requests**.
- **Custom Subsegments**: Create subsegments within your code to gain detailed insights into specific operations.

3. Visualizing and Analyzing X-Ray Traces

Step 1: View Service Map
Go to the AWS X-Ray Console:

- Open the **AWS X-Ray Console** and select **Service map**.
- The service map displays a visual representation of the interactions between Lambda functions, API Gateway, DynamoDB, S3, and other integrated services.

Analyze Service Dependencies:

- The service map shows nodes representing each service and lines connecting them to indicate interactions. You can see the latency between services, errors, and request rates.
- Click on a specific node (such as a Lambda function) to view detailed metrics and traces.

Step 2: Explore X-Ray Traces
Go to the Traces Section:

- In the X-Ray Console, click **Traces** to view individual traces collected from Lambda invocations.
- Each trace contains segments representing different operations (e.g., Lambda initialization, Boto3 calls, database queries).

Analyze Trace Segments:

- Click on a trace to view its detailed segments. Each segment displays the latency, error information, and metadata for a specific operation.
- Use the **TimeLine View** to identify which segment of the request is consuming the most time.

Step 3: Identify Performance Bottlenecks

- **Look for High Latency Segments**: Identify segments where the latency is significantly higher than others. These segments may indicate network delays, inefficient code, or slow external services.
- **Check for Errors and Throttling**: If segments are marked in red, this indicates an error or exception. Click on the segment to view details and understand the cause.
- **Compare Latency Across Multiple Traces**: Look at multiple traces to identify recurring patterns of high latency or errors.

4. Best Practices for Analyzing Lambda Performance with X-Ray

4.1. Add Custom Annotations for Better Insights

Custom annotations allow you to filter and search traces based on specific business logic or conditions. For example, you can add annotations based on user IDs, order IDs, or event types.

Example of Adding Annotations:

```
from aws_xray_sdk.core import xray_recorder

def lambda_handler(event, context):
    # Add a custom annotation for user ID
    xray_recorder.put_annotation("UserId", event.get("user_id"))

    # Your business logic here
```

4.2. Create Custom Subsegments for Critical Operations

If certain operations within your Lambda function are critical, create custom subsegments to gain detailed insights into their performance. This helps you pinpoint exactly where issues occur.

Example of Using Custom Subsegments:

```
def lambda_handler(event, context):
    with xray_recorder.in_subsegment('DatabaseQuery'):
        # Perform database operations and capture the latency
        db_response = query_database(event.get("user_id"))
```

4.3. Monitor Cold Start Latency

AWS X-Ray can help you measure cold start latency by showing the time taken for initialization before the main function execution. Look for segments labeled as **Initialization** and compare them with **Invocation** segments to identify cold starts.

4.4. Use X-Ray with Other AWS Services for End-to-End Tracing

X-Ray integrates seamlessly with services like **API Gateway**, **DynamoDB**, **SQS**, and **Step Functions**. Enable tracing on these services to gain a complete picture of the request flow from entry to exit.

5. Integrating X-Ray with Other Monitoring Tools

- **Use CloudWatch Metrics and X-Ray Together**: CloudWatch provides a high-level overview with key metrics, while X-Ray offers granular insights into individual traces. Use both services in combination for comprehensive monitoring.
- **Visualize Data in AWS CloudWatch Dashboards**: Create dashboards to combine X-Ray traces with CloudWatch metrics for centralized monitoring.

AWS X-Ray is a vital tool for analyzing and optimizing the performance of serverless applications running on AWS Lambda. By enabling tracing, configuring custom segments, and monitoring service maps and traces, you can gain valuable insights into the performance and behavior of your Lambda functions and other AWS services.

Following best practices such as adding annotations, monitoring cold starts, and leveraging end-to-end tracing allows you to identify and address performance bottlenecks, reduce latency, and improve overall application reliability. With the visibility provided by X-Ray, you can ensure that your serverless applications meet the desired performance standards and deliver an optimal user experience.

Security Best Practices for AWS Lambda

S ecuring Lambda Functions with IAM and VPC
Security is a critical component when deploying serverless
applications using AWS Lambda. Given the highly distributed nature
of serverless architectures, ensuring that Lambda functions are secure from
unauthorized access and potential threats requires a combination of access
control, network security, and monitoring practices. AWS provides robust
features for managing permissions and network configurations using **IAM
(Identity and Access Management)** and **VPC (Virtual Private Cloud)**.

In this section, we will explore how to secure Lambda functions using **IAM
roles and policies** and **VPC configurations** to create a secure environment
for your serverless applications.

1. Securing Lambda with IAM Roles and Policies

IAM provides fine-grained access control over AWS resources, allowing you
to define which actions are allowed for specific users, groups, or services.
When it comes to Lambda, IAM plays a central role in controlling what your
Lambda functions can and cannot do within your AWS environment.

1.1. Understanding IAM Roles for Lambda Functions

Each Lambda function requires an **IAM role** with a set of permissions
that dictate which AWS services and resources the function can access. This
IAM role is known as the **Lambda execution role**. The principle of **least
privilege** should guide the assignment of these roles, meaning that each
Lambda function should only have the permissions necessary to perform its

specific tasks.

Key Components of IAM for Lambda:

- **Execution Role**: The IAM role that Lambda uses to execute functions.
- **Permissions Policy**: A policy document that specifies the actions a role can perform on AWS resources.
- **Resource-Based Policies**: Policies attached to AWS resources, such as S3 buckets or DynamoDB tables, to control which services can access them.

1.2. Best Practices for IAM Role Permissions
a. Apply the Principle of Least Privilege

- **Create dedicated IAM roles for each Lambda function** or group of functions with similar requirements. Avoid using overly permissive roles or reusing a single role for multiple functions unless they share identical permission needs.
- Grant the minimum required permissions using **IAM policies**. For instance, if a Lambda function only needs to read data from an S3 bucket, avoid attaching broader permissions like s3:*.

Example of a Least Privilege IAM Policy for S3 Access:

```
{
    "Version": "2012-10-17",
    "Statement": [
        {
            "Effect": "Allow",
            "Action": ["s3:GetObject"],
            "Resource": ["arn:aws:s3:::my-secure-bucket/*"]
        }
    ]
}
```

b. Use Inline Policies for Fine-Grained Control

If you need to apply specific permissions directly to a Lambda role, consider using **inline policies** for individual Lambda functions. This approach provides more granular control over access permissions compared to managed policies.

c. Restrict Role Assumption Capabilities

Configure **IAM Trust Relationships** to control which Lambda functions or users can assume specific roles. This helps mitigate the risk of privilege escalation attacks within your AWS account.

1.3. Managing Resource-Based Policies

For AWS resources such as S3 buckets or DynamoDB tables, you can enforce additional access controls using **resource-based policies**. Resource-based policies allow you to specify which Lambda functions or roles can access specific resources.

Example of a Resource-Based Policy for an S3 Bucket:

```
{
    "Version": "2012-10-17",
    "Statement": [
        {
            "Effect": "Allow",
            "Principal": {
                "AWS":
                "arn:aws:iam::123456789012:role/my-lambda-execution-role"
            },
            "Action": "s3:GetObject",
            "Resource": "arn:aws:s3:::my-secure-bucket/*"
        }
    ]
}
```

2. Securing Lambda Functions with VPC Configurations

A **Virtual Private Cloud (VPC)** allows you to define a virtual network in AWS that resembles a traditional network, with control over routing tables, subnets, security groups, and more. Lambda functions can be configured to run inside a VPC, which helps secure your functions by controlling inbound and outbound traffic.

2.1. Benefits of Running Lambda Functions Inside a VPC

- **Private Network Access**: Functions inside a VPC can communicate privately with other AWS resources like **RDS databases, Elasticache clusters**, and on-premises resources via **AWS Direct Connect** or **VPN**.
- **Controlled Inbound and Outbound Traffic**: Using **security groups** and **network ACLs (Access Control Lists)**, you can precisely control which traffic is allowed to and from your Lambda functions.
- **Enhanced Security for Sensitive Data**: Placing functions inside a private subnet in a VPC restricts them from directly accessing the internet, reducing the attack surface.

2.2. Configuring Lambda with VPC Access
Step 1: Create a VPC with Subnets and Security Groups

- **Create a VPC** in the **VPC Console** with both **public and private subnets**. Private subnets are crucial for isolating sensitive resources from direct internet access.
- **Set up security groups** to allow only necessary inbound and outbound traffic. For example, a Lambda function that accesses a database should have a security group allowing traffic to the database's port (e.g., port 3306 for MySQL).

Step 2: Attach Lambda Functions to VPC Subnets

1. **Go to the AWS Lambda Console** and select your Lambda function.
2. In the **Configuration** section, under **VPC**, choose **Edit**.
3. **Select your VPC** and specify the **subnets** where the Lambda function will operate. Choose private subnets if your function needs to communicate with resources in a private network.
4. **Choose the Security Groups** associated with the function. These

318

security groups should allow necessary traffic between Lambda and the resources it interacts with, such as databases or caches.

Important Consideration: When configuring Lambda functions inside a VPC, it's essential to provide appropriate access to other AWS services (like S3 or DynamoDB) through either a **NAT Gateway** or **VPC Endpoints**. Without these configurations, the function may not be able to reach other services due to the restricted network access of private subnets.

2.3. Best Practices for Configuring Lambda with VPC

a. Use Private Subnets for Sensitive Resources

- Place Lambda functions that handle sensitive data or require access to databases and other secure resources inside **private subnets**. This ensures that functions are not directly exposed to the internet.

b. Utilize Security Groups to Control Traffic

- Create **security groups** that specifically allow communication between Lambda functions and other services, such as databases or S3 buckets. Avoid using overly permissive rules like 0.0.0.0/0 unless absolutely necessary.

c. Minimize VPC Attachments for Functions Not Requiring Private Access

- Not all Lambda functions need to be configured inside a VPC. If a function doesn't need private network access, leave it outside the VPC to avoid unnecessary cold start latency introduced by VPC attachment.

3. Monitoring and Auditing Lambda Security

3.1. Enable AWS CloudTrail for Lambda

Enable **AWS CloudTrail** to log all API calls related to your Lambda functions and other AWS services. CloudTrail allows you to:

- **Track changes to IAM policies** or roles associated with Lambda functions.
- **Monitor VPC configurations** to detect any unauthorized changes.
- **Audit Lambda executions** and detect anomalies such as unauthorized invocations.

3.2. Use AWS Config to Enforce Security Compliance

AWS Config enables you to continuously monitor and audit the configurations of AWS resources, including Lambda functions. With AWS Config, you can:

- **Create compliance rules** to check for overly permissive IAM roles, insecure VPC configurations, and other security risks.
- **Get alerts** for any non-compliant resources and automatically remediate issues using AWS Config rules and Lambda functions.

4. Best Practices for Securing Lambda Functions with IAM and VPC

- **Apply the Principle of Least Privilege**: Always assign the minimum necessary permissions to Lambda functions using IAM policies.
- **Use Resource-Based Policies for Enhanced Security**: Define access controls at the resource level for services like S3, DynamoDB, or SNS.
- **Run Sensitive Functions in Private VPC Subnets**: Configure Lambda functions to run inside private subnets when they need secure access to databases or internal APIs.
- **Implement Security Group Best Practices**: Limit inbound and outbound rules for security groups associated with Lambda functions to

allow only necessary traffic.

- **Monitor and Audit Security Configurations**: Regularly review Cloud-Trail logs, AWS Config rules, and IAM policies to ensure compliance with security standards.

Securing AWS Lambda functions using IAM roles and VPC configurations is essential for creating a secure serverless environment. By enforcing least privilege principles with IAM policies, controlling access to resources with resource-based policies, and isolating Lambda functions inside private subnets with VPC configurations, you can significantly reduce the risk of unauthorized access and security breaches.

Following best practices such as using dedicated IAM roles, leveraging security groups for traffic control, and monitoring configurations with CloudTrail and AWS Config ensures that your Lambda functions operate securely and meet compliance requirements. With these strategies, you can confidently deploy Lambda functions while maintaining a strong security posture across your AWS environment.

Encrypting Data Using AWS KMS

Data encryption is a fundamental security practice for protecting sensitive information, ensuring that only authorized parties can access and interpret the data. In the context of **AWS Lambda**, it is essential to encrypt data both at rest and in transit. AWS provides **AWS Key Management Service (KMS)**, which allows you to manage encryption keys and control access to encrypted data efficiently.

In this section, we will explore how to secure AWS Lambda functions by using **AWS KMS** to encrypt data. We'll cover key concepts, step-by-step implementation, and best practices for effectively managing and using encryption keys within serverless applications.

1. Overview of AWS KMS

AWS Key Management Service (KMS) is a managed service that enables you to create, manage, and control encryption keys. KMS allows you to use **customer-managed keys (CMKs)** and **AWS-managed keys** to encrypt data in various AWS services, including S3, Lambda, DynamoDB, and more. AWS KMS integrates seamlessly with Lambda, making it easy to protect sensitive data.

Key Features of AWS KMS:

- **Centralized Key Management**: Provides a single interface to create and manage encryption keys.
- **Fine-Grained Access Control**: Uses IAM policies and key policies to control access to encryption keys.
- **Seamless Integration**: Works natively with AWS services like Lambda, S3, DynamoDB, RDS, and others.
- **Auditability**: Logs all key usage and management actions in AWS CloudTrail.

2. Encrypting Environment Variables in AWS Lambda

Environment variables often contain sensitive information such as API keys, database credentials, or other configuration details. AWS Lambda allows you to encrypt these environment variables using AWS KMS keys.

Step 1: Create a KMS Key
Go to the AWS KMS Console:

- Open the **AWS KMS Console** and click **Create Key**.
- Choose **Symmetric** key type (asymmetric keys are typically not needed for Lambda environment variable encryption).

Define Key Usage Permissions:

- Assign IAM users, roles, or services that can use and manage the key. Ensure that your Lambda execution role has **decrypt permissions** for the key.

Create the Key:

- Give the key a name (e.g., Lambda-Env-Encryption-Key) and click **Create** to generate the key.

Step 2: Encrypt Environment Variables Using KMS
Go to the AWS Lambda Console:

- Open the **AWS Lambda Console** and select your Lambda function.

Configure Environment Variables:

- Under **Configuration**, navigate to **Environment variables**.
- Add or edit an environment variable and specify the **KMS key** to encrypt the variable. You can use the **AWS-managed key** or the **customer-managed key** created in KMS.

Assign Decryption Permissions:

- Ensure that the **Lambda execution role** has the kms:Decrypt permission to use the selected KMS key. You can attach an IAM policy like this:

```
{
    "Version": "2012-10-17",
    "Statement": [
        {
            "Effect": "Allow",
            "Action": [
```

```
            "kms:Decrypt"
        ],
        "Resource": [
            "arn:aws:kms:region:account-id:key/key-id"
        ]
    }
  ]
}
```

Test Decryption in Lambda Function:

- When your Lambda function runs, AWS automatically decrypts the environment variables before making them available to the function code.

Example Python Code to Access Decrypted Environment Variables:

```python
import os

def lambda_handler(event, context):
    # Access the decrypted environment variable
    secret_value = os.getenv('MY_SECRET_KEY')
    return {
        'statusCode': 200,
        'body': f"The secret key is: {secret_value}"
    }
```

3. Encrypting and Decrypting Data within Lambda Functions

In addition to environment variables, Lambda functions may need to encrypt and decrypt data on the fly. AWS KMS provides an API to perform client-side encryption and decryption within Lambda functions.

Step 1: Grant IAM Role Permissions for KMS Access

Ensure that the Lambda function's IAM execution role has permissions to use the **KMS key** for encryption and decryption. Attach an IAM policy like the following:

```
{
    "Version": "2012-10-17",
    "Statement": [
        {
            "Effect": "Allow",
            "Action": [
                "kms:Encrypt",
                "kms:Decrypt"
            ],
            "Resource": [
                "arn:aws:kms:region:account-id:key/key-id"
            ]
        }
    ]
}
```

Step 2: Encrypt Data Using KMS in Python

To encrypt data within your Lambda function, use the **boto3** library to interact with AWS KMS.

Example Code for Encrypting Data:

```python
import boto3
import base64

# Initialize KMS client
kms_client = boto3.client('kms')

def encrypt_data(plain_text):
    # Encrypt the plaintext using the KMS key
    response = kms_client.encrypt(
        KeyId='arn:aws:kms:region:account-id:key/key-id',
        Plaintext=plain_text
    )
    # Return the encrypted data as a base64-encoded string
    return base64.b64encode(response['
```

```
CiphertextBlob']).decode('utf-8')

def lambda_handler(event, context):
    secret_data = "Sensitive information"
    encrypted_data = encrypt_data(secret_data)

    return {
        'statusCode': 200,
        'body': f"Encrypted data: {encrypted_data}"
    }
```

Step 3: Decrypt Data Using KMS in Python
Example Code for Decrypting Data:

```
import boto3
import base64

# Initialize KMS client
kms_client = boto3.client('kms')

def decrypt_data(encrypted_data):
    # Decode the base64-encoded ciphertext
    decoded_data = base64.b64decode(encrypted_data)

    # Decrypt the data using the KMS key
    response = kms_client.decrypt(
        CiphertextBlob=decoded_data
    )
    return response['Plaintext'].decode('utf-8')

def lambda_handler(event, context):
    # Example encrypted data (replace with your encrypted string)
    encrypted_data = event['encrypted_data']
    decrypted_data = decrypt_data(encrypted_data)

    return {
        'statusCode': 200,
        'body': f"Decrypted data: {decrypted_data}"
```

```
}
```

4. Encrypting Data at Rest with AWS KMS

Data stored in AWS services such as **S3**, **DynamoDB**, **RDS**, and **EBS** can be encrypted using AWS KMS keys. This ensures that even if data is stored persistently, it remains secure.

4.1. Encrypting Data in Amazon S3

- **Server-Side Encryption (SSE-KMS)**: When uploading data to S3, you can specify a KMS key to encrypt objects at rest. This is known as **SSE-KMS** encryption.

Example Python Code for S3 Upload with SSE-KMS:

```python
import boto3

s3 = boto3.client('s3')

def upload_to_s3(bucket_name, file_name, key_id):
    s3.upload_file(
        Filename=file_name,
        Bucket=bucket_name,
        Key=file_name,
        ExtraArgs={
            "ServerSideEncryption": "aws:kms",
            "SSEKMSKeyId": key_id
        }
    )
```

4.2. Encrypting Data in DynamoDB

- **Encryption at Rest**: AWS automatically encrypts DynamoDB tables at rest using AWS KMS keys. You can choose between an **AWS-managed key** or a **customer-managed key**.

5. Best Practices for Using AWS KMS with Lambda

- **Use Customer-Managed Keys (CMKs) for Critical Data**: Create and manage your own keys in KMS to have complete control over key policies, rotation schedules, and access permissions.
- **Rotate Encryption Keys Regularly**: Regularly rotate customer-managed KMS keys to adhere to security best practices and compliance requirements.
- **Use IAM Policies to Restrict KMS Key Access**: Implement least privilege principles when granting permissions to use encryption keys. Avoid giving broad access to multiple Lambda functions or users.
- **Enable CloudTrail for Key Management**: Monitor all key usage and management actions using AWS CloudTrail to detect unauthorized access attempts or potential misuse.

Encrypting data using AWS KMS is a crucial step in securing sensitive information within serverless applications built on AWS Lambda. By encrypting environment variables, using KMS for client-side encryption and decryption, and securing data at rest in AWS services like S3 and DynamoDB, you can significantly enhance the security of your applications.

Following best practices such as using customer-managed keys, enforcing strict IAM policies, and enabling key rotation ensures that your encryption strategy remains secure and compliant with industry standards. With AWS KMS, you can confidently manage encryption for your Lambda functions and protect sensitive data from unauthorized access.

Ensuring API Security with Lambda Authorizers

When building serverless APIs with **AWS Lambda** and **API Gateway**, security is a top priority. API Gateway provides multiple ways to secure your APIs, including **Lambda Authorizers**, which offer a highly customizable way to validate access to your APIs. A Lambda Authorizer allows you to implement custom authorization logic by calling a Lambda function to control access based on token validation, user roles, policies, or any other authentication mechanism.

In this section, we will explore how to use Lambda Authorizers to secure APIs, covering key concepts, step-by-step implementation, and best practices for API security.

1. Overview of Lambda Authorizers

A **Lambda Authorizer** is an AWS Lambda function that you create to control access to your APIs. The Lambda Authorizer function is invoked by **Amazon API Gateway** to authenticate and authorize incoming requests based on the logic you define. There are two types of Lambda Authorizers:

- **Token-Based Authorizers**: These validate a bearer token (such as a JWT token) and allow or deny access based on the validation.
- **Request-Based Authorizers**: These authorize access based on incoming request parameters like headers, query strings, or even the body.

2. How Lambda Authorizers Work

When a client makes a request to an API endpoint protected by a Lambda Authorizer, API Gateway:

1. Extracts the specified **token** or **parameters** from the incoming request.
2. Invokes the **Lambda Authorizer function** and passes the extracted data.
3. The **Lambda Authorizer** performs validation and returns an **IAM policy** specifying whether to allow or deny the request.
4. API Gateway processes the policy and either forwards the request to the backend service (Lambda function) or returns an error message to the client.

329

3. Setting Up a Lambda Authorizer

Let's explore how to set up a Lambda Authorizer using a token-based approach to validate **JWT tokens**.

Step 1: Create the Lambda Authorizer Function

Go to the AWS Lambda Console:

- Open the **AWS Lambda Console** and click **Create Function**.

Configure the Lambda Function:

- Name the function (e.g., JWTAuthorizer).
- Choose **Python 3.9** as the runtime.
- Attach an **IAM role** with basic execution permissions.

Add the Function Code:

The following example demonstrates a simple Lambda Authorizer function that validates a JWT token:

```python
import json
import jwt  # Requires the PyJWT library (install locally and
package with Lambda)

def lambda_handler(event, context):
    token = event['authorizationToken']  # Extract the token
    passed by API Gateway
    principal_id = 'user'  # Default principal ID (subject to
    change upon successful validation)

    # Define the policy document structure
    def generate_policy(principal_id, effect, resource):
        return {
            'principalId': principal_id,
            'policyDocument': {
                'Version': '2012-10-17',
```

```
        'Statement': [
            {
                'Action': 'execute-api:Invoke',
                'Effect': effect,
                'Resource': resource
            }
        ]
    }
}


    # Validate the token
(for demonstration purposes, we assume a shared secret)
    try:
        # Replace 'secret-key'
 with your JWT secret or public key for verification
        decoded_token = jwt.decode(token, 'secret-key',
        algorithms=['HS256'])
        principal_id = decoded_token
['sub']  # Extract the user ID from the JWT payload

        # Return an allow policy if the token is valid
        return generate_policy(principal_id, 'Allow',
        event['methodArn'])
    except Exception as e:
        # Deny access if the token is invalid
        return generate_policy(principal_id, 'Deny',
        event['methodArn'])
```

Explanation:

- The function extracts the token from the incoming request.
- It validates the token using a shared secret key ('secret-key'). In a real-world scenario, use a more secure method such as validating with a public key or secret stored in **AWS Secrets Manager**.
- If the token is valid, the function returns an **allow policy** that permits access to the API. Otherwise, it returns a **deny policy**.

Step 2: Attach the Lambda Authorizer to API Gateway

331

Go to the API Gateway Console:

- Open the **API Gateway Console** and select your API.

Create or Select a Method:

- Choose a method (e.g., GET) for which you want to enable the authorizer. Click **Method Request**.

Set Up the Authorizer:

- Under **Authorizers**, click **Create New Authorizer**.
- Choose **Lambda** as the authorizer type.
- Name the authorizer (e.g., JWTAuthorizer) and select the Lambda function created in Step 1.
- For the **Token Source**, specify the request header containing the token (e.g., Authorization).

1. **Associate the Authorizer with the Method**:

- Under **Method Request**, choose **JWTAuthorizer** as the authorizer for the selected method.
- Save the changes and deploy the API.

4. Testing the Lambda Authorizer

To test the Lambda Authorizer:

1. **Generate a valid JWT token** using a secret key or the appropriate signing key.
2. **Make a request to the protected API endpoint** using a tool like **Postman** or **cURL**, passing the token in the Authorization header.

For example:

```
curl -H "Authorization: Bearer
  <your-jwt-token>"
https://<your-api-id>.
execute-api.
<region>.amazonaws.
com/<stage>/<resource>
```

If the token is valid, the API should return a successful response. If the token is invalid, the API Gateway should return a 403 Forbidden response.

5. Best Practices for Securing APIs with Lambda Authorizers

5.1. Validate and Verify JWT Tokens Securely

- **Use a Secure Secret or Public Key**: Store your JWT secret or public key securely using **AWS Secrets Manager** or **AWS KMS**. Avoid hardcoding sensitive information in your Lambda function code.
- **Check Token Expiration and Audience**: When validating JWT tokens, ensure that you verify the expiration time (exp claim) and intended audience (aud claim) to prevent unauthorized access.

5.2. Implement Role-Based Access Control (RBAC)

- **Attach Role-Based Policies**: Instead of allowing or denying all users, implement role-based policies in the Lambda Authorizer. For instance, you can allow different levels of access based on roles (e.g., Admin, User, Guest) embedded in the JWT payload.
- **Use the IAM Policy Format**: Create dynamic IAM policies based on the role or user permissions in the decoded JWT token.

Example: Generate Dynamic Policies Based on Roles:

```python
def generate_policy(principal_id, effect, resource, role):
    if role == 'Admin':
        return {
            'principalId': principal_id,
            'policyDocument': {
                'Version': '2012-10-17',
                'Statement': [
                    {
                        'Action': 'execute-api:Invoke',
                        'Effect': 'Allow',
                        'Resource': resource
                    }
                ]
            }
        }
    else:
        return {
            'principalId': principal_id,
            'policyDocument': {
                'Version': '2012-10-17',
                'Statement': [
                    {
                        'Action': 'execute-api:Invoke',
                        'Effect': 'Deny',
                        'Resource': resource
                    }
                ]
            }
        }
```

5.3. Monitor and Audit API Access

- **Enable AWS CloudTrail**: Log all Lambda Authorizer invocations and API Gateway calls using CloudTrail to detect any unauthorized attempts or unusual access patterns.
- **Set Up CloudWatch Alarms**: Create alarms to notify you of repeated access denials or suspicious activity on your API endpoints.

6. Advanced Techniques for Lambda Authorizers

6.1. Integrate with Third-Party Identity Providers

If you are using a third-party identity provider such as **Cognito**, **Auth0**, or **Okta**, Lambda Authorizers can be configured to validate tokens issued by these providers. Extract the public key URL from the provider and use it to verify incoming tokens.

6.2. Use Request-Based Authorizers for Custom Validations

For scenarios where the token alone is not sufficient for authentication, use **request-based authorizers** to inspect other request attributes such as headers, query strings, or body parameters. This can be useful for validating API keys, client certificates, or other custom headers.

Lambda Authorizers provide a powerful way to secure APIs by enabling custom authentication and authorization logic in serverless applications. By validating JWT tokens, implementing role-based access controls, and integrating with third-party identity providers, you can build robust and flexible security mechanisms for your APIs.

Following best practices such as securely managing secrets, monitoring API access, and using dynamic policies ensures that your API remains secure and resilient against unauthorized access. With Lambda Authorizers, you can confidently deploy serverless APIs that meet the highest standards of security and compliance.

Implementing Logging and Monitoring for Security Compliance

Implementing comprehensive logging and monitoring is critical for maintaining **security compliance** in AWS Lambda functions. It not only helps in detecting unauthorized access and anomalies but also ensures that your serverless applications comply with industry regulations and best practices.

AWS offers several services such as **AWS CloudWatch**, **AWS CloudTrail**, and **AWS Config** to facilitate logging, monitoring, and auditing activities.

In this section, we'll explore how to set up and manage logging and monitoring for AWS Lambda functions to ensure security compliance, covering key concepts, step-by-step implementation, and best practices.

1. Key Logging and Monitoring Components

- **AWS CloudWatch Logs**: Captures Lambda function logs and provides search and visualization capabilities.
- **AWS CloudWatch Metrics**: Monitors Lambda function performance metrics like duration, error counts, and invocation counts.
- **AWS CloudTrail**: Logs API activity across your AWS account, providing insights into Lambda function deployments, configurations, and invocation events.
- **AWS Config**: Monitors configuration changes and enforces compliance rules across AWS resources.

2. Setting Up Logging with AWS CloudWatch Logs

AWS Lambda automatically creates log streams in **CloudWatch Logs** for each function invocation. These logs contain details like request and response payloads, execution times, and error messages.

2.1. Configure Lambda Function to Write Logs
Go to the AWS Lambda Console:

- Open the **AWS Lambda Console** and select your Lambda function.

Verify the Lambda Execution Role:

- Ensure that the Lambda function's execution role has permissions to write to CloudWatch Logs. The role should include the AWSLambda BasicExecutionRole policy, which provides necessary permissions for logging.

IAM Policy Example:

```
{
    "Version": "2012-10-17",
    "Statement": [
        {
            "Effect": "Allow",
            "Action": [
                "logs:CreateLogGroup",
                "logs:CreateLogStream",
                "logs:PutLogEvents"
            ],
            "Resource": "arn:aws:logs:*:*:*"
        }
    ]
}
```

Add Logging Code to Lambda Function:

Use the built-in **Python logging library** to generate logs in your Lambda function.

Example Python Code:

```
import logging

# Configure the logging format and level
logger = logging.getLogger()
logger.setLevel(logging.INFO)

def lambda_handler(event, context):
    logger.info("Lambda function invoked with event: %s", event)
    try:
        # Your business logic here
        result = process_event(event)
        logger.info("Processing succeeded with result: %s", result)
        return result
    except Exception as e:
```

```
logger.error("Error occurred: %s", str(e))
raise
```

Key Points:

- **Use the appropriate logging level** (INFO, WARNING, ERROR, etc.) to categorize log messages.
- **Avoid logging sensitive data** to comply with data protection standards.

3. Enabling AWS CloudTrail for Lambda Auditing

AWS CloudTrail provides detailed records of all AWS API calls made on your account, including Lambda functions. It records who invoked a function, which changes were made, and whether the calls succeeded or failed.

3.1. Enable CloudTrail
Go to the AWS CloudTrail Console:

- Open the **AWS CloudTrail Console** and create a new trail or use the default trail.
- Ensure that the trail includes **management events** and **data events** for Lambda functions.

Configure Logging to an S3 Bucket:

- Set up an S3 bucket to store CloudTrail logs. Ensure that the bucket is encrypted and has versioning enabled for security and compliance purposes.

3.2. Monitor Lambda Invocation and Configuration Changes
CloudTrail logs the following Lambda-related activities:

- **Function Invocations**: Tracks every time a Lambda function is invoked

and by whom.
- **Function Configuration Changes**: Logs changes to function code, environment variables, or IAM roles.
- **VPC and Security Group Changes**: Records changes to VPC configurations and security groups used by Lambda functions.

3.3. Set Up Alerts for Suspicious Activities

Use **Amazon CloudWatch Alarms** to monitor CloudTrail logs for suspicious activity, such as:

- Unauthorized IAM role changes.
- High frequency of Lambda function errors or invocations.
- Unauthorized modifications to Lambda function configurations.

Example CloudWatch Alarm for Unauthorized Changes:

- **Create a CloudWatch alarm** that triggers if CloudTrail logs show changes to sensitive Lambda functions without proper IAM authorization.

4. Using AWS Config for Compliance Monitoring

AWS Config allows you to continuously monitor your AWS resources and ensure that they comply with security and compliance policies. AWS Config tracks changes to Lambda functions and evaluates them against predefined rules.

4.1. Set Up AWS Config
Go to the AWS Config Console:

- Open the **AWS Config Console** and select **Set up AWS Config**.

Select Resources to Monitor:

- Choose **Lambda Functions** and other relevant resources like **S3 buckets**, **IAM roles**, and **security groups**.

Configure AWS Config Rules:
Example AWS Config Rules for Lambda Security:

- **IAM Role Policy Check**: Ensures that Lambda execution roles have the least privilege permissions.
- **Lambda Function VPC Configuration Check**: Verifies that sensitive Lambda functions are configured to run inside a VPC.
- **Environment Variable Encryption Check**: Ensures that environment variables containing sensitive data are encrypted using AWS KMS.

1. **Automate Remediation with AWS Config Rules**:
2. You can set up automatic remediation actions using **AWS Config** and **Lambda**. For example, if a Lambda function's environment variables are found to be unencrypted, AWS Config can trigger a Lambda function to automatically apply encryption.

5. Best Practices for Logging and Monitoring Lambda Functions

5.1. Implement Centralized Logging

- **Use a Centralized Log Aggregation Solution**: Forward CloudWatch Logs to a centralized solution like **Amazon Elasticsearch Service** or **AWS OpenSearch**. This allows you to search and visualize logs across multiple Lambda functions easily.
- **Use Log Retention Policies**: Configure retention periods for Cloud-Watch log groups based on compliance requirements. Avoid keeping logs indefinitely unless required.

5.2. Mask or Encrypt Sensitive Data in Logs

- **Use Environment Variables for Secrets**: Do not hardcode secrets or sensitive information in your Lambda code or logs. Store them securely in **AWS Secrets Manager** or **AWS Systems Manager Parameter Store** and retrieve them dynamically.
- **Mask PII or Sensitive Data**: Before logging, ensure that personally identifiable information (PII) or sensitive data is masked or encrypted.

5.3. Set Up Real-Time Monitoring with CloudWatch Alarms

- **Create Alarms for Key Metrics**: Set up CloudWatch alarms to monitor critical Lambda metrics such as **Error Count**, **Duration**, and **Throttles**.
- **Monitor CloudWatch Logs for Security Events**: Use **CloudWatch Logs Insights** to create custom queries that detect security-related events, such as unauthorized API calls or role changes.

5.4. Regularly Review and Rotate IAM Roles and Access Keys

- **Review IAM Role Policies**: Regularly review IAM policies attached to Lambda functions to ensure they adhere to least privilege principles.
- **Rotate Access Keys**: Rotate access keys used by Lambda functions and other services periodically to minimize security risks.

6. Monitoring Lambda Functions with AWS Security Hub

AWS Security Hub provides a unified view of security alerts across multiple AWS accounts. It aggregates findings from AWS services like **GuardDuty**, **Macie**, **Inspector**, and custom Lambda functions to give you comprehensive security visibility.

6.1. Integrate Lambda Findings into AWS Security Hub

- **Enable Security Hub**: In the **Security Hub Console**, enable Security Hub and configure it to integrate with other security services.
- **Forward Lambda Security Findings**: Send Lambda security findings

(such as unauthorized access attempts) to Security Hub using **custom Lambda functions** or **CloudWatch Events**.

Implementing robust logging and monitoring practices for AWS Lambda functions is essential to maintain security compliance and safeguard your serverless applications from threats. By using services like CloudWatch, CloudTrail, AWS Config, and Security Hub, you can gain comprehensive visibility into your Lambda functions, detect anomalies, and enforce security policies effectively.

Following best practices such as masking sensitive data, centralizing logs, and setting up alerts ensures that your Lambda functions are secure, compliant, and resilient to unauthorized access or misconfigurations. With these strategies, you can confidently deploy and monitor your serverless applications while adhering to security standards and regulations.

Working with Asynchronous Processing

QS and SNS Integrations for Async Processing

Asynchronous processing is a crucial part of serverless architectures, allowing applications to decouple components, handle large volumes of data, and improve scalability and reliability. **AWS Lambda** seamlessly integrates with **Amazon Simple Queue Service (SQS)** and **Amazon Simple Notification Service (SNS)** to provide asynchronous messaging and event-driven processing. These integrations enable you to offload tasks from Lambda functions, process events asynchronously, and build distributed systems without managing servers.

In this section, we'll explore how to use **SQS** and **SNS** to enable asynchronous processing with Lambda, covering key concepts, step-by-step integration, and best practices.

1. Overview of SQS and SNS for Asynchronous Processing

- **Amazon Simple Queue Service (SQS)**: A fully managed message queuing service that allows you to decouple components of a distributed application. SQS provides two types of queues: **Standard Queues** (which offer at-least-once delivery and best-effort ordering) and **FIFO Queues** (which ensure exactly-once delivery and ordered messages).
- **Amazon Simple Notification Service (SNS)**: A fully managed pub/sub messaging service that enables you to send notifications or messages to multiple subscribers, such as Lambda functions, HTTP endpoints, and SQS queues. SNS is ideal for broadcasting messages or triggering

multiple downstream processing tasks.

2. Using Amazon SQS with Lambda

2.1. How SQS and Lambda Work Together

Amazon SQS acts as a buffer between producers (such as applications generating tasks or events) and consumers (such as Lambda functions). This approach allows you to offload processing to Lambda, handle retries, and control the flow of messages to ensure smooth processing even during peak loads.

- **Producer sends messages to an SQS queue.**
- **SQS stores messages** until they are processed.
- **Lambda function polls the queue** and processes messages in batches.

2.2. Setting Up SQS and Lambda Integration
Step 1: Create an SQS Queue
Go to the AWS SQS Console:

- Open the **Amazon SQS Console** and click **Create Queue**.
- Choose the **Standard Queue** type or **FIFO Queue** based on your application's requirements.
- Name the queue (e.g., OrderProcessingQueue) and configure the default settings or customize visibility timeout, retention period, and message size as needed.

Configure Access Permissions:

- Create an IAM role with permissions to read messages from the SQS queue. The Lambda execution role must have access to the SQS queue and the required SQS actions.

Example IAM Policy for Lambda to Access SQS:

```
{
    "Version": "2012-10-17",
    "Statement": [
        {
            "Effect": "Allow",
            "Action": [
                "sqs:ReceiveMessage",
                "sqs:DeleteMessage",
                "sqs:GetQueueAttributes"
            ],
            "Resource":
            "arn:aws:sqs:region:account-id:OrderProcessingQueue"
        }
    ]
}
```

Step 2: Create a Lambda Function to Process SQS Messages
Go to the AWS Lambda Console:

- Open the **AWS Lambda Console** and click **Create Function**.
- Choose **Author from Scratch** and name the function (e.g., ProcessOrde rFunction).
- Choose **Python 3.x** as the runtime and select the IAM role created earlier.

Add Lambda Function Code:
Example Lambda Function Code:

```python
import json

def lambda_handler(event, context):
    for record in event['Records']:
        # Extract message from SQS event
        message_body = record['body']
        # Process the message (e.g., save to a database, invoke
```

```
    other services, etc.)
    print(f"Processing message: {message_body}")
return {
    'statusCode': 200,
    'body': json.dumps('Successfully processed SQS messages')
}
```

Explanation:

- The Lambda function iterates over each message received from the SQS queue and processes them.
- **SQS triggers the Lambda function** with a batch of messages, allowing efficient processing of multiple messages at once.

Step 3: Add SQS as a Trigger for the Lambda Function
Go to the Lambda Function Configuration:

- In the **AWS Lambda Console,** navigate to your Lambda function's **Configuration** section and click **Add Trigger**.
- Select **SQS** as the trigger source and choose the **OrderProcessingQueue** created earlier.
- Set the **Batch Size** (e.g., 10 messages per batch) and **Enable Trigger**.

Save the Changes:

- The Lambda function is now configured to automatically process messages from the SQS queue.

3. Using Amazon SNS with Lambda

3.1. How SNS and Lambda Work Together
Amazon SNS is designed for sending notifications and messages to multiple subscribers. SNS can trigger Lambda functions directly or send messages to SQS queues, HTTP endpoints, email addresses, and mobile

devices.

- **Producer publishes a message to an SNS topic**.
- **SNS broadcasts the message** to all its subscribers, which may include Lambda functions, SQS queues, or other endpoints.
- **Lambda functions** are invoked by SNS to process the received message.

3.2. Setting Up SNS and Lambda Integration
Step 1: Create an SNS Topic
Go to the AWS SNS Console:

- Open the **Amazon SNS Console** and click **Create Topic**.
- Choose the **Standard** or **FIFO** topic type based on your use case.
- Name the topic (e.g., OrderNotificationsTopic).

Configure Access Permissions:

- SNS topics have topic policies that define which AWS accounts or services can publish or subscribe to the topic. Ensure that your Lambda function's IAM role has permissions to subscribe to the SNS topic.

Step 2: Create a Lambda Function to Process SNS Messages
Go to the AWS Lambda Console:

- Open the **AWS Lambda Console** and click **Create Function**.
- Choose **Author from Scratch** and name the function (e.g., HandleOrde rNotification).
- Choose **Python 3.x** as the runtime and select an IAM role with permissions to receive SNS notifications.

Add Lambda Function Code:
Example Lambda Function Code:

```python
import json

def lambda_handler(event, context):
    # Extract SNS message details
    for record in event['Records']:
        sns_message = record['Sns']['Message']
        # Process the SNS message (e.g., send an alert, trigger
        other workflows, etc.)
        print(f"Received SNS message: {sns_message}")
    return {
        'statusCode': 200,
        'body': json.dumps('Successfully processed SNS messages')
    }
```

Explanation:

- The Lambda function processes messages sent by SNS by iterating over the event['Records'] array and extracting the message content.

Step 3: Add SNS as a Trigger for the Lambda Function
   Go to the Lambda Function Configuration:

- In the **AWS Lambda Console**, navigate to your Lambda function's **Configuration** section and click **Add Trigger**.
- Select **SNS** as the trigger source and choose the **OrderNotificationsTopic** created earlier.

Save the Changes:

- The Lambda function is now configured to process notifications sent to the SNS topic.

4. Best Practices for SQS and SNS Integrations with Lambda

4.1. Optimize Batch Size and Visibility Timeout in SQS

- **Batch Size**: Choose a batch size that balances the trade-off between latency and throughput. A larger batch size reduces the number of Lambda invocations but may increase processing time for individual batches.
- **Visibility Timeout**: Set the visibility timeout to be slightly longer than the maximum expected processing time for a message. This prevents the message from being processed again before the function completes.

4.2. Implement Dead-Letter Queues (DLQs)

Configure a **Dead-Letter Queue (DLQ)** for both SNS and SQS to handle messages that cannot be processed successfully after multiple retries. This helps prevent data loss and provides an opportunity to investigate failed messages.

4.3. Secure SQS Queues and SNS Topics with IAM Policies

- **Use IAM Policies**: Ensure that IAM policies attached to Lambda functions are set to least privilege. Avoid granting excessive permissions that could lead to unintended access.
- **Apply Resource Policies**: Use SNS topic and SQS queue policies to restrict access to specific AWS accounts or services.

4.4. Use Message Attributes for Filtering and Routing

- **SNS Message Filtering**: Use SNS message filtering to route messages to specific subscribers based on message attributes. This reduces the need for additional logic in Lambda functions and optimizes message distribution.
- **SQS Message Attributes**: Include metadata in SQS message attributes to simplify message processing logic in Lambda.

5. Monitoring and Troubleshooting SQS and SNS with Lambda

- **Enable CloudWatch Metrics**: Monitor key metrics such as Lambda **invocation errors**, **SQS queue size**, and **SNS message delivery failures** using CloudWatch.
- **Set Up CloudWatch Alarms**: Create alarms to notify you if the SQS queue grows beyond a certain size or if SNS messages fail to reach subscribers.
- **Enable CloudTrail for Auditing**: Use CloudTrail to track and audit API calls related to SQS and SNS, ensuring that unauthorized changes are detected.

Integrating AWS Lambda with **Amazon SQS** and **Amazon SNS** provides a robust way to build scalable, event-driven, and decoupled serverless applications. By using SQS for queue-based processing and SNS for pub/sub messaging, you can achieve asynchronous processing while offloading heavy workloads and improving application reliability.

Following best practices such as optimizing batch sizes, using DLQs, securing resources with IAM policies, and implementing message filtering ensures that your Lambda functions handle asynchronous tasks efficiently and securely. With these integrations, you can confidently design and deploy serverless architectures that handle complex event-driven workflows with ease.

Handling Asynchronous Errors and Dead Letter Queues

When implementing asynchronous processing in AWS Lambda with **Amazon SQS** and **Amazon SNS**, handling errors gracefully is crucial to ensuring reliability and maintaining data integrity. Sometimes, messages fail to process due to transient or permanent issues, such as Lambda function errors, network issues, or message format problems. To handle such failures effectively, AWS provides a feature called **Dead Letter Queues (DLQs)**, which can capture and store unprocessed messages for further inspection and reprocessing.

In this section, we'll explore how to handle asynchronous errors using Dead Letter Queues (DLQs) and discuss best practices for setting up DLQs and monitoring unprocessed messages.

1. Understanding Dead Letter Queues (DLQs)

A **Dead Letter Queue (DLQ)** is an SQS queue that stores messages that are not successfully processed after a set number of attempts. By redirecting unprocessed messages to a DLQ, you gain visibility into issues affecting your asynchronous processing and have the opportunity to inspect, analyze, and reprocess the failed messages.

Key Use Cases for DLQs:

- **Handling Permanent Failures**: Messages that consistently fail due to permanent issues like incorrect data formats, missing fields, or invalid parameters.
- **Identifying Transient Failures**: Temporary issues, such as service outages, that prevent successful processing within the retry window.
- **Analyzing and Debugging Failures**: DLQs provide a repository of failed messages, allowing developers to analyze and troubleshoot the root cause.

2. Configuring Dead Letter Queues for SQS and SNS

2.1. Setting Up a Dead Letter Queue for SQS

When working with **SQS** and **Lambda**, you can configure a Dead Letter Queue to capture messages that cannot be successfully processed after multiple attempts.

Step 1: Create a Dead Letter Queue in SQS
Go to the AWS SQS Console:

- Open the **Amazon SQS Console** and click **Create Queue**.
- Choose **Standard Queue** or **FIFO Queue** based on your requirements. Name the queue (e.g., OrderProcessingDLQ).

Configure Access Permissions:

- Ensure that the IAM role associated with your Lambda function has permissions to write messages to the DLQ.

Step 2: Associate the Dead Letter Queue with Your SQS Queue
Open Your Main SQS Queue:

- Go to the **SQS Console** and open the queue that triggers your Lambda function (e.g., OrderProcessingQueue).

Configure the Dead Letter Queue:

- In the queue configuration settings, find the **Redrive Policy** section.
- Specify the **OrderProcessingDLQ** as the target Dead Letter Queue.
- Set the **Maximum Receives** value, which determines the number of times a message can be received before being moved to the DLQ. For example, if you set **Maximum Receives** to 5, a message that fails 5 times will be moved to the DLQ.

Save the Changes:

- Save the configuration, and your SQS queue is now configured with a DLQ.

2.2. Setting Up a Dead Letter Queue for SNS

If you are using **SNS** to trigger Lambda functions or SQS queues, you can configure a Dead Letter Queue to capture failed message deliveries.

Step 1: Create a Dead Letter Queue in SQS
Go to the AWS SQS Console:

- Create a new SQS queue to act as the DLQ (e.g., NotificationDLQ).

Step 2: Associate the Dead Letter Queue with Your SNS Topic
Open Your SNS Topic:

- Go to the **Amazon SNS Console** and select the SNS topic that triggers your Lambda function (e.g., OrderNotificationsTopic).

Configure the Dead Letter Queue:

- In the SNS topic settings, find the **Delivery Policy** section.
- Specify the ARN of the **NotificationDLQ** as the Dead Letter Queue for the SNS topic.

Save the Changes:

- Save the configuration, and your SNS topic is now configured with a DLQ to handle failed deliveries.

3. Handling and Analyzing Errors in Dead Letter Queues

3.1. Monitoring DLQ Messages with CloudWatch Alarms

1. **Enable CloudWatch Metrics for DLQs**:

- AWS automatically publishes key metrics such as **ApproximateNumbe rOfMessagesVisible** and **NumberOfMessagesSentToDLQ** for SQS queues. These metrics provide visibility into the number of messages

353

stored in the DLQ.

1. **Create CloudWatch Alarms**:

- Set up **CloudWatch Alarms** to notify you when messages accumulate in the DLQ beyond a certain threshold. For example, create an alarm that triggers if **NumberOfMessagesSentToDLQ** exceeds a specified number.

Example Alarm Configuration:

- **Metric**: ApproximateNumberOfMessagesVisible
- **Condition**: Greater than 10 messages
- **Actions**: Send a notification to an SNS topic or trigger a Lambda function for automated remediation.

3.2. Analyzing Messages in the Dead Letter Queue
Access and Download Messages from the DLQ:

- Go to the **SQS Console**, open the DLQ, and use the **Send and Receive Messages** option to inspect the contents of the unprocessed messages.
- Download message bodies to analyze common issues, such as incorrect data formats, missing attributes, or invalid parameters.

Debug and Identify Root Causes:

- Review logs in **CloudWatch Logs** for the associated Lambda function to identify errors that caused the messages to fail.
- Use AWS **X-Ray** for detailed tracing of message processing paths, pinpointing failures in external API calls, database interactions, or function logic.

4. Reprocessing Messages from the Dead Letter Queue

Once the root cause of the failures has been identified and addressed, you can reprocess the messages stored in the DLQ.

4.1. Manual Reprocessing
Download and Review Messages:

- Manually download the failed messages from the DLQ and review them for correctness.
- Modify messages if necessary to correct data formatting or attribute issues.

Send Messages Back to the Main Queue:

- Use the **AWS SQS Console** or a script to resend the corrected messages to the main SQS queue. This triggers the Lambda function to reprocess the messages.

4.2. Automated Reprocessing Using a Lambda Function
Create a Reprocessing Lambda Function:

- Develop a Lambda function that reads messages from the DLQ, performs validation or correction, and sends the messages back to the main queue.

Example Lambda Function for Reprocessing Messages:

```
import boto3

sqs = boto3.client('sqs')
dlq_url =
'https://sqs.region.amazonaws.com/account-id/OrderProcessingDLQ'
main_queue_url =
```

```
'https://sqs.region.amazonaws.com/account-id/OrderProcessingQueue'

def lambda_handler(event, context):
    # Receive messages from the DLQ
    response = sqs.receive_message(
        QueueUrl=dlq_url,
        MaxNumberOfMessages=10,
        WaitTimeSeconds=5
    )

    for message in response.get('Messages', []):
        # Validate or correct the message (optional step)
        corrected_message = message['Body']

        # Send the corrected message to the main queue
        sqs.send_message(
            QueueUrl=main_queue_url,
            MessageBody=corrected_message
        )

        # Delete the message from the DLQ after successful
        reprocessing
        sqs.delete_message(
            QueueUrl=dlq_url,
            ReceiptHandle=message['ReceiptHandle']
        )
    return {
        'statusCode': 200,
        'body': 'Successfully reprocessed messages from DLQ'
    }
```

5. Best Practices for Handling Asynchronous Errors and DLQs

5.1. Set Appropriate Maximum Receives Limits

- Choose a **Maximum Receives** value based on your application's tolerance for transient errors. For example, a value of 3-5 retries is common
  to avoid excessive retries in case of persistent failures.

5.2. Monitor DLQ Metrics and Set Alerts

- Set up **CloudWatch Alarms** to monitor the number of messages in the DLQ. Establish alerts to notify relevant teams or trigger automated remediation workflows when messages accumulate in the DLQ.

5.3. Automate Remediation with Lambda Functions

- Create automated workflows using **Lambda** to perform corrective actions on failed messages, such as fixing data issues or reprocessing messages in batches.

5.4. Implement Logging and Tracing for Error Analysis

- Ensure that Lambda functions are configured to **log errors** and **trace execution paths** using CloudWatch Logs and AWS X-Ray. This provides visibility into what went wrong and enables faster debugging.

Handling asynchronous errors and implementing Dead Letter Queues (DLQs) is essential for maintaining the reliability and resilience of serverless applications. By configuring DLQs for both SQS and SNS, you can capture unprocessed messages and gain insights into recurring issues affecting your asynchronous workflows.

Following best practices such as setting appropriate maximum receives limits, monitoring DLQ metrics, automating remediation, and logging errors ensures that your serverless architecture can gracefully handle failures while maintaining data integrity. With these strategies in place, you can build robust and scalable applications that meet the demands of modern, distributed environments.

Scaling and Concurrency Management for Event-Driven Architectures

Event-driven architectures rely heavily on AWS Lambda and related services such as **Amazon SQS**, **Amazon SNS**, and **Amazon Kinesis** to handle asynchronous tasks and scale based on demand. However, managing scaling and concurrency efficiently is essential to ensure optimal performance, prevent throttling, and control costs.

In this section, we'll explore best practices and strategies for managing scaling and concurrency in event-driven architectures using AWS Lambda. We will cover key concepts such as Lambda scaling behavior, concurrency limits, reserved concurrency, provisioned concurrency, and handling burst workloads.

1. Understanding Lambda Scaling and Concurrency

AWS Lambda is designed to automatically scale horizontally based on the incoming rate of events. When an event occurs, Lambda creates a new execution environment (up to the **account concurrency limit**) to handle the incoming request. Lambda can scale nearly instantaneously to handle thousands of events, but it's essential to understand how concurrency is managed to optimize performance and avoid issues.

1.1. Key Concepts of Concurrency in Lambda

- **Concurrency**: Refers to the number of Lambda function instances that are running at any given time. If there are 10 concurrent invocations of a Lambda function, there are 10 separate instances of that function running simultaneously.
- **Burst Concurrency**: Lambda can instantly increase the number of concurrent function executions, but there are limits to the initial burst and sustained concurrency growth.
- **Account Concurrency Limit**: The total maximum number of concurrent Lambda instances that your account can run across all functions.

358

This limit can be adjusted through a support request to AWS.

- **Function Concurrency**: You can reserve a portion of the total account concurrency for a specific Lambda function using **Reserved Concurrency** or keep a minimum number of instances ready with **Provisioned Concurrency**.

2. Lambda Scaling Behavior and Concurrency Controls

2.1. Burst Concurrency and Sustained Scaling

AWS Lambda initially supports a burst of up to 1,000 concurrent executions per region, allowing functions to rapidly scale up to meet demand. Beyond this initial burst, Lambda's scaling behavior is managed by an additional concurrency allocation rate.

- **Burst Scaling**: Lambda supports an immediate burst of 500 to 3,000 new concurrent executions depending on the region.
- **Sustained Scaling**: After the initial burst, Lambda scales by an additional 500 instances per minute to meet the increase in workload.

2.2. Reserved Concurrency

Reserved Concurrency is used to limit the number of concurrent executions for a specific Lambda function. This feature ensures that critical functions do not consume all available concurrency, leaving other functions starved for resources.

When to Use Reserved Concurrency:

- **Protect Critical Functions**: Reserve concurrency for high-priority functions that must always have available capacity.
- **Prevent Unintentional Spikes**: Limit concurrency for functions that may unintentionally consume a large number of resources, affecting other parts of your application.

Setting Reserved Concurrency:

1. **Go to the AWS Lambda Console** and select the function.
2. In the **Configuration** section, select **Concurrency**.
3. **Set a reserved concurrency limit** (e.g., 50) to reserve capacity for the function.

2.3. Provisioned Concurrency

Provisioned Concurrency allows you to pre-warm a specific number of execution environments so that they are always ready to handle requests with minimal cold start latency. This is especially useful for latency-sensitive applications such as APIs or real-time processing tasks.

When to Use Provisioned Concurrency:

- **For Low-Latency APIs**: When you need to reduce cold start times for user-facing applications.
- **Handling Predictable Traffic Patterns**: If your application experiences consistent traffic spikes at specific times (e.g., during business hours or promotional events).

Setting Provisioned Concurrency:

1. **Go to the AWS Lambda Console** and select the function.
2. In the **Configuration** section, select **Concurrency** and choose **Add Provisioned Concurrency**.
3. **Specify the number of concurrent instances** to provision (e.g., 100) and click **Save**.

3. Concurrency Management in Event-Driven Architectures

3.1. Scaling with Amazon SQS

Amazon SQS automatically scales to handle an increasing number of messages. Lambda functions process these messages in batches, with the batch size configurable based on your application's needs.

Best Practices for SQS Scaling:

- **Optimize Batch Size**: Choose an appropriate batch size to balance throughput and latency. A larger batch size reduces the number of Lambda invocations but may increase processing latency.
- **Use Dead Letter Queues (DLQs)**: Implement DLQs to handle unprocessed messages, preventing them from being retried indefinitely.
- **Monitor Queue Depth**: Use **CloudWatch metrics** such as **ApproximateNumberOfMessagesVisible** to monitor queue length and trigger scaling or alarms if messages accumulate.

3.2. Scaling with Amazon SNS

Amazon SNS uses a publish-subscribe model to deliver messages to Lambda functions, HTTP endpoints, SQS queues, or other subscribers. When using Lambda as an SNS subscriber, ensure that your function can handle the concurrent load generated by SNS notifications.

Best Practices for SNS Scaling:

- **Set Up Retry Policies**: Define retry policies for Lambda functions that process SNS messages to handle transient errors.
- **Control Throttling**: Monitor Lambda metrics for throttling and adjust reserved concurrency if your function is consistently exceeding concurrency limits.

3.3. Scaling with Amazon Kinesis

Amazon Kinesis enables real-time processing of streaming data. Lambda functions process records from Kinesis streams in parallel, but there are concurrency limits tied to the number of shards in a Kinesis stream.

Best Practices for Kinesis Scaling:

- **Distribute Load Across Multiple Shards**: Add more shards to your Kinesis stream to increase the number of records processed concurrently by Lambda.
- **Monitor Iterator Age**: Use **CloudWatch** to track the **GetRecords.IteratorAgeMilliseconds** metric, which indicates the delay in processing

records. If the iterator age is increasing, consider adding more shards or increasing Lambda concurrency.

4. Managing Throttling and Burst Workloads

4.1. Avoiding Throttling with Reserved Concurrency

Throttling occurs when a Lambda function exceeds the maximum concurrency limit, resulting in requests being denied temporarily. Throttled requests return a **429 Too Many Requests** error. By reserving concurrency, you can reduce the risk of throttling for critical functions.

- **Set Appropriate Reserved Concurrency**: Reserve a portion of the account concurrency limit for critical functions to ensure they always have available capacity.
- **Use Retries and Exponential Backoff**: Implement retry logic in your application with exponential backoff to handle temporary throttling gracefully.

4.2. Handling Burst Workloads with Provisioned Concurrency

For workloads that experience sudden spikes in demand, **Provisioned Concurrency** can pre-warm execution environments to handle bursts effectively. Additionally, using **API Gateway throttling** and **rate limiting** can help control the incoming load on Lambda functions.

5. Monitoring and Optimizing Lambda Scaling

5.1. Monitor Key CloudWatch Metrics

Monitor key metrics to ensure that Lambda functions are scaling appropriately and not exceeding concurrency limits or experiencing performance issues. Important metrics include:

- **ConcurrentExecutions**: Tracks the number of concurrent executions for your Lambda function.

- **Throttles**: Indicates the number of requests throttled due to exceeding the concurrency limit.
- **Errors**: Monitors the number of errors encountered by the function.
- **Duration**: Measures the execution duration of each function invocation.

5.2. Use AWS X-Ray for Tracing

Enable **AWS X-Ray** to trace Lambda invocations and gain insights into the latency and execution paths of your functions. X-Ray helps you identify bottlenecks, debug issues, and optimize performance.

6. Best Practices for Scaling and Concurrency Management

- **Use Reserved and Provisioned Concurrency Wisely**: Reserve concurrency for critical functions and use provisioned concurrency for low-latency applications or predictable workloads.
- **Optimize Batch Sizes for Asynchronous Processing**: Balance batch size and latency to optimize throughput for SQS and Kinesis-triggered Lambda functions.
- **Implement Retry Strategies**: Use retry policies with exponential backoff for functions triggered by SQS, SNS, and other sources.
- **Monitor Lambda Metrics and Set Alarms**: Create CloudWatch alarms for key metrics such as **ConcurrentExecutions**, **Throttles**, and **Errors** to proactively detect and respond to scaling issues.
- **Leverage DLQs for Error Handling**: Use Dead Letter Queues to capture and analyze failed messages, preventing indefinite retries and data loss.

Effective scaling and concurrency management are essential for building resilient, high-performance, event-driven architectures using AWS Lambda. By understanding Lambda's scaling behavior, configuring reserved and provisioned concurrency, and optimizing asynchronous processing with SQS,

SNS, and Kinesis, you can create scalable applications that handle varying workloads efficiently.

Implementing best practices such as monitoring key metrics, using Dead Letter Queues, and avoiding throttling ensures that your Lambda functions can handle both regular traffic and unexpected bursts. With these strategies in place, you can confidently build and maintain scalable, cost-effective, and highly available serverless architectures.

Machine Learning with AWS Lambda

Running Lightweight ML Models in Lambda
AWS Lambda provides a highly scalable, serverless computing environment that can be an excellent choice for running lightweight machine learning (ML) models. Lightweight models, which are typically small, fast, and designed to make inferences on-the-fly, fit well within Lambda's execution and memory constraints. Leveraging AWS Lambda for ML tasks allows developers to deploy models at scale without worrying about infrastructure management.

In this section, we'll explore how to deploy and run lightweight ML models in AWS Lambda, covering key concepts, implementation strategies, and best practices for optimizing Lambda for machine learning inference tasks.

1. Why Use AWS Lambda for ML Inference?

AWS Lambda is ideal for running lightweight ML models for several reasons:

- **Cost-Effective**: Lambda operates on a pay-per-use pricing model, which means you only pay for the compute time you consume. This is particularly advantageous for infrequent or bursty ML inference workloads.
- **Scalability**: Lambda automatically scales to accommodate concurrent requests, making it a good fit for handling unpredictable spikes in inference requests.
- **Serverless Architecture**: Deploying ML models on Lambda eliminates

the need for server provisioning, maintenance, and scaling, reducing operational overhead.

Use Cases for running lightweight ML models in Lambda include:

- Real-time recommendations (e.g., product recommendations in an e-commerce website).
- Sentiment analysis on text data.
- Image classification or object detection for low-resolution images.
- Language translation tasks for small chunks of text.
- Predictive analytics for low-volume event streams.

2. Choosing the Right ML Model for Lambda

When running ML models in Lambda, it's essential to choose models that align with Lambda's constraints on memory, execution time, and package size. Models designed for edge or mobile deployment (such as those optimized for **TensorFlow Lite**, **ONNX Runtime**, or **scikit-learn**) are generally good candidates for Lambda deployment.

Criteria for Selecting ML Models for Lambda:

- **Small Model Size**: Ensure that the model file size fits within the Lambda package size limits (typically under 250 MB, including dependencies).
- **Low Latency Requirements**: Lambda functions are best suited for models that can generate predictions quickly (ideally within a few hundred milliseconds).
- **Efficient Memory Usage**: Choose models that require minimal memory during inference, allowing you to allocate an appropriate amount of Lambda memory (between 128 MB and 10 GB).

3. Deploying and Running Lightweight ML Models in Lambda

3.1. Preparing the ML Model for Deployment

To deploy an ML model to AWS Lambda, you need to:

1. **Train and Optimize the Model**: Train your model using the desired framework (such as **scikit-learn**, **TensorFlow**, or **PyTorch**). Once trained, optimize the model for inference using techniques like model quantization or pruning.
2. **Serialize the Model**: Serialize and save the trained model in a format compatible with the chosen inference framework. For example:

- Save a **scikit-learn** model as a .pkl file using Python's pickle module.
- Export a **TensorFlow** or **Keras** model in the **SavedModel** or **HDF5** format.
- Export a **PyTorch** model to **TorchScript** format (.pt).

Example: Exporting a scikit-learn Model:

```
from sklearn.ensemble import RandomForestClassifier
import pickle

# Train the model
clf = RandomForestClassifier()
clf.fit(X_train, y_train)

# Save the model to a file
with open('/tmp/model.pkl', 'wb') as model_file:
    pickle.dump(clf, model_file)
```

3.2. Creating the Lambda Function
Go to the AWS Lambda Console:

- Open the **AWS Lambda Console** and create a new Lambda function. Choose **Python 3.x** as the runtime.

Configure the Lambda Execution Role:

- Ensure that the Lambda function's IAM role has the necessary permissions to access any required AWS resources, such as S3 for loading the model.

Upload the Model and Dependencies:

- Create a deployment package that includes the serialized model and any required dependencies. You can either:
- **Package the dependencies with the Lambda function**: Include all required libraries and the model file in a ZIP archive.
- **Use Lambda Layers**: Package and deploy dependencies separately using Lambda layers to keep the function package size small.

Write the Lambda Function Code:

- Load the model during the function's initialization phase to minimize loading time during execution.

Example Lambda Function for Running a scikit-learn Model:

```
import json
import pickle
import boto3

# Load the model during initialization
s3 = boto3.client('s3')
model = None

def load_model():
    global model
    if model is None:
        # Download the model from S3 (if stored in S3)
        s3.download_file('my-bucket', 'model.pkl',
```

```
        '/tmp/model.pkl')
        with open('/tmp/model.pkl', 'rb') as model_file:
            model = pickle.load(model_file)

# Lambda handler function
def lambda_handler(event, context):
    load_model()

    # Extract features from the event
    features = event['features']

    # Make a prediction
    prediction = model.predict([features])

    return {
        'statusCode': 200,
        'body': json.dumps({'prediction': int(prediction[0])})
    }
```

4. Optimizing ML Models for Lambda Inference

Running ML models in Lambda requires careful optimization to stay within the constraints of memory, execution time, and cold starts. Below are some techniques to optimize your models for Lambda:

4.1. Use Lightweight Frameworks and Libraries

- **Choose Efficient ML Libraries**: If possible, use optimized libraries like **TensorFlow Lite**, **ONNX Runtime**, or **sklearn-porter** (for converting scikit-learn models to portable Python code).
- **Reduce Model Size**: Apply techniques such as model quantization (using tools like **TensorFlow Model Optimization Toolkit** or **ONNX Quantization**) or pruning to reduce model size without sacrificing too much accuracy.

4.2. Optimize Memory and Execution Time

369

- **Allocate Appropriate Memory**: Use the AWS Lambda console to experiment with different memory configurations. Increasing memory also allocates proportional CPU resources, potentially reducing inference time.
- **Leverage Lambda Layers**: Package common ML dependencies like **numpy**, **scipy**, and **sklearn** in a Lambda Layer to keep your function code small.

4.3. Reduce Cold Start Latency

- **Provisioned Concurrency**: Use **Provisioned Concurrency** to pre-warm Lambda execution environments, reducing cold start latency for latency-sensitive applications.
- **Warm the Model During Initialization**: Load and initialize the ML model during the cold start phase (outside of the handler function) to avoid unnecessary loading delays during execution.

5. Deploying Lambda Functions with ML Models Using the AWS CLI

You can deploy Lambda functions and associated models using the **AWS CLI** for better version control and automation.

Example Deployment Steps Using AWS CLI:
Create a deployment package:

```
zip -r9 lambda_function.zip lambda_function.py model.pkl
```

Deploy the function using the AWS CLI:

```
aws lambda create-function \
    --function-name my-ml-lambda \
    --runtime python3.9 \
    --role arn:aws:iam::123456789012:role/execution_role \
```

```
--handler lambda_function.lambda_handler \
--zip-file fileb://lambda_function.zip
```

Update the Lambda function code:

```
aws lambda update-function-code \
    --function-name my-ml-lambda \
    --zip-file fileb://lambda_function.zip
```

6. Best Practices for Running ML Models in Lambda

- **Use Pre-trained Models**: For many tasks, such as sentiment analysis or image recognition, pre-trained models can be used effectively. This saves training time and leverages well-established architectures.
- **Minimize Dependency Size**: Keep your Lambda package size small by using Lambda Layers for common dependencies and removing unnecessary libraries.
- **Use Efficient Data Formats**: When exchanging data with Lambda functions, use efficient formats such as **JSON**, **Parquet**, or **Apache Arrow** to reduce serialization/deserialization overhead.

7. Monitoring and Logging ML Inference in Lambda

- **Enable CloudWatch Logs**: Ensure that logging is enabled to capture key metrics such as inference time, input parameters, and prediction results.
- **Monitor Performance with CloudWatch Metrics**: Track metrics like **Duration**, **Memory Usage**, and **Error Count** to identify performance bottlenecks.
- **Use AWS X-Ray for Tracing**: Integrate **AWS X-Ray** to trace execution paths and understand latency issues during model inference.

Running lightweight ML models in AWS Lambda is an effective approach to deploying scalable, cost-efficient, and serverless machine learning applications. By carefully selecting models, optimizing memory and execution time, and using efficient ML frameworks, you can leverage Lambda to handle various inference tasks without managing infrastructure.

Following best practices such as minimizing cold start latency, using lightweight frameworks, and monitoring performance metrics ensures that your Lambda-based ML models perform reliably and efficiently. With these strategies, you can confidently deploy ML models at scale and meet the demands of real-time applications while minimizing costs.

Integrating Python with AWS SageMaker for AI/ML Applications

While AWS Lambda excels at running lightweight machine learning models, **Amazon SageMaker** offers a more comprehensive and scalable platform for training, deploying, and managing a wide range of ML models. Integrating Python-based Lambda functions with **Amazon SageMaker** enables developers to combine the power of serverless computing with SageMaker's advanced ML capabilities, creating highly scalable and efficient AI/ML applications.

In this section, we will explore how to integrate **AWS Lambda** with **Amazon SageMaker** using Python. We'll cover the basics of SageMaker, steps to deploy and manage models in SageMaker, and how to invoke these models from Lambda functions.

1. Overview of Amazon SageMaker

Amazon SageMaker is a fully managed service that provides all the tools necessary to build, train, deploy, and manage machine learning models. SageMaker offers a variety of features, including:

- **Managed Jupyter Notebooks** for experimentation and model development.

- **Built-in Algorithms** and support for popular frameworks like TensorFlow, PyTorch, MXNet, and scikit-learn.
- **Automatic Model Tuning** to find the optimal hyperparameters for your models.
- **One-Click Deployment** to deploy models as scalable and secure endpoints.
- **Model Monitoring** and **Drift Detection** to ensure models stay accurate over time.

By integrating SageMaker with Lambda, you can automate workflows, handle asynchronous tasks, or trigger model inference in response to events.

2. Why Integrate Lambda with SageMaker?

Integrating AWS Lambda with SageMaker allows you to:

- **Invoke SageMaker endpoints for real-time predictions** from Lambda functions, enabling serverless ML-based applications.
- **Trigger model training jobs** from Lambda in response to events such as new data being uploaded to S3.
- **Automate SageMaker workflows** using Lambda to orchestrate data preprocessing, model training, tuning, and deployment.

3. Setting Up and Deploying a SageMaker Model

3.1. Train and Deploy a Model in SageMaker
To integrate with SageMaker, you first need to train a model using SageMaker's built-in algorithms or by bringing your own code. Let's take a look at the steps involved.

Step 1: Train a Model in SageMaker
Open the SageMaker Console:

- In the **AWS Management Console**, navigate to **Amazon SageMaker** and open **SageMaker Studio**.

Create a Notebook Instance:

- Launch a Jupyter Notebook in SageMaker Studio for training and experimentation.
- Use SageMaker's built-in algorithms or custom scripts to train your model.

Train the Model:

Example Python Code for Training in a Jupyter Notebook:

```python
import sagemaker
from sagemaker import get_execution_role
from sagemaker.sklearn.estimator import SKLearn

# Define the SageMaker role and session
role = get_execution_role()
session = sagemaker.Session()

# Define the training script
script_path = 'train_script.py'

# Set up the estimator
sklearn_estimator = SKLearn(
    entry_point=script_path,
    role=role,
    instance_count=1,
    instance_type='ml.m4.xlarge',
    framework_version='0.23-1',
    py_version='py3'
)

# Fit the model using training data in S3
sklearn_estimator.fit({'train': 's3://your-bucket/training-data/'})
```

Deploy the Trained Model:

Once the model is trained, deploy it as a **SageMaker Endpoint** to enable real-time predictions.

Example Python Code for Deployment:

```
# Deploy the trained model
predictor = sklearn_estimator.deploy(
    initial_instance_count=1,
    instance_type='ml.m4.xlarge',
    endpoint_name='sagemaker-sklearn-endpoint'
)
```

Step 2: Configure the Endpoint and Permissions
Configure IAM Permissions:

- Ensure that the SageMaker endpoint has the necessary IAM role with permissions to access S3, SageMaker services, and other required AWS resources.

Test the Endpoint:

- Use the predictor object in your notebook to test predictions and ensure that the endpoint is working correctly.

4. Invoking a SageMaker Endpoint from AWS Lambda

After deploying the model as a SageMaker endpoint, you can invoke it from a Lambda function using **boto3**, AWS's Python SDK. This allows you to perform real-time predictions in response to various events.

4.1. Creating a Lambda Function to Invoke SageMaker
Step 1: Create a New Lambda Function
Go to the AWS Lambda Console:

- In the **AWS Lambda Console**, create a new Lambda function. Choose

Python 3.x as the runtime.

Configure the Lambda Execution Role:

- Attach an IAM role to the Lambda function with permissions to invoke the SageMaker endpoint and read data from S3 if needed. The IAM policy should include sagemaker:InvokeEndpoint permission.

Step 2: Write the Lambda Function Code
Write the Python Code to Invoke the Endpoint:
Example Lambda Function Code:

```
import json
import boto3

# Initialize SageMaker runtime client
sagemaker_runtime = boto3.client('sagemaker-runtime')

def lambda_handler(event, context):
    # Extract features from the incoming event
    input_data = json.dumps(event['features'])

    # Invoke the SageMaker endpoint
    response = sagemaker_runtime.invoke_endpoint(
        EndpointName='sagemaker-sklearn-endpoint',
        Body=input_data,
        ContentType='application/json'
    )

    # Parse the response
    result = json.loads(response['Body'].read().decode())

    return {
        'statusCode': 200,
        'body': json.dumps({'prediction': result})
    }
```

Test the Lambda Function:

- Deploy the Lambda function and use the **Test** feature in the AWS Lambda Console to invoke the function with sample input data.

Step 3: Configure Triggers for the Lambda Function

- You can set up triggers such as S3 events, API Gateway, or CloudWatch Events to invoke the Lambda function automatically based on certain conditions. For example, use an **S3 event** to trigger model inference whenever new data is uploaded to a specific S3 bucket.

5. Automating Model Training and Deployment with Lambda

AWS Lambda can also be used to automate model training and deployment tasks in SageMaker. For example, you can create a Lambda function that triggers a SageMaker training job whenever new training data is uploaded to an S3 bucket.

5.1. Creating a Lambda Function to Trigger a Training Job
Example Lambda Code to Start a SageMaker Training Job:

```
import json
import boto3

# Initialize SageMaker client
sagemaker_client = boto3.client('sagemaker')

def lambda_handler(event, context):
    # Define the SageMaker training job parameters
    training_job_name = 'my-sklearn-training-job'
    training_image =
    '811284229777.dkr.ecr.us-west-2.amazonaws.com/sklearn:0.23-1-cpu-py3'

    response = sagemaker_client.create_training_job(
        TrainingJobName=training_job_name,
        AlgorithmSpecification={
```

```
        'TrainingImage': training_image,
        'TrainingInputMode': 'File'
    },
    RoleArn='arn:aws:iam::123456789012:role/SageMakerRole',
    InputDataConfig=[
        {
            'ChannelName': 'train',
            'DataSource': {
                'S3DataSource': {
                    'S3DataType': 'S3Prefix',
                    'S3Uri': 's3://your-bucket/training-data/',
                    'S3DataDistributionType': 'FullyReplicated'
                }
            },
            'ContentType': 'text/csv'
        }
    ],
    OutputDataConfig={
        'S3OutputPath': 's3://your-bucket/output/'
    },
    ResourceConfig={
        'InstanceType': 'ml.m5.large',
        'InstanceCount': 1,
        'VolumeSizeInGB': 50
    },
    StoppingCondition={
        'MaxRuntimeInSeconds': 3600
    }
)

return {
    'statusCode': 200,
    'body': json.dumps(f'Training job {training_job_name}
    started.')
}
```

Explanation:

- This Lambda function triggers a SageMaker training job using the specified training image and input data configuration.

- You can set up an S3 event trigger to invoke this function whenever new training data is uploaded to the designated S3 bucket.

6. Best Practices for Integrating Lambda with SageMaker

- **Use IAM Roles and Policies Wisely**: Ensure that the Lambda execution role has minimal privileges necessary to invoke SageMaker endpoints and perform S3 operations. Follow the principle of least privilege.
- **Optimize Data Serialization**: When passing data between Lambda and SageMaker, use efficient data formats like JSON or CSV to minimize overhead.
- **Monitor SageMaker Endpoints and Lambda Functions**: Use **CloudWatch** to monitor key metrics such as endpoint latency, error rates, and Lambda execution duration. Set up alerts for anomalous behavior.
- **Handle Timeouts Gracefully**: For longer-running tasks such as training jobs, ensure that Lambda has an appropriate timeout configuration and handle errors gracefully with retries if necessary.

Integrating AWS Lambda with Amazon SageMaker provides a powerful combination for building scalable and cost-effective AI/ML applications. By leveraging Lambda's serverless compute capabilities alongside SageMaker's model training, deployment, and management features, you can create automated workflows, invoke real-time predictions, and orchestrate complex ML tasks.

Following best practices such as optimizing IAM roles, efficient data handling, and monitoring performance ensures that your Lambda-SageMaker integration is reliable, secure, and scalable. With these strategies in place, you can confidently build and deploy sophisticated machine learning solutions using AWS Lambda and SageMaker.

Deploying Pre-trained Models Using Lambda and API Gateway

Pre-trained machine learning models can be efficiently deployed using **AWS Lambda** in combination with **Amazon API Gateway**. This architecture allows developers to create serverless, scalable, and cost-effective RESTful APIs that serve predictions in real-time. By leveraging **Lambda's auto-scaling capabilities** and **API Gateway's routing and security features**, you can deploy pre-trained models with minimal overhead and infrastructure management.

In this section, we'll explore how to deploy pre-trained models using AWS Lambda and API Gateway, covering key concepts, deployment steps, and best practices.

1. Why Use Lambda and API Gateway for Model Deployment?

Deploying pre-trained models using Lambda and API Gateway offers several advantages:

- **Serverless Scalability**: Lambda automatically scales with the number of concurrent requests, ensuring that your API can handle fluctuating demand without manual intervention.
- **Cost Efficiency**: You only pay for the compute resources used by Lambda during model inference, making it an economical choice for APIs with varying or unpredictable traffic.
- **Ease of Integration**: API Gateway provides easy integration with Lambda and includes features such as **rate limiting**, **authentication**, **CORS configuration**, and **logging**.
- **Security and Access Control**: API Gateway allows you to control access to your models through **IAM policies**, **Cognito User Pools**, **API keys**, or **Lambda Authorizers**.

2. Preparing the Pre-trained Model

Before deploying the model using Lambda and API Gateway, you need to:

Train and Optimize the Model: Use a machine learning framework like **scikit-learn**, **TensorFlow**, or **PyTorch** to train the model. Optimize the model by pruning unnecessary weights, quantizing it, or using lightweight versions like **TensorFlow Lite** or **ONNX**.

Serialize and Save the Model: Serialize the model into a portable format, such as **pickle** for scikit-learn, **HDF5** for TensorFlow/Keras, or **TorchScript** for PyTorch.

Example: Saving a scikit-learn Model:

```
from sklearn.ensemble import RandomForestClassifier
import pickle

# Train the model
clf = RandomForestClassifier(n_estimators=100)
clf.fit(X_train, y_train)

# Save the model to a file
with open('/tmp/model.pkl', 'wb') as model_file:
    pickle.dump(clf, model_file)
```

3. Creating the Lambda Function

Step 1: Create a Lambda Function in AWS Console
Go to the AWS Lambda Console:

- Open the **AWS Lambda Console** and click **Create Function**. Choose **Author from Scratch**.

Configure the Lambda Function:

- **Runtime**: Select **Python 3.x**.

- **Role**: Create a new role with basic Lambda permissions or use an existing role. Ensure the role has permissions to access any necessary AWS resources, such as **S3** if your model is stored there.

Upload the Model and Dependencies:

- You can either:
- **Include the model file** and all necessary dependencies within the deployment package, or
- **Use Lambda Layers** to separate common dependencies, reducing package size and simplifying updates.

Step 2: Write the Lambda Function Code
Load the Model during Initialization:

- The model should be loaded during the initialization phase to reduce inference time and avoid repeated loading during each function invocation.

Define the Lambda Handler Function:
  Example Lambda Function Code:

```python
import json
import pickle
import boto3

# Load the model during initialization
model = None

def load_model():
    global model
    if model is None:
        # If using S3 to store the model, download it first
        s3 = boto3.client('s3')
        s3.download_file('your-bucket-name', 'model.pkl',
```

```
        '/tmp/model.pkl')
        with open('/tmp/model.pkl', 'rb') as model_file:
            model = pickle.load(model_file)

def lambda_handler(event, context):
    # Ensure model is loaded
    load_model()

    # Extract features from the incoming event
    features = json.loads(event['body'])['features']

    # Make predictions using the loaded model
    prediction = model.predict([features]).tolist()

    return {
        'statusCode': 200,
        'body': json.dumps({'prediction': prediction})
    }
```

4. Creating the API Gateway

Step 1: Create a New API in API Gateway
Go to the API Gateway Console:

- Open the **API Gateway Console** and create a new **REST API**. Provide a name for the API (e.g., ModelInferenceAPI).

Define a New Resource and Method:

- Create a new **Resource** (e.g., /predict).
- Under this resource, create a **POST** method, which will accept feature data in the request body and return the model prediction.

Step 2: Configure Integration with Lambda
Select Integration Type:

- Set the integration type as **Lambda Function** and choose the Lambda function you created in the previous step.

Configure Lambda Proxy Integration:

- Enable **Lambda Proxy Integration** to pass the incoming request as-is to the Lambda function, allowing the function to handle all HTTP details (such as parsing the request body and returning the response).

Deploy the API:

- Create a new deployment stage (e.g., prod) and deploy the API. Note the **Invoke URL**, which will be used to call the API.

5. Testing the Deployed Model API

Invoke the API using a Tool like Postman:

- Send a **POST request** to the API Gateway endpoint URL with JSON input containing the model features.

Example Request:

```
POST
https://your-api-id.execute-api.region.amazonaws.com/prod/predict

{
    "features": [5.1, 3.5, 1.4, 0.2]
}
```

Verify the Response:

- Check that the Lambda function processes the request correctly and returns the model prediction as expected.

6. Handling Security and Access Control

Use IAM Roles and Policies:

- Ensure that the Lambda execution role has appropriate permissions to access resources like S3, SageMaker, or other AWS services.

Configure API Gateway Authorization:

- You can use **Cognito User Pools**, **IAM Roles**, **API Keys**, or **Lambda Authorizers** to restrict access to your API.

Enable CORS:

- If your API needs to be accessed from a web application, configure **Cross-Origin Resource Sharing (CORS)** settings in API Gateway.

7. Best Practices for Deploying Pre-trained Models

- **Optimize Model Size**: Ensure that your model fits within Lambda's size and memory limits. If the model is too large, consider using **model compression** techniques or deploying it on **SageMaker** and invoking it from Lambda.
- **Minimize Cold Starts**: Use **Provisioned Concurrency** if your API needs to handle frequent requests with low latency. This will reduce cold start times by keeping execution environments warm.
- **Monitor and Scale**: Set up **CloudWatch alarms** to monitor key metrics such as **Lambda function duration**, **memory usage**, **throttling errors**, and **API Gateway errors**.
- **Log Key Metrics**: Use **CloudWatch Logs** to log prediction requests, model inputs, and outputs. This will help you analyze and debug issues in production.

8. Handling Common Issues and Troubleshooting

- **Lambda Function Timeout**: If your Lambda function is timing out frequently, increase the **timeout limit** in the function configuration. Ensure that the model loading and inference steps are efficient to stay within the time limits.
- **Memory Constraints**: If the model or the inference process exceeds Lambda's memory limits, consider optimizing the model or increasing the memory allocation in the Lambda configuration.
- **Model Loading Errors**: Ensure that the model file is properly stored in S3 and that the Lambda function has the necessary permissions to read from the S3 bucket.

Deploying pre-trained models using AWS Lambda and API Gateway provides a scalable, cost-effective, and serverless solution for serving real-time predictions. By following best practices such as optimizing model size, minimizing cold starts, and using efficient data handling, you can build robust and secure APIs for machine learning inference.

Integrating Lambda with API Gateway offers flexibility in handling various use cases, including real-time analytics, recommendation systems, image classification, and predictive maintenance. With these strategies, you can confidently deploy and manage machine learning models in a serverless environment using AWS Lambda and API Gateway.

Real-World ML Use Cases for Lambda

AWS Lambda is an excellent choice for deploying lightweight, serverless machine learning models that need to handle real-time predictions, process streaming data, or perform on-demand analysis. Combining AWS Lambda's serverless infrastructure with other AWS services allows developers to create cost-effective and scalable ML solutions. In this section, we'll explore several real-world ML use cases where Lambda can play a critical role.

1. Real-Time Sentiment Analysis for Customer Feedback

Use Case Description:

Companies often need to analyze customer feedback, such as social media comments, product reviews, or support tickets, to understand customer sentiment. Real-time sentiment analysis allows businesses to respond proactively to negative feedback or identify opportunities for improvement.

Solution Architecture:

- **Data Source**: Feedback data from social media platforms (using a streaming service like **Amazon Kinesis**), product reviews, or support tickets.
- **Lambda Function**: Hosts a pre-trained sentiment analysis model, such as a model trained using **scikit-learn**, **NLTK**, or **HuggingFace Transformers**. The model predicts sentiment scores for each incoming text.
- **API Gateway**: Provides a RESTful API endpoint for submitting text data.
- **CloudWatch**: Logs key metrics, including average sentiment scores and counts of positive, neutral, or negative feedback.

Example Workflow:

1. Customers submit product reviews or comments, which are ingested into an **Amazon Kinesis** stream.
2. A **Kinesis Data Firehose** triggers a Lambda function for each new record.
3. The Lambda function processes the text, makes a prediction, and stores the sentiment score in **Amazon DynamoDB** or **Amazon S3**.

2. Personalized Product Recommendations

Use Case Description:

E-commerce platforms can provide personalized product recommendations based on a user's browsing history, purchase patterns, and behavior. This approach increases sales by improving the relevance of the product suggestions.

Solution Architecture:

- **Data Source**: User interaction data stored in **Amazon DynamoDB** or **Amazon Redshift**.
- **Lambda Function**: Uses a pre-trained recommendation model (such as collaborative filtering with **scikit-learn** or **XGBoost**) to generate recommendations for a given user.
- **API Gateway**: Exposes an endpoint to request product recommendations for a specific user ID.
- **SageMaker**: Optionally used for training and deploying the recommendation model.

Example Workflow:

1. A user logs in to the e-commerce website, triggering a request to the **API Gateway** for product recommendations.
2. The Lambda function fetches user interaction data from DynamoDB, processes it through the recommendation model, and returns a list of recommended products.
3. The website displays the recommended products to the user in real-time.

3. Image Classification for Real-Time Quality Inspection

Use Case Description:

Manufacturing companies need to inspect products for defects in real-time to maintain quality standards. By deploying a lightweight image classification model on Lambda, companies can automate quality checks without relying on on-premises infrastructure.

Solution Architecture:

- **Data Source**: Images captured by inspection cameras uploaded to an **Amazon S3** bucket.
- **Lambda Function**: Hosts a pre-trained image classification model (e.g., using **TensorFlow Lite**, **MXNet**, or **PyTorch**) to classify images and detect defects.
- **S3 Event Notifications**: Triggers the Lambda function whenever a new image is uploaded.
- **DynamoDB**: Stores the classification results and metadata for each inspected product.

Example Workflow:

1. A camera captures images of products on a conveyor belt and uploads them to an **S3 bucket**.
2. The **S3 bucket** triggers a Lambda function with each uploaded image.
3. The Lambda function processes the image through the classification model and stores the inspection results in **DynamoDB**.

4. Voice-Based Sentiment Analysis for Call Center Recordings

Use Case Description:

Call centers need to analyze customer interactions to gauge customer satisfaction and improve service quality. By integrating AWS Lambda with speech-to-text and sentiment analysis models, call centers can automate sentiment analysis for recorded calls.

Solution Architecture:

- **Data Source**: Recorded customer calls uploaded to **Amazon S3**.
- **Lambda Function 1**: Invokes **Amazon Transcribe** to convert speech

recordings into text.

- **Lambda Function 2**: Uses a pre-trained sentiment analysis model (e.g., using **HuggingFace Transformers**) to analyze the transcribed text.
- **API Gateway**: Allows authorized users to query sentiment scores for specific calls.
- **S3 and DynamoDB**: Stores the transcribed text and sentiment analysis results.

Example Workflow:

1. A call recording is uploaded to **Amazon S3**, triggering a Lambda function.
2. The Lambda function invokes **Amazon Transcribe** to convert the recording to text.
3. Another Lambda function processes the text through a sentiment analysis model and stores the results in **DynamoDB**.

5. Anomaly Detection for IoT Data

Use Case Description:
Industries using IoT sensors need to detect anomalies in real-time to prevent equipment failures and minimize downtime. Lambda functions can be used to process streaming IoT data and identify anomalies using machine learning models.

Solution Architecture:

- **Data Source**: IoT sensor data ingested via **AWS IoT Core** or **Kinesis Data Streams**.
- **Lambda Function**: Hosts an anomaly detection model (such as **Isolation Forest** or **LSTM** model) to process incoming data and flag anomalies.
- **DynamoDB or S3**: Stores sensor data and anomaly detection results for historical analysis.
- **CloudWatch**: Monitors anomaly counts and triggers alerts.

Example Workflow:

1. Sensor data is ingested into an **AWS IoT Core** topic or **Kinesis Data Stream**.
2. A Lambda function processes the data in real-time and applies an anomaly detection model to identify abnormal patterns.
3. Anomalies are logged in **DynamoDB** or **S3**, and alerts are sent via **Amazon SNS** if an anomaly is detected.

6. Dynamic Pricing for E-commerce Platforms

Use Case Description:
Dynamic pricing models allow e-commerce companies to adjust product prices based on demand, supply, competition, and other market factors. Lambda can run lightweight dynamic pricing models that update prices in real-time.

Solution Architecture:

- **Data Source**: Historical sales data and competitor pricing information stored in **Amazon Redshift**.
- **Lambda Function**: Runs a dynamic pricing model (e.g., using **scikit-learn** or **XGBoost**) to calculate updated product prices.
- **API Gateway**: Provides an endpoint to trigger price updates manually or based on specific events.
- **DynamoDB**: Stores updated prices and logs changes for auditing.

Example Workflow:

1. An e-commerce platform periodically triggers a Lambda function via a **CloudWatch event**.
2. The Lambda function fetches sales and competitor data, applies a dynamic pricing model, and updates product prices in **DynamoDB**.
3. The updated prices are reflected on the platform's website in real-time.

7. Predictive Maintenance for Industrial Equipment

Use Case Description:

Industrial equipment requires predictive maintenance to prevent unexpected failures and reduce downtime. By deploying predictive maintenance models in Lambda, companies can analyze sensor data and predict equipment failure.

Solution Architecture:

- **Data Source**: Sensor data streams from equipment collected via **AWS IoT Core** or **Kinesis**.
- **Lambda Function**: Hosts a predictive maintenance model (such as **LSTM** or **Random Forest**) to process sensor data and predict equipment failure.
- **DynamoDB**: Stores predictions and metadata for each equipment instance.
- **CloudWatch Alarms**: Sends alerts to maintenance teams if a failure is predicted.

Example Workflow:

Sensor data is ingested into an **AWS IoT Core** topic or **Kinesis stream**.

A Lambda function processes the data, makes predictions, and stores the results in **DynamoDB**.

CloudWatch Alarms notify maintenance teams if a potential failure is detected.

AWS Lambda provides an ideal environment for running lightweight ML models in real-time and on-demand use cases. By integrating Lambda with other AWS services like **API Gateway, S3, DynamoDB**, and **Kinesis**, you can build serverless applications that are cost-effective, scalable, and resilient. From real-time sentiment analysis and anomaly detection to dynamic pricing and predictive maintenance, Lambda enables a wide range of machine learning use cases.

Following best practices such as optimizing model size, implementing secure API endpoints, and monitoring key metrics ensures that your ML applications are reliable and performant. With these use cases as a guide, you can confidently explore and deploy ML models using AWS Lambda for various business scenarios.

Debugging and Monitoring Lambda Functions

ebugging Locally with AWS SAM CLI and Docker
When developing and testing AWS Lambda functions, local debugging is crucial for identifying and fixing issues before deploying the code to the cloud. The **AWS Serverless Application Model (SAM) CLI** combined with **Docker** provides a powerful environment for testing and debugging Lambda functions locally. By replicating the AWS Lambda execution environment on your local machine, you can debug your functions, inspect their behavior, and gain confidence before pushing the code to production.

In this section, we'll explore how to use the **AWS SAM CLI** and Docker for local debugging of Lambda functions. We will cover key concepts, installation steps, and provide a comprehensive walkthrough of setting up and running a local debugging session.

1. Overview of AWS SAM CLI and Docker for Local Debugging

The **AWS Serverless Application Model (SAM)** is an open-source framework designed to build, test, and deploy serverless applications. It extends AWS CloudFormation, providing a simplified syntax for defining serverless resources. The **AWS SAM CLI** allows you to run your Lambda functions locally using Docker, simulating the AWS Lambda execution environment on your machine.

Key Features of AWS SAM CLI:

- **Local Execution**: Run Lambda functions locally using Docker, with full support for different runtimes such as Python, Node.js, Java, and more.
- **Local Debugging**: Attach debuggers to your code to inspect variable states, set breakpoints, and step through code execution.
- **API Gateway Emulation**: Simulate API Gateway locally to test Lambda functions integrated with RESTful APIs.
- **Local Event Testing**: Trigger functions with various AWS events (e.g., S3 events, SNS messages, DynamoDB streams) to validate behavior.

Why Use Docker? The AWS SAM CLI uses Docker containers to simulate the Lambda runtime environment on your local machine. This provides a nearly identical environment to the one in AWS, allowing you to catch issues related to dependencies, runtime configurations, or Lambda execution constraints.

2. Setting Up AWS SAM CLI and Docker

2.1. Prerequisites

Before you can start debugging locally, ensure you have the following installed on your machine:

- **AWS SAM CLI**: Download and install the AWS SAM CLI.
- **Docker Desktop**: Download and install Docker.
- **AWS CLI** (optional): For deploying functions to AWS after local debugging.

2.2. Installing AWS SAM CLI
Verify Docker Installation:

- Ensure that Docker Desktop is running on your machine. Test the installation by running:

```
docker --version
```

Install SAM CLI:

- Follow the installation instructions specific to your operating system from the AWS SAM CLI documentation.

Verify SAM Installation:

- After installation, verify that SAM CLI is working by running:

```
sam --version
```

3. Creating a Lambda Function for Local Debugging

3.1. Initialize a New SAM Application
Initialize a New SAM Project:

```
sam init
```

This command prompts you to choose a runtime, template, and project name. Choose a runtime (e.g., **Python 3.9**) and a starter template.

Example Selection:

```
Which runtime would you like to use?
1 - nodejs14.x
2 - python3.9
3 - java11
4 - go1.x
...
```

```
Runtime: 2

What template source would you like to use?
1 - AWS Quick Start Templates
...
Template selection: 1
```

Navigate to the Project Directory:

```
cd your-project-name
```

Examine the Generated Project: The SAM CLI generates a project with a basic Lambda function, a template file (template.yaml), and other required files.

Example template.yaml:

```yaml
AWSTemplateFormatVersion: '2010-09-09'
Transform: AWS::Serverless-2016-10-31
Resources:
  HelloWorldFunction:
    Type: AWS::Serverless::Function
    Properties:
      Handler: app.lambda_handler
      Runtime: python3.9
      CodeUri: hello_world/
      Events:
        HelloWorld:
          Type: Api
          Properties:
            Path: /hello
            Method: get
```

Open the Function Code (hello_world/app.py): This file contains a basic handler function that responds to an HTTP request. Modify it as needed for your use case.

4. Running and Debugging the Function Locally

4.1. Running the Function Locally without Debugging

To test the Lambda function locally without attaching a debugger, use the sam local invoke command.

Invoke the Function Locally:

```
sam local invoke HelloWorldFunction --event events/event.json
```

This command runs the Lambda function inside a Docker container and simulates an AWS Lambda execution environment. The —event flag specifies the input event to pass to the function.

Check the Output: The output includes the function logs and the response returned by the Lambda function.

4.2. Setting Up Debugging with AWS SAM CLI

Install Debugger Extension (for IDE):

- For **VS Code**, install the **Python** extension and the **AWS Toolkit** extension.
- For **PyCharm**, use the **Python** debugger built into the IDE.

Configure the Debugger (VS Code Example): Create a .vscode/launch.json file with the following configuration:

```
{
    "version": "0.2.0",
    "configurations": [
        {
            "name": "Debug Lambda",
            "type": "python",
            "request": "attach",
            "port": 5858,
            "host": "localhost",
            "pathMappings": [
```

```
        {
            "localRoot": "${workspaceFolder}/hello_world",
            "remoteRoot": "/var/task"
        }
    ]
  }
  ]
}
```

Explanation:

- This configuration tells VS Code to attach to the Lambda function running inside the Docker container on port 5858.
- The localRoot and remoteRoot map your local directory to the container's working directory.

Run SAM in Debug Mode:
  Start the Function in Debug Mode:

```
sam local invoke HelloWorldFunction -d 5858
```

This command starts the Lambda function in debug mode, exposing port 5858 for debugging connections.
  Attach the Debugger from Your IDE:

- Open your IDE (e.g., **VS Code**) and start the debugger using the configuration you defined in launch.json.
- Set breakpoints in your code and step through the execution.

5. Debugging Lambda Functions with Docker

5.1. Building a Custom Docker Image for Lambda

If your function requires specific dependencies or a custom runtime, you can use **AWS Lambda custom runtimes** with Docker. The SAM CLI supports building and running custom Docker images locally.

Create a Dockerfile in your project directory:

Example Dockerfile:

```
FROM public.ecr.aws/lambda/python:3.9

COPY app.py requirements.txt ./
RUN pip install -r requirements.txt

CMD ["app.lambda_handler"]
```

Build the Docker Image:

```
docker build -t my-lambda-function .
```

Run the Docker Container Locally:

```
docker run -p 9000:8080 my-lambda-function
```

Invoke the Function: Use curl or Postman to send a request to the container's local endpoint:

```
curl -X POST
"http://localhost:9000/2015-03-31/functions/function/invocations"
-d '{}'
```

6. Best Practices for Local Debugging with SAM CLI

- **Use Meaningful Test Events**: Create realistic event data for testing Lambda functions locally. Use JSON files to simulate actual data from services like S3, DynamoDB, or API Gateway.
- **Leverage Docker for Dependency Testing**: If your function relies on specific dependencies, use Docker containers to emulate the Lambda

runtime environment accurately.

- **Check CloudWatch Logs for Production Issues**: After deploying your function, always check **CloudWatch Logs** for unexpected errors that might not surface during local testing.
- **Version Control Your SAM Templates**: Maintain your template.yaml and deployment scripts in version control to track infrastructure changes and collaborate effectively.

Debugging Lambda functions locally using the **AWS SAM CLI** and **Docker** is a powerful way to replicate the AWS Lambda runtime environment on your machine. This approach enables you to catch issues early, understand the function's behavior, and validate its integration with other AWS services before deploying it to production.

By following best practices such as setting up realistic test events, using Docker for dependency emulation, and leveraging IDEs for interactive debugging, you can streamline the development process and reduce the chances of encountering issues in production. With this comprehensive approach to local debugging, you can confidently build and maintain reliable serverless applications using AWS Lambda.

Setting Up Custom CloudWatch Alarms and Metrics

Amazon CloudWatch provides a robust set of monitoring and alerting capabilities that are crucial for maintaining and troubleshooting AWS Lambda functions. By setting up custom **CloudWatch Alarms** and **CloudWatch Metrics**, you can proactively monitor the health and performance of your serverless applications, receive notifications when issues arise, and take automated actions to prevent system failures.

In this section, we'll explore how to set up and manage custom CloudWatch metrics and alarms for Lambda functions. We'll cover key concepts, the step-by-step process of creating alarms, and best practices for leveraging these capabilities.

1. Understanding CloudWatch Metrics and Alarms

Amazon CloudWatch automatically collects key metrics for AWS Lambda functions, such as **invocation count**, **duration**, **error count**, and **throttles**. However, there are scenarios where you may need to create custom metrics and set up alarms for more granular monitoring.

Key CloudWatch Metrics for AWS Lambda:

- **Invocations**: The number of times a Lambda function is invoked.
- **Duration**: The amount of time a Lambda function takes to execute (in milliseconds).
- **Errors**: The number of times a Lambda function invocation fails due to an unhandled error.
- **Throttles**: The number of times Lambda throttled the function due to concurrency limits.
- **ConcurrentExecutions**: The number of function instances that are running concurrently.
- **IteratorAge (for stream-based invocations)**: The age of the last record processed from a stream (e.g., Kinesis or DynamoDB).

2. Creating Custom CloudWatch Metrics for Lambda

2.1. Using CloudWatch Embedded Metrics Format (EMF)

You can create custom metrics in Lambda by using **CloudWatch Embedded Metrics Format (EMF)**. EMF enables you to embed custom metric data directly within your Lambda logs, which are automatically processed by CloudWatch to generate metrics.

Example Python Code for Creating Custom Metrics:

```python
import json
import boto3
import time
import logging

# Set up logging for the Lambda function
logger = logging.getLogger()
logger.setLevel(logging.INFO)

# Function to create and log custom metrics
def log_custom_metrics(success_count, failure_count,
processing_time):
    metrics = {
        "_aws": {
            "CloudWatchMetrics": [
                {
                    "Namespace": "MyLambdaApp",
                    "Dimensions": [["FunctionName"]],
                    "Metrics": [
                        {"Name": "SuccessCount", "Unit": "Count"},
                        {"Name": "FailureCount", "Unit": "Count"},
                        {"Name": "ProcessingTime", "Unit":
                        "Milliseconds"}
                    ]
                }
            ],
            "Timestamp": int(time.time() * 1000)
        },
        "FunctionName": "MyLambdaFunction",
        "SuccessCount": success_count,
        "FailureCount": failure_count,
        "ProcessingTime": processing_time
    }

    # Log the custom metrics as a JSON string
    logger.info(json.dumps(metrics))

def lambda_handler(event, context):
    try:
        # Your function logic here
```

```
        start_time = time.time()

        # Simulating some logic with success and failure
        success_count = 1
        failure_count = 0

        # Log custom metrics
        processing_time = int((time.time() - start_time) * 1000)
        log_custom_metrics(success_count, failure_count,
        processing_time)

        return {
            "statusCode": 200,
            "body": json.dumps("Success")
        }
    except Exception as e:
        logger.error(f"Error: {str(e)}")
        log_custom_metrics(0, 1, 0)
        raise
```

Explanation:

- **Log Custom Metrics**: The function logs metrics to **CloudWatch Logs** in the EMF format, which automatically converts these logs into custom CloudWatch metrics.
- **Dimensions**: Dimensions are used to filter and aggregate metrics, allowing you to slice and dice data effectively.
- **Namespace**: Custom metrics should be placed in a logical namespace to distinguish them from default AWS Lambda metrics.

3. Creating CloudWatch Alarms for Lambda Metrics

3.1. Setting Up Alarms Using the CloudWatch Console
Go to the CloudWatch Console:

- In the AWS Management Console, navigate to **CloudWatch** and select

Alarms from the left-hand menu.

Create a New Alarm:

- Click **Create Alarm** and select **Browse** to find the metric that you want to monitor (e.g., Errors, Duration, or your custom metric).

Choose a Metric:

- Select the **Namespace** and **Metric Name** from the available options. For custom metrics, choose the namespace you used when creating the metric (e.g., MyLambdaApp).

Configure the Alarm:

- Define the **threshold** for the alarm. For example, you can set an alarm to trigger if the number of errors exceeds 5 within a 5-minute period.
- Choose the **statistic** to evaluate (e.g., **Sum, Average, Maximum**), the **period**, and the **comparison operator** (e.g., **Greater than**).

Set Up Notifications:

- Configure actions to take when the alarm state changes, such as sending an email using **Amazon SNS** or executing a Lambda function to perform automated remediation.

Review and Create the Alarm:

- Review your settings and click **Create Alarm**.

3.2. Example: Creating an Alarm for Lambda Errors
Select the Errors Metric from the **AWS/Lambda** namespace.
Define the Alarm:

- **Threshold**: If the Sum of Errors exceeds 3 in a 5-minute period.
- **Notification**: Send an alert to an SNS topic or trigger an automated remediation Lambda function.

Save and Activate the Alarm.

4. Best Practices for Setting Up Custom CloudWatch Alarms

4.1. Monitor Key Metrics and Set Thresholds

Identify critical metrics that indicate the health of your Lambda functions. Create alarms for key metrics such as:

- **Errors**: Monitor for increases in error rates, indicating potential issues in the function logic or external dependencies.
- **Duration**: Set alarms to detect unusually long execution times, which could indicate performance bottlenecks or slow dependencies.
- **Throttles**: Track the number of throttled invocations to detect issues related to concurrency limits or scaling constraints.
- **Custom Business Metrics**: Create alarms for business-specific metrics, such as processing times, success rates, or incoming request volumes.

4.2. Use Dimensions for Granular Monitoring

Leverage **dimensions** to filter and aggregate metrics based on specific attributes, such as function names, environment types, or invocation sources. This allows you to set more precise alarms tailored to individual functions or deployments.

4.3. Automate Responses to Alarms

Configure CloudWatch Alarms to trigger automated actions in response to threshold breaches:

- **Invoke Remediation Lambda Functions**: For example, if an alarm detects excessive errors, trigger a Lambda function to reset connections, clean up resources, or escalate to on-call personnel.

- **Send Notifications Using Amazon SNS**: Send notifications to relevant stakeholders when alarms are triggered, ensuring prompt action.

4.4. Monitor Custom Metrics with Dashboards

Create **CloudWatch Dashboards** to visualize both standard and custom metrics in a single view. Use widgets to track key metrics over time and identify patterns or trends in your Lambda function's performance.

5. Automating CloudWatch Alarms with AWS SAM

If you are using the **AWS SAM CLI**, you can define CloudWatch Alarms and custom metrics directly in your SAM template to automate the setup during deployment.

Example template.yaml with CloudWatch Alarm Definition:

```
Resources:
  HelloWorldFunction:
    Type: AWS::Serverless::Function
    Properties:
      Handler: app.lambda_handler
      Runtime: python3.9
      Events:
        ApiEvent:
          Type: Api
          Properties:
            Path: /hello
            Method: get

  LambdaErrorAlarm:
    Type: "AWS::CloudWatch::Alarm"
    Properties:
      AlarmDescription: "Alarm for monitoring Lambda function
      errors"
      Namespace: "AWS/Lambda"
      MetricName: "Errors"
      Dimensions:
```

```
        - Name: "FunctionName"
          Value: !Ref HelloWorldFunction
        Statistic: "Sum"
        Period: 300
        EvaluationPeriods: 1
        Threshold: 3
        ComparisonOperator: "GreaterThanThreshold"
        AlarmActions:
          - !Ref SNSAlertTopic

    SNSAlertTopic:
      Type: "AWS::SNS::Topic"
      Properties:
        DisplayName: "Lambda Error Alerts"
```

Setting up custom CloudWatch Alarms and Metrics for AWS Lambda functions allows you to proactively monitor your serverless applications and receive timely alerts when issues arise. By leveraging CloudWatch's built-in capabilities, defining custom metrics with EMF, and creating alarms based on key performance indicators, you can ensure the reliability and health of your Lambda functions.

Following best practices such as monitoring critical metrics, using dimensions for granular control, and automating responses to alarms helps you maintain observability and stability in your serverless architecture. With these tools in place, you can confidently deploy and monitor Lambda functions in production environments.

Analyzing Lambda Errors and Failures

Efficiently analyzing errors and failures in AWS Lambda functions is crucial for identifying issues, improving function reliability, and reducing downtime. AWS offers various tools and techniques to help you track, monitor, and debug Lambda errors, enabling you to maintain a high level of observability in your serverless applications. By utilizing **AWS CloudWatch**, **AWS X-Ray**, and detailed **logging strategies**, you can gain deep insights into the causes of errors and failures.

In this section, we'll explore how to analyze AWS Lambda errors and failures effectively, covering common error types, strategies for capturing detailed error information, and using AWS services for tracing and troubleshooting.

1. Understanding Common Lambda Error Types

Before diving into the analysis, it's essential to understand the common types of errors encountered in Lambda functions:

- **Invocation Errors**: These occur when a Lambda function fails to execute due to invalid input, missing parameters, or service-level issues.
- **Runtime Errors**: These include exceptions raised during the execution of the function, such as ValueError, TypeError, or missing dependencies.
- **Timeout Errors**: Occur when a Lambda function exceeds its configured timeout duration, often due to inefficient code, blocking operations, or slow external service calls.
- **Permissions Errors**: These result from incorrect IAM role configurations, preventing the function from accessing AWS resources like S3, DynamoDB, or Kinesis.
- **Throttling Errors**: Triggered when the function's concurrency limit is exceeded, causing some requests to be denied.

2. Capturing and Logging Detailed Error Information

2.1. Logging Best Practices

Detailed logging is critical for effective error analysis. AWS Lambda automatically captures logs and sends them to **Amazon CloudWatch Logs**, but you can enhance this by implementing structured logging and capturing contextual information.

Example: Enhanced Logging with Contextual Information:

```python
import json
import logging

# Configure logger
logger = logging.getLogger()
logger.setLevel(logging.INFO)

def lambda_handler(event, context):
    try:
        # Log event details and context information
        logger.info(f"Event received: {json.dumps(event)}")
        logger.info(f"Lambda Request ID: {context.aws_request_id}")
        logger.info(f"Function Name: {context.function_name}")

        # Simulate processing logic
        if "key" not in event:
            raise ValueError("Missing 'key' in event data")

        result = process_event(event)  # Your function logic here
        return {
            "statusCode": 200,
            "body": json.dumps(result)
        }

    except Exception as e:
        logger.error(f"Error occurred: {str(e)}")
        logger.exception("Detailed traceback for debugging")
        raise
```

Explanation:

- **Log Context Information**: Capture details like the **request ID, function name**, and other context attributes to correlate errors with specific invocations.
- **Use Structured Logs**: Logging structured data (e.g., JSON) allows for easier searching, filtering, and analysis in CloudWatch Logs.

410

2.2. Configuring CloudWatch Log Groups and Retention Policies

Each Lambda function creates a dedicated **log group** in **CloudWatch Logs**. Ensure that log retention policies are configured appropriately based on your monitoring and compliance requirements.

Steps to Configure Retention Policies:

1. Open the **CloudWatch Console** and navigate to **Log Groups**.
2. Select the log group for your Lambda function (e.g., /aws/lambda/my-function).
3. Click **Actions** and select **Edit Retention**.
4. Choose a retention period (e.g., 7 days, 30 days, or custom period) based on your needs.

3. Using AWS CloudWatch Insights for Log Analysis

Amazon CloudWatch Logs Insights is a powerful tool for querying and analyzing logs. It provides a structured query language that allows you to extract meaningful insights from large volumes of log data.

Example: Query for Analyzing Errors:

```
fields @timestamp, @message
| filter @message like /(?i)error/
| sort @timestamp desc
| limit 20
```

Explanation:

- **Filter for Errors**: This query searches for logs containing the word "error" (case-insensitive) and lists the most recent entries.
- **Include Contextual Information**: By logging relevant metadata in your function code, you can extend this query to include details like **request IDs** or **event attributes** for deeper analysis.

4. Setting Up CloudWatch Alarms for Error Monitoring

As covered in the previous section, **CloudWatch Alarms** are essential for monitoring key Lambda metrics like **Error Count**, **Throttles**, and **Duration**. Create alarms that notify you via **Amazon SNS** whenever errors exceed a certain threshold, allowing you to respond proactively to issues.

5. Tracing Lambda Functions with AWS X-Ray

AWS X-Ray helps you trace and analyze distributed applications, including AWS Lambda functions. It allows you to visualize the flow of requests through your serverless architecture, identify bottlenecks, and pinpoint errors.

5.1. Enabling X-Ray for Lambda Functions
Open the Lambda Console:

- Select the Lambda function you want to trace.

Go to the Monitoring and Operations Tools Section:

- Enable **Active Tracing** with **AWS X-Ray**.

Configure Sampling Rules (Optional):

- Go to the **X-Ray Console** and define sampling rules if you only want to trace a percentage of requests.

5.2. Analyzing X-Ray Traces

- **Trace Segments**: Each trace contains segments representing different services, Lambda functions, or external calls. You can inspect each segment to see detailed metadata, execution times, and exceptions.
- **Error and Fault Indicators**: X-Ray highlights error segments in red,

making it easy to spot issues in the trace map.

Example: Detecting an External Service Latency: If your Lambda function calls an external API or database, X-Ray traces can show which part of the request is causing latency or failures. You can view details like HTTP status codes, response times, and retry attempts.

6. Analyzing and Resolving Lambda Timeouts

Timeouts are a common cause of Lambda failures. They often occur due to long-running operations, such as waiting for slow database queries or external API calls. Here's how you can approach resolving timeout issues:

Increase the Timeout Setting:

- In the **Lambda Console**, go to the **General Configuration** and increase the function timeout if your operations require more time.

Identify Slow Operations:

- Use **X-Ray** or **CloudWatch Logs** to identify which part of your function is taking the most time. For example, a database call or file upload to S3 may be the root cause.

Optimize Code and Dependencies:

- Review your code for any unnecessary loops, blocking calls, or inefficient operations.
- Consider using asynchronous approaches or batch processing to minimize blocking operations.

7. Leveraging CloudWatch Metrics for Root Cause Analysis

CloudWatch provides default metrics such as **Duration, Error Count**, and **Throttles** for Lambda functions. Analyzing these metrics over time can help identify patterns and root causes of failures.

Steps for Root Cause Analysis:

1. **Plot Error Metrics**: Visualize the **Error Count** and **Duration** metrics on a CloudWatch Dashboard to spot spikes or unusual trends.
2. **Correlate Metrics with Events**: If your function is triggered by events (e.g., API Gateway, S3, or Kinesis), correlate Lambda metrics with these trigger sources to identify patterns.
3. **Drill Down into Individual Invocations**: Use **X-Ray Traces** and **CloudWatch Logs** to drill down into individual function invocations for detailed error information.

8. Implementing Custom Error Handling in Lambda Functions

Custom error handling allows you to gracefully handle exceptions and prevent unhandled errors from causing function failures. Use **try-except blocks** in Python or equivalent constructs in other languages to handle errors effectively.

Example: Graceful Error Handling and Fallback Logic:

```python
import json
import logging

logger = logging.getLogger()
logger.setLevel(logging.INFO)

def lambda_handler(event, context):
    try:
        # Example processing logic
        result = perform_critical_operation(event)
```

```python
        if not result:
            raise ValueError("Critical operation failed")

        return {
            "statusCode": 200,
            "body": json.dumps({"message": "Success"})
        }

    except ValueError as ve:
        logger.error(f"Validation Error: {str(ve)}")
        return {
            "statusCode": 400,
            "body": json.dumps({"message": "Validation Error",
            "details": str(ve)})
        }

    except Exception as e:
        logger.error(f"Unhandled Exception: {str(e)}")
        logger.exception("Full stack trace for debugging")
        return {
            "statusCode": 500,
            "body": json.dumps({"message": "Internal Server
            Error"})
        }
```

Explanation:

- **Validation Error**: Returns a **400** response with an error message for validation failures.
- **Unhandled Exception**: Logs the full stack trace and returns a generic **500** response for unexpected issues.

Analyzing errors and failures in AWS Lambda functions is essential for maintaining the reliability and performance of your serverless applications. By leveraging detailed logging, CloudWatch Insights, X-Ray tracing, and custom error handling techniques, you can gain deep insights into your functions' behavior and efficiently troubleshoot issues.

Continuous Deployment and Version Control

Automating Lambda Deployments with AWS CodePipeline

In modern software development, implementing **Continuous Deployment (CD)** is essential for maintaining agility, reducing release cycle times, and ensuring that code changes are deployed reliably. For AWS Lambda functions, automating deployments with **AWS CodePipeline** helps you achieve efficient CI/CD practices, enabling automated testing, version control, and deployments without manual intervention.

AWS CodePipeline is a fully managed service that automates the build, test, and deployment phases of your application's release process. It integrates seamlessly with other AWS services such as **CodeCommit, CodeBuild, CodeDeploy**, and **CloudFormation**, making it ideal for automating Lambda deployments.

In this section, we'll explore how to automate Lambda deployments using **AWS CodePipeline**, covering key concepts, step-by-step implementation, and best practices for achieving efficient and secure CI/CD pipelines.

1. Why Use AWS CodePipeline for Lambda Deployments?

AWS CodePipeline provides several advantages for automating Lambda deployments:

- **Automated Deployments**: Reduces manual intervention by automating the entire deployment process, including code changes, testing, and versioning.

- **Integrated Version Control**: Supports integration with popular version control systems like **AWS CodeCommit**, **GitHub**, and **Bitbucket**.
- **Consistent Releases**: Ensures consistent and error-free deployments by enforcing automated tests and checks before code is promoted to production.
- **Scalability and Security**: Provides a scalable framework for deploying Lambda functions while following best practices for security and access control.

2. Overview of the CodePipeline Architecture for Lambda

A typical CodePipeline setup for Lambda deployments includes the following stages:

1. **Source Stage**: Retrieves the latest code changes from a source repository like **AWS CodeCommit**, **GitHub**, or **Bitbucket**.
2. **Build Stage**: Uses **AWS CodeBuild** to package the Lambda function and its dependencies. The build output includes a deployment package or **CloudFormation template**.
3. **Test Stage (Optional)**: Executes automated tests (e.g., unit tests, integration tests) on the packaged code using **CodeBuild**.
4. **Deploy Stage**: Uses **AWS CloudFormation** or **AWS CodeDeploy** to deploy the Lambda function to the target environment.

3. Setting Up CodePipeline for Lambda Deployment

3.1. Prerequisites

Before setting up a pipeline, ensure you have the following prerequisites:

- **An AWS Account** with permissions to create and manage CodePipeline, CodeBuild, CodeDeploy, Lambda, and IAM resources.

- **A Version Control Repository** in **AWS CodeCommit, GitHub,** or **Bitbucket**.
- **AWS CLI** or **AWS Management Console** access.

3.2. Step-by-Step Setup of AWS CodePipeline
Step 1: Create a Source Repository
Create a CodeCommit Repository:

- Go to the **CodeCommit Console** and create a new repository. Clone the repository to your local machine and push your Lambda code.

```
git clone
https://git-codecommit.us-east-1.amazonaws.com/v1/repos/MyLambdaRepo
cd MyLambdaRepo
# Add your Lambda function code and push to CodeCommit
git add .
git commit -m "Initial commit"
git push origin main
```

Alternatively, Use GitHub or Bitbucket:

- Link your GitHub or Bitbucket account to CodePipeline when setting up the pipeline.

Step 2: Create an S3 Bucket for Build Artifacts
Create an S3 Bucket:

- Go to the **S3 Console** and create a bucket to store build artifacts and deployment packages (e.g., my-lambda-artifacts-bucket).

Step 3: Create a Build Specification File (buildspec.yml)
Define the Build Specification:

419

- Create a buildspec.yml file in your project root directory to define the build steps for CodeBuild. This file specifies how to package your Lambda function and dependencies.

Example buildspec.yml:

```
version: 0.2

phases:
  install:
    runtime-versions:
      python: 3.8
    commands:
      - pip install -r requirements.txt -t .

  build:
    commands:
      - zip -r lambda-function.zip .

artifacts:
  files:
    - lambda-function.zip
```

Include Dependencies:

- If your Lambda function requires specific dependencies, list them in a requirements.txt file.

Step 4: Create a CodeBuild Project
Go to the CodeBuild Console:

- Create a new build project and specify the **source repository** (Code-Commit, GitHub, or Bitbucket).

Configure the Build Environment:

- Choose the **runtime version** (e.g., Python 3.8) and specify the build-spec.yml file path.

Set Up Artifacts:

- Specify the S3 bucket to store the build output (lambda-function.zip).

Step 5: Define a Deployment Strategy with CodeDeploy or CloudFormation

Create a Deployment Configuration:

- For simple deployments, use a **CloudFormation template** to create or update the Lambda function. For more complex scenarios, use **CodeDeploy** with a canary or linear deployment strategy.

Define the Deployment Template:

- Create a **CloudFormation template** (template.yaml) to define the Lambda function, role, and permissions.

Example template.yaml:

```
AWSTemplateFormatVersion: '2010-09-09'
Transform: AWS::Serverless-2016-10-31
Resources:
  MyLambdaFunction:
    Type: AWS::Serverless::Function
    Properties:
      FunctionName: MyLambdaFunction
      Handler: app.lambda_handler
      Runtime: python3.8
      CodeUri: s3://my-lambda-artifacts-bucket/lambda-function.zip
      Role: arn:aws:iam::123456789012:role/MyLambdaRole
```

Step 6: Create the CodePipeline

Go to the CodePipeline Console:

- Create a new pipeline and define the pipeline stages.

Add the Source Stage:

- Select **CodeCommit**, **GitHub**, or **Bitbucket** as the source provider and choose the repository.

Add the Build Stage:

- Select **AWS CodeBuild** and choose the build project you created earlier.

Add the Deploy Stage:

- For the deployment, use **AWS CloudFormation** or **AWS CodeDeploy** as the provider. Specify the deployment configuration and artifacts.

Review and Create the Pipeline:

- After reviewing your configurations, create the pipeline.

4. Configuring Automated Tests in CodePipeline

To ensure that only high-quality code is deployed, configure an additional **Test Stage** in the pipeline:

- **Unit Tests**: Run unit tests using **pytest** or another testing framework in the CodeBuild phase.
- **Integration Tests**: Simulate real-world scenarios to validate Lambda function behavior.
- **Security Tests**: Perform security checks, such as validating IAM roles and resource access policies.

Example buildspec.yml with Tests:

```
version: 0.2

phases:
  install:
    runtime-versions:
      python: 3.8
    commands:
      - pip install -r requirements.txt -t .

  pre_build:
    commands:
      - pytest tests/  # Run unit tests

  build:
    commands:
      - zip -r lambda-function.zip .

artifacts:
  files:
    - lambda-function.zip
```

5. Managing Versions and Rollbacks

AWS Lambda supports versioning, allowing you to create and manage multiple versions of your functions. You can also define **aliases** to represent stable versions (e.g., prod, beta).

5.1. Creating Lambda Versions Automatically

1. **Update template.yaml to Publish Versions**:
2. **Example template.yaml**:

```
Resources:
  MyLambdaFunction:
    Type: AWS::Serverless::Function
    Properties:
      FunctionName: MyLambdaFunction
      Handler: app.lambda_handler
      Runtime: python3.8
      CodeUri: s3://my-lambda-artifacts-bucket/lambda-function.zip
      Role: arn:aws:iam::123456789012:role/MyLambdaRole
      AutoPublishAlias: prod  # Automatically publish a new
      version with each deployment
```

Automate Rollbacks:

- Use **CodeDeploy** to define a rollback strategy in case of failed deployments.

6. Best Practices for Automating Lambda Deployments

- **Enable Notifications**: Set up **Amazon SNS** notifications to alert relevant teams of pipeline failures or manual approval requests.
- **Secure Access to Resources**: Use **IAM roles** with the principle of least privilege to grant pipeline permissions.
- **Implement Approval Stages**: For critical environments, add manual approval stages to the pipeline to ensure deployments are reviewed by authorized personnel.
- **Monitor Pipelines and Logs**: Use **CloudWatch** and **CodePipeline Logs** to track pipeline executions, build logs, and deployment outcomes.

Automating Lambda deployments with **AWS CodePipeline** streamlines your CI/CD process, reduces manual effort, and improves code quality through consistent testing and deployment practices. By integrating version control, automated tests, and deployment strategies, CodePipeline enables efficient and reliable releases of Lambda functions.

Managing Function Versions and Aliases

When deploying AWS Lambda functions, it's essential to manage different versions of your code and establish stable references for production, staging, or development environments. AWS Lambda provides built-in support for **versioning** and **aliases**, allowing you to organize, reference, and promote your Lambda functions efficiently.

In this section, we'll explore how to use Lambda versions and aliases to enhance deployment flexibility, implement safe rollbacks, and simplify application updates.

1. Understanding Lambda Function Versions

AWS Lambda versions allow you to create immutable snapshots of your Lambda function code and configuration. Each published version is assigned a unique version number and cannot be changed, ensuring consistency across different environments.

Key Characteristics of Lambda Versions:

- **Immutable**: Once a version is published, it cannot be modified. This immutability guarantees that the code and configuration remain consistent.
- **Default Version**: When you create or update a function without specifying a version, you are working with the $LATEST version. This represents the most recent code and configuration.
- **Explicit Publishing**: You must explicitly publish a new version to generate a version number.

2. Creating and Publishing Lambda Versions

2.1. Publishing a New Version Manually
Open the Lambda Console:

- Navigate to the **AWS Lambda Console** and select your function.

Review Changes:

- Ensure that all changes to your function code and configuration have been saved in the $LATEST version.

Publish a New Version:

- Click **Actions** and select **Publish new version**. You will be prompted to provide an optional description for the new version.
- Once published, your function will have a new version number (e.g., 1, 2, 3, etc.).

Accessing Versions:

- You can view and manage versions in the **Versions** tab within the Lambda console.

2.2. Publishing Versions Using CloudFormation or SAM
You can automate version publishing using **AWS CloudFormation** or **AWS Serverless Application Model (SAM)** templates.
Example CloudFormation Template:

```
Resources:
  MyLambdaFunction:
    Type: AWS::Serverless::Function
    Properties:
```

```
FunctionName: MyLambdaFunction
Handler: app.lambda_handler
Runtime: python3.8
CodeUri: s3://my-bucket/my-lambda-code.zip
Role: arn:aws:iam::123456789012:role/MyLambdaRole
AutoPublishAlias: live
```

Explanation:

- **AutoPublishAlias**: Automatically creates a new version and publishes an alias (live) pointing to the new version each time the function is updated.

2.3. Publishing Versions with AWS CLI

You can also use the **AWS CLI** to publish new versions programmatically.
Example Command:

```
aws lambda publish-version --function-name MyLambdaFunction
--description "My new stable version"
```

3. Working with Lambda Aliases

Aliases are pointers to specific Lambda versions, allowing you to abstract away version numbers and refer to your function by a meaningful name, such as prod, staging, or beta.
Key Benefits of Aliases:

- **Simplify Deployment**: Abstract the complexity of version numbers by using aliases in application configurations or API calls.
- **Implement Canary Releases**: Gradually shift traffic from one version to another using weighted aliases.
- **Roll Back Safely**: Easily revert to a previous version by changing the alias's version reference.

427

4. Creating and Managing Aliases

4.1. Creating an Alias Manually
Open the Lambda Console:

- Navigate to your Lambda function and select the **Aliases** tab.

Create a New Alias:

- Click **Create alias** and specify the alias name (e.g., prod) and the version number to which the alias should point (e.g., 1).
- Optionally, add a description for the alias.

Manage Alias Versions:

- To update the alias to point to a new version, select the alias, click **Edit alias**, and change the version reference.

4.2. Creating Aliases Using AWS CLI
Example Command:

```
aws lambda create-alias --function-name MyLambdaFunction --name
prod --function-version 1 --description "Production alias"
```

Updating an Alias:

```
aws lambda update-alias --function-name MyLambdaFunction --name
prod --function-version 2
```

5. Implementing Canary Deployments with Aliases

AWS Lambda supports **weighted aliases,** allowing you to gradually shift traffic between two versions of your function. This approach is known as a **canary deployment** and helps minimize risk during updates by gradually increasing the percentage of traffic directed to the new version.

5.1. Setting Up a Weighted Alias
Create or Update an Alias:

- In the **Lambda Console**, go to the **Aliases** tab and create or update an alias.

Enable Traffic Shifting:

- In the alias settings, specify a **second version** and a **traffic weight**. For example, you can allocate 90% of traffic to version 1 and 10% to version 2.

Example CLI Command for Weighted Alias:

```
aws lambda update-alias --function-name MyLambdaFunction --name
prod --routing-config '{"AdditionalVersionWeights": {"2": 0.1}}'
```

Explanation:

- This command routes 10% of incoming requests to version 2 while keeping 90% directed to the current alias version.

6. Best Practices for Managing Lambda Versions and Aliases

- **Use Meaningful Alias Names**: Name your aliases based on environment or deployment stages, such as dev, staging, prod, or canary.
- **Automate Versioning**: Incorporate versioning into your CI/CD pipelines using **CloudFormation** or **AWS SAM** to automatically publish new versions with each deployment.
- **Implement Canary Deployments**: Use weighted aliases to perform gradual rollouts and monitor new versions before fully shifting traffic.
- **Monitor Version Performance**: Set up **CloudWatch Alarms** and **AWS X-Ray** traces for each version and alias to track key metrics like **errors**, **duration**, and **concurrent executions**.
- **Enable Rollbacks**: In case of failures, quickly roll back to a stable version by updating the alias reference.

7. Example Deployment Strategy with Aliases

Suppose you have a Lambda function that serves API requests through **Amazon API Gateway**. You can define the following strategy using versions and aliases:

1. **Initial Deployment**: Deploy the initial version and create a prod alias pointing to version 1.
2. **Deploy a New Version**: After making changes, deploy the updated function as version 2.
3. **Canary Deployment**: Update the prod alias to shift 10% of traffic to version 2. Monitor performance for errors or latency issues.
4. **Full Deployment**: If version 2 is stable, shift 100% of traffic to version 2 by updating the alias. If issues are detected, revert the alias to version 1.

Managing function versions and aliases in AWS Lambda provides powerful tools for organizing, deploying, and updating serverless applications. By using versions to create immutable snapshots and aliases to create meaningful references, you can simplify deployments, implement safe rollbacks, and execute controlled releases.

Zero-Downtime Deployments Using Canary Releases

One of the key challenges in deploying new versions of a service is ensuring that there is minimal disruption to users. AWS Lambda offers a deployment strategy known as **canary releases** which allows you to gradually shift traffic from an old version to a new version, minimizing the risk of deploying updates. This strategy helps achieve **zero-downtime deployments**, allowing you to test and monitor new versions in a production environment without affecting all users.

In this section, we'll explore how to implement zero-downtime deployments using canary releases for AWS Lambda functions, covering the key concepts, benefits, implementation steps, and best practices.

1. What is a Canary Release?

A **canary release** is a deployment strategy where you release a new version of your application to a small subset of users (or traffic) before rolling it out to the entire user base. This helps detect issues in the new version without impacting all users, reducing the risk associated with changes.

Key Benefits of Canary Releases:

- **Minimizes Risk**: Only a small percentage of users experience the new version initially, allowing you to identify and fix issues before full deployment.

431

- **Enables Real-Time Testing**: Allows you to test new features in a live environment with real traffic.
- **Supports Zero-Downtime**: Gradually shifting traffic reduces the impact of bugs or performance issues.

2. How Canary Releases Work in AWS Lambda

In AWS Lambda, you can use **aliases** to manage versions and traffic shifting. An alias can point to one or more versions of a Lambda function, and you can define a **routing configuration** to distribute traffic between these versions. By allocating a small percentage of traffic to the new version, you can observe how it behaves in production before gradually increasing the traffic.

3. Implementing Canary Releases for Lambda Functions

3.1. Creating Lambda Versions and Aliases
Publish a New Version:

- After making changes to your Lambda function, publish a new version using the AWS Management Console, **AWS CLI**, or **CloudFormation**.

```
aws lambda publish-version --function-name MyLambdaFunction
--description "New version with feature updates"
```

Create or Update an Alias:

- Create an alias (e.g., prod) that initially points to the stable version (e.g., version 1).

```
aws lambda create-alias --function-name MyLambdaFunction --name
prod --function-version 1 --description "Production version"
```

3.2. Setting Up a Canary Release
Update the Alias with Routing Configuration:

- To set up a canary release, update the alias to shift a small percentage of traffic to the new version (e.g., version 2). This can be done using the **AWS CLI** or the **Lambda Console**.

Example CLI Command:

```
aws lambda update-alias --function-name MyLambdaFunction --name
prod --routing-config '{"AdditionalVersionWeights": {"2": 0.1}}'
```

Explanation:

- This command routes 10% of incoming requests to version 2, while the remaining 90% are routed to version 1.

Monitor and Analyze Performance:

- After implementing the canary release, use **CloudWatch Metrics**, **CloudWatch Logs**, and **AWS X-Ray** to monitor the new version's performance. Look for metrics like:
- **Error Count** and **Error Rate** for each version.
- **Invocation Duration** to detect any latency changes.
- **X-Ray Traces** to identify bottlenecks or exceptions.

Gradually Increase Traffic to the New Version:

- If the new version is stable, incrementally increase the traffic weight allocated to the new version using the update-alias command or the

Lambda Console. For example:

```
aws lambda update-alias --function-name MyLambdaFunction --name
prod --routing-config '{"AdditionalVersionWeights": {"2": 0.5}}'
```

This command shifts 50% of the traffic to version 2.

Fully Shift Traffic to the New Version:

- Once you're confident in the new version's stability, shift all traffic to it by updating the alias to reference only the new version.

```
aws lambda update-alias --function-name MyLambdaFunction --name
prod --function-version 2
```

4. Using AWS CodeDeploy for Automated Canary Releases

AWS **CodeDeploy** provides an automated way to implement canary releases with Lambda functions. CodeDeploy allows you to define **deployment strategies** like canary, linear, or all-at-once, and it automatically manages traffic shifting and rollback operations.

4.1. Defining a Canary Deployment Strategy in CodeDeploy

Create an Application in CodeDeploy:

- In the **AWS CodeDeploy Console**, create a new application and choose **AWS Lambda** as the compute platform.

Create a Deployment Group:

- Create a deployment group and specify the Lambda function, alias, and

434

deployment configuration.

Choose a Deployment Configuration:

- CodeDeploy provides pre-defined configurations such as:
- **Canary10Percent5Minutes**: Shifts 10% of traffic to the new version, waits 5 minutes, and then shifts the remaining 90%.
- **Canary10Percent30Minutes**: Shifts 10% of traffic to the new version, waits 30 minutes, and then shifts the remaining 90%.

You can also define custom configurations to fit your specific needs.

Deploy the Lambda Function:

- Trigger a deployment in CodeDeploy, which automatically shifts traffic according to the defined canary configuration.

5. Monitoring and Rolling Back Canary Releases

5.1. Monitoring Canary Releases
Use CloudWatch Metrics and Alarms:

- Set up **CloudWatch Alarms** to monitor key metrics like **Errors**, **Throttles**, and **Duration** for the new version. If any threshold is breached, CodeDeploy can automatically trigger a rollback.

Enable X-Ray for Tracing:

- Enable **AWS X-Ray** to trace requests through the Lambda function, allowing you to identify slow or failing components.

5.2. Rolling Back Canary Releases
Automatic Rollbacks in CodeDeploy:

- CodeDeploy supports automatic rollbacks based on CloudWatch Alarms. If an alarm is triggered during a canary release, CodeDeploy reverts to the previous stable version.

Manual Rollback Using Aliases:

- If you're not using CodeDeploy, you can manually roll back a canary release by updating the alias to point to the previous version:

```
aws lambda update-alias --function-name MyLambdaFunction --name
prod --function-version 1
```

6. Best Practices for Zero-Downtime Deployments with Canary Releases

- **Start Small and Gradually Increase**: Begin by shifting a small percentage of traffic (e.g., 5-10%) to the new version. If the new version is stable, gradually increase traffic to minimize risk.
- **Monitor Key Metrics**: Use **CloudWatch Metrics, CloudWatch Alarms**, and **AWS X-Ray** to monitor function performance and detect anomalies early.
- **Automate with CodeDeploy**: Use AWS CodeDeploy to automate canary deployments, define rollback conditions, and simplify the release process.
- **Test in a Staging Environment First**: Before deploying to production, test the new version thoroughly in a staging environment that mirrors your production setup.
- **Define Custom CloudWatch Alarms**: Set up custom alarms to detect application-specific issues like increased latency, higher error rates, or unexpected behavior in external dependencies.

Zero-downtime deployments using canary releases are an effective strategy for rolling out new versions of AWS Lambda functions without disrupting users. By gradually shifting traffic to the new version and monitoring performance metrics, you can minimize risks and identify issues early.

AWS Lambda's support for aliases and traffic routing, combined with the automation capabilities of AWS CodeDeploy, provides a flexible and scalable framework for implementing canary releases. By following best practices and leveraging AWS tools effectively, you can achieve safe and reliable deployments in your serverless applications.

Rolling Back Deployments in Production

Despite rigorous testing and canary releases, issues can still arise when deploying new versions of Lambda functions in production. To maintain service reliability, it's crucial to have an effective rollback strategy. Rolling back deployments quickly helps restore functionality and minimizes the impact on users.

AWS Lambda offers robust tools for rolling back to a previous version, either manually or automatically. In this section, we'll explore best practices and techniques for rolling back Lambda deployments in production environments.

1. Understanding the Need for Rollbacks

Rollbacks are necessary when:

- **New deployments introduce errors** such as unhandled exceptions, missing configurations, or incompatibilities with external services.
- **Performance issues arise** due to inefficient code, increased memory consumption, or prolonged execution times.
- **New features cause unintended consequences**, like negatively affect-

ing user experience or breaking key workflows.

2. Manual Rollbacks Using Lambda Aliases

AWS Lambda's **aliases** make manual rollbacks straightforward. If a new version fails or causes issues, you can quickly update the alias to point to a stable previous version.

2.1. Step-by-Step Manual Rollback
Identify the Stable Version:

- Review the **versions** of your Lambda function in the **Lambda Console**. Identify the last stable version (e.g., version 1).

Update the Alias to Point to the Previous Version:

- In the Lambda Console, go to the **Aliases** tab and select the alias used in production (e.g., prod).
- Click **Edit alias**, and change the **function version** to the stable version.

Save the Changes:

- Save the alias configuration. This will immediately route all traffic to the previous stable version.

2.2. Rollback Example Using AWS CLI
You can also perform rollbacks using the **AWS CLI**.
Example Command:

```
aws lambda update-alias --function-name MyLambdaFunction --name
prod --function-version 1
```

Explanation:

- This command updates the prod alias to point to version 1, effectively rolling back the function to the last stable state.

3. Automated Rollbacks with AWS CodeDeploy

AWS CodeDeploy supports automated rollbacks based on **CloudWatch Alarms**. If an alarm threshold is breached during deployment, CodeDeploy automatically reverts to the last successful version, reducing downtime and user impact.

3.1. Setting Up Automated Rollbacks
Configure CloudWatch Alarms:

- Create CloudWatch Alarms to monitor key Lambda metrics such as:
- **Error Count**: Trigger an alarm if the number of errors exceeds a predefined threshold.
- **Duration**: Set an alarm if execution time significantly increases.
- **Throttles**: Monitor for increased throttling due to concurrency issues.

Link Alarms to CodeDeploy:

- In your **CodeDeploy deployment group**, specify the CloudWatch Alarms that should trigger an automatic rollback.

Deploy the Lambda Function Using CodeDeploy:

- Initiate a deployment with CodeDeploy using a **canary** or **linear** deployment strategy. CodeDeploy will automatically monitor the deployment and execute rollbacks if alarms are triggered.

Example Deployment Configuration:

```
Resources:
  MyLambdaFunction:
    Type: AWS::Serverless::Function
    Properties:
      FunctionName: MyLambdaFunction
      Handler: app.lambda_handler
      Runtime: python3.8
      CodeUri: s3://my-bucket/my-lambda-code.zip
      Role: arn:aws:iam::123456789012:role/MyLambdaRole
      AutoPublishAlias: live
      DeploymentPreference:
        Type: Canary10Percent30Minutes
        Alarms:
          - !Ref LambdaErrorAlarm
```

Explanation:

- **DeploymentPreference**: Specifies a canary deployment strategy where 10% of traffic is shifted to the new version over 30 minutes.
- **Alarms**: Lists the CloudWatch Alarms that trigger a rollback if breached.

4. Implementing Rollbacks with CloudFormation and SAM

When using **AWS CloudFormation** or **AWS Serverless Application Model (SAM)**, rollbacks are managed automatically if a deployment fails. If CloudFormation detects a deployment failure, it reverts all resources to their previous state.

4.1. CloudFormation Stack Rollbacks
Deploy the Lambda Function Using CloudFormation:

- Deploy your Lambda function using a CloudFormation template or an AWS SAM template.

```
aws cloudformation deploy --template-file template.yaml
--stack-name MyLambdaStack --capabilities CAPABILITY_IAM
```

Automatic Rollbacks:

- If the stack deployment fails, CloudFormation automatically reverts all changes. This includes reverting the Lambda function to its last stable version.

Monitor Deployment Status:

- Monitor the deployment in the **CloudFormation Console** or use the AWS CLI to check the stack status:

```
aws cloudformation describe-stacks --stack-name MyLambdaStack
```

5. Best Practices for Managing Rollbacks in Production

5.1. Maintain Stable Versions as Baselines

- **Always retain at least one known stable version** of your Lambda function. This baseline should serve as the fallback point in case of issues with new deployments.

5.2. Set Up Robust Monitoring and Alerts

- **Define meaningful CloudWatch Alarms** based on your function's key performance indicators (KPIs). This includes monitoring error counts, execution duration, memory usage, and custom business metrics.
- **Configure notifications** to alert stakeholders when a rollback is triggered or when alarms breach critical thresholds.

5.3. Automate Testing and Rollback Verification

- **Run automated tests** after each deployment to verify that the new version is functioning as expected. These tests should cover all critical paths and common user flows.
- **Validate rollback success** by monitoring performance and error metrics immediately after a rollback is executed.

5.4. Document and Communicate Rollback Procedures

- **Create a rollback plan** that details how to revert deployments, update aliases, and restore stable versions. Ensure that all team members are familiar with this plan.
- **Communicate rollback events** to relevant stakeholders, including operations teams, development teams, and business leaders, to maintain transparency.

6. Example Rollback Scenario

Let's walk through a hypothetical rollback scenario to illustrate these concepts:

Scenario: You've deployed a new version (3) of your Lambda function to the prod alias using a canary release strategy. After shifting 20% of traffic to version 3, you notice an increase in error rates and a decline in performance.

Actions Taken:

1. **Monitor Alarms**: A CloudWatch Alarm linked to the deployment detects the increased error count and triggers an automatic rollback in **AWS CodeDeploy**.
2. **Rollback Execution**: CodeDeploy reverts the prod alias to the previous stable version (2), effectively restoring service stability.
3. **Post-Rollback Analysis**: You review X-Ray traces and CloudWatch Logs to identify the root cause of the issues in version 3.

4. **Communicate with Stakeholders**: Notify stakeholders of the rollback, including details on the issue and the plan for future fixes.

Rolling back deployments in production is an essential capability for maintaining service reliability and minimizing the impact of unexpected issues. AWS Lambda's built-in versioning and alias features, combined with automated rollback mechanisms in **AWS CodeDeploy** and **CloudFormation**, provide a flexible and robust framework for handling rollbacks.

Serverless Frameworks for AWS Lambda

I ntroduction to the Serverless Framework
The rapid rise of serverless computing has fundamentally changed how applications are built and deployed, with AWS Lambda playing a pivotal role. However, as serverless architectures grow more complex, managing resources manually or through basic scripts can become cumbersome. This is where **Serverless Framework** comes into play—a powerful, open-source framework designed to simplify the development and deployment of serverless applications.

In this section, we will explore the Serverless Framework in detail, covering its features, advantages, key concepts, and how it fits into the serverless development lifecycle.

1. What is the Serverless Framework?

The **Serverless Framework** is an open-source deployment and automation tool that enables developers to build and deploy serverless applications across multiple cloud providers, including AWS, Azure, Google Cloud, and more. It provides a **YAML-based configuration** file to define serverless functions, resources, and their configurations, making it easier to manage and deploy serverless architectures.

Key Features of the Serverless Framework:

- **Multi-Provider Support**: Compatible with AWS, Azure, Google Cloud, and other cloud providers.

- **Declarative Configuration**: Uses a YAML-based configuration file (serverless.yml) to define infrastructure, making it easier to understand and maintain.
- **Automated Deployments**: Deploys serverless applications and manages Lambda functions, IAM roles, API Gateway configurations, and more.
- **Extensibility with Plugins**: Offers a wide variety of community-built and official plugins for additional features like monitoring, security, and CI/CD integrations.
- **Supports Local Development**: Provides local testing and debugging capabilities.

2. Why Use the Serverless Framework?

The Serverless Framework provides several benefits over manually deploying serverless applications or using basic AWS CLI commands. Let's explore why using this framework is advantageous:

2.1. Simplified Infrastructure as Code

With the Serverless Framework, you can define your entire serverless infrastructure using a single, declarative YAML configuration file. This Infrastructure as Code (IaC) approach enables you to version-control your infrastructure, replicate environments quickly, and reduce configuration errors.

2.2. Faster Deployment and Management

The framework automates the deployment process, allowing you to deploy Lambda functions, create or update API Gateway endpoints, configure DynamoDB tables, and manage IAM roles in a single command. This automation saves time and reduces the chances of manual errors.

2.3. Improved Collaboration and Extensibility

Since the framework is open-source and widely adopted, it has a large community and extensive plugin ecosystem. Plugins allow you to extend the framework's capabilities for various use cases, such as monitoring with **Serverless Dashboard**, integrating with **CI/CD pipelines**, or adding security checks.

3. Key Concepts in the Serverless Framework

To effectively use the Serverless Framework, it's essential to understand its core concepts and terminology:

3.1. Service

A **Service** is the fundamental unit in the Serverless Framework. It represents your entire application or a component of it. A service contains functions, events, and resources defined in a single configuration file (serverless.yml).

3.2. Functions

Functions are the building blocks of a serverless application. Each function corresponds to an AWS Lambda function and has its own handler code and configuration. Functions are defined under the functions section of the serverless.yml file.

3.3. Events

Events define the triggers that invoke your functions. These triggers can be HTTP endpoints, S3 bucket events, DynamoDB table updates, scheduled events (like cron jobs), or other AWS services. The Serverless Framework allows you to easily bind events to functions.

3.4. Resources

Resources define additional AWS infrastructure components needed for your application, such as DynamoDB tables, S3 buckets, or IAM roles. You can declare resources using the **AWS CloudFormation syntax** directly within the serverless.yml file.

3.5. Plugins

Plugins extend the core functionality of the framework. They allow you to add new features, perform additional operations during deployment, or integrate with third-party services. The Serverless Framework has a rich plugin ecosystem with numerous official and community-contributed plugins.

4. Setting Up the Serverless Framework

4.1. Prerequisites

Before you can use the Serverless Framework, ensure you have the following:

- **Node.js**: The Serverless Framework runs on Node.js. You can install it from nodejs.org.
- **AWS Account and IAM Permissions**: Ensure you have an AWS account and an IAM user with sufficient permissions to create Lambda functions, API Gateway endpoints, and other AWS resources.
- **AWS CLI**: You should configure the AWS CLI with your IAM credentials.

4.2. Installing the Serverless Framework
Install the Serverless Framework Globally using npm:

```
npm install -g serverless
```

Verify the Installation:

```
serverless --version
```

Configure AWS Credentials:

```
aws configure
```

5. Creating Your First Serverless Service

5.1. Initializing a New Service
Create a New Service:

```
serverless create --template aws-nodejs --path my-serverless-app
cd my-serverless-app
```

This command generates a new service using the **AWS Node.js template** and creates a directory named my-serverless-app.

Explore the Generated Files:

- **serverless.yml**: The main configuration file defining the service, functions, events, and resources.
- **handler.js**: A sample Lambda function handler file.

5.2. Modifying the serverless.yml File
Open the serverless.yml file and review its structure:

```
service: my-serverless-app

provider:
  name: aws
  runtime: nodejs14.x

functions:
  hello:
    handler: handler.hello
    events:
      - http:
          path: hello
          method: get
```

Explanation:

- **service**: Defines the name of the service.

- **provider**: Specifies the cloud provider (AWS) and the runtime for Lambda functions.
- **functions**: Defines a function named hello, specifying the handler code (handler.hello) and an HTTP event that triggers the function on a GET request to /hello.

5.3. Deploying the Service

Deploy the Service to AWS:

```bash
serverless deploy
```

This command packages the code, uploads it to AWS, and provisions the necessary AWS resources, including the Lambda function and API Gateway endpoint.

View the Deployment Output: After the deployment is complete, the output will display the endpoints created:

```
endpoints:
  GET -
  https://xxxxxxx.execute-api.us-east-1.amazonaws.com/dev/hello
```

Test the Deployed Function:

- Open your browser or use a tool like Postman to access the endpoint: https://xxxxxxx.execute-api.us-east-1.amazonaws.com/dev/hello.

6. Managing and Monitoring Serverless Deployments

The Serverless Framework provides built-in tools and integrations for managing, monitoring, and scaling serverless applications:

6.1. Serverless Dashboard

449

The **Serverless Dashboard** offers a visual interface for managing services, monitoring function invocations, tracking errors, and configuring alerts. You can link your Serverless Framework account to the dashboard to gain deeper insights into your serverless applications.

1. **Sign Up for a Serverless Dashboard Account** at app.serverless.com.
2. **Link Your Service** to the dashboard by running:

```
serverless login
serverless
```

6.2. Serverless Offline Plugin for Local Development

During development, it's often beneficial to test your functions locally. The **Serverless Offline plugin** emulates API Gateway on your local machine, allowing you to test Lambda functions without deploying them.

Install the Serverless Offline Plugin:

```
npm install serverless-offline --save-dev
```

Add the Plugin to serverless.yml:

```
plugins:
  - serverless-offline
```

Run the Service Locally:

```
serverless offline
```

Access Local Endpoints:

- Open your browser and access the local endpoint (e.g., http://localhost:3 000/hello).

7. Best Practices for Using the Serverless Framework

- **Use Version Control for serverless.yml**: Keep your configuration file (serverless.yml) in version control to track changes and collaborate effectively.
- **Implement Staging Environments**: Create separate environments (e.g., dev, staging, prod) using the —stage option during deployment:

```
serverless deploy --stage staging
```

- **Leverage Plugins**: Explore the **Serverless Plugin Directory** to find plugins that add functionality such as security checks, performance optimizations, or integration with third-party services.
- **Monitor and Optimize Costs**: Use the **Serverless Dashboard** to track invocation metrics, errors, and cost estimations for each function.

The Serverless Framework provides a comprehensive and developer-friendly way to manage serverless applications. Its intuitive YAML-based configuration, automated deployments, and support for multi-cloud environments make it an essential tool for building modern serverless architectures.

Deploying with the Serverless Framework and Zappa

When building serverless applications, efficient deployment tools are crucial for managing infrastructure and function lifecycles. While the **Serverless Framework** is a widely adopted tool for managing serverless applications across multiple cloud providers, **Zappa** is another powerful Python-based tool specifically designed for deploying web applications (like Flask and Django) to AWS Lambda.

In this section, we will cover the deployment workflows using the Serverless Framework and Zappa, discussing their respective advantages, use cases, and step-by-step guides for deploying serverless applications.

1. Introduction to Serverless Framework Deployment

The **Serverless Framework** offers a streamlined way to deploy serverless applications, enabling you to manage functions, events, and AWS resources from a single configuration file. It automates the entire deployment process, including creating or updating Lambda functions, setting up API Gateway routes, and provisioning other required AWS services.

1.1. Prerequisites for Serverless Framework Deployment

- **Node.js** and **npm** installed on your system.
- **Serverless Framework** installed globally (npm install -g serverless).
- An **AWS account** with appropriate permissions (configured with the AWS CLI).
- Basic knowledge of **YAML** for managing the serverless.yml file.

1.2. Step-by-Step Deployment with the Serverless Framework
Initialize the Project:
Create a new Serverless Framework project using an AWS Node.js template:

```
serverless create --template aws-nodejs
 --path my-serverless-project
cd my-serverless-project
```

Edit the serverless.yml File:
Open serverless.yml and define your service name, provider settings, and functions:

```
service: my-serverless-app

provider:
  name: aws
  runtime: nodejs14.x

functions:
  hello:
    handler: handler.hello
    events:
      - http:
          path: hello
          method: get
```

Explanation:

- The service section defines the name of your application.
- The provider section specifies AWS as the cloud provider and the runtime as Node.js 14.x.
- The functions section defines a single function named hello that handles HTTP GET requests on the /hello path.

Deploy the Application:

Run the deployment command to provision and deploy the application:

```
serverless deploy
```

This command packages your code, uploads it to AWS, and sets up the necessary infrastructure. The console output provides details about the deployed endpoints and resources.

Test the Deployed Application:

After deployment, you will see an endpoint URL in the output. Test your function by visiting the URL in a web browser or using a tool like Postman:

```
GET https://xxxxxxx.execute-api.us-east-1.amazonaws.com/dev/hello
```

Update and Redeploy:

Make changes to the code or serverless.yml file as needed, then redeploy using:

```
serverless deploy
```

Remove the Deployed Resources:

To clean up and remove all resources created by the deployment, run:

```
serverless remove
```

2. Introduction to Zappa for Python Web Applications

Zappa is a deployment tool designed specifically for deploying Python web applications (such as Flask and Django) to AWS Lambda and API Gateway. It abstracts away much of the complexity involved in deploying serverless web applications by automating infrastructure provisioning and deployment.

2.1. Prerequisites for Zappa Deployment

- **Python 3.6+** installed on your system.
- **Zappa** installed globally using pip (pip install zappa).
- An **AWS account** configured with the AWS CLI.
- A web application built using **Flask**, **Django**, or another compatible Python framework.

2.2. Step-by-Step Deployment with Zappa
Install Zappa:

```
pip install zappa
```

1. **Create and Configure a Python Web Application**:
2. Let's assume you have a simple **Flask** application (app.py):

```
from flask import Flask

app = Flask(__name__)

@app.route('/')
def index():
    return "Hello, Zappa!"

if __name__ == '__main__':
    app.run()
```

Initialize Zappa:

In the root directory of your project, initialize Zappa:

```
zappa init
```

This command prompts you to configure various settings, such as:

- The name of your project.
- The AWS region to deploy to (e.g., us-east-1).
- The S3 bucket for storing deployment artifacts.
- The type of web framework you're using (e.g., Flask, Django).

Deploy the Application:

Once initialization is complete, deploy your application with:

```
zappa deploy production
```

This command packages your application, uploads it to AWS Lambda, and creates the necessary API Gateway endpoints. The console output displays the URL of your deployed application.

Test the Deployed Application:

After deployment, test the application by visiting the provided URL in a web browser:

```
https://xxxxxxx.
execute-api.us-east-1
.amazonaws.com/production/
```

Update and Redeploy:

Make changes to your application code as needed, then update the deployment with:

```
zappa update production
```

Rollback and Remove:

To rollback to a previous deployment, use:

```
zappa rollback production
```

To remove the deployed resources and clean up:

```
zappa undeploy production
```

3. Serverless Framework vs. Zappa: When to Use Each?

Both the **Serverless Framework** and **Zappa** are popular deployment tools for serverless applications, but each serves different use cases and programming languages.

3.1. Serverless Framework Use Cases

- **Multi-Language and Multi-Provider Support**: Ideal for projects that involve Node.js, Python, Go, or other runtimes. It supports multiple cloud providers (AWS, Azure, Google Cloud).

- **Complex Infrastructure Needs**: Suitable for applications that require complex infrastructure configurations involving multiple AWS services such as API Gateway, DynamoDB, SNS, and more.
- **Plugin Ecosystem**: Offers a robust plugin ecosystem for added functionality, such as CI/CD integrations, security checks, and local testing.

3.2. Zappa Use Cases

- **Python Web Applications**: Tailored for deploying Python-based web applications, especially those built using Flask or Django.
- **Simple Deployments**: Zappa abstracts away many AWS-specific configurations, making it ideal for developers looking for a straightforward deployment process for web applications.
- **Quick Prototyping**: Excellent for quickly deploying proof-of-concept applications and MVPs without worrying about extensive configurations.

4. Best Practices for Deploying with Serverless Framework and Zappa

4.1. Best Practices with Serverless Framework

- **Use Version Control for serverless.yml**: Keep your configuration in a version-controlled repository to track changes and collaborate effectively.
- **Automate Staging and Production Deployments**: Define separate stages for development, staging, and production using the —stage option:

```
serverless deploy --stage staging
```

- **Leverage Plugins**: Use plugins to enhance functionality, such as serverless-offline for local testing or serverless-plugin-canary-deployments for automated canary releases.

4.2. Best Practices with Zappa

- **Optimize Cold Starts**: For Django applications, consider using django-zappa for optimizations related to session management and database connections.
- **Use Environment Variables**: Store configuration details such as API keys and database URIs in environment variables instead of hardcoding them.
- **Monitor and Log Errors**: Enable **AWS CloudWatch** logging for detailed monitoring and troubleshooting of deployed applications.

Deploying serverless applications with the **Serverless Framework** and **Zappa** simplifies the entire development lifecycle, from infrastructure provisioning to deployment and monitoring. While the Serverless Framework is versatile and supports multiple runtimes and cloud providers, Zappa excels at deploying Python-based web applications with minimal configuration.

Using AWS SAM for Multi-Service Applications

The **AWS Serverless Application Model (AWS SAM)** is an open-source framework designed to simplify the building, testing, and deployment of serverless applications. AWS SAM extends AWS CloudFormation to provide a more streamlined syntax for defining serverless resources like AWS Lambda functions, API Gateway endpoints, DynamoDB tables, and more.

When working on **multi-service applications**, AWS SAM provides the flexibility to manage complex serverless architectures that consist of multiple Lambda functions, APIs, databases, queues, and other resources. In this section, we will explore how to use AWS SAM for multi-service applications, covering key concepts, setting up a project, and best practices for building scalable and maintainable serverless applications.

1. Overview of AWS SAM

AWS SAM enables you to define and deploy serverless applications using a simple YAML configuration file (template.yaml). It supports defining resources, permissions, and event triggers in a concise and structured manner. AWS SAM integrates seamlessly with other AWS services and tools like **AWS CodePipeline**, **AWS CloudFormation**, **AWS CloudWatch**, and **AWS X-Ray**.

Key Benefits of AWS SAM:

- **Simplified Syntax**: Provides a simplified CloudFormation syntax for serverless resources.
- **Local Development and Debugging**: Offers SAM CLI for local testing and debugging of Lambda functions.
- **Comprehensive Resource Management**: Allows you to define multiple serverless functions and related services in a single template.
- **Built-In Best Practices**: Implements AWS best practices for security, scalability, and monitoring.

2. Multi-Service Architecture with AWS SAM

Multi-service applications typically consist of several independent or loosely-coupled Lambda functions, each responsible for handling different parts of the application's logic. AWS SAM allows you to define and manage these functions, along with associated resources, in a unified configuration file.

Example Multi-Service Use Cases:

- **Event-Driven Architectures**: Multiple Lambda functions processing different types of events (e.g., S3 uploads, DynamoDB streams, SNS notifications).

459

- **Microservices**: Each Lambda function represents a microservice that handles a specific domain or feature.
- **ETL Pipelines**: Lambda functions working together to extract, transform, and load (ETL) data between sources.

3. Setting Up a Multi-Service Project with AWS SAM

3.1. Prerequisites

Before setting up your project, ensure you have:

- **AWS Account** with appropriate IAM permissions.
- **AWS CLI** installed and configured with your credentials.
- **AWS SAM CLI** installed on your machine.

3.2. Initializing a SAM Project
Initialize a New SAM Project:

```
sam init
```

This command prompts you to choose a runtime, project template, and project name. For a multi-service project, you can start with a basic runtime like Python or Node.js.

Example Selection:

```
Which runtime would you like to use?
1 - python3.8
2 - nodejs14.x
3 - java11
...
Runtime: 1

What template source would you like to use?
1 - AWS Quick Start Templates
2 - Custom Template Location
```

Choose a runtime (e.g., Python 3.8) and a quick start template to create a basic project structure.

Navigate to the Project Directory:

```
cd my-multi-service-project
```

Explore the Project Structure:

AWS SAM creates the following default structure:

```
my-multi-service-project/ ┌──────
  hello-world/         # Sample Lambda function
  directory │ ┌──────
     app.py            # Lambda function handler │ ┌──────
     __init__.py       # (if using Python) │ └──────
     requirements.txt  # Dependencies └──────
  template.yaml         # AWS SAM template
```

4. Defining Multiple Functions and Resources in template.yaml

Open template.yaml and define multiple functions, events, and resources based on your multi-service architecture.

Example template.yaml for Multi-Service Application:

```yaml
AWSTemplateFormatVersion: '2010-09-09'
Transform: AWS::Serverless-2016-10-31

Resources:
  GetUsersFunction:
    Type: AWS::Serverless::Function
    Properties:
      FunctionName: GetUsers
      Handler: get_users.app
      Runtime: python3.8
      Events:
```

```
        ApiGetUsers:
          Type: Api
          Properties:
            Path: /users
            Method: get


  CreateUserFunction:
    Type: AWS::Serverless::Function
    Properties:
      FunctionName: CreateUser
      Handler: create_user.app
      Runtime: python3.8
      Events:
        ApiCreateUser:
          Type: Api
          Properties:
            Path: /users
            Method: post


  UserTable:
    Type: AWS::DynamoDB::Table
    Properties:
      TableName: Users
      AttributeDefinitions:
        - AttributeName: UserId
          AttributeType: S
      KeySchema:
        - AttributeName: UserId
          KeyType: HASH
      ProvisionedThroughput:
        ReadCapacityUnits: 5
        WriteCapacityUnits: 5

Outputs:
  GetUsersApiUrl:
    Value: !Sub "https://$
{ServerlessRestApi}.
execute-api.$
{AWS::Region}.
amazonaws.
```

```
com/Prod/users"
  CreateUserApiUrl:
    Value: !Sub "https://$
{ServerlessRestApi}.
execute-api.${AWS::Region}.
amazonaws.com/Prod/users"
```

Explanation:

- **GetUsersFunction**: A Lambda function to handle GET requests to fetch user information. The function is triggered by an API Gateway event.
- **CreateUserFunction**: A Lambda function to handle POST requests to create a new user. It uses the same DynamoDB table (UserTable).
- **UserTable**: A DynamoDB table to store user information.
- **Outputs**: Defines URLs for the API endpoints created by API Gateway.

5. Building and Deploying the Multi-Service Application

Build the Project:

```
sam build
```

1. This command packages your Lambda functions and dependencies into a build directory.
2. **Deploy the Project**:

```
sam deploy --guided
```

1. The —guided option prompts you for deployment details, such as the stack name, AWS region, and permissions. After the first deployment, you can deploy updates without —guided.

2. **View the Deployment Output**:

3. Once deployment is complete, you'll see the URLs for your API endpoints in the output section. Use these URLs to test the different functions.

6. Testing and Monitoring Multi-Service Applications Locally

6.1. Local Testing with SAM CLI

AWS SAM provides built-in support for testing Lambda functions locally using Docker containers. This allows you to replicate the Lambda runtime environment on your machine.

Invoke a Lambda Function Locally:

```
sam local invoke GetUsersFunction
--event events/get-users.json
```

The —event flag specifies an event file containing mock input data.

Test HTTP Endpoints Locally:

```
sam local start-api
```

This command starts a local API Gateway on your machine, allowing you to test HTTP requests at http://localhost:3000.

6.2. Monitoring with CloudWatch

- **Enable Logging**: AWS SAM automatically sends Lambda logs to **CloudWatch Logs**. Review logs in the CloudWatch Console to identify errors or performance issues.
- **Enable X-Ray Tracing**: Add the Tracing configuration to your Lambda functions to enable distributed tracing with **AWS X-Ray**.

7. Best Practices for Multi-Service Applications with AWS SAM

7.1. Modularize and Organize Your Code

Organize your codebase by separating Lambda functions into different folders based on their purpose. For example:

```
my-multi-service-project/ ├──────
 get-users/               # Lambda function for getting
 users │ ├──────
    app.py │ └──────
    requirements.txt ├──────
 create-user/             # Lambda function for creating
 users │ ├──────
    app.py │ └──────
    requirements.txt └──────
 template.yaml            # AWS SAM template
```

7.2. Use IAM Policies with Principle of Least Privilege

Define IAM policies that grant each Lambda function the minimum set of permissions it needs to operate. This helps improve security and minimize the impact of compromised functions.

Example IAM Policy for Lambda Function:

```
Role:
  Type: AWS::IAM::Role
  Properties:
    AssumeRolePolicyDocument:
      Version: '2012-10-17'
      Statement:
        - Effect: Allow
          Principal:
            Service: lambda.amazonaws.com
          Action: sts:AssumeRole
    Policies:
```

```
- PolicyName: LambdaDynamoDBPolicy
  PolicyDocument:
    Version: '2012-10-17'
    Statement:
      - Effect: Allow
        Action:
          - dynamodb:GetItem
          - dynamodb:PutItem
        Resource: !GetAtt UserTable.Arn
```

7.3. Automate Deployments with CI/CD Pipelines

Use **AWS CodePipeline** or other CI/CD tools to automate builds, tests, and deployments of your SAM-based projects. This ensures that all changes are tested and reviewed before being pushed to production.

7.4. Implement Rollback Strategies

Integrate AWS SAM with **AWS CloudFormation** to leverage rollback strategies in case of failed deployments. Define CloudWatch Alarms to detect issues early and trigger rollbacks automatically.

AWS SAM provides a comprehensive framework for managing multi-service serverless applications. By using SAM's simplified syntax, integrated testing, and deployment capabilities, you can efficiently build and deploy complex serverless architectures on AWS.

Automating Testing and Deployments

In serverless application development, automated testing and deployments are key to ensuring reliability, speed, and consistency. AWS SAM, combined with modern CI/CD practices, allows you to build, test, and deploy your serverless applications automatically. This section explores how to automate testing and deployments for AWS SAM projects, focusing on CI/CD pipeline design, testing strategies, and leveraging AWS tools like **CodePipeline** and **CodeBuild**.

1. Why Automate Testing and Deployments?

Automating testing and deployments offers several benefits:

- **Consistency**: Automates repetitive tasks to eliminate manual errors and inconsistencies.
- **Speed**: Increases the speed of delivering new features and fixes to production.
- **Quality**: Incorporates testing at every stage of the pipeline to catch issues early.
- **Reliability**: Provides rollback mechanisms to handle failures automatically.

2. Setting Up a CI/CD Pipeline for AWS SAM Projects

A typical CI/CD pipeline for AWS SAM projects consists of:

1. **Source Stage**: Fetches the latest code from a version control system (e.g., GitHub, CodeCommit).
2. **Build Stage**: Builds and packages the serverless application using **AWS SAM CLI**.
3. **Test Stage**: Runs unit tests, integration tests, and security checks.
4. **Deploy Stage**: Deploys the application to a staging or production environment using **AWS CloudFormation**.

AWS **CodePipeline** integrates these stages seamlessly, automating each step from source to deployment.

2.1. Prerequisites

- An **AWS Account** with IAM permissions to create and manage Code-

Pipeline, CodeBuild, Lambda, CloudFormation, and related services.
- **AWS CLI** and **SAM CLI** installed on your machine.
- A **Version Control Repository** (e.g., CodeCommit, GitHub, Bitbucket) to store your code.

2.2. Creating a CI/CD Pipeline with CodePipeline

Create a CodeCommit Repository (or use GitHub/Bitbucket):

```
aws codecommit create-repository --repository-name MySAMProjectRepo
```

1. **Set Up a Build Specification File (buildspec.yml):**
2. In your SAM project, create a buildspec.yml file to define the build steps for **AWS CodeBuild**. This file specifies how to build and package the application using **SAM CLI**.
3. **Example buildspec.yml:**

```
version: 0.2

phases:
  install:
    runtime-versions:
      python: 3.8
    commands:
      - pip install aws-sam-cli
      - pip install -r requirements.txt

  build:
    commands:
      - sam build
      - sam package --output-
template-file packaged.yaml
--s3-bucket my-deployment-bucket

artifacts:
```

```
files:
  - packaged.yaml
```

Explanation:

- **Install Phase**: Installs required dependencies, including the AWS SAM CLI.
- **Build Phase**: Uses sam build to package Lambda functions and dependencies.
- **Package Phase**: Uses sam package to upload the packaged artifacts to an S3 bucket.

Create a CodeBuild Project:

1. Go to the **CodeBuild Console** and create a new build project. Choose your repository as the source and specify the **buildspec.yml** file as the build specification.
2. **Create a CloudFormation Template for Deployment**:
3. In your SAM project, use the existing template.yaml file or modify it as needed to define the resources, functions, and permissions required.
4. **Create the CodePipeline**:
5. Go to the **CodePipeline Console** and create a new pipeline. Specify the following stages:

- **Source Stage**: Choose CodeCommit, GitHub, or Bitbucket as the source.
- **Build Stage**: Select the CodeBuild project you created earlier.
- **Deploy Stage**: Use **AWS CloudFormation** to deploy the output of the build to your AWS environment.

Deploy to Multiple Environments:
Define multiple deployment stages (e.g., **Staging** and **Production**) in CodePipeline. You can configure manual approvals between stages to enforce review processes before deploying to production.

3. Automating Tests with SAM CLI and CodeBuild

3.1. Writing Unit Tests for Lambda Functions

For Python-based Lambda functions, use a testing framework like **pytest** to write unit tests. Store these tests in a separate directory (e.g., tests/) and include them in your project's requirements.

Example Unit Test with pytest:

```python
import app  # Import the Lambda handler file

def test_lambda_handler():
    event = {"key": "value"}  # Mock event data
    response = app.lambda_handler
(event, None)  # Call the handler function
    assert response["statusCode"] == 200
```

3.2. Defining Unit Tests in buildspec.yml

Add a **test phase** to your buildspec.yml file:

```yaml
version: 0.2

phases:
  install:
    runtime-versions:
      python: 3.8
    commands:
      - pip install aws-sam-cli
      - pip install -r requirements.txt
      - pip install pytest

  pre_build:
    commands:
      - pytest tests/  # Run unit tests

  build:
    commands:
      - sam build
```

```
      - sam package --output-
template-file packaged.yaml
--s3-bucket my-deployment-bucket

artifacts:
  files:
    - packaged.yaml
```

Explanation:

- **pre_build Phase**: Runs unit tests using pytest to validate the Lambda function logic before proceeding to the build phase.

3.3. Integration Tests and Mock Events

For integration tests, create mock events that simulate real-world scenarios. Use these mock events to invoke Lambda functions locally with **SAM CLI** or during a CodeBuild run.

Example Integration Test:

```
sam local invoke MyFunction
  --event events/my-integration-event.json
```

Store these mock event files in a dedicated directory (events/) for easy access.

4. Deploying to Staging and Production Environments

Automate deployments to separate **staging** and **production** environments using AWS SAM and CodePipeline.

4.1. Multi-Environment Setup in template.yaml

Add environment-specific parameters to your **template.yaml** file to differentiate between staging and production environments:

Example Parameters in template.yaml:

```
Parameters:
  Environment:
    Type: String
    Default: "staging"
    AllowedValues:
      - "staging"
      - "production"

Resources:
  MyLambdaFunction:
    Type: AWS::Serverless::Function
    Properties:
      FunctionName: !Sub "my-function-${Environment}"
      Handler: app.lambda_handler
      Runtime: python3.8
      Environment:
        Variables:
          TABLE_NAME: !Sub "my-dynamodb-table-${Environment}"
```

4.2. Automate Environment-Specific Deployments

Define deployment configurations for each environment in CodePipeline, using different parameter values for staging and production:

```
deploy:
  staging:
    command: sam deploy
--template-file packaged.yaml -
-stack-name my-stack-staging
--parameter-overrides Environment=staging
  production:
    command: sam deploy
--template-file packaged.yaml
  --stack-name my-stack-production --parameter-overrides
  Environment=production
```

Use manual approval steps in CodePipeline to enforce human review before deploying to production.

5. Best Practices for Automated Testing and Deployments

- **Implement Robust Unit and Integration Tests**: Ensure that each Lambda function is covered by unit tests and end-to-end integration tests. Use mock events to validate behavior under different scenarios.
- **Use Environment Variables for Configuration**: Avoid hardcoding environment-specific values in Lambda functions. Use environment variables and SAM parameters to manage configuration differences between staging and production.
- **Enable Rollback Mechanisms**: Configure **CloudFormation** stack policies and CloudWatch alarms to trigger automatic rollbacks in case of deployment failures.
- **Incorporate Security Scans**: Use tools like **AWS CodeBuild Reports** and third-party plugins to perform security scans during the build phase.

Automating testing and deployments for AWS SAM-based projects improves development agility, application reliability, and consistency in your serverless applications. By leveraging AWS tools like **CodePipeline**, **CodeBuild**, and **SAM CLI**, you can build robust CI/CD pipelines that streamline the entire serverless development lifecycle.

Troubleshooting Common AWS Lambda Issues

Memory Leaks and Timeout Issues
AWS Lambda is a powerful serverless computing service, but like all serverless applications, it can encounter certain runtime issues, particularly **memory leaks** and **timeout issues**. These problems can lead to performance degradation, increased costs, and unexpected failures in production. Understanding the causes and solutions for these common issues is essential for building reliable serverless applications.

In this section, we will explore what causes memory leaks and timeout issues in AWS Lambda functions, how to diagnose them, and best practices for preventing and resolving these problems.

1. Understanding Memory Leaks in AWS Lambda

Memory leaks occur when an application continuously allocates memory without releasing it. In AWS Lambda, memory leaks can lead to an increase in memory consumption over time, which can eventually cause a function to exceed its allocated memory limit and be terminated by the Lambda runtime.

Causes of Memory Leaks:

- **Improper Resource Management**: Forgetting to release or close resources like database connections, file streams, or network connections.
- **Global Variables Holding State**: Retaining stateful objects or large

datasets in global variables that persist across Lambda invocations.
- **Circular References in Code**: Object references pointing to each other, preventing garbage collection from freeing them.

2. Diagnosing and Resolving Memory Leaks

2.1. Monitoring Memory Usage with CloudWatch Metrics

AWS Lambda automatically tracks and reports memory usage to **Amazon CloudWatch**. You can use CloudWatch Metrics to monitor memory consumption and set up alarms for functions that exceed their expected limits.

- **Metric to Monitor**: MaxMemoryUsed
- This metric shows the maximum amount of memory used during each invocation.

Create a CloudWatch Alarm:

- Go to the **CloudWatch Console**.
- Select **Alarms** and click **Create Alarm**.
- Choose the MaxMemoryUsed metric for your Lambda function.
- Set a threshold that is close to or exceeds your function's allocated memory (e.g., 90% of the allocated memory).

Review Memory Trends:

- Analyze the MaxMemoryUsed metric over time to identify whether memory usage increases consistently across multiple invocations. This could indicate a memory leak.

2.2. Debugging Code for Memory Leaks
Check Global Variables:

- Review your code for global variables that hold references to large objects. AWS Lambda reuses execution environments for performance optimization, which means global variables persist between invocations.

Example Issue:

```
# Problematic Code
connections = []

def lambda_handler(event, context):
    conn = create_db_connection()  # Simulated database connection
    connections.append(conn)  # Storing connection in a global list
    ...
```

Solution: Avoid accumulating connections or state in global variables.

Release Resources Properly:

- Ensure that you close or release any open resources, such as file handles, network connections, or database connections, at the end of each invocation.

Example Fix:

```
def lambda_handler(event, context):
    conn = create_db_connection()
    try:
        # Your logic here
        ...
    finally:
        conn.close()  # Close the connection to release memory
```

Inspect Circular References:

- In languages like Python, circular references can prevent garbage collection. Use debugging tools or profilers to identify objects that are not

476

being freed.

Example: If two objects refer to each other, the garbage collector may fail to release them.

```
class A:
    def __init__(self):
        self.ref = None

class B:
    def __init__(self, a):
        self.ref = a

a = A()
b = B(a)
a.ref = b  # Creates a circular reference
```

Use Runtime Tools for Debugging:

- Tools like **AWS Lambda Powertools** for Python and **Node.js memory profiling tools** can help you identify memory leaks by capturing memory snapshots and analyzing heap usage.

3. Understanding Timeout Issues in AWS Lambda

AWS Lambda functions have a configurable timeout setting that defines the maximum duration a function can run. If the function exceeds this timeout, it is forcibly terminated, which can lead to incomplete processing and data loss.

Causes of Timeout Issues:

- **Long-Running Loops or Recursion**: Infinite loops or deep recursion can lead to functions running indefinitely.
- **Network Latency**: Slow responses from external services or databases can increase function execution time.

- **Inefficient Code or Blocking Operations**: Slow processing logic, unoptimized database queries, or blocking I/O operations can cause delays.

4. Diagnosing and Resolving Timeout Issues

4.1. Monitoring and Analyzing Duration Metrics

AWS Lambda tracks the duration of each invocation, which is reported as a **CloudWatch Metric**.

- **Metric to Monitor**: Duration
- This metric shows the execution time of each Lambda function invocation in milliseconds.

Create a CloudWatch Alarm:

- Create an alarm for the Duration metric to notify you if the function execution time approaches or exceeds the configured timeout value.

Review and Analyze Trends:

- Look for invocations where the execution time approaches the function's timeout limit. If the duration varies significantly between invocations, it could indicate inconsistent performance or inefficient code.

4.2. Optimizing Code to Reduce Execution Time
Increase the Timeout Setting:

- If your function requires more time to complete processing, consider increasing the **timeout setting**. This can be configured in the **Lambda Console** or in your deployment configuration (e.g., AWS SAM or Serverless Framework).

```
Resources:
  MyLambdaFunction:
    Type: AWS::Serverless::Function
    Properties:
      Timeout: 60  # Timeout set to 60 seconds
```

Optimize Database Queries and External Calls:

- Review database queries or external API calls to identify slow or inefficient operations. For example, reduce unnecessary database queries by batching them or optimizing SQL queries.

Example Issue:

```python
python

# Inefficient Code
for user_id in user_ids:
    user = fetch_user_from_db(user_id)  # Separate database call
    for each user
```

Solution: Use batch processing to reduce the number of calls.

```
# Optimized Code
users = fetch_users_from_db(user_ids)  # Batch processing with a
single database call
```

Use Asynchronous or Parallel Processing:

- Where possible, use asynchronous techniques or multi-threading to perform time-consuming tasks in parallel.

Example (Python):

479

```
import asyncio

async def fetch_data():
    await asyncio.gather(
        fetch_data_from_service_a(),
        fetch_data_from_service_b()
    )

def lambda_handler(event, context):
    asyncio.run(fetch_data())
```

Implement Caching:

- Use caching strategies to avoid redundant calculations or repeated data retrievals from slow sources. AWS offers caching services like **Amazon DynamoDB Accelerator (DAX)** or **Amazon ElastiCache** for this purpose.

5. Best Practices for Preventing Memory Leaks and Timeout Issues

Set Realistic Timeout Values: Choose a timeout value that aligns with your function's expected execution time. Monitor this value periodically to adjust as needed.

1. **Use Idempotency and Checkpoints**: When performing long-running operations, design your Lambda functions to be idempotent and utilize checkpoints. This allows functions to resume processing in case of interruptions.
2. **Log and Monitor Lambda Performance**: Implement detailed logging in your Lambda functions to capture key events, durations, and resource usage. Use CloudWatch Logs to analyze and troubleshoot performance issues.
3. **Limit Resource Usage in Global Scope**: Avoid storing large objects

or retaining unnecessary connections in the global scope of Lambda functions, as these persist between invocations.

Memory leaks and timeout issues are common challenges in AWS Lambda applications, but with the right monitoring, debugging, and coding practices, they can be effectively managed. By using **CloudWatch Metrics**, **runtime debugging tools**, and following best practices for efficient code and resource management, you can prevent memory leaks and reduce the likelihood of timeout errors.

Debugging Dependencies and Package Size Limitations

In AWS Lambda, managing dependencies effectively is critical to ensure your serverless functions run smoothly and stay within the platform's size constraints. Poor management of dependencies can lead to bloated packages, increased cold start times, and deployment failures. This section dives into understanding and resolving common issues related to dependencies and package size, with a focus on debugging, optimization, and best practices for maintaining efficient deployment packages.

1. Common Issues with Dependencies and Package Size

When developing AWS Lambda functions, especially in Python or Node.js, you may encounter several challenges related to dependencies and package size:

- **Package Size Limit Exceedance**: AWS Lambda limits the size of your deployment package. If your zipped package exceeds 50 MB, Lambda won't accept it directly, requiring you to rethink your deployment strategy.

- **Unused or Heavy Dependencies**: Including unused libraries or unnecessary heavy dependencies can inflate the package size and slow down cold starts.
- **Dependency Conflicts**: Mismatched versions or conflicting packages can cause runtime errors or unexpected behavior.
- **Native Module Compatibility**: Dependencies requiring native binaries must be compatible with the Lambda runtime environment, which can be challenging to debug and build locally.

2. Debugging and Analyzing Package Size

2.1. Identifying and Analyzing Dependencies
List Installed Packages and Their Versions:

- For Python, use pip freeze to list all installed packages and their versions:

```
pip freeze
```

- For Node.js, use npm list to achieve a similar outcome:

```
npm list --depth=0
```

Review the list to spot unnecessary or heavy dependencies.
Visualize Dependencies Using Dependency Trees:

- Use tools like **pipdeptree** for Python or **npm's dependency tree** feature to see a visual representation of your dependency hierarchy.

Example for Python:

```
pip install pipdeptree
pipdeptree
```

This command helps you find nested dependencies that might unnecessarily bloat your deployment package.

Check Package Sizes Locally:

- Navigate to the directory where dependencies are installed and use the du command (in Linux/Mac) to check the size of each directory:

```
du -sh *
```

This approach provides insight into which dependencies are taking up the most space, enabling you to consider alternatives or optimizations.

2.2. Reducing Dependency Size

Remove Unused Dependencies:

- Manually review your requirements.txt or package.json and remove any dependencies that are not used in your Lambda function's code.

Use Lightweight Alternatives:

- Opt for lightweight alternatives to heavy packages. For example, if you only need a basic HTTP client, consider using requests instead of boto3 (in Python) or axios instead of larger Node.js HTTP clients.

Use Tree-Shaking or Minification for Node.js:

- For JavaScript/TypeScript-based Lambda functions, use tools like **Webpack** or **Parcel** to tree-shake and minify your dependencies. This helps eliminate dead code and unused modules, reducing the overall package size.

Example Webpack Configuration:

```
const path = require('path');

module.exports = {
  entry: './src/index.js',
  output: {
    filename: 'bundle.js',
    path: path.resolve(__dirname, 'dist')
  },
  optimization: {
    minimize: true,
  }
};
```

Split Large Packages with Lambda Layers:

- Move large, shared, or reusable dependencies to a **Lambda Layer**. This not only reduces the size of your core deployment package but also allows you to share dependencies across multiple Lambda functions.

Example Workflow for Python:

```
mkdir -p python/lib/python3.8/site-packages
pip install requests -t python/lib/python3.8/site-packages/
zip -r my-layer.zip python/
```

Use AWS Lambda's Docker Runtime for Native Dependencies:

- For packages with native dependencies, build them inside an Amazon Linux Docker container to match Lambda's execution environment:

```
docker run -v "$PWD":/var/task -it amazonlinux:2 bash
```

Inside the container, install the native dependencies using your preferred package manager (pip or npm).

3. Debugging Compatibility Issues

3.1. Simulating the Lambda Runtime Locally
Use Virtual Environments for Python:

- Create a virtual environment that matches the Lambda runtime's Python version:

```
python3.8 -m venv venv
source venv/bin/activate
```

This allows you to install dependencies and test your Lambda function in an environment similar to AWS Lambda.

Use Docker Containers for Native Dependencies:

- Use Docker to create an environment that mimics the Lambda runtime. This is especially useful for debugging compatibility issues with native binaries or platform-specific packages.

Example Docker Command:

```
docker run -v "$PWD":/var/task -it amazonlinux:2 bash
```

1. Inside the container, build and test your deployment package.

3.2. Addressing Version Conflicts
Specify Exact Package Versions:

485

- In your requirements.txt or package.json, lock package versions explicitly to prevent version drift:

```
# requirements.txt example
boto3==1.18.0
requests==2.26.0
```

1. **Use pip check or npm audit**:

- For Python, run pip check to identify conflicts between installed package versions. For Node.js, use npm audit to check for security vulnerabilities and potential conflicts:

```
pip check
npm audit
```

4. Optimizing Deployment Packages with AWS SAM and Serverless Framework

4.1. Deployment with AWS SAM
Use the requirements.txt Approach:

- Define all dependencies in a requirements.txt file, and let AWS SAM handle the packaging.

Example requirements.txt:

```
boto3
pandas
```

1. **Example template.yaml**:

```
Resources:
  MyLambdaFunction:
    Type: AWS::Serverless::Function
    Properties:
      Handler: app.lambda_handler
      Runtime: python3.8
      CodeUri: .
      Layers:
        - !Ref CommonLayer
```

Build and Package Efficiently:

```
sam build
sam deploy --guided
```

This command automatically packages your dependencies and uploads them to S3, optimizing the deployment process.

4.2. Deployment with Serverless Framework
Use Serverless Plugin for Python Requirements:

- If you're using the Serverless Framework, the serverless-python-requirements plugin can help manage Python dependencies and package them efficiently:

Install the Plugin:

```
npm install serverless-python-requirements --save-dev
```

Configure the Plugin in serverless.yml:

```
plugins:
  - serverless-python-requirements

custom:
  pythonRequirements:
    dockerizePip: true
```

1. This configuration builds Python dependencies inside a Docker container, ensuring compatibility with the Lambda runtime.
2. **Use Exclusions and Whitelisting**:

- The Serverless Framework allows you to exclude unnecessary files and folders from the deployment package, keeping it lean:

```
package:
  exclude:
    - node_modules/**
    - test/**
```

Alternatively, you can whitelist only essential files using the include option.

5. Best Practices for Managing Dependencies and Package Size

1. **Modularize Your Code**: Break down your Lambda functions into smaller, specialized functions to reduce the number of dependencies required for each function.
2. **Optimize Your Imports**: Avoid importing entire libraries when only specific modules are needed. This helps reduce the footprint of your deployment package.

3. **Automate Dependency Management**: Use CI/CD pipelines to automate dependency checks and packaging. This reduces the risk of introducing redundant or outdated dependencies.
4. **Monitor and Test Regularly**: Set up monitoring for Lambda cold start times and memory usage to identify if large dependencies are affecting performance. Regular testing can catch compatibility issues before they reach production.

Handling dependencies and package size limitations in AWS Lambda is essential to maintaining performance and reliability. By understanding the constraints, optimizing dependencies, and using tools like Lambda Layers, Docker, and the Serverless Framework, you can effectively manage and reduce the complexity of your deployment packages.

Debugging compatibility and package size issues requires a proactive approach, including monitoring dependency sizes, simulating the Lambda runtime, and automating dependency management. With these strategies in place, you can build leaner, faster, and more efficient serverless applications on AWS Lambda.

Solving Execution Time Limits

One of the most common issues in AWS Lambda is hitting the **execution time limit**, which is set by AWS to ensure efficient utilization of resources. AWS Lambda functions have a maximum timeout of **15 minutes**, and if a function exceeds this duration, it is forcibly terminated. This can result in incomplete processing, corrupted data, or user dissatisfaction.

In this section, we will explore the causes of timeout issues, strategies for optimizing execution time, and best practices to ensure your Lambda functions execute efficiently within the allowed time limits.

1. Understanding Execution Time Limits in AWS Lambda

Timeouts are an essential mechanism in AWS Lambda to prevent runaway or infinite loops and manage computing resources effectively. By default, the timeout for a Lambda function is set to **3 seconds**, but you can configure it to be anywhere between **1 second to 15 minutes** (900 seconds).

Common Causes of Timeout Issues:

- **Heavy or Long-Running Operations**: Processing large datasets, complex calculations, or deep recursive operations.
- **Network Latency**: Waiting for responses from external services, databases, or APIs with significant latency.
- **Unoptimized Code**: Inefficient loops, excessive data transformations, or blocking I/O operations.
- **Resource Contention**: Simultaneous Lambda invocations leading to resource contention or throttling.

2. Diagnosing Timeout Issues

2.1. Analyzing CloudWatch Logs and Metrics

AWS Lambda automatically generates logs and reports key metrics to **Amazon CloudWatch**. These logs and metrics are crucial for diagnosing the causes of timeout issues.

1. **Review CloudWatch Logs for Timeout Events**:

- Look for log entries indicating that the function execution was terminated due to a timeout:

```
Task timed out after X seconds
```

1. This message indicates that the Lambda function exceeded its configured timeout duration.
2. **Monitor the Duration Metric**:

- The **Duration** metric in CloudWatch provides the execution time for each invocation. If the duration is consistently near the configured timeout value, it suggests that the function is likely hitting its execution limit.

Set Up CloudWatch Alarms for Duration:

- Create an alarm in CloudWatch to trigger notifications if the duration exceeds a predefined threshold. This allows you to detect when functions are at risk of timing out and take corrective action.

2.2. Identifying Bottlenecks in Code
Profile Execution Time:

- Use custom **CloudWatch Logs** to capture timestamps at critical points in your code. This helps identify slow operations or bottlenecks in your function logic.

Example (Python):

```python
import time
import logging

logger = logging.getLogger()
logger.setLevel(logging.INFO)

def lambda_handler(event, context):
    start_time = time.time()

    # Process step 1
```

```
step_1_time = time.time()
logger.info(f"Step 1 completed in {step_1_time - start_time}
seconds")

# Process step 2
step_2_time = time.time()
logger.info(f"Step 2 completed in {step_2_time - step_1_time}
seconds")
```

Enable AWS X-Ray Tracing:

- X-Ray provides distributed tracing capabilities, allowing you to see a detailed breakdown of your function's execution time, including external API calls, database operations, and more.

Enable X-Ray by adding the following configuration to your template.yaml (for AWS SAM):

```
Resources:
  MyLambdaFunction:
    Type: AWS::Serverless::Function
    Properties:
      Tracing: Active
```

1. X-Ray visualizes the execution flow and highlights slow segments, enabling you to pinpoint the exact cause of timeouts.

3. Strategies for Solving Execution Time Limits

3.1. Optimize Code and Data Processing
Reduce Iterations and Loop Complexity:

- If your function performs repeated calculations or iterates over large datasets, try to optimize the logic. For instance, use vectorized operations or batch processing to reduce loop iterations.

Example Improvement:

```
# Inefficient: Separate processing for each item
for item in data:
    process_item(item)

# Optimized: Batch processing
process_batch(data)
```

Minimize Blocking Operations:

- Replace synchronous I/O operations with asynchronous ones to prevent the function from waiting unnecessarily. This is especially relevant for Node.js and Python applications.

Example (Python with Asyncio):

```
import asyncio

async def fetch_data():
    # Perform asynchronous I/O
    ...

def lambda_handler(event, context):
    asyncio.run(fetch_data())
```

Avoid Excessive Data Transformations:

- Minimize the number of transformations or conversions applied to data. For example, avoid unnecessary serialization and deserialization operations when interacting with databases or APIs.

3.2. Break Down Large Tasks into Smaller Functions

Use Step Functions for Long-Running Tasks:

- **AWS Step Functions** allow you to break down complex workflows into smaller, independent Lambda functions. Each function performs a discrete task, and Step Functions orchestrate the entire process, effectively overcoming the 15-minute Lambda execution limit.

Example Use Case:

- A data processing pipeline where each Lambda function handles one step, such as data ingestion, transformation, and storage.

Leverage SQS for Asynchronous Processing:

- If your Lambda function processes large payloads or handles intensive tasks, consider offloading the work to **Amazon SQS** (Simple Queue Service). Use SQS to queue tasks, and Lambda functions to process them asynchronously.

Example Workflow:

- An API Gateway request triggers a Lambda function to enqueue a message in SQS. A separate Lambda function consumes and processes messages from the queue.

Implement Chained Invocations:

- For tasks that exceed the maximum duration, consider using **chained invocations**, where one Lambda function triggers another upon completion. This allows you to process large datasets incrementally.

Example:

```
def lambda_handler(event, context):
    # Process a portion of the data
    process_partial_data(event["start"], event["end"])

    # Trigger the next Lambda function if there is more data to
    process
    if event["end"] < TOTAL_DATA_SIZE:
        invoke_next_lambda(event["end"], event["end"] + CHUNK_SIZE)
```

3.3. Optimize Interactions with External Services
Use Bulk or Batch Operations:

- When interacting with databases or external APIs, use batch operations to minimize the number of requests. This can significantly reduce execution time and prevent hitting rate limits.

Example (DynamoDB Batch Writes):

```
import boto3

dynamodb = boto3.client('dynamodb')

def batch_write_items(items):
    dynamodb.batch_write_item(RequestItems={'MyTable': items})
```

Implement Caching:

- Caching frequently accessed data using services like **Amazon Elasti-Cache** or **DynamoDB Accelerator (DAX)** can help reduce repeated fetches, speeding up execution.

Use Retry Mechanisms for Unreliable Services:

- If your Lambda function depends on an external API with variable latency, implement exponential backoff or retries using the **boto3** library in

Python or native retry mechanisms in Node.js.

4. Increasing the Timeout Value Strategically

If none of the above strategies solve your timeout issue, you may consider increasing the Lambda function's timeout value.

4.1. Configuring the Timeout Setting
In the Lambda Console:

- Go to the **AWS Lambda Console**, select your function, and navigate to **Configuration > General Configuration**. Increase the timeout value to a reasonable duration, considering the estimated execution time.

In template.yaml with SAM:

```
Resources:
  MyLambdaFunction:
    Type: AWS::Serverless::Function
    Properties:
      Timeout: 300  # Timeout set to 300 seconds (5 minutes)
```

1. **In serverless.yml with Serverless Framework**:

```
functions:
  myFunction:
    handler: handler.lambdaHandler
    timeout: 300  # Timeout set to 300 seconds (5 minutes)
```

4.2. Best Practices for Setting Timeouts

- **Balance Execution Time and Costs**: Remember that longer execution times can increase Lambda costs. Set the timeout just above your

function's maximum estimated runtime to avoid unnecessary expenses.
- **Monitor Timeouts Regularly**: Use CloudWatch alarms to notify you if functions regularly approach their timeout limits. This indicates the need for optimization or refactoring.

Execution time limits in AWS Lambda are crucial for maintaining cost efficiency and avoiding runaway functions. Solving timeout issues requires a combination of **code optimization, efficient resource handling**, and **proper architectural design**. By monitoring key metrics, profiling execution time, and leveraging serverless patterns such as Step Functions, you can ensure that your Lambda functions stay within their execution limits.

Common Pitfalls and How to Avoid Them

When developing with AWS Lambda, there are several common pitfalls that developers can encounter. These pitfalls can lead to inefficient code, increased costs, runtime errors, or even security vulnerabilities. In this section, we'll explore some of the most frequent mistakes made in AWS Lambda development and provide best practices to avoid them.

1. Neglecting IAM Permissions and Security Configurations

The Pitfall:

- One of the most common pitfalls is configuring overly permissive IAM (Identity and Access Management) roles for Lambda functions. Granting wide permissions, such as AdministratorAccess, increases the risk of security breaches. Another common issue is hardcoding sensitive information like API keys or database credentials within the Lambda code.

497

How to Avoid It:

- **Principle of Least Privilege**: Assign only the necessary permissions that the Lambda function requires to perform its tasks. Use **IAM Policies** with explicit resource ARNs (Amazon Resource Names) and limited actions.
- **Example IAM Policy**:

```
{
  "Version": "2012-10-17",
  "Statement": [
    {
      "Effect": "Allow",
      "Action": "dynamodb:PutItem",
      "Resource":
      "arn:aws:dynamodb:us-east-1:123456789012:table/MyTable"
    }
  ]
}
```

- **Environment Variables for Secrets**: Store sensitive information like API keys, database credentials, or encryption keys in **environment variables** and use **AWS KMS (Key Management Service)** to encrypt them.

```
Environment:
  Variables:
    DATABASE_PASSWORD: !Sub
    "{{resolve:secretsmanager:MySecretKey:SecretString:password}}"
```

- **Regular Policy Reviews**: Conduct regular reviews of IAM policies assigned to Lambda functions to ensure that permissions are still appropriate as the function evolves.

2. Overlooking Error Handling and Retries

The Pitfall:

- Ignoring error handling or failing to account for common runtime errors can cause Lambda functions to fail silently or result in unexpected behavior. Additionally, retry logic for network calls or external API requests is often not implemented, leading to transient failures.

How to Avoid It:

- **Graceful Error Handling**: Use try-catch blocks to handle exceptions and provide informative error messages for easier troubleshooting.
- **Example** (Python):

```
try:
    response = fetch_data_from_api()
except Exception as e:
    print(f"Error fetching data: {str(e)}")
    raise e  # Re-raise the exception if necessary
```

- **Configure Retry Policies**: AWS services like SQS and EventBridge support automatic retry mechanisms. Configure them to automatically retry failed invocations.
- **Example with SQS**:

```
SQSQueue:
  Type: AWS::SQS::Queue
```

```
Properties:
  RedrivePolicy:
    deadLetterTargetArn: !GetAtt DeadLetterQueue.Arn
    maxReceiveCount: 5
```

- **Use AWS Lambda Destinations**: Leverage AWS Lambda Destinations to route successful invocations to another service (like SNS or SQS) or failures to a dead-letter queue for further investigation.

3. Ignoring Cold Start Optimization

The Pitfall:

- Cold starts can lead to increased latency during the initial invocation of Lambda functions, especially in the context of user-facing applications. This can impact user experience and overall function performance.

How to Avoid It:

- **Right-Size Your Memory Allocation**: Allocate sufficient memory to your Lambda function. Increasing memory also proportionally increases the CPU power, leading to reduced execution time and faster cold starts.
- **Keep Dependencies Light**: Only include necessary libraries and avoid using heavy frameworks. Move large or shared dependencies to **Lambda Layers**.
- **Use Provisioned Concurrency**: For critical or latency-sensitive applications, enable **Provisioned Concurrency** to keep a specified number of instances initialized and ready to serve requests immediately.

4. Not Implementing Logging and Monitoring Properly

The Pitfall:

- Inadequate logging and lack of monitoring can make it difficult to debug issues or identify performance bottlenecks. Not having visibility into your Lambda function's execution can lead to longer troubleshooting times.

How to Avoid It:

- **Use Structured Logging**: Log critical events using structured JSON logging to make it easier to query and analyze using tools like **CloudWatch Logs Insights**.
- **Example Structured Logging**:

```
import json
import logging

logger = logging.getLogger()
logger.setLevel(logging.INFO)

def lambda_handler(event, context):
    logger.info(json.dumps({"message": "Processing started",
    "event": event}))
```

- **Enable CloudWatch Alarms**: Set up alarms for key metrics such as duration, error count, and memory usage to get real-time alerts on function issues.
- **Enable AWS X-Ray**: Use **AWS X-Ray** to trace the execution of your Lambda functions and analyze requests across distributed services for latency and bottlenecks.

5. Hardcoding Configuration Values

The Pitfall:

- Hardcoding configuration values such as endpoint URLs, environment-specific variables, or resource names within your Lambda function's code can make it difficult to update or deploy functions across multiple environments.

How to Avoid It:

- **Use Environment Variables**: Store configuration values like URLs, environment names, and resource identifiers in environment variables instead of hardcoding them in the code.

```
Environment:
  Variables:
    DATABASE_URL: "https://mydatabase.amazonaws.com"
    API_ENDPOINT: "https://api.example.com"
```

- **Use Parameter Store or Secrets Manager**: For more complex configurations or sensitive values, store them securely in **AWS Systems Manager Parameter Store** or **AWS Secrets Manager**.

6. Inadequate Testing Strategy

The Pitfall:

- Insufficient testing, especially for Lambda functions that integrate with other AWS services, can lead to unexpected failures or missed edge cases. Over-reliance on manual testing can also introduce errors.

How to Avoid It:

- **Automate Unit and Integration Tests**: Implement a testing framework (like **pytest** for Python or **Jest** for Node.js) to write automated unit and integration tests. Test isolated function logic as well as integrated flows with mock services.
- **Example with pytest**:

```
def test_lambda_handler():
    event = {"key": "value"}
    result = lambda_handler(event, None)
    assert result["statusCode"] == 200
```

- **Use SAM CLI or LocalStack for Local Testing**: AWS SAM CLI and LocalStack allow you to emulate AWS services locally, making it easier to test Lambda functions and their interactions with other services before deploying them to the cloud.
- **Perform Load Testing**: Use tools like **Artillery** or **AWS Distributed Load Testing** to stress test your Lambda functions and see how they behave under heavy loads.

7. Not Using Deployment Stages and Versioning

The Pitfall:

- Deploying directly to production without proper staging environments and version control can lead to unstable releases and downtime. Additionally, rolling back to a previous version without function versioning becomes difficult.

How to Avoid It:

- **Define Multiple Deployment Stages**: Create separate stages for development, staging, and production using SAM, CloudFormation, or the Serverless Framework.
- **Example**:

```
sam deploy --stack-name my-app-dev --parameter-overrides
Environment=dev
sam deploy --stack-name my-app-prod --parameter-overrides
Environment=prod
```

- **Use Lambda Versioning and Aliases**: Deploy Lambda functions as new versions and use **aliases** to point to the desired version. This allows you to perform gradual rollouts and rollbacks seamlessly.
- **Example**:

```
aws lambda create-alias --function-name my-function --name prod
--function-version 2
```

AWS Lambda offers powerful capabilities for building serverless applications, but there are common pitfalls that can hinder your development and operations. By understanding and avoiding these pitfalls, you can improve the performance, reliability, and security of your Lambda-based applications.

Adhering to best practices like following the principle of least privilege, implementing comprehensive error handling, optimizing cold starts, and managing configurations effectively will enable you to build resilient and scalable serverless applications. With a proactive approach to security, monitoring, testing, and deployment, you can avoid these common pitfalls and maximize the benefits of serverless architecture with AWS Lambda.

Scaling Lambda for High Traffic Applications

Understanding Lambda's Auto-Scaling Mechanism
AWS Lambda provides a highly scalable serverless computing service that automatically adjusts capacity based on incoming requests. Unlike traditional server-based architectures, Lambda dynamically scales horizontally by creating new instances to handle increases in demand, allowing developers to focus on writing code without worrying about provisioning or managing servers.

However, while Lambda's auto-scaling capabilities provide significant benefits, understanding how this mechanism works is crucial for building efficient, cost-effective, and responsive applications. This section provides a comprehensive look at how AWS Lambda's auto-scaling works, what factors impact scaling behavior, and best practices for designing Lambda functions that scale effectively with high traffic.

1. How AWS Lambda Auto-Scaling Works

AWS Lambda uses an event-driven model where each request is processed independently by invoking a Lambda function. When a function is invoked, Lambda allocates an execution environment and assigns memory, CPU, and storage based on the function's configuration. When incoming requests increase, AWS Lambda automatically scales by creating additional execution environments, allowing multiple invocations of the same function to run concurrently.

Key Points of Lambda's Auto-Scaling:

- **Concurrency Model**: AWS Lambda scales by increasing the number of concurrent executions to handle incoming traffic.
- **Cold Starts**: Each new execution environment incurs a brief initialization period called a **cold start**.
- **Execution Environment Reuse**: After a cold start, execution environments can be reused for subsequent requests, reducing latency.

2. Concurrency in AWS Lambda

2.1. What is Concurrency?

Concurrency in AWS Lambda refers to the number of instances of a function that are executing at a given time. Lambda functions can handle multiple invocations concurrently, and AWS manages the creation of new instances based on the volume of incoming requests.

For example, if you receive 100 requests in one second, and each invocation takes 1 second to process, AWS Lambda creates 100 concurrent instances of your function to handle each request simultaneously.

2.2. Types of Concurrency
Reserved Concurrency:

- **Reserved Concurrency** allows you to limit the number of concurrent executions for a Lambda function. This is useful to protect downstream services, databases, or APIs from being overwhelmed by a sudden spike in traffic.
- When you set reserved concurrency, AWS ensures that only the specified number of concurrent executions are allowed, and any additional invocations are throttled.

Example: If you set a reserved concurrency of 50, the Lambda function can handle a maximum of 50 concurrent executions at a time. Additional requests will be throttled.

Provisioned Concurrency:

- **Provisioned Concurrency** pre-allocates a specified number of execution environments, ensuring that they are initialized and ready to handle incoming requests immediately. This significantly reduces cold start latency, making it suitable for latency-sensitive applications like real-time APIs or chatbots.
- With provisioned concurrency, you essentially "warm up" a specific number of Lambda instances to avoid cold starts.

Example: If you set provisioned concurrency to 100, AWS maintains 100 warm execution environments at all times, ready to process incoming requests without the cold start delay.

Unreserved Concurrency (Default):

- By default, Lambda functions have a **soft concurrency limit** of **1,000 concurrent executions per region** (which can be increased by request). This means that if you do not set a reserved concurrency limit, AWS Lambda will dynamically scale up to this limit based on incoming traffic.

3. Scaling Factors in AWS Lambda

Several factors influence how AWS Lambda scales in response to incoming traffic:

Function Execution Duration:

- Functions with shorter execution durations can scale more effectively because they free up execution environments faster, allowing them to serve more requests within the same time period.
- Long-running functions consume concurrency resources for extended periods, reducing the capacity available for other invocations.

Burst Concurrency Limits:

- AWS Lambda supports **burst scaling** by allowing up to 500 new execution environments per minute in most regions. After reaching this burst limit, Lambda scales linearly by adding 500 additional environments per minute until the regional concurrency limit is reached.

Throttling:

- If a function's concurrency limit is reached (either due to reserved concurrency settings or regional concurrency limits), Lambda starts throttling incoming requests. Throttled requests either fail immediately or are retried based on the event source configuration.

1. **Key Metric to Monitor: Throttles** in **CloudWatch Metrics**.
2. **Cold Starts and Warm Environments**:

- Cold starts occur when Lambda initializes a new execution environment. The duration of cold starts can vary depending on the runtime, memory allocation, and initialization tasks such as dependency loading.
- Warm environments are reused for subsequent requests, reducing the impact of cold starts on average latency.

4. Best Practices for Optimizing Lambda Auto-Scaling

4.1. Optimize Function Duration

- **Reduce Execution Time**: Aim to minimize the execution duration by optimizing code logic, reducing unnecessary processing, and optimizing interactions with external services.
- **Leverage Asynchronous Processing**: Offload non-critical or long-running tasks to **asynchronous services** like SQS, SNS, or EventBridge to reduce the time functions spend handling each request.

4.2. Implement Efficient Concurrency Management

- **Use Reserved Concurrency for Critical Functions**: Set reserved concurrency limits for functions that handle critical business processes. This ensures that these functions always have sufficient capacity to process requests without being impacted by traffic spikes on other functions.
- **Set Up Provisioned Concurrency for Latency-Sensitive Workloads**: For functions that are part of user-facing applications or have strict SLAs, use provisioned concurrency to pre-warm execution environments and reduce cold start latency.

4.3. Manage Downstream Dependencies

- **Avoid Overloading Downstream Services**: When Lambda scales, it can overwhelm downstream resources like databases or APIs. Implement throttling and rate-limiting logic in your code or at the API Gateway level to prevent cascading failures.
- **Use Caching and Batch Operations**: Implement caching strategies using services like **ElastiCache** or **DynamoDB Accelerator (DAX)** to reduce redundant requests. Similarly, use batch operations to minimize the number of interactions with external services.

4.4. Optimize Cold Starts

- **Keep Deployment Packages Lean**: Reduce the size of your deployment package by including only necessary dependencies. This speeds up initialization and reduces cold start latency.
- **Use Efficient Runtimes and Frameworks**: Some runtimes (like Python and Node.js) have shorter cold start times compared to others (like Java). Choose the appropriate runtime based on your application requirements.

5. Monitoring and Scaling Alerts

5.1. Key Metrics to Monitor in CloudWatch

- **Invocations**: Number of times your Lambda function is invoked. Monitor this metric to understand traffic patterns and plan for scaling.
- **ConcurrentExecutions**: Number of concurrent executions across all functions in your account. Monitor this to identify when your functions are approaching concurrency limits.
- **Throttles**: Number of throttled invocations. High throttle counts indicate that the function is reaching its concurrency limits.
- **Duration**: Average execution time of your Lambda functions. Longer durations can reduce scalability, so focus on optimizing this metric.

5.2. Setting Up Alarms for Scaling

1. **Concurrency Alarms**: Set alarms on **ConcurrentExecutions** to notify you when the number of concurrent executions approaches the account-level concurrency limit.
2. **Throttling Alarms**: Create alarms for **Throttles** to detect when Lambda functions are throttling requests, indicating that the function's concurrency limit has been reached.
3. **Provisioned Concurrency Utilization**: Monitor and set alarms on the utilization of provisioned concurrency to ensure that your configuration matches actual usage patterns.

AWS Lambda's auto-scaling mechanism provides automatic horizontal scaling in response to incoming requests, making it ideal for handling high-traffic applications without manual intervention. By understanding how Lambda scales, managing concurrency effectively, and optimizing cold starts, you can design functions that scale efficiently and maintain consistent performance under varying loads.

Managing Concurrency and Provisioned Concurrency

In AWS Lambda, **concurrency** plays a critical role in determining how your Lambda functions handle incoming requests. Effective management of concurrency ensures that your functions can scale to meet demand without overloading downstream services or exhausting AWS resources. Understanding how to manage both **default concurrency** and **provisioned concurrency** is crucial to achieving optimal performance and reliability in high-traffic applications.

In this section, we will explore different types of concurrency, their implications, and best practices for configuring and managing concurrency in AWS Lambda.

1. Understanding Concurrency in AWS Lambda

1.1. What is Concurrency?

Concurrency refers to the number of Lambda function instances that can execute simultaneously. AWS Lambda allocates a new execution environment for each concurrent request to a function. If the demand exceeds the available concurrent execution capacity, AWS Lambda either scales up or throttles additional requests based on the concurrency configuration.

Key Points:

- **Default Concurrency**: AWS Lambda can handle up to **1,000 concurrent executions per region** by default, which can be increased by contacting AWS support.
- **Reserved Concurrency**: Allows you to reserve a specific number of concurrent executions for a Lambda function, ensuring that other functions don't consume all available concurrency.
- **Provisioned Concurrency**: Pre-allocates and initializes a specified number of execution environments, ensuring that a certain number of

instances are always warm and ready to handle requests.

2. Default Concurrency and Reserved Concurrency

2.1. Default Concurrency Limits

By default, Lambda dynamically scales the number of concurrent executions up to the regional limit (1,000 by default). This means that if a sudden spike in traffic occurs, Lambda can automatically create up to 1,000 concurrent instances to handle incoming requests. If the default concurrency limit is reached, subsequent invocations are throttled.

Impact of Default Concurrency:

- Functions that consume all available concurrency can cause **throttling** for other functions.
- Unexpected spikes in one function's traffic can exhaust the default concurrency limit, affecting unrelated Lambda functions within the same account and region.

2.2. Using Reserved Concurrency

Reserved Concurrency allows you to allocate a specific number of concurrent executions exclusively to a Lambda function. This guarantees that the function always has a minimum capacity reserved and helps to protect critical functions from being affected by high-traffic spikes in other functions.

Benefits of Reserved Concurrency:

- **Prevents Resource Exhaustion**: Protects critical functions by reserving concurrency exclusively for them.
- **Limits Resource Consumption**: Prevents a single Lambda function from consuming all available concurrency, which can cause throttling of other functions.

How to Set Reserved Concurrency:
Via the Lambda Console:

- Go to the **AWS Lambda Console**.
- Select your function and go to **Configuration > Concurrency**.
- Set the **Reserved concurrency** value to the desired number of concurrent executions.

Using AWS CLI:

```
aws lambda put-function-concurrency --function-name
MyLambdaFunction --reserved-concurrent-executions 100
```

This command reserves 100 concurrent executions exclusively for My-LambdaFunction.

Example Use Case: If you have a function that interacts with a rate-limited API, reserving concurrency can prevent Lambda from overwhelming the API with too many requests at once.

3. Provisioned Concurrency for Latency-Sensitive Applications

3.1. What is Provisioned Concurrency?

Provisioned Concurrency allows you to pre-allocate and keep a specified number of Lambda execution environments warm and ready to handle requests immediately. This significantly reduces cold start latency, making it ideal for latency-sensitive applications such as real-time APIs, chatbots, or financial transaction processing systems.

Benefits of Provisioned Concurrency:

- **Reduced Cold Start Latency**: By keeping environments warm, provisioned concurrency ensures that incoming requests are handled without the cold start delay.
- **Predictable Performance**: Provides a consistent and predictable response time for critical functions with strict SLAs.

3.2. How to Configure Provisioned Concurrency

Set Provisioned Concurrency in the Lambda Console:

- Go to the **AWS Lambda Console** and select your function.
- Under **Configuration** > **Concurrency**, choose **Add provisioned concurrency**.
- Specify the desired number of provisioned concurrent instances.

Using AWS CLI:

```
aws lambda put-provisioned-concurrency-config \
  --function-name MyLambdaFunction \
  --qualifier $LATEST \
  --provisioned-concurrent-executions 50
```

This command sets the number of provisioned concurrent executions for MyLambdaFunction to 50.

Using AWS SAM or Serverless Framework: You can define provisioned concurrency in your SAM template (template.yaml) or Serverless Framework configuration (serverless.yml).

Example SAM Configuration:

```
Resources:
  MyLambdaFunction:
    Type: AWS::Serverless::Function
    Properties:
      Handler: app.lambda_handler
      Runtime: python3.8
      ProvisionedConcurrencyConfig:
        ProvisionedConcurrentExecutions: 20
```

3.3. When to Use Provisioned Concurrency

- **Low-Latency APIs**: Provisioned concurrency is beneficial for functions that must respond in real-time or with low latency, such as payment gateways, gaming applications, or live streaming services.

- **Predictable Traffic Patterns**: If you know that your function receives predictable bursts of traffic at specific times (e.g., during business hours or promotional events), provisioned concurrency ensures that functions are ready to handle these bursts efficiently.

4. Managing Concurrency Effectively

4.1. Balancing Reserved and Provisioned Concurrency

- **Reserved Concurrency**: Use reserved concurrency to control and limit the number of concurrent executions for functions that interact with sensitive or rate-limited resources (e.g., databases, third-party APIs). This prevents overwhelming these resources during traffic spikes.
- **Provisioned Concurrency**: Apply provisioned concurrency to functions that require low latency and predictable performance.

4.2. Monitoring Concurrency Metrics

Monitoring concurrency metrics in **CloudWatch** is essential for ensuring that Lambda functions are scaling appropriately and not hitting concurrency limits.

Key Metrics to Monitor:

- **ConcurrentExecutions**: Number of concurrent executions across all functions in the account and region.
- **ProvisionedConcurrentExecutions**: Number of execution environments that have been provisioned and are ready to handle requests.
- **Throttles**: Number of throttled invocations due to reaching the concurrency limit.
- **ProvisionedConcurrencyUtilization**: Percentage of provisioned concurrency capacity being utilized.

4.3. Setting Up Alarms for Concurrency
Concurrency Limit Alarms:

515

- Set up alarms for **ConcurrentExecutions** to get alerts when the number of concurrent executions approaches the account-level limit.

Throttling Alarms:

- Create alarms for **Throttles** to detect when functions are being throttled due to reaching concurrency limits. High throttling rates indicate that the concurrency limit needs to be increased or that traffic management strategies should be reviewed.

Provisioned Concurrency Utilization Alarms:

- Monitor the **ProvisionedConcurrencyUtilization** metric to ensure that the provisioned concurrency settings are aligned with actual demand. If utilization is consistently low, consider reducing provisioned concurrency to save costs.

5. Best Practices for Concurrency Management

- **Use Rate Limiting and Circuit Breakers**: Implement rate-limiting logic in your application or at the API Gateway level to avoid overwhelming Lambda functions or downstream resources during high-traffic periods.
- **Decouple Workloads Using Asynchronous Messaging**: Offload non-critical or heavy tasks to asynchronous messaging services like SQS, SNS, or EventBridge. This helps reduce contention for concurrency resources and improves the overall responsiveness of your Lambda functions.
- **Conduct Load Testing**: Regularly perform load testing on Lambda functions to identify bottlenecks and ensure that concurrency settings align with expected traffic patterns.

Effective concurrency management in AWS Lambda is essential for building scalable, high-performance applications that can handle sudden spikes in traffic and meet latency requirements. By understanding and configuring reserved and provisioned concurrency appropriately, you can optimize your Lambda functions for both scalability and cost-efficiency.

Leveraging CloudWatch metrics and alarms, implementing efficient resource controls, and aligning concurrency configurations with traffic patterns are key strategies to ensure reliable performance in high-traffic applications. By following these best practices, you can confidently scale your serverless architecture with AWS Lambda to handle even the most demanding workloads.

Handling Throttling and Rate Limits

AWS Lambda provides the capability to handle high levels of concurrent executions and dynamic scaling. However, in high-traffic scenarios, managing throttling and rate limits becomes critical. Throttling can occur when your Lambda function exceeds its configured concurrency limits or if it hits an external service's rate limits. Understanding these constraints and implementing strategies to mitigate their effects is crucial for building robust and resilient applications.

In this section, we'll discuss the causes of throttling, how to identify it, and best practices for handling throttling and rate limits effectively.

1. What is Throttling in AWS Lambda?

Throttling occurs when AWS Lambda hits the concurrency limit configured for a specific function or the account-level limit. When a function is throttled, additional invocations are denied and fail with a 429 status code. Throttling can lead to increased error rates, slowdowns, and potentially data loss if not handled properly.

Types of Throttling:

- **Function-Level Throttling**: Occurs when a function's reserved concurrency is exceeded.
- **Account-Level Throttling**: Occurs when all functions within an account and region collectively exceed the account's total concurrency limit.
- **Downstream Throttling**: Happens when Lambda functions call external services or APIs that have their own rate limits (e.g., AWS API Gateway, DynamoDB, or third-party services).

2. Causes of Throttling in AWS Lambda

1. **Exceeding Function Concurrency Limits**: When a Lambda function exceeds its reserved concurrency limit or hits the account-level concurrency limit, AWS Lambda starts throttling additional requests.
2. **Exceeding Account Concurrency Limits**: If the total concurrent executions across all functions exceed the account-level concurrency limit, throttling occurs across all functions.
3. **Rate Limits of External Services**: Many AWS services and third-party APIs impose rate limits. Exceeding these limits can result in request throttling or service outages.
4. **Unexpected Traffic Spikes**: High-traffic events or unexpected spikes in requests can overwhelm your functions, causing them to exceed concurrency limits or overwhelm downstream services.

3. Identifying Throttling Issues

3.1. Monitor CloudWatch Metrics for Throttling

AWS Lambda provides key metrics in **Amazon CloudWatch** that help you detect and analyze throttling issues:

- **Throttles**: This metric tracks the number of invocations that were throttled due to exceeding concurrency limits. If this metric rises, it indicates that the Lambda function is hitting its concurrency limit.

- **ConcurrentExecutions**: This metric shows the number of concurrent executions across all Lambda functions in your account. If this approaches the account limit, throttling may occur.
- **Duration**: Monitoring the average and maximum duration of function executions can help identify if long-running functions are causing concurrency limits to be exhausted.

3.2. Setting Up CloudWatch Alarms for Throttling
Create a Throttling Alarm:

- Go to the **CloudWatch Console**, choose **Alarms**, and create a new alarm.
- Select the **Throttles** metric for your Lambda function.
- Set the threshold to a non-zero value to be alerted whenever throttling occurs.

Set Up Concurrency Limit Alarms:

- Create an alarm on **ConcurrentExecutions** to notify you when the total number of concurrent executions is approaching the account limit. This allows you to proactively address potential throttling issues before they impact your application.

4. Strategies to Mitigate Throttling in AWS Lambda

4.1. Optimize Lambda Concurrency and Scaling
Increase Reserved Concurrency:

- If you notice consistent throttling, consider increasing the **reserved concurrency** for the function to ensure it has enough capacity to handle peak loads.

Example Using AWS CLI:

```
aws lambda put-function-concurrency --function-name
MyLambdaFunction --reserved-concurrent-executions 200
```

Use Provisioned Concurrency for Critical Functions:

- For functions that require low-latency responses or that experience frequent cold starts due to scaling, use **provisioned concurrency**. This helps maintain a warm pool of execution environments, reducing throttling caused by sudden traffic spikes.

Optimize Function Execution Time:

- Shorten the duration of Lambda executions by optimizing code, leveraging asynchronous processing, and using batch operations. Shorter execution times free up concurrency resources more quickly, reducing the likelihood of throttling.

4.2. Implement Rate Limiting and Circuit Breakers
Use Rate Limiting at the API Gateway Level:

- If your Lambda function is triggered via API Gateway, set up **rate limiting** or **throttling rules** at the API Gateway level. This prevents the function from being overwhelmed by excessive requests.

Example API Gateway Throttling Settings:

- **Rate**: Limit the number of requests per second.
- **Burst**: Limit the number of requests in a burst period.

Implement a Circuit Breaker Pattern:

- Use the **circuit breaker pattern** to protect your Lambda functions and downstream services from overload. A circuit breaker monitors failed requests, and if failures exceed a threshold, it opens the circuit and temporarily stops new requests to prevent further overload.

Example Circuit Breaker with Python:

```
from circuitbreaker import circuit

@circuit(failure_threshold=3, recovery_timeout=60)
def call_external_service():
    # Make an external API call
    ...
```

4.3. Manage Downstream Service Limits
Use Exponential Backoff and Retry Logic:

- For calls to rate-limited services like DynamoDB or third-party APIs, implement **exponential backoff** and retry logic. This allows your Lambda function to automatically retry failed requests, reducing the risk of hitting downstream rate limits.

Example with Boto3 in Python:

```
import boto3
from botocore.config import Config

my_config = Config(
    retries={
        'max_attempts': 10,
        'mode': 'adaptive'
    }
)

dynamodb = boto3.client('dynamodb', config=my_config)
```

Use Queues to Decouple Processing:

- Decouple your Lambda functions from downstream services by using **Amazon SQS** or **Amazon SNS**. This helps absorb traffic spikes and prevent Lambda functions from overwhelming external services.

Example Workflow:

- Place messages in an SQS queue and have another Lambda function process them asynchronously. This approach smooths out spikes in traffic and prevents hitting service rate limits.

5. Handling Throttling in Asynchronous Invocations

AWS Lambda automatically retries throttled invocations when functions are triggered asynchronously (e.g., by S3 events or SNS notifications). However, if throttling persists, Lambda eventually drops messages after the maximum retry limit is reached.

5.1. Configure Dead-Letter Queues for Failed Invocations
Set Up a Dead-Letter Queue (DLQ):

- Configure a DLQ (using SQS or SNS) to capture messages that fail to process after the maximum number of retries. This allows you to review and manually reprocess failed messages.

Example Configuration:

```
Resources:
  MyLambdaFunction:
    Type: AWS::Serverless::Function
    Properties:
      Handler: app.lambda_handler
```

```
Runtime: python3.8
DeadLetterConfig:
  TargetArn:
  arn:aws:sqs:us-east-1:123456789012:MyDeadLetterQueue
```

Monitor DLQ Metrics:

- Set up CloudWatch alarms to notify you if the number of messages in the DLQ exceeds a certain threshold, indicating persistent throttling or errors.

6. Best Practices for Managing Throttling and Rate Limits

- **Plan for Peak Traffic**: Use traffic forecasting and historical data to anticipate peak traffic times and adjust concurrency limits or provisioned concurrency settings accordingly.
- **Limit Concurrent Executions on Critical Functions**: Implement reserved concurrency to protect critical functions and ensure they have enough capacity during peak loads.
- **Use Async Processing for Resource-Intensive Tasks**: Offload resource-intensive or long-running tasks to asynchronous services like SQS, SNS, or Step Functions.
- **Regularly Review and Update Concurrency Limits**: Reassess your Lambda concurrency limits periodically based on changing traffic patterns, application usage, and new features or updates.

Throttling and rate limits are crucial considerations when designing scalable and resilient AWS Lambda applications. Understanding the causes of throttling and proactively implementing strategies to handle it can help maintain reliable performance under varying load conditions. By effectively managing concurrency, implementing rate limiting, and using asynchronous patterns, you can build serverless applications that handle high traffic gracefully and avoid overloading downstream services.

Using AWS Step Functions for Complex Workflows

AWS Step Functions is a fully managed service that makes it easier to coordinate multiple AWS services into serverless workflows. By defining workflows as state machines, Step Functions allow you to break down complex processes into smaller, manageable tasks while maintaining reliability, scalability, and ease of troubleshooting. Using AWS Step Functions with AWS Lambda enables the orchestration of complex workflows that involve multiple AWS services, including conditional logic, error handling, retries, and parallel execution.

In this section, we will explore how AWS Step Functions work, their benefits, and best practices for using Step Functions to manage complex workflows.

1. Overview of AWS Step Functions

AWS Step Functions allow you to create workflows that coordinate the execution of multiple services, such as Lambda, DynamoDB, ECS, SNS, and more. Each workflow is represented as a **state machine**, which defines a sequence of steps to be performed, the conditions for transitioning between steps, and any error-handling or retry logic required.

Key Components of Step Functions:

- **States**: The individual steps within a workflow. States can be tasks, parallel branches, choices, or wait states.
- **Tasks**: The individual units of work performed by a specific service or Lambda function.
- **State Machine**: The entire workflow definition that includes all states, transitions, and error-handling mechanisms.

2. Benefits of Using AWS Step Functions

- **Simplifies Complex Workflows**: Breaks down complex tasks into smaller, modular states with well-defined transitions and logic.
- **Built-in Error Handling and Retries**: Provides built-in error handling and retry capabilities, reducing the need for custom retry logic in your Lambda functions.
- **Visual Workflow Representation**: Step Functions provide a graphical interface to visualize the entire workflow, making it easier to understand and troubleshoot.
- **Supports Asynchronous and Parallel Execution**: Allows the concurrent execution of multiple states or branches, enabling faster processing of large workloads.

3. Creating a Step Functions Workflow

To create a Step Functions workflow, you define a **state machine** using **Amazon States Language (ASL)**. ASL is a JSON-based language that allows you to describe the workflow's states, transitions, and associated actions.

3.1. Example State Machine Definition

Here is an example of a state machine that orchestrates a simple data processing workflow using AWS Lambda:

```
{
  "Comment": "A simple Step Functions example for data processing",
  "StartAt": "FetchData",
  "States": {
    "FetchData": {
      "Type": "Task",
      "Resource":
      "arn:aws:lambda:us-east-1:123456789012:function:FetchDataLambda",
      "Next": "ProcessData"
    },
```

```
    "ProcessData": {
      "Type": "Task",
      "Resource":
      "arn:aws:lambda:us-east-1:123456789012:function:ProcessDataLambda",
      "Next": "SaveData"
    },
    "SaveData": {
      "Type": "Task",
      "Resource":
      "arn:aws:lambda:us-east-1:123456789012:function:SaveDataLambda",
      "End": true
    }
  }
}
```

Explanation:

- **StartAt** defines the first state of the workflow.
- **States** section defines three states: FetchData, ProcessData, and SaveData, each of which corresponds to a Lambda function.
- Each state uses a Type of "Task", indicating that it performs a specific action (i.e., invoking a Lambda function).
- **Next** specifies the next state to transition to, and **End** marks the end of the workflow.

4. Types of States in AWS Step Functions

Step Functions support various state types that allow you to build complex workflows with advanced control flow and error handling. Some key state types include:

4.1. Task State

A **Task State** performs a specific action, such as invoking a Lambda function or calling an AWS service.

Example:

```
"FetchData": {
  "Type": "Task",
  "Resource":
  "arn:aws:lambda:us-east-1:123456789012:function:FetchDataLambda",
  "Next": "ProcessData"
}
```

4.2. Choice State

A **Choice State** allows you to define branching logic based on conditions. This is useful for implementing workflows with conditional flows or alternative paths.

Example:

```
"CheckCondition": {
  "Type": "Choice",
  "Choices": [
    {
      "Variable": "$.isValid",
      "BooleanEquals": true,
      "Next": "ProcessData"
    },
    {
      "Variable": "$.isValid",
      "BooleanEquals": false,
      "Next": "HandleInvalidData"
    }
  ]
}
```

4.3. Parallel State

A **Parallel State** allows you to execute multiple states simultaneously, which can significantly reduce processing time for large workloads or independent tasks.

Example:

```json
"ProcessDataInParallel": {
  "Type": "Parallel",
  "Branches": [
    {
      "StartAt": "Task1",
      "States": {
        "Task1": {
          "Type": "Task",
          "Resource":
          "arn:aws:lambda:us-east-1:123456789012:function:Task1Lambda",
          "End": true
        }
      }
    },
    {
      "StartAt": "Task2",
      "States": {
        "Task2": {
          "Type": "Task",
          "Resource":
          "arn:aws:lambda:us-east-1:123456789012:function:Task2Lambda",
          "End": true
        }
      }
    }
  ],
  "Next": "FinalProcessing"
}
```

4.4. Wait State

A **Wait State** introduces a delay before proceeding to the next state. This is useful when workflows require a specific delay between steps.

Example:

```json
json

"WaitForData": {
  "Type": "Wait",
```

```
  "Seconds": 300,
  "Next": "ProcessData"
}
```

5. Error Handling and Retry Strategies

AWS Step Functions provide built-in mechanisms for handling errors and implementing retry logic. You can define retry policies for specific states or set up fallback states using the Catch and Retry fields.

5.1. Implementing Retries

You can use the Retry field in a task state to specify retry behavior in case of transient errors.

Example:

```
"FetchData": {
  "Type": "Task",
  "Resource":
  "arn:aws:lambda:us-east-1:123456789012:function:FetchDataLambda",
  "Retry": [
    {
      "ErrorEquals": ["Lambda.ServiceException",
      "Lambda.AWSLambdaException"],
      "IntervalSeconds": 2,
      "MaxAttempts": 3,
      "BackoffRate": 2.0
    }
  ],
  "Next": "ProcessData"
}
```

5.2. Catching Errors

You can use the Catch field to handle errors gracefully by defining fallback states or alternative actions when a specific error occurs.

Example:

```
"FetchData": {
  "Type": "Task",
  "Resource":
  "arn:aws:lambda:us-east-1:123456789012:function:FetchDataLambda",
  "Catch": [
    {
      "ErrorEquals": ["Lambda.ServiceException",
      "Lambda.AWSLambdaException"],
      "ResultPath": "$.errorInfo",
      "Next": "HandleError"
    }
  ],
  "Next": "ProcessData"
}
```

6. Best Practices for Using Step Functions with AWS Lambda

- **Decouple and Modularize Tasks**: Break down large workflows into smaller, independent tasks. Use Step Functions to orchestrate these tasks, making them easier to understand, test, and maintain.

- **Implement Error Handling and Retries**: Leverage Step Functions' built-in error-handling and retry features to manage transient errors and provide fault tolerance.

- **Optimize Parallel Execution**: When processing large workloads, use parallel states to execute multiple tasks simultaneously and reduce overall workflow duration.

- **Monitor and Visualize Workflows**: Use the Step Functions console to visualize workflows and monitor state transitions, errors, and task execution times. This makes debugging and troubleshooting easier.

7. Real-World Use Cases for AWS Step Functions

7.1. ETL Pipelines

In an **Extract-Transform-Load (ETL) pipeline**, Step Functions can orchestrate the extraction of data from various sources, transformation using Lambda functions or AWS Glue, and loading into data warehouses like Redshift or S3.

7.2. Order Processing Workflows

For e-commerce applications, Step Functions can manage order processing workflows, including order validation, inventory checks, payment processing, and shipment notifications.

7.3. Serverless Microservices Orchestration

In serverless architectures, Step Functions can orchestrate microservices that are implemented as Lambda functions or ECS services. This enables communication and coordination between multiple microservices, while providing fault tolerance and error handling.

AWS Step Functions provide a powerful way to orchestrate complex workflows in a serverless architecture. By breaking down tasks into smaller, manageable steps and using built-in error handling, retry logic, and parallel execution, you can build scalable, fault-tolerant applications. Leveraging Step Functions with AWS Lambda allows you to create reliable workflows that are easy to visualize, monitor, and maintain.

Optimizing AWS Lambda Costs

Pricing Structure of AWS Lambda

AWS Lambda is priced based on a pay-as-you-go model, which charges for the compute time and the number of requests to your functions. While this pricing structure allows for cost efficiency by aligning costs with actual usage, understanding the various factors that influence Lambda costs is crucial to optimizing expenses and preventing unexpected charges.

In this section, we'll explore AWS Lambda's pricing model in detail, including key components such as request pricing, compute charges, additional cost factors, and pricing variations for different usage scenarios.

1. Key Components of AWS Lambda Pricing

The AWS Lambda pricing model consists of two primary components:

1. **Request Charges**: The cost incurred based on the number of times your Lambda function is invoked.
2. **Duration Charges**: The cost incurred based on the amount of time your Lambda function runs, calculated in milliseconds.

Both these components work together to determine the overall cost of running a Lambda function.

2. Request Pricing

Request Charges are calculated based on the number of times your Lambda function is invoked. AWS offers a **free tier** for up to 1 million requests per month. After exceeding the free tier limit, you will be charged based on the number of additional requests.

Pricing Breakdown:

- **First 1 million requests per month**: Free.
- **After 1 million requests**: $0.20 per 1 million requests.

Example Calculation: If your Lambda function receives 5 million invocations in a month:

- 1 million requests are free.
- The remaining 4 million requests are billed at $0.20 per 1 million requests.

Total Request Cost: 4×0.20=0.804 \times 0.20 = 0.804×0.20=0.80 USD

3. Duration Pricing

Duration Charges are based on the total compute time consumed by your Lambda function. Duration is calculated from the time the function starts executing until it returns or terminates. The duration charge is calculated in increments of 1 millisecond, with a minimum execution time of 1 millisecond.

AWS Lambda pricing for duration depends on the amount of **memory allocated** to the function, and the cost is expressed in **GB-seconds**.

Pricing Breakdown:

- **Compute Time**: Billed in GB-seconds, based on the memory allocation and the execution time.
- **Pricing**: $0.00001667 per GB-second.

Formula for Duration Charges:

Cost=Number of Executions×Memory Allocated (GB)×Execution Time (seconds)×Price per GB-second\text{Cost} = \text{Number of Executions} \times \text{Memory Allocated (GB)} \times \text{Execution Time (seconds)} \times \text{Price per GB-second}Cost=Number of Executions×Memory Allocated (GB)×Execution Time (seconds)×Price per GB-second

Example Calculation: Let's say you have a Lambda function with the following specifications:

- **Memory Allocated**: 512 MB (0.5 GB).
- **Number of Executions**: 2 million.
- **Average Execution Time**: 200 milliseconds (0.2 seconds).
- **Pricing per GB-second**: $0.00001667.

Duration Charges:

Cost=2,000,000×0.5×0.2×0.00001667=3.334 USD\text{Cost} = 2,000,000 \times 0.5 \times 0.2 \times 0.00001667 = 3.334 \text{ USD}Cost=2,000,000 ×0.5×0.2×0.00001667=3.334 USD

4. Additional Factors Affecting AWS Lambda Costs

4.1. Memory Allocation

AWS Lambda allows you to allocate memory in 64 MB increments, from a minimum of 128 MB to a maximum of 10,240 MB. When you increase memory allocation, AWS automatically allocates proportional CPU power. Higher memory allocations result in higher GB-second charges, but can also lead to faster execution times.

- **Lower Memory**: Lower memory allocation reduces the cost per execution but may lead to longer durations.
- **Higher Memory**: Higher memory allocation increases the cost per GB-second but may significantly reduce execution time, improving overall efficiency.

Cost-Optimization Tip: Test different memory allocations to find the optimal balance between execution time and memory cost for your specific workload.

4.2. Provisioned Concurrency Charges

For applications requiring low latency or with strict SLAs, AWS Lambda offers **Provisioned Concurrency**. This feature keeps a specific number of execution environments initialized and ready to handle requests, reducing cold start latency.

Provisioned Concurrency Pricing:

- **Provisioned Concurrency Execution Time**: $0.0000041667 per GB-second.
- **Provisioned Concurrency Requests**: $0.000009722 per invocation.

Example Calculation: If you have a function with 1 GB of memory and a provisioned concurrency of 100, running for a month (30 days):

- **Compute Time Cost**: $100 \times 1 \times 30 \times 24 \times 60 \times 60 \times 0.0000041667 = 1{,}036.8100$ \times 1 \times 30 \times 24 \times 60 \times 60 \times 0.0000041667 = 1{,}036.8100 \times 1 \times 30 \times 24 \times 60 \times 60 \times 0.0000041667 = 1{,}036.8 USD
- **Request Cost**: For 10 million invocations, the cost would be $10{,}000{,}000 \times 0.000009722 = 97.22$ $10{,}000{,}000 \times 0.000009722 = 97.22$ $10{,}000{,}000 \times 0.000009722 = 97.22$ USD

5. Data Transfer Charges

While data transfer within AWS Lambda (from the function to other AWS services in the same region) is free, certain types of data transfers may incur additional charges:

- **Data Transfer Out to the Internet**: Charges apply when transferring data from AWS Lambda to the internet.
- **Data Transfer Across Regions**: Charges apply when transferring data

between AWS Lambda functions or services located in different AWS regions.

Cost-Optimization Tip: Keep data transfers within the same region and utilize regional services like Amazon S3 or DynamoDB to minimize data transfer costs.

6. Lambda@Edge Pricing

Lambda@Edge is a feature that lets you run Lambda functions at AWS locations closer to the end users, improving latency and user experience. Lambda@Edge pricing includes two additional charges beyond standard Lambda pricing:

- **Execution Charges**: Calculated based on the number of requests and the duration of execution at the edge location.
- **Replication Charges**: There are additional costs for replicating Lambda@Edge functions across multiple AWS locations.

7. Free Tier and Pricing Variations

AWS Lambda offers a **free tier** that provides up to 1 million free requests and 400,000 GB-seconds of compute time per month. This free tier applies on a per-region basis, and any usage beyond the free tier is billed according to the standard Lambda pricing.

Pricing Variations by Region

AWS Lambda pricing may vary slightly between AWS regions, due to differences in infrastructure costs. When planning for large-scale deployments, it is essential to consider regional pricing variations and choose regions that align with both latency requirements and cost efficiency.

8. Optimizing Costs Based on Pricing Structure

Understanding the Lambda pricing structure provides opportunities to optimize costs and improve efficiency. Some effective strategies include:

- **Right-Sizing Memory Allocation**: Experiment with different memory configurations to find the optimal balance between duration and memory cost.
- **Using Provisioned Concurrency Selectively**: Apply provisioned concurrency only to critical functions where latency is a concern.
- **Minimizing Execution Time**: Optimize code to reduce execution time, leveraging batch operations, asynchronous processing, and efficient data handling.
- **Leveraging the Free Tier**: Take advantage of the free tier for development, testing, and low-volume workloads.
- **Reducing Data Transfer Costs**: Design architectures that minimize data transfer between regions or to external endpoints.

The pricing structure of AWS Lambda is designed to provide cost-effective compute services that scale with your workload. By understanding the key components of Lambda pricing—request charges, duration charges, memory allocation, and provisioned concurrency—you can make informed decisions to optimize costs while maintaining the performance and reliability of your serverless applications.

Strategically managing memory allocation, leveraging the free tier, and minimizing data transfer costs can help you achieve the right balance between cost and efficiency in your Lambda functions. With these insights, you are well-equipped to design and optimize serverless applications that deliver value without exceeding your budget.

Cost Reduction Techniques for Lambda Functions

Optimizing costs for AWS Lambda involves strategically managing the key factors that influence pricing. By understanding the pricing model and utilizing cost-efficient design and architectural techniques, you can significantly reduce expenses without compromising performance or scalability. This section covers effective cost reduction techniques for Lambda functions.

1. Right-Sizing Memory Allocation

The Challenge:

AWS Lambda charges based on memory allocation and duration, where higher memory allocations increase cost per millisecond. However, allocating too little memory can lead to longer execution times, increasing overall costs.

The Solution:

Perform memory profiling and allocate memory based on your function's actual requirements. Sometimes, increasing memory can reduce execution time, resulting in a lower overall cost.

Steps to Right-Size Memory:

1. **Measure Execution Time at Different Memory Levels**: Test your Lambda function with various memory configurations (e.g., 128 MB, 256 MB, 512 MB, etc.) to find the point where execution time drops significantly without increasing costs unnecessarily.
2. **Calculate GB-Second Costs for Each Memory Level**: Multiply memory allocation by execution time and the cost per GB-second to identify the optimal configuration.

Example:

If a function with 256 MB of memory takes 1 second to run but takes only 0.4 seconds with 512 MB, increasing the memory allocation might reduce costs even if the per-GB charge is higher.

2. Optimize Function Execution Time

The Challenge:

Longer execution times increase Lambda duration costs. Inefficient code, unnecessary computations, or excessive data processing can contribute to longer runtimes.

The Solution:

Streamline your code to reduce execution time and avoid unnecessary processes. Key strategies include:

- **Use Asynchronous Processing**: Offload non-critical or long-running tasks to asynchronous services like SQS, SNS, or Step Functions.
- **Minimize Data Transformations**: Reduce the number of times data is serialized, deserialized, or reformatted during processing.
- **Avoid Redundant I/O Operations**: Minimize calls to external services or databases within the same invocation.

Example: If your function repeatedly fetches the same data from a database, consider caching the data locally within the function to reduce redundant fetch operations.

3. Batch Processing of Data

The Challenge:

Processing a large number of individual records or events using separate Lambda invocations can lead to high invocation and duration costs.

The Solution:

Wherever possible, use batch processing to reduce the number of invocations and improve efficiency. AWS services like SQS, Kinesis, and DynamoDB Streams support batch processing with Lambda, allowing multiple records to be processed in a single invocation.

Benefits of Batch Processing:

- **Reduces Number of Requests**: Fewer invocations mean lower request charges.
- **Improves Efficiency**: Processing multiple records in a single invocation reduces per-record processing overhead.

Example: When processing Kinesis stream events, configure the batch size for Lambda to fetch and process multiple records at once.

4. Use Provisioned Concurrency Selectively

The Challenge:

Provisioned Concurrency incurs additional costs to keep execution environments initialized, which can increase expenses if not used efficiently.

The Solution:

Reserve provisioned concurrency only for critical functions that require low-latency response times. For non-critical functions, rely on the default on-demand concurrency to save costs.

Best Practices:

- **Monitor Provisioned Concurrency Utilization**: Use CloudWatch metrics to track the actual utilization of provisioned concurrency and adjust the settings to match peak traffic periods.
- **Schedule Provisioned Concurrency**: Enable provisioned concurrency only during high-traffic hours using scheduled scaling.

5. Leverage Lambda Layers for Shared Dependencies

The Challenge:

Bundling dependencies with each Lambda function can lead to bloated deployment packages and increased costs due to longer cold start times.

The Solution:

Use **Lambda Layers** to share common dependencies across multiple functions. This reduces deployment package sizes, improves cold start times, and can lower overall duration costs.

Example: If multiple Lambda functions use the same Python or Node.js library, move the library to a Lambda Layer and attach the layer to each function.

6. Schedule Non-Critical Functions

The Challenge:

Running Lambda functions continuously or during low-demand hours can lead to unnecessary costs.

The Solution:

Use **Amazon CloudWatch Events** or **EventBridge** to schedule non-critical Lambda functions to run only at specific times or during peak demand hours. This is particularly useful for functions performing maintenance, cleanup, or batch processing tasks.

Example: Schedule a Lambda function that archives old logs or cleans up data in a database to run only once a day during off-peak hours.

7. Avoid Over-Invoking Lambda Functions

The Challenge:

Triggering Lambda functions too frequently for high-volume events, such as frequent S3 bucket changes or API Gateway requests, can lead to high request and execution charges.

The Solution:

Optimize trigger configurations to reduce invocation frequency:

- **Filter S3 Events**: When using S3 as an event source, apply S3 event filters to only trigger Lambda functions for specific file types or prefixes.
- **Use WebSockets for Real-Time Communication**: When building real-time APIs, consider using WebSockets instead of frequent API Gateway invocations.

Example: Instead of triggering a Lambda function for every small object uploaded to an S3 bucket, use event filtering to only trigger the function for files larger than a certain size or with a specific prefix.

8. Use Spot Instances for High-Volume Batch Processing

The Challenge:

Lambda can be relatively expensive for high-volume, long-running batch processing tasks.

The Solution:

For high-volume batch processing workloads that can tolerate interruption, consider using **EC2 Spot Instances** in conjunction with AWS Batch. This approach can be much more cost-effective for long-running or CPU-intensive tasks compared to using Lambda.

Example: Use Lambda for real-time triggers or lightweight operations, and delegate heavy batch processing to AWS Batch running on EC2 Spot Instances.

9. Implement Idle Function Cleanup

The Challenge:

Leaving unused or obsolete Lambda functions active can result in unnecessary charges for storage, monitoring, or data retention.

The Solution:

Implement an automated cleanup process to identify and remove unused or deprecated Lambda functions periodically. This not only reduces clutter but can also lower ongoing maintenance and monitoring costs.

Example: Use an automated script to identify Lambda functions that have not been invoked in over 90 days and notify developers for potential cleanup.

10. Monitor and Review Lambda Cost Reports Regularly

The Challenge:
Cost optimizations are not a one-time task. Without regular reviews, Lambda costs can escalate due to unexpected traffic, new deployments, or architectural changes.

The Solution:
Set up regular reviews of AWS Lambda cost reports using **AWS Cost Explorer** and **CloudWatch Billing Metrics**. Look for trends, unexpected spikes, or anomalies in Lambda costs and take corrective action as needed.

Steps for Regular Monitoring:

1. **Set Up Cost and Usage Reports**: Use AWS Cost Explorer to break down costs by function, region, and time period.
2. **Configure Billing Alerts**: Create billing alerts in CloudWatch to notify you when Lambda costs exceed a predefined threshold.

Optimizing AWS Lambda costs requires a comprehensive understanding of Lambda's pricing structure and the factors that influence it. By right-sizing memory, optimizing execution time, leveraging batch processing, and using provisioned concurrency selectively, you can achieve significant cost reductions while maintaining performance and scalability.

Employing strategic techniques such as scheduling non-critical functions, avoiding over-invocation, and using shared dependencies effectively can further enhance your cost-efficiency. Regular monitoring and proactive reviews of Lambda costs ensure that your optimizations remain relevant as traffic patterns and workloads evolve.

With these cost reduction strategies in place, you can confidently build serverless applications that are not only performant and scalable but also cost-efficient.

Analyzing Lambda Costs with Cost Explorer

AWS **Cost Explorer** is a powerful tool that enables you to analyze and manage your AWS spending by providing visual insights into your costs and usage patterns. When working with AWS Lambda, Cost Explorer can help you identify cost trends, understand the drivers of Lambda expenses, and find opportunities for optimization. This section covers how to leverage Cost Explorer effectively to gain insights into your AWS Lambda costs.

1. Overview of Cost Explorer

AWS **Cost Explorer** is a visualization tool that helps you view and analyze your AWS costs over time. It provides customizable reports that allow you to filter and group costs based on different dimensions, such as service type, account, usage type, and tags. For AWS Lambda, you can use Cost Explorer to track costs by function, region, execution duration, and more.

Key Features of Cost Explorer:

- **Cost and Usage Reports**: View detailed reports on cost and usage trends, including a breakdown by AWS services.
- **Filtering and Grouping**: Analyze costs by applying filters for services, regions, accounts, usage types, and tags.
- **Cost Anomaly Detection**: Automatically detect and notify you of unusual spikes or drops in AWS spending.

2. Setting Up Cost Explorer for AWS Lambda

2.1. Accessing Cost Explorer

1. **Sign in to the AWS Management Console**.
2. Navigate to **Cost Management** and select **Cost Explorer**.
3. **Enable Cost Explorer** if you have not already done so.

2.2. Understanding Cost Explorer's Interface

The main **Cost Explorer Dashboard** displays an overview of your costs, with options to filter and group data based on different dimensions. For AWS Lambda, you can focus on dimensions such as **Service, Linked Account, Usage Type**, and **Tags**.

3. Analyzing Lambda Costs in Cost Explorer

3.1. Create a Lambda Cost Report

1. **Filter by Service**: In Cost Explorer, select **Filter > Service** and choose **AWS Lambda**. This filters the cost report to show expenses related only to Lambda functions.
2. **Choose a Time Period**: Set the time range (e.g., last 30 days, last month) to view cost trends over a specific period.
3. **Group by Usage Type**: To get more granular insights, group costs by **Usage Type**. Common usage types for Lambda include:

- **Requests**: Costs associated with the number of Lambda invocations.
- **Duration**: Costs based on the execution duration of your Lambda functions, measured in GB-seconds.
- **Provisioned Concurrency**: Charges for keeping execution environments initialized.

Example Report Setup:

- **Filter**: AWS Lambda
- **Time Range**: Last 30 days
- **Group By**: Usage Type

This setup will display a breakdown of Lambda costs based on the number of requests, duration, and provisioned concurrency usage over the selected time period.

3.2. Analyze Cost Trends Over Time

1. **Identify Cost Spikes**: Look for sudden increases in cost over time. Cost Explorer's visualization allows you to identify days or weeks with unusual spikes. Use these insights to correlate with deployment events, traffic changes, or newly introduced functions.
2. **Compare Costs Across Regions**: AWS Lambda costs may vary by region. In Cost Explorer, group by **Region** to identify regions with higher costs and assess if these regions align with your application's performance or redundancy needs.
3. **Track Costs by Function**: If you have tagged your Lambda functions appropriately, you can group costs by **Tag Key**. For example, if you use tags like Project or Environment, you can identify which projects or environments are driving Lambda costs.

4. Leveraging Tags for Detailed Cost Analysis

AWS Lambda supports tagging, allowing you to apply key-value tags to your Lambda functions. By utilizing tags, you can achieve more detailed cost breakdowns in Cost Explorer.

4.1. Tagging Lambda Functions

- **Apply Tags Consistently**: Create a consistent tagging strategy for your Lambda functions. Common tags include:
- **Project**: Identify costs associated with different projects.
- **Environment**: Differentiate costs by environment (e.g., production, staging, development).
- **Owner**: Assign ownership of functions to teams or individuals.

Example Tag:

- **Key**: Environment
- **Value**: Production

4.2. Analyzing Tagged Costs in Cost Explorer

1. **Filter by Tag Key**: In Cost Explorer, choose **Filter** > **Tags** and select a tag key (e.g., Environment).
2. **Group by Tag Key**: Group costs by the selected tag key to see how costs are distributed across different values (e.g., production, development).

This approach allows you to track costs for different projects or environments separately and gain insights into which functions are consuming the most resources.

5. Identifying Cost Drivers and Optimizing Lambda Expenses

5.1. Drill Down into Cost Drivers

Cost Explorer allows you to drill down into specific cost drivers to identify inefficiencies or opportunities for optimization. For AWS Lambda, key cost drivers to analyze include:

- **Request Volume**: High invocation rates can lead to significant costs, especially for chatbots, IoT applications, or high-frequency APIs.
- **Execution Duration**: Longer execution times result in higher costs, especially if functions are not optimized or if unnecessary processes are being run.
- **Provisioned Concurrency Usage**: While provisioned concurrency reduces cold starts, it comes at an additional cost. Analyze if your functions are effectively utilizing their provisioned concurrency settings.

5.2. Analyze Cost Efficiency with Cost and Usage Reports (CUR)

For more advanced analysis, AWS provides **Cost and Usage Reports (CUR)**, which offer detailed line-item billing data. You can use CUR to analyze Lambda costs at a more granular level, identify inefficient functions, and track costs by specific usage dimensions.

Example Use Cases for CUR:

- **Identify Long-Running Functions**: Use CUR to find Lambda functions with high duration charges and investigate why they are running longer than expected.
- **Assess Provisioned Concurrency Utilization**: Determine if the actual invocations match the provisioned concurrency capacity, helping you adjust provisioned concurrency settings to save costs.

6. Setting Up Cost and Usage Alerts

6.1. Create Cost Anomaly Detection Alerts

AWS **Cost Anomaly Detection** can automatically identify unusual patterns in your spending and alert you to unexpected cost spikes. Configure anomaly detection to monitor AWS Lambda costs and notify you of sudden increases in requests, duration, or provisioned concurrency charges.

Steps:

1. Go to **AWS Cost Management** and select **Cost Anomaly Detection**.
2. Create an anomaly monitor and set it to watch AWS Lambda costs.
3. Set up alert preferences to receive notifications via email or SNS.

6.2. Create Budget Alerts

AWS **Budgets** allow you to set custom budget thresholds and receive alerts when your actual or forecasted costs exceed those thresholds. This is a proactive way to manage AWS Lambda costs and avoid unexpected expenses.

Steps to Create a Budget:

1. Go to **AWS Cost Management** and select **Budgets**.
2. Create a new budget for AWS Lambda costs and set your desired monthly budget threshold.
3. Choose an alert condition and set up email or SNS notifications.

AWS Cost Explorer provides powerful capabilities for tracking, analyzing, and managing your AWS Lambda costs. By leveraging filters, grouping options, and tags, you can gain detailed insights into which functions and usage patterns are driving costs. This enables you to identify inefficiencies, optimize memory allocations, reduce over-provisioned concurrency, and improve overall cost management.

Through regular analysis of Cost Explorer reports, monitoring of tags, and proactive alert setups using Budget Alerts and Cost Anomaly Detection, you can maintain better control over your AWS Lambda expenses and make informed decisions to keep your serverless applications cost-efficient.

Optimizing Lambda Invocations for Maximum Savings

Optimizing the number of invocations in AWS Lambda is a crucial aspect of reducing costs and improving efficiency. Since AWS Lambda charges based on the number of requests and the total execution time, minimizing unnecessary invocations and optimizing existing ones can lead to significant savings. This section covers strategies and best practices to reduce the frequency of Lambda invocations and optimize function performance.

1. Use Efficient Event Filtering

The Challenge:
Many AWS services can trigger Lambda functions based on events, such as S3 file uploads, DynamoDB Streams updates, or API Gateway requests. If these triggers are configured inefficiently, you may end up with a large number of unnecessary or redundant invocations.

The Solution:
Implement event filters and constraints to trigger Lambda functions only for specific types of events or data changes. AWS provides built-in mechanisms to filter events at the source, reducing the number of invocations

and lowering costs.

Example Use Cases for Event Filtering:

1. **Filtering S3 Events**: If your Lambda function processes objects uploaded to an S3 bucket, use event filters to trigger the function only for specific file types, prefixes, or size ranges.

- **Filter Criteria**: .json files, files uploaded to a specific prefix (/uploads/), or files larger than 1 MB.
- **Example Filter Configuration**:

```
"LambdaFunctionConfigurations": [
  {
    "Id": "MyS3EventFilter",
    "Filter": {
      "Key": {
        "FilterRules": [
          { "Name": "suffix", "Value": ".json" },
          { "Name": "prefix", "Value": "uploads/" }
        ]
      }
    },
    "LambdaFunctionArn":
    "arn:aws:lambda:us-east-1:123456789012:function:ProcessS3Json"
  }
]
```

1. **Optimizing DynamoDB Streams**: If your function processes updates from a DynamoDB table, filter the events to trigger only on specific attribute changes or operation types (INSERT, MODIFY, or REMOVE).
2. **Optimizing Kinesis Stream Events**: Set up filters to process batches of records instead of individual events, reducing the number of invocations.

2. Batch Process with Amazon SQS and Kinesis

The Challenge:

When dealing with high-frequency events, triggering Lambda functions for each individual event can lead to excessive invocations and higher costs.

The Solution:

Batch process multiple events into a single Lambda invocation using services like **Amazon SQS**, **Kinesis**, or **DynamoDB Streams**. By increasing batch sizes, you can significantly reduce the number of invocations and save costs.

Best Practices for Batch Processing:

1. **Adjust Batch Size**: Configure a larger batch size in SQS, Kinesis, or DynamoDB Streams to process more records in each Lambda invocation. This approach reduces per-event overhead and lowers the total number of invocations.
2. **Handle Batches Efficiently**: Optimize your Lambda function's code to handle batches effectively by reducing loops and minimizing resource contention within each invocation.

Example Configuration for SQS:

```
BatchSize: 10  # Process 10 messages per invocation
```

3. Leverage Amazon API Gateway Caching

The Challenge:

For Lambda functions invoked through **Amazon API Gateway**, repeated calls for the same data or content can lead to redundant invocations and unnecessary costs.

The Solution:

Use **API Gateway caching** to store frequently accessed responses and reduce the number of Lambda function invocations. This is particularly useful for read-heavy APIs where data changes infrequently.

Steps to Enable Caching:

1. Go to **API Gateway** and select your API.
2. In the **Integration Request** settings, enable **Caching** and specify a cache duration (e.g., 60 seconds or 5 minutes).
3. For dynamic content, you can use **cache keys** to define which parts of the request are used to generate the cache.

4. Optimize Function Code to Minimize Duration

The Challenge:
Lambda charges are based on both the number of invocations and the total execution duration. Inefficient or unoptimized code can result in longer execution times, increasing costs.

The Solution:
Optimize your Lambda function code to minimize execution duration and improve efficiency. Key strategies include:

1. **Minimize External Calls**: Reduce the number of external calls to other AWS services or third-party APIs within each Lambda invocation. Instead, batch external calls when possible.
2. **Use Asynchronous Processing**: Offload non-critical tasks to asynchronous services like SQS or Step Functions to keep the main function's execution time short.
3. **Optimize Data Handling**: Use more efficient data handling techniques like streaming data instead of processing large datasets in memory.

5. Use Function Scaling Strategies Based on Traffic Patterns

The Challenge:

Provisioning Lambda functions inefficiently for fluctuating traffic patterns can lead to excessive costs, especially when provisioned concurrency is used for prolonged low-demand periods.

The Solution:

1. **Leverage Auto Scaling for Provisioned Concurrency**: Use **scheduled auto scaling** to adjust provisioned concurrency based on predictable traffic patterns, such as peak hours or promotional events. Reduce provisioned concurrency during off-peak periods to save costs.
2. **Use CloudWatch Alarms to Scale Dynamically**: Set up CloudWatch alarms to dynamically increase or decrease provisioned concurrency based on actual usage patterns, ensuring that your application is cost-efficient and responsive to demand.

6. Minimize Data Transfer Costs

The Challenge:

Data transfer costs can add up when Lambda functions interact with external services or when data is moved between regions or to external endpoints.

The Solution:

1. **Use In-Region Services**: Whenever possible, keep your Lambda function and related services in the same AWS region to avoid cross-region data transfer charges.
2. **Optimize Data Transfer Volume**: Use compression techniques to minimize the amount of data being transferred to and from Lambda functions.

7. Monitor and Analyze Lambda Invocation Patterns

The Challenge:
Without proper monitoring and analysis, it's challenging to identify inefficiencies or unnecessary invocations that are increasing costs.
The Solution:

1. **Set Up CloudWatch Metrics for Invocations**: Monitor key Cloud-Watch metrics such as **Invocations**, **ConcurrentExecutions**, and **Throttles** to identify unusual invocation patterns or potential inefficiencies.
2. **Analyze Cost Trends with AWS Cost Explorer**: Use **Cost Explorer** to track Lambda costs based on invocation counts and correlate with traffic spikes or deployment events.

Example: If you notice a sudden spike in Lambda invocations, investigate changes in event sources, API Gateway traffic, or newly deployed features that might be causing the increase.

8. Consolidate and Combine Lambda Functions

The Challenge:
Having too many small, fragmented Lambda functions can lead to higher invocation counts and increased complexity in managing triggers and dependencies.
The Solution:
Where appropriate, consolidate smaller functions into larger, more cohesive functions that can handle related tasks in a single invocation. This reduces the number of invocations, improves efficiency, and simplifies deployment and monitoring.
Example: Instead of creating separate Lambda functions for reading and writing to a DynamoDB table, combine these tasks into a single function that processes read and write operations based on event data.

Optimizing AWS Lambda invocations is essential to achieving cost efficiency and maximizing savings. By implementing efficient event filters, leveraging batch processing, using API Gateway caching, and optimizing function code, you can reduce unnecessary invocations and lower costs. Additionally, managing function scaling, monitoring data transfer, and consolidating functions help to further enhance cost-efficiency.

Hands-On Exercises: Developing Python Lambda Functions

I n this chapter, we will dive into practical, hands-on exercises to help you master the development of AWS Lambda functions using Python. These exercises are designed to give you real-world experience by walking you through three common Lambda use cases: building APIs, processing data, and automating tasks. By the end of this chapter, you'll have a solid understanding of how to develop, deploy, and optimize Lambda functions for various scenarios.

1. Exercise 1: Creating a Serverless API with AWS Lambda and API Gateway

In this exercise, we will build a simple RESTful API using AWS Lambda and Amazon API Gateway. The API will allow users to create, read, update, and delete items in a DynamoDB table.

Step 1.1: Create a DynamoDB Table

Go to the AWS Management Console and open the **DynamoDB** service. Click on **Create Table** and provide the following details:

- **Table Name**: ItemsTable
- **Primary Key**: ItemId (String)

Keep the default settings and click **Create Table**.

Step 1.2: Create Lambda Functions for CRUD Operations

We will create four Lambda functions for handling the API endpoints:

- **Create Item** (POST /items)
- **Get Item** (GET /items/{id})
- **Update Item** (PUT /items/{id})
- **Delete Item** (DELETE /items/{id})

Example Python Code for Lambda Functions:

Create Item Function (CreateItemLambda):

```python
import json
import boto3
import uuid

dynamodb = boto3.resource('dynamodb')
table = dynamodb.Table('ItemsTable')

def lambda_handler(event, context):
    body = json.loads(event['body'])
    item_id = str(uuid.uuid4())
    table.put_item(Item={
        'ItemId': item_id,
        'Name': body['name'],
        'Description': body['description']
    })
    return {
        'statusCode': 201,
        'body': json.dumps({'ItemId': item_id})
    }
```

Get Item Function (GetItemLambda):

```python
import json
import boto3
```

```
dynamodb = boto3.resource('dynamodb')
table = dynamodb.Table('ItemsTable')

def lambda_handler(event, context):
    item_id = event['pathParameters']['id']
    response = table.get_item(Key={'ItemId': item_id})
    item = response.get('Item')
    if not item:
        return {'statusCode': 404, 'body': json.dumps({'message':
        'Item not found'})}
    return {'statusCode': 200, 'body': json.dumps(item)}
```

Update Item Function (UpdateItemLambda):

```
import json
import boto3

dynamodb = boto3.resource('dynamodb')
table = dynamodb.Table('ItemsTable')

def lambda_handler(event, context):
    item_id = event['pathParameters']['id']
    body = json.loads(event['body'])
    response = table.update_item(
        Key={'ItemId': item_id},
        UpdateExpression="set #name=:n, Description=:d",
        ExpressionAttributeNames={'#name': 'Name'},
        ExpressionAttributeValues={':n': body['name'], ':d':
        body['description']},
        ReturnValues="UPDATED_NEW"
    )
    return {'statusCode': 200, 'body':
    json.dumps(response['Attributes'])}
```

Delete Item Function (DeleteItemLambda):

```
import json
import boto3

dynamodb = boto3.resource('dynamodb')
table = dynamodb.Table('ItemsTable')

def lambda_handler(event, context):
    item_id = event['pathParameters']['id']
    table.delete_item(Key={'ItemId': item_id})
    return {'statusCode': 204}
```

Step 1.3: Configure API Gateway

1. Open **Amazon API Gateway** in the AWS Console.
2. Create a new **REST API** and set up resources and methods for each operation (/items and /items/{id}).
3. Link each method to the corresponding Lambda function.
4. Deploy the API to a **Stage** and note the API URL for testing.

Step 1.4: Test the API

- Use a tool like **Postman** or **curl** to test your API by creating, reading, updating, and deleting items.

2. Exercise 2: Data Processing with AWS Lambda and S3

In this exercise, we will create a Lambda function that processes data files uploaded to an S3 bucket. The function will extract data from uploaded JSON files and store processed results in a DynamoDB table.

Step 2.1: Create an S3 Bucket

1. Open the **S3 Console** in AWS.
2. Create a new S3 bucket named data-processing-bucket.

Step 2.2: Create a DynamoDB Table

1. Go to the **DynamoDB Console** and create a new table named ProcessedData.
2. Set the **Primary Key** as RecordId (String).

Step 2.3: Create a Lambda Function for Data Processing
Example Python Code:

```python
import json
import boto3
import uuid

s3 = boto3.client('s3')
dynamodb = boto3.resource('dynamodb')
table = dynamodb.Table('ProcessedData')

def lambda_handler(event, context):
    for record in event['Records']:
        bucket = record['s3']['bucket']['name']
        key = record['s3']['object']['key']

        response = s3.get_object(Bucket=bucket, Key=key)
        data = json.loads(response['Body'].read())

        for item in data:
            record_id = str(uuid.uuid4())
            table.put_item(Item={
                'RecordId': record_id,
                'Name': item['name'],
                'Value': item['value']
            })
    return {'statusCode': 200, 'body':
json.dumps({'message':
'Data processed successfully'})}
```

Step 2.4: Set Up an S3 Trigger for the Lambda Function

1. In the **S3 Console**, select the bucket and navigate to **Properties**.
2. Create an event notification for **Object Created** and link it to your Lambda function.

Step 2.5: Test the Data Processing Workflow

1. Upload a JSON file to the S3 bucket with the following format:

```
[
    {"name": "Temperature", "value": 23.4},
    {"name": "Humidity", "value": 56.7}
]
```

Check the **DynamoDB table** for processed records after uploading the file.

3. Exercise 3: Automating Infrastructure Tasks with AWS Lambda

In this exercise, we will use AWS Lambda to automate the creation and deletion of EC2 instances based on a schedule.

Step 3.1: Create a Lambda Function to Start and Stop EC2 Instances
Example Python Code:
Start EC2 Instances:

```
import boto3

ec2 = boto3.client('ec2')

def lambda_handler(event, context):
    response =
    ec2.start_instances(InstanceIds=['i-0abcd1234efgh5678'])
    return {'statusCode': 200, 'body':
'Instances started: ' + str(response)}
```

Stop EC2 Instances:

```
import boto3

ec2 = boto3.client('ec2')

def lambda_handler(event, context):
    response = ec2.stop_
instances(InstanceIds=['i-0abcd1234efgh5678'])
    return {'statusCode': 200, 'body':
'Instances stopped: ' + str(response)}
```

Step 3.2: Set Up CloudWatch Events for Automation

Go to **Amazon CloudWatch** and select **Rules** under **Events**.

Create two rules:

- One rule to trigger the **Start EC2 Lambda function** at 9:00 AM every day.
- Another rule to trigger the **Stop EC2 Lambda function** at 6:00 PM every day.

Step 3.3: Test the Automation Workflow

- Verify that the EC2 instances automatically start and stop at the scheduled times based on your Lambda functions.

These hands-on exercises have demonstrated how to develop and deploy AWS Lambda functions using Python for three common scenarios: building serverless APIs, processing data, and automating infrastructure tasks. By working through these examples, you should have gained practical experience with Lambda integrations, event triggers, and automation techniques.

To deepen your understanding, try extending these exercises by adding additional features, such as implementing error handling, optimizing performance, or integrating additional AWS services. These exercises form the foundation for building scalable and efficient serverless solutions using AWS Lambda.

Real-World Challenges to Reinforce Learning

To solidify your understanding of AWS Lambda and expand your skills in developing serverless applications, it's essential to tackle real-world challenges. These challenges are designed to push your knowledge beyond basic implementation, forcing you to solve common but complex problems that you are likely to encounter in actual projects. Each challenge requires the application of the concepts covered in previous chapters, helping you gain a deeper, more practical understanding of AWS Lambda development.

Challenge 1: Building a Scalable Data Ingestion Pipeline

Scenario:

You are tasked with building a scalable data ingestion pipeline that processes and stores data from IoT devices. Each device sends JSON-formatted data to an S3 bucket every 10 minutes. The requirements are to process these files as soon as they arrive and store the data in a DynamoDB table for further analysis. You also need to ensure that the solution can scale efficiently to handle bursts of incoming data during peak hours.

Key Requirements:

1. Set up an S3 bucket to receive data files from IoT devices.
2. Create a Lambda function that processes each file uploaded to S3.
3. Extract relevant information from each JSON file and store it in a DynamoDB table.
4. Implement batching to efficiently handle large numbers of records.
5. Implement error handling and monitoring using CloudWatch.

Goals:

- Ensure that the solution scales automatically based on the incoming file volume.
- Minimize processing latency and optimize the Lambda function's execution time.
- Set up alarms to detect and respond to processing failures.

Challenge 2: Automating Resource Cleanup Based on Tags

Scenario:

Your organization has a policy that all AWS resources should have specific tags for identification and cost tracking. However, you discover that numerous EC2 instances and S3 buckets have been created without these required tags. Your task is to create an automated solution using AWS Lambda to identify and clean up resources that are missing mandatory tags.

Key Requirements:

1. Identify resources (EC2 instances, S3 buckets) that do not have the required tags.
2. Notify resource owners about the missing tags via SNS.
3. Schedule a cleanup function to automatically terminate EC2 instances or delete S3 buckets that remain untagged after a grace period of 7 days.
4. Implement logging and monitoring to track the cleanup process.

Goals:

- Build a Lambda function that runs on a schedule using CloudWatch Events.
- Implement an automated notification system using SNS.
- Ensure that cleanup operations are efficient and do not impact other resources.

Challenge 3: Creating a Serverless Order Processing System

Scenario:

You are working for an e-commerce company that wants to modernize its order processing system using AWS Lambda and other serverless services. The system must allow customers to place orders, view order status, and receive notifications upon order updates. The order processing should include inventory checks and payment verifications.

Key Requirements:

1. Create a RESTful API using API Gateway and Lambda to manage order creation, updates, and retrieval.
2. Create a Lambda function to process new orders, check inventory status, and trigger payment verification.
3. Use Step Functions to orchestrate the entire workflow for processing orders, with branches for success and failure scenarios.
4. Notify customers of order status changes using SNS or SES.
5. Store order data in a DynamoDB table and log all operations in CloudWatch.

Goals:

- Build a serverless order processing workflow using Step Functions and Lambda.
- Implement error handling and retries to ensure reliable order processing.
- Maintain scalability and low latency for a smooth customer experience.

Challenge 4: Implementing a Real-Time Event Streaming and Processing Solution

Scenario:

You need to create a real-time event streaming solution that captures user activity from a web application. User events (such as page views, button clicks, and form submissions) are streamed to Kinesis Data Streams. The solution must process these events in real time and store processed results in both a DynamoDB table for querying and an S3 bucket for analytics.

Key Requirements:

1. Set up Kinesis Data Streams to receive and buffer user events.
2. Create a Lambda function to read batches of events from the stream and process them.
3. Store the processed data in a DynamoDB table for low-latency queries and in S3 for analytics.
4. Implement aggregation logic to calculate real-time statistics, such as the number of page views per user.
5. Set up monitoring and alerts for potential issues, such as data processing delays or stream overflows.

Goals:

- Build a highly scalable solution that handles spikes in user activity efficiently.
- Ensure data integrity and consistency in both DynamoDB and S3.
- Minimize latency to provide real-time insights for the analytics team.

Challenge 5: Building a Cost Optimization Dashboard

Scenario:

You've been assigned to develop a cost optimization solution for your company's AWS Lambda usage. Your company uses several Lambda functions across multiple projects and environments, but lacks visibility into the associated costs. You are tasked with creating a cost optimization dashboard to provide detailed insights into Lambda usage and costs.

Key Requirements:

1. Create a Lambda function to aggregate cost and usage data for Lambda functions across all projects and environments.
2. Use the Cost Explorer API to retrieve detailed cost data and store it in a DynamoDB table.
3. Develop a dashboard using Amazon QuickSight or a similar visualization tool to display Lambda costs by project, environment, and function.
4. Identify cost-saving opportunities by highlighting inefficient Lambda functions or unused provisioned concurrency.
5. Set up automated alerts for cost anomalies or unexpected spikes in Lambda usage.

Goals:

- Create a comprehensive cost analysis solution that helps stakeholders optimize Lambda usage.
- Implement efficient data retrieval and storage techniques to keep costs low.
- Ensure that the dashboard provides actionable insights for optimizing costs.

These real-world challenges are designed to reinforce your learning by encouraging you to apply the concepts and techniques covered in this book. By tackling these scenarios, you will gain practical experience in developing serverless solutions that are scalable, efficient, and cost-effective. The challenges also push you to think critically about real-world considerations, such as error handling, automation, monitoring, and cost management.

Sample Solutions and Code Review

In this section, we will provide sample solutions for the real-world challenges presented in the previous chapter. Additionally, we'll conduct a code review to highlight best practices, discuss potential improvements, and identify common pitfalls to avoid. Each solution includes a detailed explanation to help you understand the reasoning behind the code and design choices.

1. Sample Solution for Challenge 1: Building a Scalable Data Ingestion Pipeline

Problem Recap:

You are tasked with creating a scalable data ingestion pipeline that processes JSON files uploaded to an S3 bucket and stores the extracted information in DynamoDB.

Solution Overview:

1. **Lambda Function** triggered by S3 events.
2. **DynamoDB Table** to store the processed records.
3. **S3 Bucket** configured with event triggers to invoke the Lambda function.

Sample Code:

Lambda Function (DataProcessorLambda):

```
import json
import boto3
import uuid

s3_client = boto3.client('s3')
dynamodb = boto3.resource('dynamodb')
table = dynamodb.Table('ProcessedData')

def lambda_handler(event, context):
```

```
for record in event['Records']:
    # Extract bucket and object key from the event
    bucket_name = record['s3']['bucket']['name']
    file_key = record['s3']['object']['key']

    # Fetch the file from S3
    response = s3_client.get_object
(Bucket=bucket_name, Key=file_key)
    file_content = response['Body'].read()
    data = json.loads(file_content)

    # Process each item in the file
    for item in data:
        record_id = str(uuid.uuid4())
        table.put_item(Item={
            'RecordId': record_id,
            'Name': item.get('name', 'NoName'),
            'Value': item.get('value', 'NoValue')
        })

return {
    'statusCode': 200,
    'body': json.dumps({'message': 'File processed
    successfully'})
}
```

Code Review and Best Practices:

1. **Error Handling**: Add error handling using try and except blocks to ensure that issues like file not found or DynamoDB write errors are caught and logged.
2. **Batch Writes**: Use DynamoDB batch write to handle large datasets efficiently. In the current solution, individual writes could result in higher costs and slower processing times.
3. **Logging**: Include detailed logging for troubleshooting, using AWS Lambda's integrated logging with **CloudWatch**.

2. Sample Solution for Challenge 2: Automating Resource Cleanup Based on Tags

Problem Recap:

You need to identify resources without mandatory tags and notify owners. If the resources remain untagged for a specified duration, automatically terminate or delete them.

Solution Overview:

1. **Lambda Function** that checks for missing tags.
2. **SNS Topic** for notifications.
3. **Scheduled Rule** in CloudWatch Events to run the function periodically.

Sample Code:

Lambda Function (TagCheckerLambda):

```python
import boto3
import json
from datetime import datetime, timedelta

sns_client = boto3.client('sns')
ec2_client = boto3.client('ec2')
sns_topic_arn = 'arn:aws:sns:us-east-1:123456789012:TagAlertTopic'

def lambda_handler(event, context):
    # Get all EC2 instances
    instances = ec2_client.describe_instances()

    # Check each instance for the required tags
    for reservation in instances['Reservations']:
        for instance in reservation['Instances']:
            instance_id = instance['InstanceId']
            tags = instance.get('Tags', [])

            # Check if the required tags are missing
            if not any(tag['Key'] == 'Project' for tag in tags):
```

```
                send_alert(instance_id)

def send_alert(instance_id):
    message = f"Instance {instance_id}
 is missing mandatory tags."
    sns_client.publish(
        TopicArn=sns_topic_arn,
        Message=message,
        Subject="Missing Tags Alert"
    )
    print(f"Alert sent for instance {instance_id}")
```

Code Review and Best Practices:

1. **Efficient Tagging Checks**: Instead of looping through all tags, consider using a set-based approach for faster lookups when there are many tags.
2. **Grace Period Handling**: Store missing tag information in a DynamoDB table and implement a Lambda function that checks for resources that have been untagged beyond a certain grace period.
3. **Resource Cleanup**: Add a function to terminate or delete resources after the grace period. Use a scheduled CloudWatch Event to periodically check and clean up these resources.

3. Sample Solution for Challenge 3: Creating a Serverless Order Processing System

Problem Recap:

You need to create a serverless order processing system using Lambda and Step Functions. The system should handle order creation, inventory checks, and payment processing.

Solution Overview:

1. **API Gateway** and Lambda functions for order management.
2. **Step Functions** to coordinate inventory checks and payment processing.

3. **DynamoDB Table** to store order information.

Sample Code:
Order Processing Workflow (Step Functions Definition):

```
{
  "Comment": "Order Processing State Machine",
  "StartAt": "CheckInventory",
  "States": {
    "CheckInventory": {
      "Type": "Task",
      "Resource": "arn:aws:lambda:
us-east-1:123456789012:
function:CheckInventory",
      "Next": "ProcessPayment",
      "Catch": [
        {
          "ErrorEquals": ["InventoryError"],
          "Next": "NotifyOutOfStock"
        }
      ]
    },
    "ProcessPayment": {
      "Type": "Task",
      "Resource":
      "arn:aws:lambda:us-east-1:123456789012:function:ProcessPayment",
      "Next": "OrderSuccess",
      "Catch": [
        {
          "ErrorEquals": ["PaymentError"],
          "Next": "NotifyPaymentFailure"
        }
      ]
    },
    "OrderSuccess": {
      "Type": "Succeed"
    },
    "NotifyOutOfStock": {
      "Type": "Task",
```

```
    "Resource": "arn:aws:lambda:us-east-1:123456789012:function:
SendOutOfStockNotification",
      "End": true
    },
    "NotifyPaymentFailure": {
      "Type": "Task",
      "Resource": "arn:aws:lambda:us-east-1:123456789012:function:
SendPaymentFailureNotification",
      "End": true
    }
  }
}
```

Code Review and Best Practices:

1. **Error Handling in Step Functions**: Leverage Step Functions' built-in error handling features to automatically route failed states to corresponding notification tasks.
2. **Idempotency**: Ensure that each Lambda function is idempotent to avoid duplicating operations in the event of retries or errors.
3. **Decoupled Notifications**: Use SNS or SES for sending notifications to customers, ensuring that the core workflow remains decoupled from the notification mechanism.

4. Sample Solution for Challenge 4: Real-Time Event Streaming and Processing

Problem Recap:
You need to create a solution that captures and processes user events in real-time using Kinesis and Lambda.
Solution Overview:

1. **Kinesis Data Stream** for capturing and buffering user events.
2. **Lambda Function** to read and process event batches from the Kinesis stream.

573

3. **DynamoDB Table** and **S3 Bucket** for storing processed data.

Sample Code:
Lambda Function (EventProcessorLambda):

```python
import json
import boto3

dynamodb = boto3.resource('dynamodb')
s3_client = boto3.client('s3')
table = dynamodb.Table('UserActivity')
bucket_name = 'user-event-analytics'

def lambda_handler(event, context):
    for record in event['Records']:
        # Decode the Kinesis record data
        payload = json.loads
(record['kinesis']['data'])

        # Store processed data in DynamoDB
        table.put_item(Item={
            'UserId': payload['userId'],
            'Event': payload['event'],
            'Timestamp': payload['timestamp']
        })

        # Optionally, store raw data in S3 for analytics
        s3_client.put_object(
            Bucket=bucket_name,
            Key=f"{payload['userId']}/
{payload['timestamp']}.json",
            Body=json.dumps(payload)
        )

    return {
        'statusCode': 200,
        'body': json.dumps
({'message': 'Events processed successfully'})
    }
```

574

Code Review and Best Practices:

1. **Data Validation**: Add input validation logic to verify the integrity and structure of incoming events. This prevents corrupt or malformed records from being stored.
2. **Batch Size**: Optimize the batch size for reading events from Kinesis to balance processing speed and function memory usage.
3. **Concurrency**: Use Lambda's concurrent execution settings to scale automatically based on incoming event volume.

5. Sample Solution for Challenge 5: Building a Cost Optimization Dashboard

Problem Recap:

You need to build a cost optimization dashboard that provides detailed insights into AWS Lambda usage and costs.

Solution Overview:

1. **Lambda Function** to aggregate cost and usage data using the Cost Explorer API.
2. **DynamoDB Table** to store aggregated data for reporting.
3. **Amazon QuickSight** for visualization.

Sample Code:

Cost Aggregation Lambda Function (CostAggregatorLambda):

```
import boto3
import datetime

cost_explorer = boto3.client('ce')
dynamodb = boto3.resource('dynamodb')
table = dynamodb.Table('LambdaCostData')

def lambda_handler(event, context):
```

```
today = datetime.datetime.today()
start_date = (today -
datetime.timedelta(days=30)).strftime('%Y-%m-%d')
end_date = today.strftime('%Y-%m-%d')

response = cost_explorer.get_cost_and_usage(
    TimePeriod={'Start': start_date, 'End': end_date},
    Granularity='DAILY',
    Metrics=['UnblendedCost'],
    GroupBy=[{'Type': 'DIMENSION', 'Key': 'SERVICE'}]
)

for result in response['ResultsByTime']:
    for group in result['Groups']:
        service = group['Keys'][0]
        amount = group['Metrics']['UnblendedCost']['Amount']

        table.put_item(Item={
            'Date': result['TimePeriod']['Start'],
            'Service': service,
            'Cost': float(amount)
        })

return {
    'statusCode': 200,
    'body': 'Cost data aggregated successfully'
}
```

Code Review and Best Practices:

1. **Data Accuracy**: Ensure that all date calculations are timezone-aware to avoid discrepancies in cost reporting.
2. **Efficient Data Storage**: Consider using efficient data types for DynamoDB (e.g., using number types for cost values) to improve query performance.
3. **Visualization**: Integrate with Amazon QuickSight to create cost analysis reports and dashboards for stakeholders.

These sample solutions demonstrate the practical application of AWS Lambda, serverless architecture, and related AWS services to solve real-world problems. The accompanying code reviews highlight key best practices, common pitfalls, and strategies for improvement. By working through these solutions and understanding the reasoning behind each approach, you can enhance your skills and confidence in building robust, scalable, and cost-efficient serverless applications.

www.ingramcontent.com/pod-product-compliance
Lightning Source LLC
LaVergne TN
LVHW080110070326
832902LV00015B/2496